BETTY'S CHILD

MELISSA,
PLEASE KEEP AN EYE
OR ROSS... :)

BEST,
DON
DEMPSEY

OMISHDON@AOL.COM

BETTY'S CHILD

Donald R. Dempsey

Dream of Things
Downers Grove Illinois USA

Betty's Child

First Dream of Things edition, February 2013
Published by Dream of Things, Downers Grove, Illinois USA
Originally published by Donald R. Dempsey in 2009.
dreamofthings.com

Dream of Things provides discounts to educators, book clubs, writers groups, and others. Contact customerservice@dreamofthings.com or call 847-321-1390.

Publisher's Cataloging-in-Publication data:
Dempsey, Donald R.
    Betty's child / Donald R. Dempsey.
    p. cm.
    ISBN 978-0-9884390-1-6
1. Dempsey, Donald R. 2. Adult child abuse victims —United States —Biography.
3. Abused children —Biography. 4. Victims of family violence —Biography.
5. Mothers and sons —Biography. I. Title.
HV6626.52 .D45 2013
306.874092 --dc23   2012951075

Book design: Susan Veach

Cover illustration: We gratefully acknowledge permission to use the cover illustration by Elizabeth "Beth" Maltbie Uyehara (1935-2010). Beth died in 2010 after a valiant battle with Amyotrophic Lateral Sclerosis (aka ALS, aka Lou Gehrig's Disease). Before Beth was diagnosed with ALS, she worked for the *Los Angeles Times* and was passionate about the art she and her husband, Paul, created in their California studios during their forty years together. One of Beth's last acts was to sign her body over to researchers to help unravel the mystery of Lou Gehrig's Disease. "We are not really humans looking for spiritual experiences," Beth once said, paraphrasing a mentor. "We are spiritual beings looking for human experiences." Beth's art continues to be shown in the United States and Europe.

DEDICATION

I would like to dedicate this book to my children. To Ross, my firstborn, who was given both the best and worst of what I am. To Gavin, who is well on his way to being the man I never managed to be. And to my daughter Rebecca, who with the first touch of her tiny hand taught me I was capable of truly loving another. I don't offer these words as an excuse, but pray they serve as some semblance of an explanation.

ACKNOWLEDGMENTS

I would like to thank Chip Brown for his constant encouragement and assistance with this book. I never would have written it if he hadn't been so stubborn and set in his principles, and I never would have finished or published it if he hadn't admitted he believed what I'd written worth the effort. I'd also like to thank Marcia Trahan, who edited this for me and encouraged me along the way, and a special thank you to Mike O'Mary and Dream of Things for believing in this book when even I had given up on it.

Most of all I'd like to thank my wife, who was really ticked that she wasn't included in my dedication, but has stood by me until I managed to come to terms with the tortured child depicted in these pages. There are no words to thank her for the life she has given me.

PROLOGUE

Most of my life has flashed by me. I have trouble with dates and names and places. It's often difficult for me to recall what year I lived in what state. I cling to moments. I remember standing on the deck of the U.S.S. Tarawa in '83 after they'd blown up the barracks, staring out across a green ocean and realizing how very little the life of a young Marine truly meant to the government running our country. I remember being more terrified than at any other time in my life the day I married my wife. The births of my children have been by far the happiest and most hopeful days I've been granted.

Yet some moments are darker. There are realizations and choices we all undergo that often leave us worse for having endured them. It was that night—the night I learned what really happened to Benji—that I understood how alone I truly was. Perhaps for the first time in my life, I fully comprehended what I was and how people saw me. My mother was a drain on her family and society in general, a woman who lived on welfare and on crime. I was nothing but a burden—a child most people assumed would mature into a man who would travel the path blazed by those who raised him.

They were wrong. I had no more room for pain. I wasn't going to beg, or need. And even though I wasn't quite sure where I was going or how I was going to learn to stand on my own, I knew I wasn't going to follow after Betty. *I'd rather die,* I vowed. People could think what they wanted of me, but I decided right then and there I didn't care one whit what they believed. I didn't need anyone. I wasn't going to need anyone, ever.

I began to form a vision in my head, a rudimentary plan of sorts. My wife would be the opposite of my mother. My children would be the opposite of me. I would succeed. My children would succeed. Everyone would see how wrong they were. No man would ever look down on me. *An eye for an eye,*

9

I promised. Only in my case it wound up being more like an elbow for an elbow, or a curse word for a curse word. Many times it wound up being a fist for a fist.

I let pain make me mean. I let hurt make me cold and indifferent. I would pay for the choices I was forming that fateful night. So would those who would one day be close to me. But I don't blame myself too much. I was backed into a corner. I was just a baby. Many years later I would be forced to see what I'd become, how mean and cruel a man I could be. In some ways I never escaped being Betty's child, but it would be a long time before the dawning of that horrible realization. For now I was just trying to survive, learning to snarl and bluff, to bleed if need be. I'd suffer just about anything so I didn't feel you'd slighted me and gotten away with it.

I like to say some dirt doesn't wash off. I still believe that. I also believe some scars never heal. I'm a calmer man today, a gentler man. I have learned that a softly spoken word is heard and remembered long after an angry outburst fades. I've come to understand that very often a measured silence is the best response to a threat. Discretion is one of the great secrets to living carefree, easy days.

But you still won't catch me turning the other cheek very often.

CHAPTER 1

"Hurry the hell up, Donny," Tommy whispered.

He was only making me that much more nervous. I was making my fourth trip across a creaky porch with at least two more to go, while all he had to do was hand off the bottles to Rupe and wait in the dark, with the safety of the alley a mere few strides away. I glared at him through the gloom, handing him two cartons of empty Pepsi bottles. He flashed that wide smile of his, broad white teeth splitting the black face I could hardly make out. I heard him laugh as he turned away, quietly but purposely clanking the glassware as I headed back to continue gathering our loot.

Of course I was *gathering* nothing. I was stealing. It was what we did. Pop bottles were our chosen and most convenient means of obtaining money, but we weren't above pilfering loose power tools, bikes, change out of the ashtrays of cars left unlocked, and even clothes drying on the line if we thought they'd fit and were worth wearing. Tommy had once ripped off a blind man's cane at the park while the old guy had been getting a drink of water, just to show it off, pretending to have a limp the next day at school.

Another groan of the rotting porch planks: I was sure someone in the house was going to hear the noise. That, or notice we'd unscrewed the exposed light bulb that had been illuminating the rear of their house. I paused for just a second, causing another whispered outburst from Tommy, and then carefully hefted two more cartons of bottles, silently cursing the last carton that waited for me.

"Why don't you just crawl?" Tommy's sarcastic tones mocked out of the night as he relieved me of my tinkling burden. "How many more?"

I resisted the urge to punch him right in the face. But I was only scared, not completely out of my freaking mind. "Last trip," I whispered back.

"Last trip," he repeated, exaggerating the fear in my voice.

I heard him telling Rupe to roll, leaving me to follow them with the last of our bounty. Four steps there and another four back, a few gut-wrenching creaks that probably couldn't be heard even a few feet away, and I was hopping off the porch and trotting after them on silent feet. Another *Mission Impossible* episode lived and survived. They were worth five cents apiece and ten for the big guys. We'd hide the carts in Rupe's garage until we had them filled—which was just another job or two away—and then head for the Kroger to trade glass for cash.

Tommy was humming M.I.'s theme song as I approached. Rupe was just a slim shadow walking on the far side of the cart. I placed my carton atop the rest and fell in with them, glancing nervously behind us as we made our way through the glow of the lone streetlight brightening the alley. Our late night passage set a dog to barking on Rupe's side of the alley, adding to my trepidation.

"Stop being such a pussy," said Tommy, loud as you please. "What you got to worry about? I can outrun anybody who tries to catch us, and you run faster than me." Tommy nudged Rupe with the cart, garnering a dark glare seen even in the night. "It's old limp-along here who ought to be scared."

That was true. I doubted anybody could catch Tommy or me, but just about everybody could catch Rupe. He was the tallest of the three of us, but definitely the weakest, and by leaps and bounds the slowest. He walked with a slight limp that became more pronounced when he tried to run. His mom claimed it was because he'd broken his leg as a toddler and had to spend two months in a body cast. Tommy claimed it was just because Rupe was white. But I was white too, and I could beat our Negro amigo by a step in shorter races and completely trounce him in anything longer than a city block.

But Tommy didn't run from much of anything. He was big for his age and strong for his size, already formidable at fourteen. He stood five feet nine inches and probably weighed a buck fifty. On top of that, he'd been held back a year, so even though we were all in the seventh grade, he was supposed to be heading for the high school next year. Add a volatile temper to his solid frame, and you had a contender for the roughest boy in the middle school. He was easily one of the toughest in our neighborhood, at least among those younger than the teenage sect. Let's just say I was often glad he was my friend and not looking to pick on me.

Not that I had to fight much. I ran my mouth and talked a big game, but when it came right down to it I wasn't big enough to mix it up with any of the guys who would actually fight. If push came to shove I could take a few punches and even throw a few in the general direction of my opponent, but I usually wound up on the losing end of any confrontation. My best asset was my feet, which I had employed to flee many impending ass-whippings. My second-best defense against antagonists was Tommy Washington, who could fight and did, well and often.

My boy Rupe was church quiet and adept at avoiding almost every confrontation. He was polite and modest, and so meek it just wasn't any fun to pick on him. You could talk about his parents, his limp, his pointed nose, or make up just about anything you wanted to throw at him and still get nary a rise. If not for the trouble Tommy and I continued to bring down on him, Rupe would have been content to skate through life without a single shred of anything even remotely resembling excitement.

He was nervous now, repeatedly checking behind us to see if we were being pursued. As if the elderly couple we'd just ripped off would actually risk these alleys after midnight just to regain some empty pop bottles worth a few bucks at most. I often wondered what it was that kept Thomas Rupe hanging out with us. (We called him Rupe because Tommy was Tommy and didn't like to be called Washington. That left Rupe as Rupe whether he liked it or not.) Rupe had a mother and a father, a decent enough place to live, and a world of hurt waiting to fall on him if he was to be caught doing anything like what he was doing at this very moment. Add the fact that his parents didn't exactly care for Tommy or me, and that made our tight friendships all the more risky.

Tommy's grades were terrible, and his behavior was borderline criminal. My grades were passable, but my attendance kept me threatened with summer school and juvenile hall almost daily. Well, at least they threatened me when I was actually *at* school. Rupe never skipped and always made the honor roll. And he never, ever purposely made his parents' lives more difficult. Rupe was what the teachers called a good kid. Like I said: I often wondered what drew the boy to us.

The cart started bouncing along with more clatter as we turned onto the alley running behind Rupe's place, due to the old, uneven bricks that paved the way. Tommy slowed a bit to help calm our distraught friend's nerves, but couldn't stifle a chuckle. We couldn't help it. Neither of us had fathers around, and the thought of being afraid of our mothers was hilarious. In any case, there was no one about to hear our passage. We always planned our operations for weekday evenings, when most of our neighbors slept. Even those who didn't actually have jobs still went to sleep somewhat early if it wasn't a weekend.

"Quiet!" Rupe hissed as Tommy bumped the cart into his garage. It was a detached cinder block structure, far enough away from the house to make hearing us unlikely, but Rupe was still begging for caution. "Take it easy," he pleaded as he fumbled for the key to the lone door.

"Just open the door and shut up," warned Tommy.

He was always a little too hard on Rupe, too harsh concerning his fear of trouble with his parents. I sometimes felt Tommy was jealous of Rupe and his bond with his mother and father, but it was a sentiment I would never dare give voice to. Instead I kept my mouth shut and tried to help Rupe with the cartons as quietly as possible, while Tommy just glared at the both of us. When we were finished, Rupe locked the door and trotted toward home without a see ya later, and Tommy and I started back the way we'd come.

"A buck says he's in school in the morning, and not even late," said Tommy, his tone laden with the disdain reserved for those lame idiots who actually did homework and tried to please parents, teachers, and coaches.

"No bet," I replied. "I'll bet you five I'm not in school though." We both laughed at that, knowing without having to say it that he wasn't going to be at Central Middle School anytime today either. "You going home?"

Tommy nodded. "Yeah," he sighed. "Mom and her new dude need me to watch my little sister tomorrow. But I'm getting paid. Come on over when you get up."

Tomorrow was Friday. I rarely made it to school on Friday. "I'll be there," I said, confirming my bad habit.

We walked the blocks between our homes and Rupe's, who lived nearer the park. Here, in what was a respectable section of Columbus, some folks still tried to maintain their small city lots with pride. Rupe lived just off the circle, with its bricked roadways and curbs. Painted porches and trimmed lawns looked down on you from behind low wrought-iron fences, topped by blunted spikes that could easily be jumped over. It was an area we weren't welcome in unless we were mowing those lawns, raking leaves in the fall, or shoveling snow in the winter.

Our more decrepit houses were only minutes away, but the trash and filth we were soon stepping around made it seem like another world. Broken-down cars lined the streets; some stood on blocks that hadn't been moved in months. Crushed cans and broken bottles were strewn along the curbs.

Wadded-up cigarette wrappers and tossed butts littered the sidewalks. The alleys were dumping grounds for ruined furniture, bundled newspapers, torn trash bags full of clothes, useless engine parts, and every other kind of debris.

Even the night air couldn't disguise or subdue the reek of our alleys. The stench was a mixture of rotting garbage and spilled engine oil, discarded diapers and pooling animal waste. Many of the fences that once distinguished property lines now lay on their sides like dead carcasses, the twisted wires just waiting to snare your foot and send you sprawling. But we made our way through this without a thought, neither noticing nor caring about the poverty we lived in. We had just added a few bucks to our stash and tomorrow was Friday. And neither of us was going to school. Tonight, life was good.

"Later," Tommy sent as we made his place.

The glow of a TV flickered in one of the upstairs bedrooms, but that didn't matter. Tommy came and went as he pleased. I heard him slam the screen door as he entered the kitchen in the rear of his house, an exclamation of that very sentiment. Tommy would be rummaging around his refrigerator by now, eating anything he wanted and taking a swig of whatever he might find. Milk or a Colt 45, it didn't matter much to Tommy. His mom kept a smaller locked fridge in her bedroom to hide the hard liquor and lunch meat, and her drugs.

Without Tommy strutting along beside me, the two blocks between his place and mine suddenly loomed more menacingly, the shadows deeper and the silence threatening. My step grew quicker, and a darting cat set me to jogging. I had a pretty decent act around my peers; I wasn't scared of my mom, and nobody could make me go to school or act respectful if I didn't want to. But when I was alone and in the dark, I realized abruptly that I was just another twelve-year-old street kid out where he shouldn't be. I hadn't made the next corner before I was outright hoofing it for home with those fleet feet of mine.

Home wasn't much in the way of a haven. Our house was right off the alley, which meant we were easily accessible to the prying eyes of every passerby. There were no windows on the first floor of the alley side of the house, but we were constantly finding footprints along the rear sidewalk and beneath the single kitchen window where someone had taken a stroll and a peek, probably checking to see if there was anything of value near at hand. My mother's current sometime-live-in boyfriend had taken to parking his car in the yard as close as possible to the back door, just to hinder the enthusiasm of would-be thieves.

I scooted around that car—a beat-up El Camino Leon was always planning to fix up to sell the next weekend—and tiptoed through the front door. Betty and Leon were crashed on the sofa bed, bathed in the white noise of the TV, which was now just crackling static. The artist in me couldn't help but notice the scene and wonder how old Norman Rockwell would depict it, or name it. *Betty and Leon's Cellulite Asses,* I thought to myself.

My mother's threadbare robe was hiked up over her hip, exposing one nasty flank, and Leon was clothed in his normal pair of brown-stained, saggy underpants. Both of them were overweight, and neither was prone to bathing. Leon was covered with a coat of shaggy, coppery hair that made the swell of his belly that much more pronounced. Their mouths were hanging open as they snored. Somewhere in that mass of flesh my mother's Chihuahua mix, Tiki, was huddled up against her, trembling even in sleep. Add the blackened skin of the soles of my mother's feet and toes, and the sight of her false teeth sitting right out in the open on the coffee table, and just maybe you can appreciate the picture.

I turned away, locked the door, and flicked off the TV, then headed upstairs after draining the last of the Kool-Aid right out of the pitcher. My dog was scratching at the door before I reached the top of the steps, whining and excited. He jumped on me as soon as I let him out, and continued to pester me for attention while I peeked in on my younger brothers. Both were asleep amid a tangle of dingy sheets. I stepped over piles of dirty clothes and around the usual clutter of toys, shoes, and piecemeal furniture to push Terry, who was six, back onto the mattress he had halfway rolled off of. Chip, who was two, had balled up against the wall, the thumb he'd been sucking on now just barely fallen out of his mouth.

Benji—yeah, I was one of probably thousands of kids who named their dog after that movie—walked across the mattress to sniff at Chip, which roused him and got him noisily working on his thumb again. Terry moaned and jerked away from me after I rolled him back up off the floor, then tucked a hand into his underpants and fell motionless again. Benji jumped off the mattress and followed me back to my room, nuzzling me again for the affection he'd yet to receive.

After turning my desk light on, I rubbed his floppy ears while he kept trying to lick me in the face. In my defense, my dog *did* look a lot like the one from the movie. He was a little bigger, but he had the same droopy-mustache hair and the tangle of curls hiding his eyes. And he was just as smart. He sat, rolled over, caught balls, played tug of war and hide-and-seek. If you pointed your fingers at him like a gun and said *bang!*, he fell over and pretended to be dead, except he kept looking up at you with his eyes wide open, waiting to play some more.

I'd had him since I was nine or ten. My aunt Kathy in Indiana had given him to me on my birthday, and the mutt had been my best friend ever since. We slept together, ate the same food—often right off the same plate, bowl, or spoon—and were only apart when absolutely necessary. I'd lost him the last time my mother had been incarcerated for passing bad checks. It had only been for a few months, but the bill to get him back from the kennel he'd been boarded at was far more money than Betty would ever willingly give up for a dog, especially since he was *my* dog. Fortunately, my tears aroused pity from the wife of the guy who owned the place, and she let me have him with only a promise of payments from my mother. Payments that kind woman never saw. But I'm sure she knew that just as well as Betty did, even as the lies were passing her lips.

Benji was more than a dog and a friend. When I read comics, he lay next to me and enjoyed the same fantasies. When I cried, it was his fur that sopped up the tears. When I was scared, it was he who trotted ahead of me to check out what had made that noise. When I slept, he growled if one of my mom's latest buddies tried to enter my room. And his bared teeth balked anyone who got too loud or too close to me; his growl warned of consequences if a hand was raised to me. Not that either of us were big enough to do much, but while I was just bluffing, Benji wasn't. He would bite, and had.

I fell onto my own mattress, and he slipped beside me, already yawning. We rarely had bed frames, being such a transient family. Most of the time, we left our furniture behind in haste if Betty was being chased by cops with warrants. Other times, we just left it because it was only crap someone else had thrown out and wasn't worth hauling. My desk was a piece of plywood laid across matching egg crates, and my dresser was four more egg crates stacked atop one another.

While my room would probably not have been considered neat by most standards, it was by far the most livable room in the house. My dirty clothes were piled in the corner instead of strewn about the floor. My comics and baseball cards were neatly stored in boxes beside my makeshift desk. My art supplies, baseball gear, and football were on shelves in the closet, along with my pressboard box record player and Jackson Five and Donny Osmond records. In fact, I kept my belongings so neat I knew at a glance if anyone had messed with my stuff.

Replace the sheets covering the windows with curtains, wash the clothes and sweep the floors, and throw in some furniture, and my bedroom would have been quite functional. The same could not be said for the rest of the house. My mother's room was so filthy and filled with heaps of soiled clothing and boxes of ceramics, it could hardly be entered, much less used to sleep in. That was the reason she and her latest man were on the sofa bed Leon had bought at a yard sale. Her own queen-sized mattress was buried beneath a growing, reeking mound of shit that rational people would have thrown away instead of hoarding.

Add the fact that my mother's cat, Fluffy, often used the forgotten clothing as a litter box, and the stink was unbearable. Fluffy wasn't fluffy at all. The cat was ratty, spoiled, and sullen. Not that I blamed the cat much. Betty didn't buy kitty litter. She shredded old newspaper and magazines to put in the cat's box, and I guess Fluffy had her standards. Only thing I liked about the feline was that she beat the crap out of Tiki every time my mother left the poor little excuse for a dog by itself. That was hilarious.

I didn't feel like I was going to fall asleep any time soon. Our late night escapade still had me keyed up. Rolling forward, I kicked off my sneaks and pulled off my socks, tossing them on the heap in the corner. Sometime this weekend Betty would have me carting three or four loads of clothes over to the Laundromat, but most likely I would put it off and do it during the week. Any excuse to skip school was a good one. Right now I was hungry, and I headed back downstairs. After an irritated grunt, Benji rose and followed after me.

Foraging for sustenance in Betty's kitchen was an endeavor that grew more futile as the month progressed, and we were into that last week of the month now. The fridge offered a half pack of Kraft singles and a near empty pack of bologna, along with a few cans of Pepsi and one of Leon's six-packs of Miller. We still had a bag of puffed rice and a pitcher of powdered milk, and a bowl of tossed salad I could drown in French dressing. I decided to leave the lunch meat for my brothers, grabbed a Pepsi and slapped some cheese slices between bread, making two sandwiches before twist-tying the bread closed to keep out the roaches and going out onto the back step to eat.

Benji was focused intently on me. Though I couldn't see his eyes through all of that hair, I knew they were locked on the food in my hand; his tail wagged with furious anticipation. I tore his sandwich in two and tossed him the first portion, dropping the other half on the step as I sat down. I was still chewing my first bite while he deftly separated the bread and cheese and wolfed both parts of his meal down. He wanted more, but after I ignored him and took another bite he decided to go hike his leg and pee on one of Leon's worn tires, and then set off to sniff at the scant grass in our yard.

"It's the same dirt you investigate every day, boy," I told him, my voice sounding loud in the unfamiliar silence of the early morning. "Nothing's changed." He looked up at me, only curious, but then continued out to the farthest corner of our tiny patch of earth, where he started circling, preparing to take a dump.

Cheese, bread, and puffed wheat sucked, so I was looking forward to the first of the month, like every other kid who lived on welfare checks. That check was like magic, as were the allotment of food stamps. Food coupons could be used for candy, which included baseball cards and even comics if the clerk was willing to turn a blind eye. Even the Borden vendor took food stamps, which was where we got most of our real milk and all of our ice cream and Popsicles. Betty doled out the same lecture the first of every month, but we always wolfed down those supplies within the first week or so, never able to ration them out in portions that might stretch longer.

My mother was more talk than walk. She could eat a half-gallon of Neapolitan ice cream in one sitting, and had more of a sweet tooth than any of her three sons. Add in her addiction to Pepsi—one trait that she'd passed on to me—and the fact that there wasn't a toothbrush in the house, and you had an explanation for the lack of teeth in her head. Worse than this, if she had a man around, you could safely bet he'd be eating more than any of us, plus spending Betty's money on cigarettes and beer.

Betty also sold some of her food coupons for cash, like many of the other women in our neighborhood. It was a common practice, and a well-known scam. Coupons didn't buy drugs, or gas, or drinks at the bars. The rate was about two to one, and why all those stupid women were so eager to give away profits always left me puzzled. There was a better way to cash in on your own food stamps, like the guys who took theirs and bought meat to sell out of the back of a truck in the suburbs, so the upper class could barbecue in style.

Yeah, check day was a good one, second only to tax check day that mythical means by which Betty was always going to purchase a car or pay off all her mounting bills, but which usually ended up being the money we wasted running to find some other dump to live in.

Benji waddled back up the walk, and I tossed him the last bite of my cheese sandwich, yawned and stretched, feeling like I might be able to sleep. But as I walked back into the kitchen, draining the last of my Pepsi, Leon stood in the light of the open fridge, glaring at me with sleep-swelled eyes while scratching at his crotch.

I tossed the can in our cracked, nearly overflowing plastic trash bucket and tried to walk on toward the stairs, but Leon wasn't having that. "Why you up so late? Did anyone say you could have your mom's Pepsi?"

"I was doing homework," I lied.

Leon shut the fridge and popped the top on one of his beers, snorting at me. "Homework? That'll be the day." He took a long drink, still eyeing me, then wiped his mouth with the back of one hairy arm and repeated, "What about the Pepsi?"

I shrugged. "Betty doesn't care." I wished I hadn't called her Betty as soon as I said it. My mother hated when I did that, and Leon was always looking for any chance to give me shit. I could see by the hardening of his ruddy face that I was going to catch some now.

"You lie like I fart. And you're a little punk. How many times you been told to call her Mom, and show some respect?"

Benji started growling at Leon. I could see that my mom's boyfriend wasn't in any mood to be trifled with, so I snapped my fingers and pointed at the stairs. Benji looked at me and dropped his ears, but scuttled up the three stairs to the landing and sat down, still waiting for me and hoping I wouldn't force him the rest of the way. Leon glanced at the stairs and back to me. I knew he was going to start telling me how easily he could punt my dog clear across the street, or how he could whip my ass with one hand cupping his balls.

Instead he said, "Sit down a minute."

Hesitantly, I followed his example and pulled out a chair, choosing the one farthest from him and closest to the stairs. Except for a few light slaps to the back of the head, Leon had never hit me. He threatened more than most, but was more bluster than substance, at least up to this point in what I hoped would be our brief acquaintance. Only one of my mom's previous lowlife men had ever dared hit me solid. That swollen eye had won me a trip to the school nurse, who immediately sent me home with a note threatening to notify the police. The bastard scampered for the hills, so fast my mother was now quick to point out to her boyfriends that I was more trouble than I was worth.

It wasn't that Leon didn't look tough enough. He was overweight but burly, with big arms and a thick chest. His hands were big and strong, which he'd proven with some occasional roughhousing. A truck driver by trade, he wore jeans with the chains hanging off his wallet and a silver buckle shaped like a reclining nude woman. Of course, at present all he wore was that pair of stained, baggy underwear and the covering of fur that could easily get him through a harsh winter.

"Your mom asked me to speak with you," he began, a little nervous. I almost grinned at the tone of his voice. *He's trying to sound paternal,* I realized. "The school called her at the diner last night."

"The school?" I repeated, feigning ignorance.

To his credit, Leon continued his efforts to be fatherly. "Yes, Donny, the school. You know, the place you rarely go?" He sat his beer on the table, and then leaned back in his chair. "You really need to listen up. A few more weeks and you'll be on summer vacation. Can't you stick it out for that long? You want to be held back?"

"They won't hold me back," I insisted, pulling at the loose piece of chrome stripping on our kitchen table. It was another of Leon's special deliveries, straight from someone's garage sale, or so he claimed. It was one of those cheap laminate jobs with chromed curvy legs and stripping, complete with four cheap chairs with vinyl seats and backings, all cracked, the rips held in place with duct tape. He'd probably dug it out of some trash bin and told Betty he'd had to pay for it, just to make her think he cared.

"And I won't have to go to summer school either, so don't worry. Betty— I mean *Mom* will have her free baby-sitting service to rely on real soon now."

"That mouth of yours is going to override your ass one day, little boy," he warned, but I could tell he was ready to wrap this up, as was I. It was just too weird having one of Betty's studs actually trying to act like my dad. He glanced at his watch; I remembered he had to head out for an overnight run, which meant he'd be glad to get this conversation out of the way. "Could you just do me a favor and promise to go to school every day until it lets out? They're threatening to call juvie and getting your mom all upset."

That was going to be difficult, considering I already had plans for today that didn't include Central. Besides, I had the whole school thing all figured out. I always tested high on the aptitude tests; very high. I never did homework but always scanned the books and did well on the quizzes I took. At the end of the year, I would study up and ace the finals, and the teachers were always more than happy to move me on. With all the kids in their school who actually couldn't read or write—my compatriot Tommy, for example— why hold back a kid who could? Passing me made them look like they were actually teaching some of us a little something every now and then.

It was late. I was tired. "Sure," I said with a shrug.

"Good," Leon said, lightly slapping the table and rising. "I'll tell your mom we settled this. I got to get going to work." He checked his watch again and headed back into the living room, probably in search of his clothes. I was relieved he hadn't tried to hug me or expected us to touch in any way. I bolted up the stairs the moment his back was turned.

I checked in on my brothers again. Terry was back off the mattress, but I decided to leave him there. I held my nose and ducked into the bathroom to take a quick pee, flushed and checked my face in the mirror while the water swirled around before being swallowed by the rusty pipes. The same sandy-haired kid who always stared back at me was there: tired blue eyes above a smattering of light freckles, marred only by a couple of pimples that would spread into many more as I became a teenager. My hair needed washing, my teeth brushing, and my face scrubbing, but I didn't notice. Bathing was a maybe once-a-week thing for my brothers and me, and even less frequent for Betty.

I shut the door to my room and turned off the light before falling back onto my mattress. I scratched Benji's ears for a little while, listening to the murmur of voices below me. The sound increased in volume, threatening to swell into an outright fight, but soon became almost inaudible again. *Leon needing money for the road,* I surmised. He always promised to return the money when he got paid. Friday was payday, but Leon wouldn't show up until late Saturday or even Sunday, dead drunk and near broke by the time Betty saw him again.

She never learned. Married guys she met working at Bob's Big Boy—usually over-the-road truckers—drunks, bored bosses, and other lowlifes were

Betty's suitors. Few of them hung around long, and none of them were ever good to her for more than a few weeks. She'd been robbed, beaten, abused, and lied to so often that a man who just took her money and came and went as he pleased seemed like a prince. Most of them were here but a night or two before jetting off back to their own families. Maybe the sight of Betty without her makeup and teeth was more than they bargained for.

She'd been pretty once. I'd seen the pictures to prove it. My father had married her when she'd gotten pregnant with me, but then left her after finding out she had trouble keeping her legs crossed around his sailor buddies. There was even some question as to my true parentage, even though the man's last name of Davis was legally mine. I was even a junior; Donald Raymond Davis Jr. I'd never met him, but I thought almost every night about what he might be like. He never wrote or sent cards. Now and then I would get a five or a ten from his current wife—a lady named Grace—in a card signed by her and two half-brothers and a half-sister who lived out in Indiana. I acted like I hated those cards and pictures, but I kept them neatly hidden away in a shoe box. And I studied them too often.

I told so many lies concerning my father that I couldn't possibly keep up with them: He called me today. I was going to spend the summer with him. He had money. I was with him on his boat once. He was coming to see me. He was going to buy me a car when I was old enough. So on and so on. I also made up lies about having an older brother who would kick your ass if you messed with me. I lied about a lot of things. I told stories and embellished on those stories. It was a bad habit that followed me long into adulthood, a mechanism for dealing with internal scars that probably did more harm than good. But it seemed to work when I was a kid.

Tommy and Rupe knew I was lying most of the time, but neither called me on it. I guess they knew what I was doing better than I did myself. Street kids have better instincts than most. They have to or else they won't get very far. Not that they have that far to go. Rupe didn't talk much and Tommy was prone to spinning whoppers himself on occasion, so we got along well. Besides, who did it hurt that I liked to pretend someone really cared about me?

My brothers' last name was Williams. Betty had been married to their father for quite a few good years. They were the only pleasant times I could even vaguely remember. Terrance Williams had treated me like a son. But drugs, alcohol, and being blown out of a helicopter in Viet Nam turned him into a different man upon his return home. Throw in the fact that Betty had been having that leg-crossing problem again while he was overseas, and that marriage was over, even though they tried off and on to stay together. All that effort got Betty was some severe ass-beatings and Chip, the baby brother sucking his thumb in the next room, before Terrance left the country and moved to Australia, where he lived without having to pay child support.

So I listened to Betty and Leon downstairs, thankful they were only talking and not making some of the more vulgar noises I was accustomed to hearing, feeling sorry for myself. As it grew quiet again, I remembered our haul tonight, and that I was skipping school and would be spending the day with Tommy. Those were better thoughts. We would turn in our bottles soon, and I'd have a little cash. The first of the month was coming, and we'd have plenty to eat. Summer was coming, and we would be running all our scams, making money and having fun.

This was the same battle I fought every night. The same unanswered questions about my father were racing around in my brain, but instead of dwelling on what I didn't have, I planned on what little I could control. I looked forward to the best I had to grab on to. A car rolled through the alley, the headlights brightening the sheet hanging over the window, casting my room in weird shadows. I didn't care. I was tired, and I had Benji. Still, I didn't fall asleep until I heard the loud rumble of Leon's El Camino pulling out of the yard.

CHAPTER 2

Laundry sucked, especially when that chore included handling some guy's dirty drawers. It was bad enough to have to touch my mother's panties and bras, but Leon needed some new underwear in the worst way. The only good thing about washing Leon's clothes was occasionally finding forgotten money in his pants pockets. My scavenging this morning had turned up three mangled dollar bills and some lady named Brenda's phone number. I pocketed the money and tossed the number. Leon's choices concerning women left a lot to be desired. I was probably doing him a favor. And it would be one less thing for Betty to find and them to fight about.

Stumbling beneath the weight of a wet load of whites, I barely managed to beat a wild-eyed lady with a head full of curlers and pins to an available dryer. She cursed, and I garnered yet another evil glare, which I returned with my most innocent smile. I was an old hand at the Laundromat tactics of war. Always leave something of yours atop washing machines you'd claimed or intended to use. A magazine or a box of detergent was acceptable, even if the box was empty. If you removed clean clothes from the washer and left it unmanned while you gathered a second load? *Whoosh!* Some harried mother of six with a hundred pounds on you and a bad attitude would swoop in and claim the machine, displaying a speed that belied her bulk.

The dryers were a bit trickier. To keep a dryer called for tact and timing. The objective was to keep it running and hot by having washed clothes ready to go in even as you were taking dried clothes out. A dryer was more difficult to claim and keep than a washer. By the time the old bats needed dryers, they'd already been at the 'mat for an hour or three, chasing kids and bitching to anyone who'd listen about their pathetic lives and their countless problems. Tempers were short and the battles were often intense. There was no real rule concerning the dryers. First come first served. There were many

25

times I'd lost a dryer to some spiteful hag willing to pull rank on a kid, but I'd also witnessed some awesome fights between the beasts.

This place was open twenty-four hours, but I'd gotten here early. Today was Saturday, and it would be packed by eight or nine. It was even worse on Sunday. My mother was pulling a day shift at the Big Boy, so both of my brothers were with me. I had Chip caged in the shopping cart I'd hauled the clothes baskets in, and Terry was coloring in a book when he wasn't whining to me about wanting soda and candy out of the machines. Benji sat where I'd told him to stay near the cart, and Chip was busy trying to poke at him through the crossed wires along the bottom of his makeshift crib.

Most days the old broad who ran the place would be sitting behind her crappy little desk in the back, handing out change and watching her fuzzy black-and-white TV. I was glad she wasn't here today. She always got her wig all twisted if I brought my dog inside, or if Terry started climbing on the tables or coloring on the floor. The old bat hated her job—she probably hated her life—and was wise to any and all cons. It was no use trying to lie to her about a machine keeping your money and trying to get a free bag of M&Ms. There was no mercy coming from her, and she couldn't have cared less if a machine *did* keep your money. She'd just put a note on the thing saying it was broken and tell you to fill out a yellow slip of paper that she probably tossed as soon as you left.

"Donny, can I have my candy now?" Terry asked for the umpteenth time. He had crayon marking all over his hands, arms, and even his face. His reddish, curly hair hadn't been combed, and it was sticking out in every direction. Mattress head was an affliction my brothers and I suffered from almost daily, and a fact Rupe was always quick to point out to me as he handed over his comb.

"What did I tell you?" I snapped back.

He looked at me with those wide, brown eyes and that blank face I'd come to loathe. Younger children are born with the innate ability to piss off their older siblings. It seemed to me that Terry was better at it than most. He was always underfoot, in my stuff, eating or drinking something I'd wanted to save, whining about this or that, wandering off, or telling Betty about something I'd hidden and kept secret. We never got along, and our relationship worsened the older he got. I resented having to watch over him all the time, and he knew it. I was just a kid myself. I didn't feel much compassion for him then.

"You said if I was good. I'm being good."

"I said if you were good when I was *done,*" I retorted with more anger than necessary.

"Are you done?" he asked, as if he didn't know I still had clothes in two washers and the first load drying and a ton of folding to do.

I sighed and slammed the lid on the washer I'd just loaded after dumping in the detergent. Terry didn't even flinch. "Do I look like I'm done?"

My brother decided there just wasn't any reason to go on talking to me and headed back to the row of bolted-down plastic chairs by our cart, where he calmly continued his coloring. (Yes, the people in our neighborhood would have stolen them if they weren't actually bolted down.) I switched the knob to cold water for the colored clothes, wishing I could keep from fighting with him all the time.

I did know that life hadn't been easy for Terry. Born with cerebral palsy and a bowed spine, he'd also had a problem with the muscles in his neck. Betty had been under the care of army doctors, and they'd let her carry him for weeks past full term. Because he'd been in the womb longer than necessary, his head had been forced onto one shoulder, and he'd undergone agonizing therapy, made to use the constricted muscles to hold his head straight. Betty had tortured Terry for months after bringing him home, twisting his head back and forth to loosen the tendons. It seemed like Terry had been torturing *me* ever since, as if I was the source of his problems.

Like I said, he was always on my nerves. We warred constantly. He told on me, and I smacked him around. He got into my stuff, and I'd hold him over the second-floor handrail by his ankles until he screamed for mercy, and he'd tell on me for that. I'd put Benji in my room if I was doing something unsafe for a dog to attend, and Terry would let him out. Sometimes he made me so intensely angry that I choked him, but as of yet I hadn't followed through and actually strangled him.

Chip was the exact opposite. He looked like a smaller version of me, with blonde hair, blue eyes, and a slight build. Everyone liked my youngest brother. He was quiet and well-behaved. He never bothered what he wasn't supposed to, and usually did what he was told, making my life that much easier. His real name was Roland Leslie Williams, but we called him Chip. *Who would name a kid Roland Leslie?* I'd often asked myself. No wonder the baby was so quiet. He was probably saving energy for all the fights coming his way if the guys he hung with ever discovered his given name.

A loud, rusted-out hatchback pulled up in front, and two girls piled out, throwing open the back and lifting out baskets of dirty clothes. The driver lifted a heavy hand and waved at me, the skin of her arm flapping under duress, so I waved back. She yelled something at me, but I couldn't hear her over the rumble of the car. I let her know my difficulty by shaking my head and pointing at my ears.

"Mama wants to know why you didn't wait for us to give you a ride," Bess, the younger of the sisters, informed me as she carried her first basket inside.

Because Mama was late again, and because stuffing my clothes and my brothers and my dog and myself into that car with all of you was more frightening than the time Betty overdosed on sleeping pills and I found her naked in the bathtub. "I was in a hurry. I've got stuff to do later."

"What stuff?" she asked, nosy as always.

The car rolled away as Lynn, Bess's older sister, came in toting two baskets piled on top of one another and dragging a full bag besides. Lynn was a ruddy-faced, brawny bull of a girl. She could fight as well as any boy her age, and was mean as a hungry dog. I doubted if I could've easily managed the load she was so casually tossing onto the row of cracked plastic chairs nearest her sister, who was still standing there waiting for my response to her question.

"We're going to practice for tomorrow's football game," I explained.

Beating the guys who were involved with recreation league football or baseball was one of our passions. Rupe couldn't run so he had to be the quarterback. Luckily, the kid had a great arm. He could throw a baseball hard, too. Tommy and I did most of the work. I scored a lot of touchdowns, and he cracked heads, making savage tackles. Every now and then some old guy would approach us about playing on some team or another, but Tommy said we didn't want any part of them. Only thing was, sometimes I thought maybe I did.

Bess smiled. She was smaller than her sister, and much prettier. "Rupe going to be there?"

Of course she would ask about Rupe. Bess was sweet on him. Sometimes she was sweet on me. Other times she would be harping about some boy from her church named Gordon or Cory or some other gay-sounding guy. I didn't pay her much mind, although I often harbored sore feelings for Rupe if he started getting too interested in Bess, or if I caught him sneaking over to her apartment without taking me along, although it was okay if *I* snuck over there without *him*.

Both girls had pale complexions, strawberry hair, and freckled cheeks, and Mama Z.—that was what we called her since their last name began with a Z and was hard to pronounce—claimed she was going to marry them both off to rich doctors. Bess was a year younger than me, slight of build and pretty, with a chatty disposition and a quick smile. Lynn was a couple of years older than Bess, solid, strong, and sullen, with a temper that flared as quickly as her younger sister's inviting smile. Leon was always telling me that both of them were going to look just like their mom one day. It seemed to me that Lynn had one hell of a head start.

"Yeah, he'll be there," I told her as Terry tried to sneak closer to us. I shot him my best *you better get away from me* glare, and he retreated.

Lynn went over and rubbed Benji's head. She liked animals and was fond of my intelligent little buddy. The traitor wagged his tail and wiggled onto his back for a vigorous belly rub, which Lynn obliged. She was the only other person he let hold him, or command him to perform his arsenal of tricks. Benji treated the rest of my friends as if he couldn't hear a word they said when they tried to tell him what to do, and occasionally showed teeth if they tried too hard to touch him. But for Lynn he'd jump through hoops, and was always overjoyed to see her.

"Chip crapped himself," Lynn told me as she came back to start loading a washer.

"Great," I said, slapping myself in the forehead. I hadn't brought along any diapers. I was always forgetting something concerning my brothers. They always needed to be fed, or changed, or found, or they were crying over something stupid like falling or wanting cartoons on the TV. "Would you keep an eye on them while I run home and get a diaper?"

Lynn nodded, and Bess started chirping something, but I was already on the move. Home was four blocks. I could be there and back in a flash. Benji started to follow me, and I told him to stay. He dropped his ears but obeyed. *That'll teach you to fall all over yourself for some stupid girl,* I thought, but then dismissed the notion. Old Benji was my best and truest friend. And Lynn was a stand-up girl. Truth was, I kind of liked her, too. She baby-sat for my mom, occasionally freeing me of that tedious chore. She was also good at all card games, especially rummy, and could even throw the ball or Frisbee around if you wanted.

My feet were slapping uneven pavement as I ran for home, barely slowing down as I crossed the first street. There weren't very many cars out this time of the morning. The street we lived on was usually the most congested street in our neighborhood, but traffic was still light. Not that kids raised in the city needed to pay special attention to traffic. It was an instinct most of us were born with. Only kids I ever knew who were struck by cars were the idiots who jumped the curb, or the ones who got popped darting out from between parked cars or around a blind corner too close to an alleyway.

I jumped a section of pavement jutting awkwardly, forced skyward by the root of a huge tree, dodged a lady walking her black lab, and ducked into the alley that would leave me just two blocks from home. Now I was Archie Griffin running for the end zone. Trash cans were would-be tacklers that I avoided and leapt over, and an old refrigerator box was the last man to beat. A stiff arm and a quick sidestep, and I was flying down the sideline, the roar of the crowd deafening in the Horseshoe.

Ohio State football was huge in Columbus. In the seventies, the football program was in its heyday. Woody Hayes, Rose Bowls, Archie winning Heismans, and victories over the hated Michigan Wolverines were constant topics of conversation, even among those of us too poor to actually get tickets to the games. We may have missed out on actually seeing the contests in person, but we watched them on TV. And we could idolize our favorite players for free and pretend we were them when we played sandlot football.

The back screen was locked, so I reached in through the rip along the bottom and flipped the latch, dug the key out of my front jeans pocket and opened the door. We hardly ever bought the disposables, so I grabbed one of the few clean cloth diapers off the kitchen counter and headed back. Rupe was cruising up my walk on his skateboard as I locked the door. He noticed the diaper in my hand and the flush of my face and grinned beneath that pointy nose of his. Rupe was much more brazen when Tommy wasn't around.

"Forgot the diapers again, I see," he noted, using his best professor's voice.

"Jesus, Rupe, I never knew you were a genius," I shot back, trotting past him.

He flipped his board around and quickly caught up to me. Skateboarding was another of our pastimes, although not one Tommy shared with Rupe and me. Tommy was a late sleeper—a condition that didn't help his poor grades, since school refused to wait until he crawled out of bed, which was rarely before noon and even later during the summer. We normally hit the sloped driveway of the doctor's office over on 5th on Saturday and Sunday mornings without our burly buddy along.

It was a good time. A few other guys usually joined in, and Rupe and I would show them up. We ramped and rode wheelies, grinded the curbs and let our boards roll under obstacles we jumped over. If any upstart pulled off a trick that actually threatened to compete with us, we'd pull out the heavy artillery and show off our handstands. As yet, nobody but us had come close to riding a handstand all the way to the bottom of the drive. Both of us fervently hoped no one else ever would.

The best was a game we called *warboards*. We'd challenge any and all comers, and the objective was to knock the other guys off their boards on the ride down. We usually won at this friendly conflict, but there were some older guys who beat us as often as we did them. Those battles usually left us cut and scraped. Still, there was no better time. Except maybe when Bess tagged along and tried a trick or two, and her skirt flew up. We always pretended not to notice, but Bess never quit trying tricks and that skirt kept flying.

Bess and Lynn attended a church that didn't allow girls to wear pants. There were always people from that church knocking on your door and asking you to ride their bus, talking about God and the good times you would have if you tagged along. The kids on that bus would sing weird songs and bring home crafts and Bible lessons. I couldn't imagine anything being worth giving up half your Sunday just to take a ride out to rich people country.

Rupe followed me clear back to the 'mat without another word. He wasn't fooling me. He knew good and well that Bess was there. We found Lynn sitting out front holding Benji. I peeked in and saw why: old Blue Head was behind her desk, TV already blazing. A load of my dried clothes was waiting for me on the folding table nearest my brothers. Terry was munching something and sipping a Fanta orange soda he'd probably conned out of Lynn. Chip was still sitting in his own crap, crying and pointing at Terry's drink. My middle brother was facing him while he drank, lording his good fortune over the baby.

I motioned for Lynn to put down Benji, and told him to stay. Benji was an old hand at waiting outside for me. I could walk a store for an hour, and he'd be right where I left him. I went inside and snatched the soda from

Terry before he noticed I was back and handed it to Chip, and then I picked him up and headed for the bathroom to change him. Chip stopped crying as Terry started wailing.

Swapping my baby brother's diaper wasn't difficult. Off with the old, wipe the butt with damp toilet paper or paper towels if handy, on with the new (taking care not to stick a wriggling two-year-old with the pins), and flush the poopy wiping material. But washing out the soiled cloth diaper to use again required rinsing as much of the crap as possible in the toilet or sink, and then wringing out the diaper and keeping it around to be washed. I wasn't in the mood and simply tossed the thing in the trash container. This wasn't going to please Betty or the broad who ran the place, but I didn't care.

Before I picked Chip up, he managed to dump what was left of the orange soda down the front of his dingy T-shirt. Again, I didn't care. I tossed the can and left the mess on the floor, just taking a second or two to wipe what I could off his face. *Make my dog stay outside, will you,* I thought as I walked past the old glaring hag. She wasn't sporting her fashionable wig this morning, and I could see mottled age spots on her scalp through the wispy strands of bluish hair vainly struggling to cover her head.

Bess was giggling at something Rupe was saying as I came back. I tried to ignore them. Terry's bellowing had convinced someone to give him another soda—grape this time—and he had both hands wrapped tightly around the can, his eyes watching me intently over the rim as he gulped. He was playing games with the wrong guy; I had Leon's three bucks to spend on myself and Chip. If he thought he was getting one over on me, he was so wrong.

"No riding those things in here!" the old lady behind the desk crowed at Rupe.

He obliged, stepping off the board and scooting it under the folding table with his foot. He murmured something I couldn't hear to Bess and plopped up on the washer she was waiting for. It was running, and he grinned at the vibration beneath his backside, holding out his arms like wings and saying, "Here comes the Red Baron, making another run." His voice sounded weird due to the shaking of the machine, causing Bess to giggle like an idiot again.

"No sitting on the washers, either!" the hag called out, ending Rupe's antics. He gave the old lady a dark glare, but he jumped off and settled for only leaning against the washer.

"Shot down again," he said, but the vibration was no longer strong enough to affect his voice, and not so funny after being cowed by the nag and her watchful eye.

I checked on Benji under the onslaught of blue hair's evil glare. She was just waiting and hoping I'd try to bring him back in. "*Go ahead, dearie, bring in your little dog,*" I said, doing my best imitation of the Wicked Witch of the West. Chip laughed and grabbed at my lips while everyone else just looked at me like I was losing my mind, including my dog.

I plopped the baby back in the cart and snatched up his empty bottle, Terry eyeing me suspiciously all the while. After a return trip to the bathroom—which was already reeking—to wash out the bottle, I got change from the hag and bought two grape sodas and two Hershey bars. I filled up the bottle and peeled the wrapping off Chip's chocolate, enjoying the sight of Terry's horror-stricken face as he finally realized the error of his ways.

"Knock yourself out, kid," I told the baby, filling his reaching hands.

Terry's bawling was sweet music. *Keep messing with me, little brother.*

"He's going to make a mess of that," Lynn warned me.

"Yeah, I know."

Bess pursed her lips and shook her head at me. "Why are you always so mean to him?" she asked.

I shrugged. "I told him to be good and wait," I explained, walking over to the table and starting my first load of folding. I smiled tightly at her. "He should have waited."

"You didn't pay for anything," scolded Lynn.

I checked my washers, finding one on the last spin. My dryer was churning away, and no one appeared to have an eye on it. "And you didn't pay for anything I just bought, either," I returned easily. "But that's not the point, is it?"

"And just what is the point?" Rupe asked. His nose wasn't just pointed; it was also sticking into business where it didn't belong. And I hadn't forgotten Bess's giggling.

"He should do what he's told. Not run behind my back and get what he wants from somebody else."

"Are you God?" Rupe asked, magnanimous in front of the girls, showing off for Bess. *That's it, buddy.* He had this coming.

"Nope, just his favorite."

Rupe snorted, still playing for the crowd. "If you're God's favorite, what are you do—"

Whatever he was going to say was lost as I spun and threw a pair of Betty's shimmering oversized panties directly into his face. Rupe convulsed and threw himself off the machine he was still leaning on, throwing the offending undergarment back at me and howling like he'd been stung by a whole swarm of bees. He stood there gawking at me, wiping at his face.

"What… what the hell are you doing!" he stammered.

Rupe was cute when he was bewildered. I bent over and carefully picked up the underwear, watching Rupe closely. Now and again he'd rise up, and I'd have to thrash him; I was hoping now wasn't one of those times. That Bess was here was a good thing. Rupe wouldn't want his ass kicked in front of her. But he just stood in place, reddening as both Lynn and Bess giggled. They weren't the only ones laughing. I could hear a lady behind me chortling as well, and I was sure I'd caught a brief glimpse of a smile from the old bat behind her desk.

"I ought to—"

"Rupe, you tick me off and I'll shove this right in your mouth," I promised, holding up the panties to further emphasize my point.

And that ended anything more from Rupe. I felt a little bad about embarrassing him like that, but only a little. Bess was more of a sore spot for me than I wanted to admit, even to myself. And I didn't want anybody giving me grief over Terry.

"You two are sick," mumbled Lynn.

"Definitely," Bess agreed.

Who was I to argue? I waited for a grin from Rupe, which came with much reluctance. Lynn started helping me fold my clothes while I pulled more dry ones out of my dryer and added the load that had just finished. I put a few more dimes in the thing and clicked the knob each time, wondering how much whoever owned this place made off these machines. He probably had a house out in richville, just sitting around while we dumped our money in machines we couldn't afford to own. In fact, he probably had more than one set up just like this joint in more neighborhoods like ours. *What a racket.*

I was always wondering why other people lived better than we did. How they afforded big homes and new cars. Why their lawns and houses looked so clean while ours looked like… Well, why it looked like it did. Why so many of the moms in those yards were pretty and trim, while most of ours strutted around in protesting spandex with cigarettes hanging out of their mouths and last night's booze still glistening in their eyes. Not that I didn't understand the concept of working. It was the working at what and the how I was missing.

I guessed that having a father around was important to any chance at a life like that. Betty rarely even paid the rent or utilities, and never made a car payment. We usually paid enough to get into a place, then just rode out the storm until the landlord managed to convince us to leave, or forced us to with an eviction notice. Once Betty had money in her hands, she spent it on what she wanted, not what we needed. We wouldn't still be in the rat trap we were currently living in if Leon hadn't caught Betty up on the rent and paid to have the lights turned back on.

And writing bad checks was Betty's most persistent downfall. She would get checking accounts from multiple banks, write as many rubber checks as she could—usually for junk like ceramics, Avon, or clothes—and skip out when the heat came down.

She had warrants in three or four states that I knew of. Last summer we'd blown out of Florida faster than a gulf hurricane, leaving behind almost everything we owned. Not that anything we owned amounted to much. I had rarely completed a school year in the same place, and was often moving on to a different school before my records from the last one even caught up. The threat of being held back was always hanging over my head, but fortunately, I'd always been smart enough to be moved on. At least up to this point in my young life.

"Will you guys come to church with us tomorrow?" Bess asked as I came back to help Lynn with my folding. She was always hounding us, and especially me, to ride her bus and check out her church. That was another cool thing about Lynn; she didn't bother me about her religion.

"Nah," Rupe gently rebuffed. "My family attends a Methodist church. My dad says Baptists are nothing but snake charmers and raving lunatics who bathe in piss-filled rivers. He'd have a heart attack if I ever went to your church."

"You're not a Methodist," Bess told me. I didn't even know what a Methodist was. For that matter, I didn't know what a Baptist was either.

"No, but I'm sure Betty's slept with some man who was. That's the same thing."

"You're horrible," Bess scolded.

Rupe laughed. I was always the comedian, and an expert at mom joke warfare. Few kids had the ammo I did when it came to material.

"You shouldn't talk bad about your mother," Lynn mumbled.

"That's in the Bible," added Bess.

"Not his mom," said Rupe. That was a good one. We both laughed.

I couldn't resist. "Sure she is. Isn't there some story about a prostitute Jesus saves from being stoned to death?"

I knew more than a few Bible stories from a book I'd read. It was full of pictures and fantastic tales about Jesus and other men. Jesus performed miracles but never really socked it to anybody. A guy named Moses dumped a whole sea on some soldiers who were chasing him. The stories about David were my favorites. I never really understood why Jesus was considered more important than all of the others, especially since they killed him at the end of the book.

David was more like the superheroes in the comics I adored. He killed a giant called Goliath, and fought wars. He stole women and did just about anything he wanted. Everyone loved David. Even though he made a mistake or two, God still called David his favorite. I figured if David was okay with God after the stuff he'd done, could be I still had a pretty good chance as well.

"Couldn't have been your mom, who would pay to sleep with her?" Rupe said through his laughter.

I had to give him credit. He was on a roll. I decided not to come back at him. Rupe was touchy where his mom was concerned. And I didn't care if you berated Betty. Besides, I'd already hit him in the face with my mother's bloomers. That was punishment enough for almost any crime committed by man. I let Rupe have his fun.

Bess started telling some story about a family at church while Lynn and I folded. That girl could talk, and talk fast. She required very little feedback and either didn't notice or didn't care whether you were interested in her chosen topic. Her voice had a little squeak to it that set your teeth on edge after a thousand words or so, and it almost took an event of catastrophic proportions to interrupt her once she really got going, something akin to a gunshot or an earthquake.

Bess paused for breath, and Rupe dove into the brief moment of silence. "You going to board today?"

"I can't. My mom's pulling a day shift." Waiting tables was the one job Betty was good at, although she wasn't exactly dependable. Customers provided tips, which afforded her ready cash for immediate needs like Pepsi or gas money for Leon, and she usually brought us kids home something from the kitchen. (That is, we got whatever Leon or some other guy didn't want.) Waitressing also presented my mother with a constant source of men. She had her choice of gap-toothed truckers, bored and desperate married guys looking for something quick on the side, greasy mechanics, out-of-work laborers, and other lowlifes.

Leon was one of the truck drivers, although he also worked on the side as one of the greasy mechanics. He'd been around for about four or five months, off and on. As far as Betty's suitors went, he wasn't all that bad. He hadn't hit me or my brothers, or stolen anything from us that my mom hadn't freely given away. He ate a lot, and took up the entire couch when he watched TV. The worst was his tendency to walk around in underwear that should have been tossed years ago, with his balls occasionally slipping out for the world to see. I did think it was funny when he'd notice and tell them to get back where they belonged before tucking himself away. I had to say Leon was one of the more decent men to ever spend time around Betty and her brood.

A few of her live-ins hadn't been nearly so manageable. One or two had been downright scary. Betty wasn't above dragging home the occasional child molester or ax murderer. I made sure both my brothers slept in my room when one of these creeps was around; I didn't hate Terry so much that I would have wanted to see him get hurt. Benji was a fail-safe warning device if anyone tried to sneak into my room. I'd been slapped a time or two, but so far threatening to call the cops had kept her more aggressive male friends at bay.

"You can go for an hour or two," Lynn offered. "I'll finish up for you and haul Terry and Chip home. Just don't be gone too long."

I didn't want to take advantage of Lynn, but I'd done it before. "What about your clothes, and Bess?"

"I'll stay here until we're done. Bess can call Mama from your house."

I wanted to go, but I knew it was wrong of me. "How are you going to get all these clothes in one shopping cart?"

Lynn shrugged. "It's not that far. The boys can walk, and I can carry a basket or two while Bess pushes the cart."

I looked at Bess, who only nodded without talking. *Thank God.*

"The Miller brothers are there already, wanting to roll a round of *warboards*," Rupe told me.

And that was it. I couldn't deny the Miller boys. "You have your key?" I asked Lynn, inching toward the door. She nodded. "Here." I handed over what was left of my change, more than enough to finish the drying. "Use what's left to buy them something to keep 'em quiet. I won't stay long. I promise."

Bess started talking again, so I told my brothers to mind, darted outside and patted my thigh, letting Benji know to come with me. Rupe may have been more interested in Bess than I was, but he gathered his board and left her blabbing away in the 'mat. Battling the Miller boys was still a stronger urge than the allure of a girl when you were twelve.

CHAPTER 3

When you were nearing your teen years and had never owned a toothbrush, the day when the health teacher decided everyone had to chew those stupid chalk tablets that revealed how much plaque was on your teeth was brutal. I dreaded health class, and hated those little pills most of all. Of all the days I chose not to skip! But I had to take two finals. I was feeling so good, knowing I'd aced both of them. With math and English out of the way, I just had science and health to get past, but this humiliating ritual had caught me completely unawares.

Jenny Tolliver was right in front of me. She smiled into the little hand mirror Mrs. Perkins held and showed off a mouth full of white teeth, traced with pinkish lines at the edges. *Why did you get behind the girl with the Colgate smile?* I asked myself. I'd managed to miss this exercise last year. As a matter of fact, quite a few of us had. *No doubt the reason she kept it so secret this time around,* I noted. I'd always liked Mrs. Perkins. I couldn't be sore at her for only doing her job. Worst of all, this was my last class of the day. I could've skipped out early and missed this aggravation, had I known.

"Smile, Donny," she instructed, showing me how to do so.

Mrs. Perkins had tiny, perfect teeth, ivory white and straight as any movie-star smile. Then again, everything about her was perfect. Her clothes were always businesslike but eye-catching. Her dark, glossy hair was always pinned up but stunning. You knew her hair must be gorgeous when set loose and flowing around her shoulders. Her posture was stiff but somehow still friendly, her manner aloof but approachable.

Her face was smooth, and her makeup was barely noticeable. It looked to me like she was something right off the cover of one of my mom's magazines. She wasn't tall, but her skirts usually fit her shapely form snugly, and her body commanded attention. Those of us too young to really understand why we were looking still did, hoping she'd be the one to give us our first clue. Even the girls worshipped her, since she was young enough to relate to them. What I loved most about her were her eyes; they reminded me of the big, soft, brown eyes of a deer.

Once, I'd almost told her she was beautiful. A lot of other guys actually had. Tommy had even invited her to a party. We cracked up at the way the male teachers in our school fell all over themselves when Mrs. Perkins graced them with her presence in the lunchroom. The principal, old cranky Davenport, was by far the most obvious, and dense, of her adoring fans. We'd nearly died the time he spilled his tray, craning his neck to check her out as she strutted primly by.

I parted my lips a bit and tried to leave, but that wasn't good enough for her. "Wider," she instructed, one slender hand taking my arm and drawing me back. Reluctantly, I looked into the mirror and tightly pulled back my lips. My teeth glowed like Christmas bulbs. The only portions of my mouth that weren't a bright red from the tablets were the darker lines that I assumed had to be the minute spaces between my teeth. Mrs. Perkins flinched, but to her credit she let me go after only saying, "Well, I see."

"Damn, it looks like you been drinking blood," Butch, the boy behind me said before I could get away, breaking up the class.

"What about that, Donny, you a vampire?" Mike asked from his desk.

"Butch, Mike, I will see you both after class," Mrs. Perkins informed them, abruptly silencing their fun. "Shall I be having any other visitors?" No one volunteered, and she continued down the line, leaving me to find my desk in shame. The only thing worse than being beaten up was getting two guys who *could* beat you up in trouble, and then knowing you were going to take a beating later. Both of them gave me knowing looks that promised just that.

Butch I could maybe square things with. He was one of the guys I always sold my free lunch tickets to. I would add the change I got from him to whatever I'd stolen out of the pants pockets of one of Betty's boyfriends and buy lunch. If I didn't have the money, I didn't eat. I would love to tell you it was a pride thing, but it wasn't. When you told as many lies about a rich father or a cool older brother who made sure you never wanted for anything as I did, free lunch tickets just didn't fit.

Thinking back, I'm sure I wasn't fooling anyone. My clothes were never new and rarely clean. There were no sports jerseys or new Nikes when I was growing up. I didn't even own a pair of Levis. My jeans were those thinning or patched corduroys that Betty dug out of some church basement or happened across at the Goodwill. The Keds I was wearing currently had duct tape along the inner sole, a desperate attempt to keep the rips along the inseams from splitting further. I never had a real haircut—Betty just gave us those bowl cuts, and I'm not shitting you, she actually used the bowl—and I've already described my teeth.

No, they knew I was dirt poor. What probably saved me a heap of persecution was that many of my peers weren't much better off. The kids like Rupe, lucky enough to have two parents, fared better than most, and others had grandparents or well-off aunts and uncles who made life easier for them. What really got to me were the guys who had single moms but didn't have the same crap to deal with that I did. Somehow their moms managed to keep them clothed, fed, and safe from creeps without falling into the same pits Betty was always crawling out of.

Mike Collins was going to be a problem. He was a two-parent kid with an attitude. He played on the school's football, basketball, and baseball teams as a seventh grader, and was always rubbing elbows with the coaches, He would be one of their starters again next year, when we came back in the fall. He was popular with the teachers, and more popular with the girls. Mike pretty much did what he pleased, and knocked around anyone who didn't please him. In this case, that anyone was soon going to be me.

When the bell rang to send us home, I was actually thankful Mrs. Perkins was holding Mike after class. I would have at least a one-day reprieve. Going to Tommy for help wasn't an option. Guys just didn't do that—unless you were a younger brother or cousin—if you were going to keep the respect of your peers. Tommy would expect me to stand up to Collins and go toe-to-toe. If, by some miracle, I managed to actually win the fight, Tommy would leave it alone. If I lost—which I was most assuredly going to—Mike Collins versus Tommy Washington would be an anticipated clash of titans. Tommy would make up an excuse to confront Mike and then soundly thrash him, but as great as that was going to be, it did little to ease my present state of mind.

Mrs. Perkins asked me, Kyle Tracy, and the quiet Spanish kid whose name I could never remember (much less pronounce) to come up to her desk before I could get away. Everyone else filed out save Butch and Mike, who still sat at their desks. I could feel their eyes on my back as I walked up to the front of the class. The blackboard behind Mrs. Perkins was washed clean, a polished black that mocked me still. Last year she'd written down the day we'd undergo this humiliation on that very board. *At least it's over,* I told myself.

And then she opened her drawer and pulled out kits containing a toothbrush and a tube of Crest. I stood there, watching in stupefied horror as she explained how we were to brush our teeth in a circular manner, making sure to reach the molars in the back. The snickers from Butch and Mike erased every kind or admiring thought I'd ever held for the beautiful young woman sitting before us. She handed the others her gift and smiled at them when she was through. I'd never hated any teacher more. I didn't extend my hand to take her offering.

Mike would have a field day with this. It was going to be one of those humiliating events that followed you for years, like a retarded little brother you just couldn't ditch. Something this embarrassing would be difficult to live down, and impossible to defend against. I could think of about a zillion yellow teeth one-liners without even straining.

I had a dim memory of being dragged to the nurse's office in first or second grade. We'd lived in a lice-infested trailer at the time, and of course I'd hauled the nasty little buggers to school and passed them on to many of my classmates. I remembered being scrubbed and having crap dug out of my ears, and then I was dusted with a strong-smelling powder. What I remembered most was the disgust on the nurse's face, and my teacher's, and the anger of the other moms at the bus stop.

"I hear you're leaving next year," I said to Mrs. Perkins.

My remark caught her off guard. "Yes, I am," she admitted, her pretty smile fading a bit. "I will be teaching at New Castle High next year."

"Finally tired of slumming?" I said. "Going out to richville to teach kids who are more like you?"

Her pity-laden smile was all gone now. "I happen to live in New Castle. I was raised there. I've always wanted to teach there, and my husband already..."

"You don't have to explain to me," I said, lifting my hands and waving off her explanation. "I wouldn't want to hang around here with us either. All the good teachers leave for better kids and schools."

That was true. Central was only a brief stopping point for teachers waiting for positions in better schools. The older teachers who'd been here for years were just clock-watching paper-pushers, barely more animated than the desks they huddled behind. We disliked them, and we knew they absolutely hated us. As if we were somehow responsible for the dead-end job that had grown up around them, the source of the violence and disdain instead of a product of it.

"You are mistaken, Donny," she told me, her jaw set firmly and her eyes flashing. Mad as I was, I felt my heart hammering in the thin bones of my chest. She was prettier than ever when angry. "All professionals seek better positions. That's just the way it is. When you're older you will understand this to be true as well."

"Don't worry, Mrs. P. Nobody blames you for getting out of here," I finished, turning away from her and walking toward the exit.

Mike and Butch were still looking at me, but at least they weren't laughing anymore. Mrs. Perkins didn't speak up to stop me from leaving. I made the safety of the hallway and quietly closed the door to health class before breaking into a run. Activity was already light in the halls, so I dashed for the south doors and the streets toward home. There was no telling how long she would hold Mike and Butch. Especially after she noticed I'd never taken her damn toothbrush and paste.

I thought about what Mrs. P. was trying to do as I walked home, and I was sure she didn't mean anything demeaning by her actions. But that was how it was. Either adults looked right through you, acting as if you were already only a year or two away from prison, as if you really didn't concern them and had no place in their perfect little world. Or they pitied you. Pity was by far the worst.

As a health teacher, it was Mrs. Perkins's job to teach us how to take care of ourselves, and I supposed she should probably get some credit for still trying while so many others didn't care to. But I needed more aggravation in my life like Betty needed unemployed boyfriends. And if she really needed to pull something like that, I'd have preferred she did it when we were completely alone. As mad as I was, though, for some reason I kept seeing Betty's false teeth lying on the coffee table, like some nasty and foreboding vision.

Was I genetically coded to the same fate as my biological mother? Would I wind up toothless, clueless, and broke because of heredity—or because of where and how we lived? Both? I didn't want to wind up here on these streets, running from cops for the rest of my life. I wanted a career and a big house and new cars. I loved animals, especially dogs. Maybe I could be a veterinarian? I wanted a TV family, complete with the hot wife and the perfect kids who always got good grades and never did the stupid shit me and my friends were always into.

Question was, how to get what I wanted? Who was I going to ask? Who cared to tell me? All of my relatives were welfare poor and in and out of trouble. Those who weren't in jail were just a step or two ahead of those who'd put them there. My mother's father was a retired Navy man who also worked for the state of Florida, but Betty had sucked so much out of him the poor guy probably keeled over every time his phone rang.

He'd set her up in Florida a couple years earlier, finding us a house with a yard to rent and even getting her a decent-paying job with the state. But Betty was Betty. Checking accounts with too many gullible banks had been a lure she couldn't resist. Before her spending spree was over, my mother had bought a kiln in which she was going to bake her own ceramic figures and pottery, and hundreds of dollars-worth of materials. In the end she'd had to leave all that crap behind when we raced north, just ahead of the police and more than one active warrant.

I was wondering how close we were to taking flight again when I saw Tommy and the guys starting up a game of football. The sides looked about normal for the status quo. Most of the "rec" league guys on one squad and the neighborhood gang on the other. Tommy's black face split wide when he saw me, showing his large white teeth and shaking his head as he waved me over. No one protested. I was always on the neighborhood side. So was Rupe, who grinned at me as well as I approached.

"I hear Collins is going to kick your little ass as soon as he sees you," Tommy teased when I was close enough.

Didn't bad news travel fast? Every kid in the school had probably heard about health class by now. Even if Mike had wanted to reconsider, he'd have no choice since everyone was talking about it. If he didn't whip up on me, the guys would say he was afraid. I shrugged as if I wasn't concerned, all bravado, but I could feel my heart skip and my pulse quicken as the reality of the upcoming confrontation suddenly loomed, imminent.

"Just what did you say?" Rupe asked.

"I didn't say anything," I responded too quickly.

Some of the other guys were grinning at me now. I glared back and a few of them averted their gazes. Being afraid of Mike Collins was one thing, but none of these kids were anyone I had to duck. Tommy was, of course.

I wouldn't have tangled with Tommy Washington even if it meant being an outcast from Central for the rest of my days in the school.

"It was Mrs. Perkins. She made them stay after for popping off."

Tommy glanced at the other team. They were yelling at us to get ready to receive the ball. He and I moved to the rear to take the kickoff. "Fuck Collins," he told me when we were out of earshot of the others. "And fuck tight-assed Mrs. P., too," he added. "When Collins steps up to you, just hit him first. Aim for his throat. And then just keep punching, kicking, and biting like you some crazy motherfucker."

I wanted to ask just how I was supposed to pull off the throat thing, but the ball was already in the air, turning end over end as it headed in my direction. I had to run up a few long steps to get under it, but not too far, and I caught the ball clean and on the run. I faked left and started around the end, checking to see if Tommy was going to lag behind and demand a pitch, but he loped in front of me and did his best to kill some poor kid with a savage block before I got run out of bounds at about midfield.

Rupe took charge in the huddle. He was always the quarterback because he was so slow, but he also had the best arm. Tommy could throw as hard, but not nearly with the accuracy of our speed-challenged buddy. Tommy was still hyped up from his first hit, so he demanded the ball out of the backfield and we all just nodded. And the game was on.

We were playing seven on seven, with three guys hanging out on the line from each team. This left an extra defender to roam around. A five-Mississippi count and the extra guy on defense could rush the quarterback, but Rupe never let anybody close enough to hit him. If one of us didn't get open in due time, he just hurled the ball out of bounds as soon as any threat to his body crossed the line of scrimmage. You were also allotted one blitz per series, but I was always cutting quickly into my friend's line of sight if someone screamed out *blitz!* and charged, giving our team an easy completion and sparing Rupe physical harm.

Three completions and your team earned a first down and a new series of plays, which meant running plays were risky. Once the quarterback handed the ball off, the line of scrimmage was no longer honored, and rushing across without counting didn't cost your team its blitz. This made completing three passes difficult. But if Tommy wanted to run the ball, we gave it to him. Sometimes his temper and determination to run right through the other team cost us the game, though none of us dared to tell him that.

I thought about Collins as the game got underway, wondering if I could avoid him for the next couple of days. This Thursday was the last of the school year, and a long, lazy summer beckoned, a mere day and a half away. *Maybe you could skip.* But no, I had those finals tomorrow. And, of course, health was one of the last tests I had to take. I couldn't bomb it either. *That'll teach you to skip so much and not turn in your homework.*

"Donny, wake up, man!" Rupe barked at me as the huddle dispersed.

I didn't have a clue what the play was, so I just ran down field, darting past the freckled kid trying to guard me like he wasn't even there, ducking his feeble attempt to jam me at the line. I didn't know the guy's name, but he raced after me and gave me an elbow in the small of the back as I slowed down. Rupe dumped the ball off to Taylor Johns, another of the neighborhood kids who usually played on our team. Freckles and I made our way back, pushing and shoving each other while Johns clamored to his feet from beneath a pile of "rec" league pukes.

"You better talk someone else into guarding me, turtle boy," I warned my new friend as I left him.

"I hear you talking," he sent back.

But he was nervous. I heard it in the preteen squawk of his voice. We both knew he didn't have a chance in hell of staying with me.

"Dump one off to me," I told Rupe as we broke the huddle.

I had purposely waited for everyone else to start away, leaving no one to refute my suggestion. Rupe nodded, almost imperceptibly.

"Here it comes, lard ass," I laughed, striking my best impersonation of a sprinter's stance in the blocks.

Freckles said something that I ignored. All I was aware of was the three or four steps backward he took, hoping to give himself a better chance of staying with me down the length of the field for the bomb he knew was about to come. *Elementary, Watson,* I silently mused, trying not to grin.

When the ball was snapped I took two quick steps, sending my defender stumbling like a drunkard. Rupe tossed me the football as Freckles stopped himself and desperately lurched toward me. One quick sidestep and I was racing down field to score untouched. I laughed at lard ass and flipped the ball in his general direction as I trotted away, cocky as always, shaking my head at him and enjoying myself immensely while his teammates cussed and complained at how easily I'd just scored.

We continued to jaw at each other from that point on. Freckles even tried to catch a pass in my vicinity, which I almost intercepted but easily knocked down, leaving our opponents to punt the ball away. They were putting pressure on him to switch up and let somebody faster guard me, but turtle boy was mad and having none of that. I kept giving it to him every chance I got, smiling and heckling, sure of myself, loving his humiliation.

"Down out and up that fool, Donny," Tommy insisted in our next huddle.

Everybody laughed. We were killing them today. Another touchdown or two and someone would start a fight, ending the game.

"Give me a good fake, Rupe. This idiot's going to bite like a hungry shark," I told my quarterback with an evil chuckle. We clapped and broke the huddle. Turtle boy tried to get up on me tight at the line, his sweaty face so red I could scarcely make out his freckles. "You ready for another lesson?" I asked him. But he only cursed vehemently by way of reply, causing me to laugh out loud.

The ball was snapped, and he tried to shove me, but that was old hat. I slapped his hands down and spun around him, so clean he barely managed to get a little piece of my shirt. I darted out toward the sideline as Rupe rolled my way—if you could call his ungainly limping trot a *roll* by any standard—where he gave me a good pump fake. Poor old Freckles bit hard, and I turned up field, leaving my defender well behind yet again.

Rupe laid the ball out in front of me with the timing of a maestro. One of those tosses so perfect, the spiral so tight, that you're actually afraid for a split second you're going to muff the catch and blow it. Add the fact that I was so wide open and had set my defender up so cleanly… Well, you just knew I was going to drop the ball. Only I wasn't. I was going to catch the ball and drop it at turtle boy's feet, laughing and mocking all the while.

At least that's what I *intended* to do. I had my eyes glued to the ball, my arms outstretched and waiting. I could hear my hapless defender huffing and puffing somewhere behind me, and my mind was already working on the jokes my lips were soon going to let fly. But as that football came within reach, lightning flashed nearby, and I was sent spinning, rocked off my feet by the blinding jolt. I hit hard and rolled to a stop with my face in the dirt, then managed to flop over on my back, trying to find air and gather my wits. Squinting, I sat up and ran a hand across my ribs, which were smarting, wondering if I'd run into something I hadn't noticed on the playing field.

Mike Collins was the something I hadn't noticed.

He stood over me as I rose unsteadily to my feet, Butch standing slightly behind him with a small mob of guys I hardly knew. Most of them were athletic types from the eighth grade. A few I recognized from the high school. They'd probably tagged along for the promise of a fight, wanting to enjoy the show. The kids we'd been playing against fell in with them, already anticipating bloodshed. A few of the faces weren't quite so avid. It surprised me to find that Freckles actually appeared to be expressing sympathy of some kind. He hung back, but stayed to watch what was about to take place just the same.

Only Tommy and Rupe came to my defense. The others who'd been on my team hung back far enough to let everyone know they weren't taking sides. Tommy came on the run, the whites of his eyes glistening in anger, while Rupe approached with caution, his long hands twitching apprehensively at his sides. Violence wasn't exactly Rupe's thing. It wasn't exactly my thing either.

"Nice blindside, Collins," spat Tommy as he approached.

"Fuck off, Washington," one of the larger guys from the high school crowd said from the safety of the throng.

Mike Collins wasn't daunted in the least by my large friend's presence. *And that was my last hope,* I realized. "You going to fight his battles for him?" Mike asked Tommy.

After some hesitation, Tommy decided on, "Not today I won't."

But everyone knew there would be another fight after this one. And one Mike Collins wouldn't be nearly so eager to engage in. Tommy stared at me hard, willing me to do as he'd earlier instructed, then moving reluctantly away. Rupe backed off quickly, looking at me with an expression of utter fear. Rupe was probably hoping I'd just survive this encounter, let alone hold my own against Collins.

I'd like to tell you I hit Mike in the throat and he fell over gagging, while I warned him never to dare step up to me again. I'd like to tell you I walked away the hero and my friends were bragging on me and all the kids in school thought I was cool for taking down one of the most pompous assholes of the popular sect. But that's not how it happened. In fact, I don't think I ever even landed a solid blow against Mike Collins.

Mike was intimidating for a kid heading into the eighth grade. He was tall and already developing lean muscle in his arms and chest. A thin growth of hair glistened menacingly above his upper lip. He stood there confident and assured, his mouth twisted into an ugly sneer and his fists coming up at the ready. My heart pounded wildly as he advanced. I could tell with no doubt that he meant to give the crowd a good show and beat the holy snot out of me.

I was overcome by that surge of adrenaline which pure fear loans the human body. Unfortunately, that adrenaline is wasted if you panic and start flailing about wildly in a futile effort to throw punches at a guy forty or fifty pounds heavier than you are. Mike also had a longer reach, and he was more experienced when it came to fighting. I'd never been in a real fight. Truth be told, if Tommy hadn't been standing behind me, I would have handled this altercation the same way I'd always reacted in the past: I would have run like hell.

I forgot to swing first, as Tommy had instructed. I also forgot about aiming for anything at all, much less Mike's throat. He threw a clumsy right hand at me, and I ducked and stumbled away, turning my back on my opponent. (Only a few years later in life, I found out this tactic is a really big no-no when it comes to fisticuffs.) Collins charged me and threw another punch that I barely managed to dodge. And another that grazed the top of my head. And another that hit me square on the side of my jaw and practically buckled my knees.

In a blind panic, and with the wild cries of the throng in my ears, I lowered my ringing head and charged, hoping to grab him around the waist and turn this boxing match I was sorely losing into more of a wrestling fight. But Mike brought his knee up and caught me in the face, and hit me another good one before I fell to the ground. Everyone was laughing as I rose, standing on swaying feet as blood gushed from my nose. Mike paused at the sight of my blood, the way most boys do when the reality of serious injury intrudes upon their fun.

But Tommy wasn't laughing. "Go crazy, Donny!" I heard him cry out.

And I did. I charged again, throwing wild punches at my larger adversary with everything I had. I wasn't as scared now. I mean, I was already bleeding, and he had taken his best shot. How much worse could it get? I hit him a few times, mostly striking his shoulders after he blocked my awkward roundhouse swings. I ducked a few more of his punches, too. But all that punching and ducking came to an end when Mike Collins reached back and drove a purposeful right hand through my pitiful defenses, splitting my eye.

The blow didn't knock me completely out, but it might as well have. I was vaguely aware of someone screaming at us to break it up. It was a man's voice. The crowd dispersed, albeit slowly. Someone kicked dirt on me, and I heard Tommy cursing. Collins said something. Tommy said something back. I heard more cursing. I wasn't sure what exactly was going on. I was just thankful I wasn't being punched anymore.

"Jesus, kid, didn't your dad ever show you how to keep up your dukes?" a sweaty man in running shorts and a tie-dyed T-shirt asked me as my foggy brain began to clear.

He had a ponytail and a tattoo on his shoulder of a naked woman entwined with a snake. His face was burned red from sun and wind, and he wore a scraggly beard and whiskers. One of his front teeth was broke near in half, but his eyes were kind. He pulled a red bandana off of his head and pulled his hair through it, then started mopping at the mess of my face. Dazed as I was, I recognized the man. He was one of the guys from the motorcycle house over near Sid's Tavern.

"His dad doesn't live with him," Rupe told my new friend.

Motorcycle man just nodded his understanding. "You need to watch more boxing and less cartoons, kid," he instructed with a grin. I winced at his probing. "Your chin's cool, but that eye might need a stitch or two."

There was another, younger dude standing behind my grizzled nurse. He had a square jaw and was clean-shaven, with bright blue eyes and a neater hair style, although he didn't look any less tough than the guy kneeling in front of me. He was jogging in place, but not acting impatient to be off. I noticed a leather strap around his wrist and well-worn army boots on his feet. I figured the guy did time in Nam, like my brothers' father had.

Tommy's face swam into view. "Nah, he'll be fine, man," he told my nurse.

"Are you a doctor?" Rupe asked from behind me. I realized he was propping me up, holding me in his lap like a helpless baby. *You were helpless, dumb ass,* I reminded myself.

"No, but *you* going to need one if you keep flapping those gums," Tommy warned Rupe.

"I can see you guys have this handled," the biker said with a chuckle. He pressed the bloody rag against my still-seeping eye and put my hand gently upon it, silently instructing me to keep it there with a little push. "Bob and weave, little man," he told me as he rose. "Never trade blows with a bigger man," he added before jogging away.

"Yeah, he's right," agreed Tommy.

I looked up at him and spit something out of my mouth, hoping it wasn't a tooth. "What happened to hit first and aim for the throat?" I asked. My jaw hurt, and my lips felt swelled and numb.

Tommy winced and shook his head. "You didn't do so good at that," he explained needlessly.

Everyone else was gone. Rupe helped me stand when I tried to get up, and I was surprised to find I could walk under my own power. We headed toward my house, wrapped in an uncomfortable silence. Rupe was afraid to say anything. I was whipped and embarrassed. And Tommy was probably ashamed at my poor effort, although he hadn't said so. People stared at us as we walked by. I must have been a sight. My shirt was covered with blood.

Rupe mumbled something about going home a couple of blocks later and left, slipping down an alley after quickly patting me on the shoulder. I knew he'd come by sometime when Tommy wasn't around, lecturing me about keeping my mouth shut and staying out of trouble. Keeping quiet and doing what you were told was Rupe's answer to almost every problem. It was a theory that seemed to prove out where his life was concerned, but didn't work so well for me. I hadn't said anything to Collins at all. Problem was, Tommy's hit-first solution wasn't working so well for me, either.

We cut across the Texaco station. Tommy stomped twice on the line that rang the bell, just to piss off the attendants inside, but I didn't see anyone glare from behind the dirty glass of the office or hear the usual growl to "cut it out" emanate from the service bay. Another couple of blocks and we were at my place. Benji pushed his way through the screen on the front door and bounded down the steps, greeting me like he always did.

"Don't worry 'bout Collins," Tommy finally said, breaking our long silence.

"I'm not," I lied.

School was going to be hell. My face was going to be a mess. Collins was going to rip into me, and I was going to have to take it. If I said anything back I'd just look more foolish than I already did. And I surely didn't want to piss him off again. Mrs. Perkins would know what had happened for sure, but I'd have to deny it. Anyone who ran to teachers for help lost all respect from the guys, and that was far worse than having the crap beat out of you now and again.

Tommy grimaced and nodded toward the porch. "What is that shit?" he asked.

I didn't know what he meant at first. Then I realized he was referring to Betty's music. *That's the way, uh huh uh huh I like it, uh huh, uh huh,* streamed through the screen and out into the street, the speakers of our old stereo cracking and popping under the strain of KC and the Sunshine Band's lyrics. My mother's taste in music was often a source of ribbing for me, especially her Engelbert Humperdinck and Tom Jones albums.

I never would have admitted it, but I liked them too. Many was the time I crooned along with Engelbert, howling *Please release me, let me go!* And one of my favorite acts was to stuff a dishtowel down my pants and strut around singing *What's new, pussycat, whoa, whoa!,* until Betty begged me to stop, on the verge of peeing herself. I could also do a mean version of Hank Williams' "Walking the Floor over You."

"Later, man," Tommy said as he left.

"You don't want to come in?" I called after him. "What? You don't like my mom's music?"

He laughed and threw up a hand, starting down the alley. "I don't dig nothin' you ain't going to hear on *Soul Train*, brother," he shot back, sauntering away.

I picked up my dog and headed in. Benji started sniffing at the blood on my shirt in earnest, clawing at my chest like he was trying to climb right up inside my hurt. He whined and scurried after me when I set him down inside. I kicked off my shoes and made my way to the kitchen, thankful Leon wasn't around. After the other night's fatherly talk, he might have actually wanted to take me out back for some boxing lessons.

Terry trotted down the steps, took one look at me, and ran back up, screaming at the top of his lungs. I peeled off my ruined shirt as Betty emerged, leaving the baby wailing somewhere upstairs. She screamed when she saw me. She always screamed at the sight of my blood, which she saw often. I'd step on a nail or get bitten by a dog. I was pretty much covered with scars.

My most common method of hurting myself was to crack open my head. Once, I'd split my upper lip so wide it had taken three or four doctors and nurses to hold me down while they stitched me up. I could barely remember that incident, but I did recall the police stopping Betty on the way to the hospital, the officer taking one look at my screaming face spraying blood all over the car, and then escorting us the rest of the way to the emergency room, siren blaring as he led the way.

"What happened?" she asked, leading me to the sink and turning on the water.

I thought that a foolish question. "I was hit by a bus," I told her.

But I let her clean me up. The water was cool and soothing, and her touch was lighter and more loving than that of my previous nurse. Betty could be quite motherly when panicked. I could tell she wanted to ask detailed questions, but she settled for my short answers and concentrated on my wounds instead. We both knew there was nothing more she was going to do for me, and no words of wisdom she might pass down. But I wasn't forgetting the bob-and-weave advice the motorcycle man had passed on.

That night was one of those rare, pleasant family evenings. Leon never showed, and Betty made a huge bowl of salad covered with French dressing and croutons. My mother always felt bad when I was hurt, at least for a day or two. She was always sorry when she did something wrong, too, but only until the trouble caused by whatever she'd done passed over. She reminded me of a leaf skirling in a brisk autumn wind, tossed wherever by chance and circumstance, in control of nothing and at the mercy of everything.

Despite the nagging pain left in the wake of Mike Collins, that was a good night. I played with my brothers and got along with Terry, who actually expressed real concern for me. Betty and I played rummy and shared the tossed salad. We listened to Elvis music (The King dominated my mother's stack of albums) and laughed as the baby tottered around the sofa bed, trying his best to dance.

Before bed I checked myself in the mirror. Swelling and bruises were kind of cool at twelve. I didn't look that bad. I brushed up on my health and science for the next day's finals, trying not to think about what the rest of my school day would bring. As an afterthought, I took a look at my teeth. None of them were broken or chipped any more than they already had been, but they weren't all that clean, and I could see at least two cavities eating away at my molars. Maybe Mrs. P. wasn't such a bitch after all, but I still wasn't going to take her charity.

"We can steal our own toothbrush," I told Benji as I jumped onto my mattress. He just cocked his head, not understanding what I wanted. That was rare, because my dog was smarter than Lassie. "I needed you today," I said, rubbing his head after he crawled in beside me. It was a good feeling, having his warm body next to me. If my little buddy had been there today, Collins would have been bitten twice for every punch he threw in my general direction.

I fell asleep imagining just that.

CHAPTER 4

Sid's wasn't owned by anyone named Sid at all. In fact, whoever Sid had been was so long gone that Pops, the half-dead old dude who owned the place, didn't even know how his bar had gotten its name. The peeling and faded sign hanging out front called the joint a tavern, but there was no kitchen to serve up food. Pops offered whiskey and beer from the tap or bottled, usually Colt 45 or Miller, but there were a lot of Bud and Schlitz drinkers sitting at the poker tables, too.

They played beneath a constant cloud of drifting cigarette and cigar smoke, the hum of conversation occasionally broken by coarse laughter or bitter cursing, depending on who won or lost a hand. Cards were what Sid's was known for. Every Friday and Saturday night the place was crammed with the same faces at the same tables. They played until well after midnight, and often hours past. A few of the players always drank too much and lost their money, but most of the guys—and the few women among the sordid collection—were serious about their cards and stayed close enough to sober to maintain their wits.

A busted and dusty jukebox stood silently beside the splintered and tattered bar, strips of dried maroon leather torn away and hanging clear to the dingy brass footrest. The overhead lights were dim and crusted with long dead-and-dried insects lying on the inner casings of the glass. Pops had installed fluorescent lights above the tables so his aging patrons could see their cards. They hung just above the concentrating faces, the long cylindrical bulbs exposed and humming quietly.

Both doors stood wide open, and a pair of window air conditioners droned along the alley wall. Six-foot standing fans swiveled back and forth just inside each opening, the blades turning just enough to kick up a gentle breeze. Rupe and I sat on stools near the alley door, next to Pops, while Tommy hung out in a lawn chair just outside the front, his bare feet resting on the rusty rail of the few concrete steps one had to climb in

I cursed and slapped a mosquito off my arm. "Why do bother them?" I asked Pops.

The old man twisted his lips in a toothless smile, the hanging loosely out of the corner of his mouth. "The smoke, stared at the cloud of wafting vapor beneath the lights, while Rupe nodded.

"I suppose you already knew that?" I asked him.

I hated when Rupe tried to act like he was smarter than I was. He would always bring up who got the better grades, but we both knew the reasons for that.

"Of course I did. My dad burns smoke at our picnics to keep away the mosquitoes," he explained defensively, anticipating an argument.

I supposed he might actually be telling the truth and dropped the subject.

I was in too good a mood to waste the night arguing. School was over, and the summer waited for me, an endless span of carefree nights and lazy days. The ordeal with Collins had blown over and left me better off than anticipated, thanks to Mrs. Perkins. She'd somehow gotten the whole story out of some of the kids who'd witnessed the fight and hauled Mike and me down to the principal's office, where I had been strenuously coerced to give Collins up and rat on him for the beating he'd given me.

In truth, no one really wanted to have to deal with our fight. Not the principal, who wanted the year to be over with, nor the cop they called in to explain how I would be protected if I wanted to tell my story, and especially not Mike's parents or coaches, who couldn't believe the golden boy could possibly do such a horrible thing as to beat the crap out of some kid so much smaller than himself. It made things worse for Mike that he didn't have a scratch on him, while I looked like I just went ten rounds with Ali. Who would have thought that being so inept at defending yourself could actually wind up being a good thing?

Except for Mrs. P., who had some difficulty handling the whipping I'd taken. She blamed herself for the altercation because it started with those stupid tablets in her class. At first I'd been pleased by her consternation, but I sure wasn't pleased when the grueling interrogation came down. She had actually shed tears of frustration during my refusal to admit what had happened. In the end, my obstinate attitude actually garnered me some measure of respect with my peers, and even Collins, who begrudgingly thanked me before we parted ways the last day of school.

o, tonight I was feeling too good to bother sniping with Rupe. I was leading for eighth grade next year, which meant fewer older guys to worry about. I was thinking I might even go out for the football or baseball team. I always entertained that notion but never followed through with it. Just like I was always going to sign up for summer ball and never did. I blamed it on the fact that we were always moving, but the truth was I lacked the confidence to go out for any team. Sandlot ball was one thing. Proving your worth to a coach was quite another matter.

Old Pauley lifted a gnarled, bony finger, and Rupe jumped off his stool and hobbled over. The old guy only wanted another beer, so he brought back an empty Miller can and paid Pops, who twisted around on his creaky barstool to reach into one of the row of churning refrigerators behind him. Rupe served up the unopened can and collected a tip, usually a dime or maybe a quarter if the customer was doing well at the table, before moving back to his seat beside me.

"Tommy's gotten more minutes at the door," Pops informed us.

We smiled at each other and nodded. The old guy was always worried about being raided, but as far as we knew he'd never had any trouble with the police. Sexy Sarah claimed a patrolman had come in looking for someone once, but years ago. Even though the officer had only passed a picture around and asked a couple of questions, Pops nearly had a stroke. We didn't mind. Pops trusted us to work the room and watch the doors, and we usually raked in between ten and fifteen dollars apiece every Friday and Saturday night. It made it that much harder for any other kids to try and horn in our racket if he mistrusted them.

He snuffed out his smoke in the ashtray, adding another butt to the graveyard that displayed his chain-smoking habit. His quick, yellowed fingers lit another Marlboro and had it dangling from his lower lip before he took another breath. Other than the procedure required to light a stick, Pops was never very animated. He rarely came out from behind the bar. At the end of the night we swept the floor, wiped the tables, and threw all the trash—which was mostly empty beer cans and bottles—in the Dumpster out back. Pops dozed behind the bar until we were done, woke long enough to lock up when we left, and slipped upstairs to his private rooms above the tavern.

I knew Pops could barely see, and not just because his dark brown eyes were rheumy and always leaking, or because he didn't move around very much. Sarah had told me he was almost blind. She did all his grocery shopping and helped him write the checks that paid his bills. As far as I knew, Pops never left the safety of Sid's walls, which was probably one of the reasons he was so fearful of the cops shutting down his little gambling house. He probably had nowhere else to go, and no one to help him if he lost what livelihood Sid's and the poker nights provided.

I thought of Pops as a black guy, but Tommy said he was a mulatto. Usually, that meant he had a white father or mother, but I'd recently discovered that many light-skinned black people had white grandparents or even white ancestors from farther back than that. Sarah claimed all black folks had white blood running in them from somewhere in their past. She often said *slave owners couldn't keep their peckers in their pants back in them days.*

But Tommy said any black person with light skin was a mulatto. He also claimed there was absolutely *no* white blood in him. Personally, I believed he was jealous of anyone of his race with brown complexions because he was so dark-skinned and always being teased about it. There was no quicker way to get that boy fighting mad than to get on him about being so black. Of course, referring to him as *boy* angered him pretty quickly, too. I rarely used the word boy around Tommy, and I never referred to anyone as a nigger, no matter how flippantly or affectionately they tossed that incendiary word around.

Sexy Sarah—who was maybe darker-skinned than Tommy—used that word all the time. With her, it was always *this nigger said...* and *that nigger did...* but I had learned long ago to avoid that particular trap. You said that word one day and the black guys laughed. You said it the next day and you got the living shit beat out of you. I teased my black friends about their mother's wigs or garish fingernails, or brought up their questionable parentage or constant abuse of the English language. I was always kidding Tommy whenever his afro got all out of whack and looked more like a burnt bush than a head. But I stayed well behind the line when it came to that particular controversial word.

Tommy strolled in, and Rupe hobbled off to take his place in the lawn chair outside. He pointed at Pops' pack of smokes, and the old man flicked them across the bar. Tommy knocked a cigarette loose and plucked it, and then lit up with a practiced grace that rivaled Pops himself. He'd started smoking only the past school year, but lately my friend was choking down about half a pack a day. And those were just the ones I knew about.

"Smoke?" he asked, knocking another loose and extending it in my direction. I just shook my head, striving for nonchalance. "Pussy," Tommy said with a smirk, sliding the Marlboros back to Pops.

"Leave him alone," Pops said. "Man don't want to smoke, that's his choice."

Tommy laughed at that, winking at me spitefully. "See his face, Pops? That look like the face of a man?" I was thankful to find Pops didn't find my buddy's joke all that funny. "Nah, Donny ain't no man. He don't smoke—" Tommy picked up Pops' half-filled whiskey glass and drained it before the old man could stop him "—and he don't drink. Hell, he ain't even got his dick wet yet. That sound like a *man* to you, Pops?"

"Leave that alone, Washington," Pops ordered, snatching the empty shot glass and glancing nervously at both doors. "You trying to get me shut down?"

Tommy tapped the bottle setting in front of Pops, grinning at me. "Ahhh. Jack Daniel's straight up. Now, that will stiffen that limp, little, white willy of yours, Donny."

I was embarrassed at the mention of my bruised face (and my willy, which at the time *was* limp, white, and kind of little), but I wasn't going to take his shit without fighting back. "Good thing you can remember the name, cause you sure as hell can't be reading the label," I told him. That did make Pops laugh.

"Lot of good it's going to do you," he snapped back, but I was pleased to find I'd struck a nerve and put him on the defensive. Tommy hated any reminder of his being held back a grade, or his inability to read and write very well. "You going to get a job reading comic books?"

"At least I'm going to get a job," I said calmly, not wanting to infuriate my hot-tempered friend.

He leaned in closer and blew smoke directly into my face, making me cough. The stink was awful. *That's why I don't smoke.* "How 'bout I finish what Collins started?" he asked.

"How 'bout I let you do your own school work next year and go off to high school without you?" I asked, imitating him almost to perfection. Pops cackled and even Tommy grinned. He loved when I imitated him, especially when I mimicked his saunter and strutted around singing like James Brown.

"You two settle down. I don't want no trouble in here," Pops said when he was done laughing.

"No trouble, Pops. Donny here's my man." Tommy held up his smoke and wiggled it. "Tell him, Pops. How long you been smoking?"

The old man scratched the thinning, coarse gray curls covering the rear of his scalp. "I'll be seventy-four in the spring, and I started smoking when I was about your age. That makes it about…"

"Sixty-two years," I said, just to fill the blank looks on their faces. Math wasn't Tommy's strong suit either.

"Ain't hurt him none," offered Tommy, as if that little fact would convince me to light right up. He gestured around the bar. "Most all of them smoke, and they old as hell. They drink, too." Tommy glanced at the door and shrugged. "Even Rupe lights up now and then."

Yeah, because he's too afraid to tell you he doesn't want to. "I don't care. No thanks. What are you, a Marlboro spokesman?"

Tommy liked that idea. He stuck the cigarette in his mouth and struck a pose, grinning like a fool. We laughed together, and he turned back to Pops, asking, "Smoking hurt you any, Pops?"

"Gives me a nasty cough every morning," the old man admitted. "Nothing a shot or two of Jack don't drown right up." He laughed at his own joke, but looked at us more soberly afterward. "I tell you straight, boys. Smoking, drinking, and loose women ruin a man. I had it to do over… Well, I'd latch onto a good churchgoing woman and walk the straight and narrow."

"Like shit, Pops," Tommy retorted harshly. "What fun would that be? You know you'd smoke and drink again. Besides, if you really mean it, why not give it up now?"

His creased face looked sad to me, but Pops just looked out over the smoky room and said, "It's too late for me, but you boys got your whole life ahead of you. Less bad habits you drag along, easier and farther you going to travel."

Tommy didn't like being told that acting older and assuming bad habits early wasn't cool. "Where we going to go, Pops?" He took another drag to emphasize his point. "My old man's upstate, and my brother's still in county. Donny here ain't even ever met his dad. You think cause I smoke or don't going to matter to my future?" He snorted and then repeated, "Where we going to go?"

"Ain't like that, Tom," Pops said with some compassion. *Please, go on,* I urged the old man. Tommy was only giving voice to my own dismal outlook on the future. If Pops had a better plan, I sure wanted to hear it. "Times have changed. You boys get through school and there plenty of options. I got a grandson been in the Navy most twenty years now. He doing real fine."

"Not me," Tommy denied him flat out. "They kicked my brother out of the Army in less than a year. He told me the service is for suckers. Said they don't pay squat and treat you like a slave."

Pops was tired of arguing. "Suit yourself, Washington. But I know your brother, and I knew your father, too. You go on like you are and you going to be joining them behind bars."

"Too smart for that," Tommy replied with a shake of his head. "Pigs are stupid and slow. You ain't never going to see me locked up." He reached for Pops' bottle, and the old man slapped his hand. "Come on, Pops. Maybe I'll take over this place when you kick off. Who knows, Sarah might want a younger man who can keep up with her."

"You watch that sassy mouth of yours, little nigger," Pops snapped, bristling, but there was a twinkle in his running eyes. He loved when we talked dirty to him about Sexy Sarah. "I've forgot more about pleasing women than you ever like to learn."

Tommy flinched when Pops lifted a shaky fist as if to slug him, pretending to be cowed. "Easy, Pops, I'm sorry," he said.

We all laughed, and Tommy tried again for the bottle, only to have his hand slapped away one more time. Denied, he settled for another smoke.

I noticed one of the players motioning for service. I left Pops and Tommy to their bickering and hopped down to go pocket a little money, waving at the putrid cloud of smoke in a vain attempt to breathe something that didn't taste like it came out of the muffler of a sputtering semi.

It was Mary Higgins Thompson Clark Robbins who wanted something. She liked to recite the last names of all her departed husbands. Mary claimed she buried them all, but Ralph the garbage man said only the first one had died. She'd run off the other three. He also said the one who had died hung himself in her basement because Mary was so mean. I didn't know who to believe, but Mary was always nice to me and tipped well.

"Donny, baby, be a dear and run over to the mart for me. I want a bag of plain chips and a Coke," she said, handing me a dollar.

Pops had Coke and Pepsi in one of his refrigerators, but Mary refused to pay his trivial markup. I could have pointed out that she normally lost money by sending me out, if she added in her tip, but I would have been stupid to do so. Mary smiled at me from beneath her tight bun of gray hair. Her teeth were sparsely spaced and yellow but still her own, and her wrinkled face was coated heavily with makeup, including lipstick so bright and so red I was always on the verge of asking her where she hid the electrical cord.

She had a large wicker bag beside her, crammed full of bingo supplies, magazines, and oodles of Avon material. Mary and Sexy Sarah were bingo fanatics. They were always talking about hitting the jackpot and bragging about how much they'd won. Pops said the two of them had already blown enough money to buy the priest his own personal golf course. Mary sold Avon to a lot of women in our neighborhood, including Betty, but I didn't know how profitable the racket was. My mother was an Avon junkie, so I guess she was helping that priest out with his golfing, too.

"Get me a bag of pretzels," Tubbs added, sliding me a couple of quarters. "A big bag of the fat ones," he added needlessly. I knew what Tubbs liked. I knew what they all liked.

Sarah raised her hand and motioned for me to stop by. The guys never let her and Mary play at the same table, or even close to each other, because they talked so much. I thought a lot of the men talked just as much as the ladies, but with less squabbling. The men just didn't want to hear about bingo, or who missed church, or where so and so bought that expensive dress, or why this daughter or that son wasn't calling enough, or how this medicine worked better than that one for certain aches and pains.

Some skinny Italian guy I didn't know raised, and Sarah had to think a moment, fingering her cards. I was always amazed at how dexterously she handled them, considering the fact that she wore those stupid Lee Press-on Nails my mother sometimes toyed with but never managed to keep on. Sarah must not have liked her chances. She cussed at the new guy and tossed in her cards before sliding me a quarter to buy her a pack of mint Lifesavers.

"Oooh, what you said," I teased her.

She smiled up at me but kept her eyes on the new guy, watching him closely and hoping to see what he'd had to raise her with. Sarah was one of the good card players. Pops said she made more money in his place than she received in her monthly check, but I wasn't exactly sure who was sending her money every month. I doubted it was the same welfare check Betty was always waiting on. My mother received a check because she had kids and couldn't afford to feed them. I was pretty sure Sarah's monthly income had something to do with her supposedly being too old to work.

"Just you never mind," she playfully scolded me as I rubbed at my stinging eyes. Trying to sleep after working a night at Pops' was sheer hell. The smoke seeped into your eyes and dried them out, leaving you weeping most of the night and well into the next day. "You need to let me hit you with some eye drops 'fore you go home, baby. This ain't no place for you boys to be hanging out, no way."

"It's not that bad," I lied, but she was already perusing her next hand, staring at the new guy over her fanned cards as if she meant to bite him the first chance she got.

"Who busted you up, kid?" he asked me, chuckling.

His eyes were dark and too close together. They glared at me from above his large, angled nose. I didn't like him, and I didn't like his laugh. It wasn't playful or even condescending. It was just plain mean.

"You and your girlfriends been fighting?" he continued, trying to taunt me.

He jabbed his thumb toward Tommy and giggled spitefully at his little jest, oblivious to the fact that nobody else was laughing with him.

Word sparring with me was a bigger mistake than playing cards with Sexy. "I didn't have change for a quarter," I returned casually, shrugging.

His stupid face went slack. He couldn't help but take the bait. "What the hell does having change for a quarter have to do with getting your ass kicked?"

I smiled, all innocence. "Your mom charges a nickel, and she wasn't worth a tip."

That was a good one. Everyone thought so but my adversary. The whole table was tittering, except for him.

"You have a smart mouth on you. How about I add to your bruises?"

I just kept on grinning. "What's the matter? Don't you want to play anymore?"

"You leave that baby alone and play cards," Sarah told him. "You started up with him first."

"Those boys can toss some mom jokes, now," Eugene warned from his seat next to Sexy, his baritone voice as big and deep as his expansive belly.

Eugene was cool. He was one of those slow, smooth-talking black guys who sported thick, bushy sideburns and wore his shades even at night. He had a pair of heavy, shiny rings on his right hand that he'd won by throwing perfect games in his bowling league. Nothing made Gene happier than letting him tell you all about how good he was at bowling. He would go through all the motions, describing how he'd won those rings, prancing around like he was throwing that last perfect ball and explaining how difficult it was to handle such incredible pressure. I'd never bowled in a league before, but how hard could it be to roll a ball?

"He won't be so funny with my foot in his ass," my new pissed off friend warned, still fuming. I had to choke down about a dozen comebacks to that. Pops wouldn't like me riling up his customers, and this fellow was way past riled.

"Clean him out, Sexy," I told Sarah as I left.

"Plan to," she sent after me.

"Making a run?" Rupe asked as I leapt down the steps in one bound.

"Nah, Pops fired me," I sent back. "I'm off to file for unemployment."

"That won't be so funny when you're actually standing in that line of losers," he shot back, but I just flipped him the bird over my shoulder and didn't look back.

Outside, the air smelled clean. It had rained earlier, dampening the odor of filth and decay that normally hung over our neighborhood. The rundown duplexes and sagging apartments didn't look so bad in the gloom, with much of the missing bricks and peeling paint concealed by darkness. The cars lining the curb disguised their age and condition, pretending they were newer automobiles sitting in the drives of rich people out in the suburbs.

I made my way through one of the bays of the car wash on the corner before crossing the street, my sneakers crunching on broken glass because someone had shattered the overhead light bulbs. I was startled by the movement of some wino taking a leak in the shadows just at the edge of the streetlight's glare. He coughed and mumbled something, but I ignored him and kept on. There wasn't a storm strong enough to wash this place clean. *Even a toilet looks fresh right after you flush it,* I thought to myself. *That's a good one. You got to remember to tell that to Rupe.*

The corner mart was run by an old Korean dude who hardly spoke English. He lived above the place with his wife, who used to run the register and spoke our language more clearly than he did, but we never saw her much anymore. They'd been robbed last summer, and one of the men holding up the store had punched his wife to silence her yammering. We heard she lost some teeth and spent a couple days in the hospital, and she'd rarely shown herself since.

That was actually a blessing for us. She'd always been shrewd and observant, and very watchful of us when we were in her store. It had been almost impossible to rip her off. She was one of those adults who just knew what you were up to and didn't mind telling you straight out that she was onto you. But her husband wasn't nearly so canny or mistrustful. In fact, this store was my constant supply of Topps baseball cards, and gum or other candy on occasion.

He was sitting behind the counter reading a well-worn paperback when I came in, and we shared a nod. He was used to us coming in and out on the weekends, due to Pops' little gaming house. I checked the comics rack, expecting nothing new and finding no surprises. I knew what days my comics hit the stores—I stole them from the Walgreens by the high school—and I had more than a week to wait for any new releases.

I slipped down the candy aisle for the Lifesavers, taking a moment to slide three packs of baseball cards down the front of my pants. The next aisle offered up the plain chips and fat pretzels, and the last stop was at the cooler for Mary's Coke. My heart didn't even skip a beat as I paid for my stuff. I was such an old hand at thievery. It was nerves got you busted. If you were smooth and quick, almost anything could be taken right out from under the noses of most store attendants. Just about all of them were only bored people pulling hours for minimum wage at a job they hated. Most of them probably stole from the store themselves.

Before checking out, I grabbed a couple of boxes of Cracker Jacks for my brothers. They were still young enough to appreciate the stupid toy they dug out of the caramel corn, although Terry was starting to complain more and more every day. It really sucked when you got old enough to figure out how poor you were. Fortunately, the kid wasn't too bright; I'd known where Betty and her brood stood in the hierarchy of life as long as I could remember. *I guess ignorance really is bliss.*

I was tickled not to find Leon's car in the yard when I got home. It was near the end of the month. Money and food were scarce. That meant Leon would be scarce, too. Betty got mean when she was needy. I hid the boxes of candy behind the lone remaining bag of puffed wheat in the pantry, just in case Leon did pop in and was too drunk to care that he was swiping food from babies.

I heard Betty get up and head for the stairs, the creaking floorboards of her upstairs bedroom and the groaning steps heralding her arrival like the corny sound effects in a midnight black-and-white thriller. I quickly tucked a five and a couple of ones into my sneaker before she made her way down. Benji had met me at the door, and he was still hopping around, waiting to be loved on. I rolled a piece of bologna and a Kraft single together, bit half of it off and tossed him the rest.

"I told you about giving that dog people food," Betty murmured sleepily.

My mother didn't like to watch my dog eat, especially if he was eating something she might have devoured herself. Tiki, safe in the crook of Betty's arm, glared at Benji's food. I could swear my dog looked right at the smaller, spoiled animal and ate even more slowly, drawing out Tiki's agony.

"Pretend I ate the whole thing and you'll feel better," I said pleasantly.

"How'd you do tonight?" she asked outright, dropping the whole dog-and-food thing without another word. *Wanting something, Betty?* I asked silently, proud of the insight I'd shown by tucking away that cash in my shoe. My mother was like a ghetto IRS, always demanding a chunk of anything I managed to earn. "I get my paycheck middle of the week, and we need a few things to tide us over."

"Wow. No *hello?* No *have you had enough to eat?* I'll settle for a *where the hell have you been? It's half past two in the morning! Do you know how dangerous this neighborhood is?*" I could never resist ribbing her for her motherly shortcomings, especially when she needed something from me. "Did I tell you I was mugged on the way home?"

She was getting pissed. One eye was starting to work its way all the way open. She was glaring at me from that eye now, her head tilted to give that baleful orb a better view. "Oh, you were not," she said. "I don't need much, just five or maybe ten to get us through."

"I'm just teasing," I told her, trying to sound serious. "Actually, Mary cornered me before she left and made me pay her for the Avon you owe her for."

That opened up the other eye. "You didn't give her the money, did you?" she asked, panic creeping into her voice. To Betty, the notion of handing over money because you owed it was ridiculous. Handing over money near the end of the month was absolutely insane. "I told that old biddy I'd pay her first of the month."

"Mary's not an old biddy, and you've been telling her that for a couple of months now," I reminded her.

"Do you have any money or not?" she snapped. "Your brothers having food to eat is more important than paying for any damn Avon." I wanted to point out that she didn't need to scam me, but I knew doing so would only throw her into a rage. *Easy, boy, she's on the edge*, I warned myself. "Well? Are you going to help out or not?"

I stood up, and Benji jumped onto my vacant seat, as near to my hands as he could possibly get. "Oh, Betty," I scolded her as I finally relented and began scratching under my dog's hairy chin. Before she could cuss at me for calling her by her first name, I dug into both my pockets and dumped everything I had on the table.

At the sight of the money, my mother forgot her irritation with me. I watched her as she counted out my night's work. She was a wreck. Her hair was wild and tangled, and the skin of her pallid cheeks hung loosely from the sides of her mouth. Without her teeth in, the woman had a puckered, sunk-in look that added at least a decade to her true age.

"Twelve dollars and forty-five cents," she announced, now wide awake.

I was tired and in no mood to dicker with her. "Take ten. I'll get you a little more tomorrow night."

I had to make our bargaining look good, or else she'd get suspicious and figure I was holding out. It wouldn't do to have her digging around in my stuff, searching for money I might have stowed away.

She accepted my terms without another thought, and no questions, probably hoping to pay me back with some form of food stamp allowance. She slid much of the loose change back to me, keeping all the folding money and quarters. Then she climbed back up the stairs, peed noisily with the bathroom door wide open, and fell onto her cluttered mattress.

"You're welcome," I muttered, scooping what was left back into one of my pockets and going into the living room.

I turned the TV on and found some old movie. There was only one channel that wasn't static this late at night. Benji snuggled up beside me on the Leonless couch. Even with my eyes stinging and already starting to seep, I was asleep before even figuring out what I was watching.

CHAPTER 5

"Give me one good reason why you won't ride our bus to church," he asked yet again.

"We have a lot of fun activities," his wife added.

I kept on walking away from them, but slowly enough that they had little trouble keeping pace with me. "I need my sleep," I repeated, actually telling the truth. "Do you know how late I'm up on a normal Saturday night?"

The pretty one with the blonde hair—a real golden yellow, not the dirty wheaten strands my mother had passed down—stepped in front of me and smiled sweetly. Her name was Holly. She was tall but shapely, even in her long dress and thin, baggy sweater. Her eyes were blue, and her mouth was wide and perfect. She sang songs for the children riding the church bus, and usually had most of them singing along by the return trip home. Billy Holmes said she sounded like she could be on the radio. He said her voice was even prettier than she was, but I was going to have to hear that for myself to believe it.

Just about every guy in the neighborhood was in love with her. I knew I was, even if I couldn't begin to tell anyone what being in love actually meant. If I ever did ride that damn bus, it would be to get closer to Holly, and for no other reason. I kept on acting like they were just bothering the hell out of me, as if I had places to be and people to see. In truth, I always looked forward to them begging me to come out and visit their church. Looking back, I'm sure they knew perfectly well I enjoyed their little visits. I craved any attention I could find.

"Couldn't you come out just once?" Holly asked. She gave me a heart-wrenching smile and cocked her head, crossing her lovely arms across her chest. "Not even for me?"

That was downright dirty, using pretty girls to get guys to go to church. I wanted to tell her no way. *So tell her.* But she was looking at me so sweet. *Just say no.* She was practically begging. It would be rude to just flat out refuse her, so I decided to be nice and give her a little hope. *Sucker.*

"I'll think about it," I proposed.

"How about thinking about this Sunday?" the man with them asked. He was always pushing, always impatient to get you on that bus. "Your brothers seem to like it."

"One of my brothers is still in diapers and can barely talk," I reminded him. "The other one still picks his nose and eats it. But only after careful examination."

He had to laugh at that. His name was Dave Jones, and I liked him, even if he *was* pushy. He was pretty cool, and could hit a baseball farther than me or any of the guys. He'd messed around with us one Saturday afternoon, hanging out with us for a little while in the hopes that he might talk somebody into coming to church. He had a noticeable white swatch of hair above his forehead that made him hard to forget. I'd asked him about it once, and he'd told me it was caused by a birthmark on his scalp.

His wife was laughing too. She was pretty, but not as pretty as Holly. Her hair was brown, not yellow, and her name was Jewel, and she wasn't as tall or as striking as Holly. But she was nice enough, and I liked the way she laughed. Besides, she was married, and Holly wasn't. I was thinking that maybe if I started riding that bus, Holly might get to liking me. Of course, I was too young to realize how much older than me she was. I was also too young to realize angelic Holly was only working her magic on me to get my reluctant backside into one of those bus seats.

"I like your dog," said Jewel. She stooped to pet him. Benji stepped cautiously away, but then sniffed at her extended hand. He must have liked what he smelled, because Benji allowed her to scratch his head. "I'll bet that feels good."

Traitor. Benji had a short list of people he allowed to touch him. That he so quickly took to Jewel told me all I needed to know about her. Dave thought he would be so privileged as well, and bent down to take a turn. All he got for his efforts were bared teeth and a throaty growl that let him know he might be missing a finger or two if his hand moved much closer. Dave wisely pulled his fortunate extremity away and stood back up.

Jewel giggled and continued to love on my mutt. "Dogs have real good instincts," she told her husband, enjoying his discomfort.

"Don't let it bother you," I told Dave. "He barely lets anybody touch him, and trusts girls mostly."

Bess and Lynn came toward us from the other side of the street. Bess's mouth was already running a mile a minute by the time she reached us, informing Dave that she was sure she had at least three or four new kids riding this coming Sunday. Lynn trudged along behind her, sullen and quiet. She carried the Bible in her hand as if she meant to bludgeon someone with it. Benji saw Lynn and scampered toward her, tail wagging and behind twitching as she squatted to rub on him.

"How's my good boy?" Benji responded by jumping up and giving her a good tongue bath. Lynn made a face when he licked her mouth, but only laughed and gently pushed him back down. "You settle now."

For some reason Dave caught my eye. While the girls prattled on about my dog and who Bess had been talking to, the two of us shared a long, almost intense stare. There was nothing threatening in the way he was looking at me, nothing that suggested harm. But something in his eyes still made me uneasy, leaving me oddly curious. It was as if he knew something and wanted to tell me, only he couldn't, or wouldn't. At least not right now, this moment.

He stepped nearer and put a strong hand on my bony shoulder, squeezing with earnest affection. "I would really appreciate it if you'd ride out with us on Sunday."

"I need my sleep—"

"You can sleep on the bus." He was back to being pushy, almost forceful. His eyes were piercing and intense. I felt like the guy was trying to look inside me instead of at me. "Both ways," he added with a smirk.

Benji was a little uneasy with Dave's close proximity to me. He was also picking up on my nerves. But before he could express his displeasure with the situation, Lynn scooped him up and gave Dave room to continue our confrontation, leaving my dog to grumble at us from her secure arms. Even Bess had fallen silent, which was kind of like a God-proving existence miracle thing in itself.

I wanted out of here. This was getting a little weird. He was seriously intent on getting me on that bus to visit his church. He kept staring, waiting for the response he wanted. Bess, Holly, and Jewel were looking at me too, hopeful and expectant. Even Lynn seemed to want me to give in.

"I'll think about it, I promise," I said, hoping that would be enough.

"You can do better than that," Dave persisted. "Just come out tomorrow. Just try it once."

"Okay, okay, I'll come this Sunday," I said, lying through my teeth. I had no intention of following through, but this guy was seriously freaking me out. If he didn't let me out of here, I was going to sic my dog on him.

As if he could read my deceitful mind, Dave asked, "You wouldn't lie to me, would you?"

"What?" I knew he was just trying to be nice, but I also knew *he* knew I was lying. "Are you from a church or a police station?"

Dave was giving me that piercing, intense stare again. "What I'm asking is…" He paused for emphasis, giving me a moment to reflect on whether or not I wanted to lie to him again. "Was that a promise?"

"Sure, it's a promise," I returned without blinking.

He didn't look at all convinced, but he had no choice but to accept. "Okay then. We'll see you tomorrow." He was still looking doubtful as he left.

Bess jumped up and down and started clapping and chattering like a monkey, but Lynn cast me a knowing glance that said she knew I wouldn't be riding that bus in the morning. I only grinned back as innocently as my doomed soul would allow. *Come on, Lynn, you know my mother. In our family, lying is not a sin, it's a tradition.* She twisted her mouth and shook her head at me, letting me know she meant to coerce my sorry carcass as best she was able to board that bus. I was just hoping not to get whacked with her Bible before she followed after the others.

That promise stuck with me like the smell of dog crap when it gets stuck in the cracks of the soles of your sneakers and you just can't get it dug out. Bess and Lynn came over that afternoon to remind me to be ready in the morning, and then Bess came back again later. She was all excited that I was coming to church for the first time, and kept telling me all about the people I was going to meet. I didn't have the heart to tell her I wasn't going to be home in the morning, and wouldn't be riding her stupid bus.

Betty thought it was just peachy keen that I'd gotten myself cornered. She kept laughing at me every time Bess and Lynn weren't looking. After Bess left for the second time—and the last, I fervently hoped—Betty started singing "Jesus Loves Me" and giggling like a kid. Even Terry got a little fired up at the thought of me riding along with him. He wanted me to make some kid named Henry stop picking on him.

"You better lay out what you're going to wear," my mother instructed with a corny smile.

"I don't have anything clean, and I'm not going anyway," I said.

I shouldn't have reminded her about the laundry. I knew that the moment I blurted it out, but she'd gotten me rattled with the whole church thing. "Speaking of the dirty clothes…?" It should have seemed odd, I guess. I wasn't sure how many mothers questioned their kids about the lack of clean clothes for the family. But I wasn't the only kid I knew tasked with that miserable chore. "I thought you were going to get those clothes done this weekend?"

"Monday morning, I promise," I told her. "That place is a madhouse on the weekend. I'll get in and out on Monday in half the time."

"I have a shift Sunday evening, but I guess I can find something," she finally said, buying my solid argument for putting the clothes off.

Actually, during the summer there wasn't much difference in the hag population at the 'mat from one day to the next, but my lies had gotten me a twenty-four-hour reprieve. "Why'd you tell them you'd go to church if you didn't want to?" Betty asked.

It was then I noticed the lipstick and heavy eyeliner. Makeup of any sort was a telltale sign that my mother meant to tread where children or even admitting to having children was not allowed. I could've just gone on about my business and not asked what or who she was doing, but most of the time I couldn't resist the lure of pointing out her faults, and her lies. I couldn't stand letting her get away with lying to me, not even to keep peace between us. She was traveling on the money she'd begged out of me, using my brothers' hunger as leverage.

"Going out?" I asked directly.

Her eyes narrowed, and she sucked those false teeth in, pressing her dentures tightly against her gums. It was a habit she'd developed when taxed to the point of irritation or outright anger. "I'm meeting Leon over at the truck stop for dinner," she lied. *Leon, right, like he's coming around before the first of the month.* "Don't worry. I wouldn't dare ask you to stay home and help me out by watching after your brothers."

"I'm working at Pops'. You know that." I let her wither and sweat, delighting in the rage building behind her dull eyes. I could've stopped, but my compulsion to dig at her was too strong. "Is Leon picking you up?"

She was glaring now, almost at her breaking point. "No, Ruby's giving me a ride over," she lied further, trying to get away from me by walking into the kitchen.

"If you're not going to church with us, what about Henry?" Terry asked me as I started to follow after Betty.

"Punch Henry in the mouth," I told my brother as I left.

Betty shot me a hateful glance as I followed her into the kitchen. She was piling dishes in the sink, carefully stacking them upon the crusted heap of filthy plates, bowls, and cups already there. I couldn't say why I enjoyed torturing her so, why I relished these moments when her urge to run around forced her to lie and deceive. But I did. This was a game we were playing more and more often. And the older I got, the better I became at it.

I looked at the clock on the cluttered counter next to her. "I'm leaving at eight, and I'm staying at Tommy's tonight. What time are you going out?"

"Don't worry about it," she tossed over her shoulder. I grinned at her back. There was nothing motherly in the venom of her tone. She hated me most of the time, and I liked it that way. "You go and steal shit with your friends. Just leave me the hell alone."

"Is Lynn watching the boys?" I asked.

That did it. "I told you to worry about your own shit!" she snapped, smashing a plastic Tupperware bowl against the counter and whirling on me. The bowl bounced onto the floor and rolled under the table, as if fleeing her rage. "Don't start with me," she warned, leveling a freshly painted fingernail in my direction.

Tiki bolted through the kitchen, fleeing for the safety of Betty's closet. The tiny dog could disappear into that shadowed alcove of forgotten clothing, shoes, and soiled bedclothes for days if it wanted to. Not even my brothers went after Tiki in there. I doubted the police or firefighters would have dared enter such a forbidding space. The clicking of Benji's nails on the stairs grew more audible even as Tiki's faded to nothing, one dog running away and the other hurrying to be near me in case of trouble.

The bowl might have been afraid, but I was having one hell of a time. "How are you paying Lynn?" I continued, boring right in.

Lynn didn't work for free. That meant Betty had more money than she'd let on while conning me last night. I wasn't about to let her slide on that score. She wasn't meeting Leon. She was going out to wherever loose women like her and her slut friend Ruby found new Leons. What pissed me off most was that she was using my money to do it.

"Why don't you mind your own goddamn business?" my mother screamed. I couldn't help it. Some sick, twisted part of me just loved pushing her buttons. "You're a kid! Why don't you try fucking acting like one and leave me alone!"

That was lame, but I ignored her stupid argument, at least for now. "Don't forget what happened last time. You bring some drunk asshole home again and I'm not going to stop Leon from smacking you around."

"If you don't like who I bring around, you're free to go," she told me. "At least no one I hang around with ever beat up your face like your own friends did."

My bruises were all but gone, and Betty was way wrong on that score. She *had* been beaten, a few times severely, by a drunken or temperamental beau. Just because none of her children had been hurt yet was no excuse to keep on experimenting with any stranger she chose to drag home. Sooner or later she was going to let something in that would refuse to leave. I wasn't as worried for myself as I was for my brothers.

"Maybe smacking one of the boys won't be what your new sick boyfriend wants. Could be you'll bring home another one of those creeping butt molesters you seem to be so fond of."

She knew what I was referring to. There'd been a night last year when Benji's growls had awakened me from a dead sleep, and I found Betty's latest live-in sneaking around in the hall outside my brothers' room. We stared at each other through the shadows. I was terrified by the look on his face and the absolute evil in his eyes. Benji stood his ground, though, grumbling and groaning like a beast just released from Hell, head down and eyes bulging at the pervert standing just a few feet away from me.

I told Betty what had happened the next morning, but her butt pirate had a different tale, and my mother chose to believe her latest fling instead of her own son. I kept my brothers and my dog in my room every night for the next couple of weeks, until the guy finally left. I always believed he would have skipped sooner, except he wanted something else, and not from Betty. That's another lesson kids with screwed-up parents have to learn early, or else suffer: watch your ass, because someone else is watching it, too.

Betty spun back to the sink, turning away from me. "Aren't you leaving? You hate me so much, why don't you stay gone?" She was pulling out her big gun, but way too early. "You're always threatening to leave and go find your father. Why don't you fucking go?" Her words were tight and constricted, her anger deflating the implied threat. "This is *my* house, and I'll do what I want in it as long as I pay the bills."

Oops. She wasn't very good at this. "Leon paid the rent last month, *and* the light bill. But you're behind on both of those again." I let that sink in. Her shoulders tightened as I prodded her with these silly little facts. "Using your reasoning, this is *his* house."

"Would you just go!" she screeched, whirling back around and charging.

And she would have hit me, but we were way past that. I dodged left as she swung, then ducked another clumsy attempt to slap me and stepped behind a chair. Betty screamed some unintelligible obscenity, spittle flying as she measured the distance between us. Benji was growling from under the table, but he knew better than to bite Betty. (I think he was afraid her flesh might make him sick.) Terry was wailing in the other room.

It wasn't until she saw Chip sitting on the steps, staring at us, that Betty lowered her claws and tried to wipe the insanity off her face. The baby was calm, his blue eyes almost serene and understanding. My mother tried to tell people he was quiet and good-natured because he was such a loving little boy. I just figured the kid was smart enough to see what the future held in store for him and was depressed all the time, resigned to his fate.

"Besides, if the church people come for the boys in the morning and find some naked drunk guy walking around, they might not be so gullible with their handouts," I added. She didn't say anything, so I decided to throw her into a full-blown panic. "You smeared makeup all over your face."

"Shit!" was all she could think to say, her eyes widening at the sight of the goop staining her fingers after she touched her face.

I managed not to laugh as she bolted upstairs to repair the damage, relishing in the hollow sounds of her cursing until she slammed the rickety bathroom door. I smiled at my baby brother, and he grinned back. Betty was right about *him* at least. There was something special about the boy, some placid aura of calm that seemed to defy our family and impoverished surroundings. Sometimes I was almost a little jealous of the kid, but mostly he was the only bright spot in an otherwise completely dismal family.

"Can you say stupid bitch?" I asked the baby. He smiled wider, as if he understood my joke, but didn't attempt to mimic me.

"Who's a stupid bitch?" Tommy asked, barging in the kitchen door.

"Who do you think?"

I picked up the baby while Tommy checked out the adjoining living room, making sure Betty had no visitors he needed to be aware of. Chip giggled when I tickled him, and Benji followed us into the other room, finally slinking out from beneath the table. I plopped my brother on the couch after checking his diaper, silently thanking God it was dry.

There was nothing on the TV that would hold my brothers' attention this late, and I didn't have any snacks to bribe them with.

"Your mom's freaking out?" Tommy asked.

"Always."

"Word is you're riding the magic bus in the morning," he informed me, grinning like a fool.

"I don't need to guess where you heard that," I muttered. *Damn, that girl needs to stop talking once in a while.* "I just lied to that dude to get him off my back."

"Yeah, he creeps me out, but he's been letting up on me lately," Tommy said. "But it wasn't your girl who told me. It was that Holly chick. She was rapping to me at my cousin's place today. Damn, that chick is nice."

I didn't like when he talked dirty about Holly, and I was hoping he wasn't about to start up on her again.

"Sorry, man, I shouldn't refer to that Bess chick as *your* girl. I know how afraid to pop her cherry you are. I imagine you going to wait around for Rupe to do the job, or some rich dude out at that church."

Okay, so maybe I preferred he went on about Holly instead. "C'mon, Tommy, ease up. You know I don't like when you come off like this."

"Yeah? Well, I'm just trying to tell you, man. You got to take care of business. That girl has done everything 'cept throw it at you." Tommy looked out the window, thinking the creaking sound of Betty moving upstairs was somebody out on the porch. "Now I know why you afraid of Lynn. Hell, that bitch scares me! But Bess is a sweet little thing. You and Rupe keep putting shit off, and I might just have to step up to the plate myself."

"Bess is just a girl who talks too much," I said feebly. *Then why are you getting so angry?* I could feel my neck and ears heating up.

"She wouldn't be talking if I had a hold of her," he said, pretending to hold someone down and swaying his hips back and forth. For some reason, both my brothers found his outlandish antics hysterical. Their laughter only made him pump faster.

"I said cut it out!" I snapped, louder than I'd intended.

He decided to have mercy on me and stopped, no doubt noticing the flush of my face. "Yeah, well never mind all that. We need to leave early. I got to show you something."

I nodded, relieved to change the subject. "Hey, you two be good for Lynn, and I'll bring home some Lucky Charms and Cracker Jacks," I told them. The baby smiled. He already knew what Cracker Jacks meant, and he loved digging the marshmallows out of the cereal box of Lucky Charms. Benji usually lapped up the rest of the castaway dry cereal.

"I want chocolate doughnuts," Terry insisted, never satisfied.

I gave him a light smack on the head as I headed out. "Okay, but I better get a good report from Lynn."

"Can I stay up 'til you get home?" he called after me.

"No," I returned. Benji tried to follow me out the back door, but I gently blocked his way with my sneaker. "You stay here, pal." He lowered his ears and slowly sat down, gazing at me with those beseeching brown eyes from beneath the tangle of hair. I bent down and rubbed his head before leaving. "I'll see you later tonight."

Outside, Tommy cursed as he tried to avoid the many piles of dog crap littering our little yard. I was always promising to clean them up, but rarely did so. Betty always flipped out whenever my brothers got into the mess while playing outside, threatening to get rid of my dog if I didn't clean up after him. I just told her Tiki was crapping too. It was actually kind of funny when Leon stepped in a pile of shit, especially if he was too drunk to notice and left with the stink of it following him into the lounge or truck stop he was off to.

"What's so important?" I asked Tommy.

"Just you wait," Tommy insisted, holding my curiosity off. "I found the fucking mother lode."

I was pretty sure I knew what he'd found. A few blocks later my guess was proven correct. Tommy pointed out a detached cinder block garage. We checked out the area, especially the duplex sitting beyond the garage, until we were as certain as we could be no one was watching. Then we crept up to a broken window just off the alley.

Within the murky garage was an array of motorcycle parts, tires, and scattered tools, but I barely registered those items in my rush of excitement. In one corner of the cluttered room was stacked the largest collection of Coke and 7UP bottles I'd ever seen or even imagined. I glanced at Tommy, and he beamed like we'd stumbled on the pot of gold at the end of a rainbow. Before we left, I surveyed the exterior of the garage and the number of choppers in the yard, making mental notes to help me prepare our plan.

Tommy waited for me to mull things over, letting me chew on this a while. I was the worrier of our little pack of thieves. It was my job to plan how we would actually steal our bounty, and Rupe's job to hide what we stole in his own garage until we were ready to move it. All Tommy usually did was assist in the theft and help spend the money, although he claimed he was the one who would protect us if we were ever caught during one of our late-night endeavors.

"We won't be able to force the side door or lift the big garage door," I said, talking mainly to myself. "Both of them were locked. That means someone has to go in through the window." *And we all know who that someone's going to be.* "Just guessing, I'd say it's going to take five or six shopping carts, maybe more."

"How many nights you figure it'll take?" Tommy asked.

I stopped dead in the middle of the alley, turning to look at him. "One. You and I both know I'll be the one inside. I'm only going in once. Did you see those Harleys? I've seen those guys roaring in and out of that place. I'm not taking any more chances than I have to."

"But we only have two carts," Tommy told me unnecessarily.

"So we steal three or four more carts," I replied, heading on toward Pops'. Tommy mumbled something and fell in beside me. "I'd rather get my hand slapped for ripping off the Kroger than have my jaw broken by some badass. I go in and hand them out to you. You give them to Rupe, who'll load the carts. We hide all the carts down the alley and get them to Rupe's garage and out of sight the same night."

Tommy readily agreed, eager to be at it now that I'd devised the plan. "When do we go?"

I stopped again, looking at him in earnest. I knew he wasn't going to like my next statement. "The first night it rains hard, even if it storms. I'm hoping for as much loud, booming thunder as possible."

"What? I'm not hauling those bottles around in the rain! Why the hell we have to do this shit in the fucking rain?"

"Elementary, my dear Watson," I countered. "The sounds of a storm will drown out all the clanking and the clattering. Plus—and this is important, so try to keep up—those Harleys won't be blowing in and out of that backyard very often if it's raining. I'm not exactly looking to mix it up with any of those crazy biker dudes."

Tommy hadn't liked my "try-to-keep-up" comment, but I could tell by his posture that my arguments had been sound enough to convince him. All he had left to complain about was, "What about the cartons getting all wet and the bottles falling out?"

I was ready for him. "The cartons will dry out, and we can wrap up the loaded carts with pieces of one of Leon's old car covers."

"Baldy won't miss it?"

"Nah, he threw a bunch of shit in our basement that he hasn't touched since. I made the boys a tent out of one of the covers a while back, and Leon could've cared less. There's another one down there all ripped and oily. We can cut that one up, and he'll never miss it."

A cat darted across the alley in front of us. We both jumped and almost started running. "I think that was a black cat," I said with a laugh. "Isn't that bad luck or something?"

"That's bullshit," Tommy snorted. "Black cats are good luck. White people made that black cat story up. Why would a cat want to be white? They wouldn't be able to hunt for shit. How's a white cat supposed to be able to sneak around at night?"

He had a good point, but I couldn't resist acting as his straight man. "I suppose white people made up the chicken and watermelon shit, too? And I suppose black guys don't jump higher and run faster, or have bigger dicks?"

"Now all that shit's true," Tommy admitted, smiling wide in the fast-falling darkness. "But none of that pisses me off. Damn, I could use me some KFC about now."

"I wonder why the KFC doesn't sell watermelon." We both cracked up at the notion. "Probably nobody's brave enough to suggest it."

Tommy was belly-laughing, but he paused long enough to inform me that he was going to suggest that very thing the next time he bought chicken.

CHAPTER 6

Betty didn't make it home that Saturday night. Ruby was dropping her sorry-and-dragging-ass off as I came strolling home, a little before noon. I caught a glimpse of Ruby's face behind the wheel of her rusted-out Pinto just before she roared away. Unbelievably, she looked worse than my mother. I followed Betty up the crumbling concrete steps of our porch, noting the rip along the seam of her cheap skirt, her torn nylons, and the way she had to use the dangerously loose handrail to manage the stairs.

I couldn't help but reach out to steady her as she swayed near the top of the steps, and she turned to look down at me, squinting through a haze of confusion and agony. Her eyes were glassy and so puffed up she had trouble getting them open enough to see. But she could see well enough to make me out, and she wasn't so confused that she didn't know who I was. She jerked away from my hand and glared at me, opening her mouth to speak and then deciding she was better off not bothering with an attempt to form words.

Lynn had locked the door before heading out to church with the boys, and Betty couldn't manipulate the lock. I let her fumble around with her key until she begrudgingly handed it over. I thought about making her wait a while before I opened the door, perhaps even starting an argument with her while we were still outside. The light was killing her eyes, and the way she kept rubbing at her temples told me she had what she liked to call a splitting headache. But I decided to have mercy on her since she'd come home alone.

Except she had to stay out all night to manage that simple little miracle, I reminded myself.

Once inside, I carried my bag of cereal and Cracker Jacks over to the counter while my hung-over mother shuffled through the kitchen, muttering something about me telling the church people she was sick before she crawled upstairs to puke in the bathroom. (At least I hoped she made it to the bathroom.) I heard the thud of her limp body falling onto her mattress, where she would stay until her head cleared and her stomach settled. She didn't have to say anything to me. I knew the drill. In fact, I had more lies memorized than times tables, and could recite them just as easily.

If she didn't get up by the time her shift started tonight, I would have to call her off work, making sure I didn't recycle a lie before it was safe. If Leon came around I was to use a whole different set of lies. The lies I told the church people or neighbors were safe little white lies, and the lies I told the police or bill collectors were always the same, and not difficult to remember. Lying came easily to me; it was a way of life. I could lie and keep track of that lie without thinking.

I wasn't surprised when Lynn and my brothers didn't get off the church bus a little later on. Dave Jones pulled up not long after it passed, and he and his wife came up to the house with Lynn and my brothers in tow. He didn't even pretend to act pleased to see me when I let them in. He just stared at me, looking just hard enough to signal he was disappointed but not really angry. I thought about using the poor lost fatherless kid routine on him, but decided against it. This guy was too in the know for that.

"We were looking for you this morning," Dave decided on for an opening.

"Yeah, I'm sorry about that, but I forgot I had to work late, and then I had other plans," I told him, preparing for another round of deception.

Dave Jones surprised me, and that didn't happen very often. "Don't lie to me anymore. If you can't speak to me without lying, don't talk to me at all. I'm only trying to help you. If you don't trust me, just say so. You're a bright kid. If you can't tell that my interest in you is genuine and real, just stay away from me. If you're going to insist on lying to me, I'd rather you just tell me to leave you alone."

I was stunned. There wasn't any malice in his tone, and hardly any anger. He had spoken plainly, and in as matter-of-fact a tone as any schoolteacher giving a lecture. My normally active brain pan went as cold and dull as one of Betty's unwashed skillets beneath that pile of dishes in the sink. And yet I knew what the guy was doing. Somehow I knew he was playing me. He had to be. Didn't he?

"Dave, maybe…"

"Please, Jewel," her husband cut her off, firmly but gently. "This is between us, a man-to-man thing. Young master Donald here needs to be told how a man feels when he's lied to so casually. Have you been lied to before?" he asked me directly. I could only nod. "And how do you like it?" I just shook my head, still struggling to find my tongue. "Well, I feel the same way."

I was embarrassed. Something wet and hot trickled out of the corner of my eye and ran down my cheek. *You are not crying!* Lynn noticed my predicament and must have felt sorry for me. She gathered up my brothers and slipped into the kitchen. I heard them getting into the bag of goodies I'd brought home, but they sounded far away. Right now my whole world was this guy coming down on me, that tear on my face, and a white-hot rage I felt building up from somewhere deep inside of me. Somehow, this had to be Betty's fault.

"Truth? You want the truth?" I asked him. *Don't you dare reach up and wipe that tear!* "The truth is, I was working last night. I worked until almost two in the morning. I don't want to get up early enough to ride your bus. And, I don't want to go to your church, either."

I could tell he wanted to ask where a twelve-year-old kid could possibly be working in such a crappy neighborhood at two in the morning on a Saturday night, but he swallowed his question and stuck to the matter at hand. "Did you know you weren't going to go when you promised me that you were?" he asked calmly.

I hesitated, but I was in way too deep already. "Yes."

"Is it so hard to tell the truth?"

"I guess not."

Dave knelt down in front of me, looking me earnestly in the eye. "How about you and I make a deal, young man?" I only nodded. "No more lies. I want you to visit my church. I admit that. I would like to spend some time with you, maybe hang out or play some ball. I don't want anything from you but honesty. You don't have to do anything you don't want to. Maybe if you get to know me a little better, you might come to trust me a little bit."

He stuck out his hand, wanting me to shake on it. "How about it? Do we have a deal?"

I couldn't help myself. For some reason, I really liked this guy. Something about him felt... honest, to cop his own word. "Sure," I promised, shaking his hand and actually meaning to keep my word this time, even if he *had* called me Donald. I absolutely hated being called Donald. His hand was strong and firm, and I was reminded by the strength of his grip that I was still just a kid.

Chip came tottering back into the living room, all smiles. He had a mouth full of chewy marshmallows and one scrawny arm buried deep in the cereal box, digging for more. Benji was right behind him, nose down and alert, sucking any dropped pieces of cereal off the floor like a waddling, hairy vacuum cleaner. Terry was behind my mutt, his mouth smeared with the chocolate doughnuts I'd remembered to grab for him. I didn't mind seeing him eating them all that much, though. I'd stolen them last night while making a run at Pops', so I wasn't out a single penny.

Jewel laughed at the silly train they made. She had a sweet-sounding laugh, gentle and pleasant. I thought Dave was awfully lucky to have a girl like her. I was pretty sure she wouldn't be creeping around with the likes of Ruby, or coming home throwing up after a night of drinking and popping pills. You could tell she would be a nice mom, like the ones on TV. Her kids wouldn't be dirty all the time, or scared, or told to lie to everybody. But thinking like that was stupid. Dave had Jewel. My brothers and I were stuck with Betty, and that was just how things were.

"Terry here threatened to punch one of the other kids in the mouth today," Dave casually informed me, tousling my brother's hair affectionately. I looked up at him with a sheepish grin. "He tells me you gave him a little big brotherly advice."

I glanced at Terry, and he gave me a broad, sloppy smile. He'd already made a royal mess of his whole face, and was busy licking chocolate off his hands and fingers. It was even in his hair, staining the reddish curly locks around his face. I was actually kind of proud of the kid for sticking up for himself.

"He didn't actually hit him, did he?" I had to ask.

"No, but he meant to," Dave told me. "He and Henry and I had a talk, and I think the two of them are going to get along a little better now."

"Henry can be a bit feisty," Jewel added.

I liked that lady more and more. "Yeah, well, I'm sorry about that. I didn't think he'd actually do it. I was fighting with my mom when I said it, so I wasn't really paying attention to what he was saying."

"Where *is* your mom?" Jewel asked cautiously.

"Upstairs, sleeping off last night," I returned without hesitation.

You wanted honesty. I was pleased at the sudden change in Dave's expression. I figured he was feeling a little bad for coming down on me so hard. At least I hoped he was. Betty wasn't the only one who could use pity as a weapon.

"I should be going," Lynn mumbled. "Chip's probably wet," she told me, heading for the door.

"Wait up, Lynn," Jewel said before she could get away. "We'll give you a ride home." Lynn tried to protest, but Jewel was having none of it. She looked at her husband, letting him know he was to finish up, and followed Lynn outside.

"I guess we'll be getting on," Dave told me. "I want you to think about coming to church, even if it's just once." He looked at me, reluctant to leave, but I couldn't read his expression. "You *did* promise to do so. I think you owe me that much, and if you visit just once, I'll forget the whole lying thing altogether."

I wasn't about to promise anything. Not after he'd made such a big deal over one stupid little lie. "I'll think about it. I really will." That would have to be enough. I wasn't giving him any more than that.

Dave waited a moment, perhaps wondering if he wanted to press the issue, but after a time he only nodded. "Fair enough," he said. He put a hand on my shoulder and squeezed. "I'll talk to you later, if that's all right?"

"Sure," I told him before he finally left, leaving me to a tedious day of tending to my brothers' dirty faces and smelly butts.

Betty and I continued to pick at one another. I was still sore over the money she'd conned me out of, and she was still pissed because I was breathing and wouldn't shut up. Things always got tense near the end of the month. Betty's resources were limited at best. They were almost nonexistent as the calendar came closer to flipping over. Even the baby seemed to sense her dark moods at these stressful times, and was more quiet and subdued than normal.

My mother did have talent. How she juggled rent and light bills, Leons, and the long list of people and creditors she owed money to was well beyond my young means to fully comprehend. I knew the basics, though. She used who she could, lied as often as necessary, and would rob you blind if you were stupid enough to let her. When she had even a meager means to work with, she could distract herself from the enormity of our dire situation with whoever she was scamming or running from. Problem was, as the end of the month grew near, the more clearly she saw where and what we were.

Not that I wasn't old enough to understand what Leon or the other guys Betty snuggled up to wanted when they came around, but I sure couldn't comprehend why they forked over cash for the privilege. I'd heard enough sickening noises emanating from my mother's bedroom to convince me that whatever she and her perverted boyfriends did in there wasn't for the faint of heart. I even had a fairly clear picture of what she and Ruby were doing when they went out at night, and how my mother sometimes magically came up with extra cash.

But I wasn't yet old enough, or brazen enough, to challenge her on that particular front. I knew I didn't like it when she let any old man move in for a while, and hated when she came home all trashed from a night out. I popped off and acted like I wasn't afraid of these men, when they knew I was. But I wasn't afraid of my mother, and I gave it to her every chance I got because I resented her so intensely for how we had to live.

Looking back, I realize now that she'd never had much of a chance at a normal life. Her own life had been a series of bad breaks, worse decisions, and doomed marriages, leaving her handicapped by an attitude that nothing was her fault, and carrying the baggage of three children she'd never really wanted to raise. She had no respect for herself. No goals. No notion of what she truly needed to be happy, and no plan to achieve it.

What I did blame her for—and still do—was putting her own needs above those of her children. She knew what kind of men she was dealing with most of the time. That she allowed them to try and prey on her own flesh and blood was a sin I cannot forgive, nor try to.

A few days after this last outing with Ruby, Leon showed up with a real mean on, and the days that followed were terror-filled, turning our shabby little house into a full-fledged war zone. I give Leon credit, though: he never laid a hand on me or my brothers. But this time he got mad enough to beat the tar out of Betty.

Leon beat her bad enough one night that she had to make a run for it, dashing half-naked and bleeding down the alley in the middle of the night, screaming for help. Help arrived in the form of two disinterested cops who politely questioned Betty amidst a crowd of curious half-asleep neighbors. Leon was long gone by the time the cops arrived, and Betty didn't tell them he was probably at his mom's house on the south side, or even give them a license plate number or a decent description of Leon's El Camino.

My mother had no explanation for Leon's sudden physical abuse. He'd never been too rough with her before. She blamed it on his drinking, crying to the police while she pretended to be near to fainting, whimpering like a dying dog after it'd been run over by a truck but wasn't quite dead. But I'd heard enough of the fighting to know Leon had found out what she and Ruby had been doing that Saturday night, and where they'd been. He'd been enraged because she'd messed around with some truck driver named Chuck.

Betty had to go to work with a black eye, a swelled-up nose, and both lips split after that last tussle with Leon. She put on a good show for everyone, but I knew her too well to fall for my mother's woe-is-me routine. I was sure she hadn't enjoyed the actual beating, but I knew for a fact she'd get a lot of mileage out of the bruises and cuts it left behind. Betty was an actress without peer when it came to working an audience for pity, especially if she had props like hungry kids or facial bruises to work with.

And she used the aftereffects of her latest beating to get as much sympathy as possible. She didn't miss church for the next couple of weeks, and had one of her greatest theatrical performances during a wailing and whining session up at the altar after a Sunday night service. She had her boss at the Big Boy giving her rides back and forth to work, the saps she waited on tipping her more than usual, people from the church giving her money, and even elderly Mrs. Lorret from across the street making us dinner and promising to help out with us kids.

It was after one of those great dinners made by that sweet old lady that I was aroused from a deep sleep by the clinking of small pieces of gravel striking the alley-side window of my bedroom. I knew who it was before I was even awake. Only Tommy or Rupe ever got my attention using that tactic, and only Tommy would possibly be out and about this late at night. Rupe only risked the wrath of his parents at the urging and coercion of me and our big, black menacing sidekick.

I peeked out the window and waved at Tommy, letting him know to go to the rear of the house, where I'd let him in through the kitchen door. My friend was just a darker shadow in the night, barely visible in the weak glow of a streetlight burning atop a leaning pole on the other side of the alley. He lifted a hand to let me know he'd seen me and moved away. I watched him for a second. That was all it took for me to know something was wrong. Just the way he walked, some difference in his posture, told me he was hurting.

"Man, you really need to get some of the shit out of this yard," my friend complained as I opened the door.

"Jesus, Tommy. What happened?" I asked, too stunned to step aside so he might slip into our kitchen and out of the night.

"Candy happened," he said, shrugging as if his swollen jaw and closed left eye were really no big deal at all. "You going to let me in or what?"

"Oh, sorry," I stammered, stepping back and letting him enter. *Don't tell me you were skimming on Candy,* I wanted to say. But instead I just waited for any further explanation and asked, "Are you all right, man?"

"Sure," he answered. But he was holding something back. "I was hoping I could crash with you tonight? Your mom got company?"

I shook my head, but then quickly blurted, "I mean she ain't got no company. You can sleep here, no problem… But what's up?"

There was no answer forthcoming, so I closed and locked the door. Benji was busy sniffing around Tommy's feet and pant legs, quietly whining for attention. Tommy relented and bent down to scratch my insistent dog's head. After the brief contact Benji moved away, deciding a quick pat was enough. I heard Tommy grunt in pain as he stood back up, and noticed his hand as he placed it gingerly against his ribs. Obviously, the extent of my friend's injuries didn't end with his face.

I led him upstairs without speaking. I was wearing the pair of cutoff sweatpants and T-shirt I'd been sleeping in. Tommy just kicked off his shoes and lay down on my mattress once we'd quietly climbed the steps and slipped into my room. I dug a plain pillow without a pillowcase out of my closet and tossed it to him. He caught it and placed it under his head while I flopped down beside him. Benji wriggled his way in between us, forcing his head under my hand so I'd have to rub on him a little while before falling asleep. It was a nightly ritual for us.

We laid there staring up at the ceiling in silence for what seemed like a long time. I wanted to know what had happened between him and Candy, but I wasn't curious, or foolish, enough to press him if he didn't want to talk about it. Instead, I listened to the sound of our breathing and rubbed on my dog, letting Tommy fall asleep if he chose to. I'd never seen Tommy marked up this badly before. The notion that even *he* could be beaten down was going to take some getting used to.

"I hear you went out to that church," Tommy finally said, breaking the silence and startling me. His statement sounded more like an accusation than a casual comment. I had only gone one time, and hadn't wanted Tommy to know about my visit. "You ain't letting that Dave dude get to you, are you?"

"Nah," I sent back. "I just went out last Sunday to get him off my back." *Why do you sound so defensive?* I asked myself. "It's nothing."

"I don't trust that dude. He's always grabbing and touching." Tommy's words were a little slurred, and I didn't think it was caused by being sleepy. His swollen jaw was making talking difficult. "He comes rolling down here like he's the answer to all our fucking problems. Man, that fancy white dude don't know shit."

"I think Dave's okay, Tommy. He really believes God can change your whole life," I said, trying to defend my new friend.

"He's probably a fag," insisted Tommy.

"If he is, he's a fag with a real pretty wife."

For a while, we didn't say anything more. I knew Tommy wouldn't like me going to church, or trusting Dave too much. We were tight. People you could trust were tough to come by in our neighborhood. When you found someone who was going to be there for you, you were there for them, no matter who was right or wrong. We won or lost together, stole together, stayed after school in detention together, worked together, and pretended we were never hurt or scared together. Tommy didn't want Dave coming between us.

When shit was too rough for me to handle in this house, Tommy always let me hang in his room. If someone was after me at school, Tommy let them know there was easier prey to be had somewhere else. When Tommy needed money, I figured ways for us to get some. Rupe was our friend, but he had a mother and a father, and there were some things he just didn't get about how Tommy and I lived. We shared more than friendship. Tommy and I shared a bond of circumstance only children bereft of a normal, secure childhood understand but can rarely express.

"What was it like?"

"Church?"

"No, asshole, changing your brother's shitty diaper. Yeah, church. What was it like?"

Beat down or not, Tommy was still Tommy.

"Kind of weird. Most of the kids of those rich people try to act nice enough. But you know how they are. Everyone tries to make the bus kids feel special. Like we're going to forget what we have to come back to."

The thing was, you kind of *did* forget for a while. I couldn't tell Tommy, but there had been some nice people at that church. Including Holly's two pretty, younger twin sisters. The three of them had sung in front of the whole church, and dumb old Billy Holmes had been right. They did sing just like someone on the radio. They also had activities on weekday nights, including basketball, and outings with kids of the same age, and they were planning a picnic next month. Dave said they played football at their picnics, and he wanted to be my quarterback.

"You going to start going out there regular?" he asked.

"I don't think so," I told him, but I was already starting to detest the feeling of being torn between my loyalty to Tommy and my promise not to lie to Dave. A lot of what Dave kept preaching was making sense to me. He almost had me convinced that a kid like me could grow up and be somebody. "Anyway, it's no big thing," I added, hoping Tommy would drop the subject.

Benji groaned and rolled over, sleeping with his feet sticking straight up in the air. We both laughed at him, and Tommy let the whole church thing drop. *Thanks, pal. That's another one I owe you.*

I'd almost given up on him saying anything more when Tommy said softly, "Candy flipped out over a stupid twenty bucks, man. I mean, like his rich black ass can't afford to drop a twenty on a brother." Tommy's voice was subdued. I could tell he was holding back anger, and tears. "He just walked right in my pad and beat on me right in front of my mom and my cousins. Told me 'you don't take what's mines, nigger,' and just starts throwing down. My mom and Ricky and Leo just stood by and watched, too."

I almost asked him what he'd expected them to do. Candy and the brutes who worked for him pretty much ran the whole neighborhood. Nothing moved around here unless Candy said it was okay to do so. Even Pops had to have Candy's permission to operate. Candy ran girls, oversaw all the food stamp swapping, sold generic cigarettes, loaned money, and even owned the meat wagon that sold steaks and hamburger cheaper than you could buy the meat at the supermarkets. Even Betty paid Candy back if she borrowed from him, and on the same day she had the money in hand. That alone proved he was no man to be messing with.

I thought about Candy whaling on my friend, and could hardly imagine it. Candy stood probably six and a half feet tall. He had a shaved, shiny scalp and a thick, square face, and was as big as any football player I'd ever seen on TV. He smiled most of the time, flashing two gold teeth that glinted in almost any light. His smile wasn't real, though. It was just a flinch of the muscles in that black man's face, a response to try and convince all of us in the neighborhood that it was safe to deal with him. I trusted my street-bred instincts when it came to Candy, and kept my distance.

No, I didn't defend Tommy's family for not trying to help him when Candy came to call. I just kept my mouth shut and thanked Dave's God that I hadn't been there, since I would have stood there and done nothing, too. And Tommy would've held that against me forever. Candy wasn't just a man—he was a stark symbol of the reality of living in this neighborhood. Candy wasn't here because he had to be. Candy was here because he liked it, and profited from it. No skinny, twelve-year-old offspring of Betty's was going to stand in that man's way.

"Why were you short?" I had to ask, hoping it wouldn't anger him to be questioned on the fact that Candy was always supposed to be given what was his.

Tommy chuckled, then moaned and grabbed his ribs again. "I spent it on Hannah Carson at the bowling alley. She had some friends with her, and I bought some food and gave them money to play at the arcade. Hannah's sweet, man. You know that." What I *knew* was that Hannah was fifteen and had been giving it up to Tommy one way or another for a couple of months now. "We have good times, and good times cost money."

"But what about the money from Pops' this weekend?" I asked him. "Couldn't you have made up the twenty from that? You had to have pocketed… What? At least twenty?"

Tommy didn't say anything. I could tell he didn't like my line of questioning. "There was a movie later, and Hannah wanted some money, and some reefer." Tommy sighed and adjusted his pillow. "You know how bitches are," he muttered.

That was another big difference between me and Tommy. I didn't know how bitches were at all, although he liked to assume I did. Tommy was thirteen closing on twenty, with hair under his arms, plus fuzz across his lips and cheeks, and elsewhere. He drank a little, smoked a lot, and even toked a joint now and then. He'd been kissing and fondling girls for a while now, and had recently moved on to experiences I could only imagine. His all-time favorite joke was to sneak up on Rupe or me and tell us to smell his finger as he thrust it under our nose.

Me? I was twelve going on ten, my body as smooth as the day I'd been born, with the exception of the mop on my head. Rarely did I find myself larger or taller than a guy my own age. I'd been kissed once when I was about nine. She was a cute little Spanish girl at a birthday party, and we had to go into an empty refrigerator box together on a dare. Even at that, she did the kissing. I just sat there, looking stupid and feeling more so. I can honestly say, lying there with Tommy that night, that I was still years away from my first sexual experience, even one of an individual nature.

It wasn't that Bess and even Lynn hadn't let me know that they were available, should I want to try my hand or lips at the making-out thing. But I was a late bloomer, both physically and in terms of confidence. I think I was afraid of sex or anything leading up to it because of the horrible noises I'd had to hear from my mother's room since I was little. Hell, even Rupe was occasionally making out. I just hoped he wasn't swapping spit with Bess.

"Damn, Tommy, you can't spend Candy's money," I whispered. "I know he let you off for doing that before." *Because I helped you come up with the money in a hurry,* I silently recalled. "If you run weed for him, you have to deliver his end."

"No shit?" was his sarcastic reply. I knew I had to back off. When Tommy got over this whipping, he was going to have a hard-on for someone, any-one, and I sure didn't want that person to be me. "He wants that twenty in the morning."

"No problem, I've got it," I assured him. It would take almost everything I'd made at Pops', and I knew Tommy wouldn't pay me back. He tended to forget debts of a monetary nature, figuring he made up for the money in other ways. "You want me to take it over to the pool hall in the morning?"

Tommy thought on that tempting offer. "No, I better do it myself. Candy will want to rap about business and respect, and all his bullshit."

"You going to keep running weed for him?" I asked, choking down a strong desire to point out all the dangers of working for Candy.

"Yeah, sure," he said with a yawn. "The money's good, and I get to pinch the reefer." He laughed softly, tiring. "Bitches get loose on that shit, Donny. I'm telling you, man, that's where it's at. You need to step up and get with some of this."

If *this* meant being a punching bag for Candy, he could keep it. But the image of Hannah Carson acting loose was a strong argument. I may not have hit puberty yet, but I *was* male, and Hannah was definitely a lure every boy I knew would take notice of. She was stacked, and knew she attracted a lot of attention. It wasn't that I didn't understand Tommy's weakness for her. It was the fact that he could put aside any fear of Candy just to spend time with her that baffled me.

I was falling asleep when Tommy said, "Donny?"

"Yeah?" I murmured. Benji groaned again, but we were too tired to laugh.

"Thanks, man," he said. That was a first. *I'll bet that hurt,* I told myself.

"You can sleep here whenever. You know that," I told him, fishing for whatever it was he was actually thanking me for.

"Not just that. I mean… the money, you know? And all the other shit. Helping me with school this year, and getting me in at Pops'. All of it, you know…?"

"It's cool, Tommy," I said, letting him off the hook. "I know you're there for me, too."

"You my nigger, Donny," he said. After a moment's hesitation, we both laughed. "What? A white boy can't be no nigger?" I wasn't sure about the etiquette where that particular brand was used, but he had me laughing even harder. "Gran says they more white niggers than black ones."

I didn't want to disagree with Tommy's grandmother. "Well, somebody should tell all of *them*, 'cause I don't think they know about that."

We were laughing so hard I was afraid we might wake Betty. Benji raised his head and peered at us like we were nuts. After a while we settled back down and didn't say much, listening to the occasional traffic outside and considering our options for the next day. Before long we were both yawning, and Benji was nestled back against me.

Tommy snorted, already sounding more like his normal self now that we'd left the Candy issue behind. "Don't you worry 'bout Collins no more. He's got one coming."

"I think we dropped that before school was out. I think maybe I'd rather just let that go. Who needs the trouble, you know?" I hoped Tommy saw that my way. Collins was more trouble than he was worth, and he had more than a few friends to back any play he decided to make. The last thing I wanted was to get my ass kicked as soon as the next school year opened. "I think we were cool."

"We'll see," was all he gave me back. That meant he'd push on Collins a little and see where Mike and his crew wanted to take it. Tommy never gave anyone the last word, or punch. "It's weird how tight we are. I'll bet we going to be tight forever."

"Sure," I agreed.

But I was awake for a long while, listening to the sounds of Tommy's snoring. For the first time I found myself wondering just how long we *would* be friends. He was rushing headlong into a life I detested, and Dave Jones and his God kept creeping into my head. It was almost an escape, having someone tell you that all the things expected of you, all the things you were afraid of, were actually sins, and not something you were simply supposed to do.

CHAPTER 7

"Some dude in a suit was looking for you today," I told my mother as soon as she walked in the door.

"A cop?" she asked, stiffening.

"I don't think so. He was sneaking around and tried to talk to Mrs. Phillips next door, but she told him to get stuffed."

I watched Betty's reactions closely. Something serious was going down.

"I think he was trying to serve you with court papers." If that was true, which I was sure it was, it wouldn't be long until they caught up with her at work. "Anything I should know?"

"Anything you need to know, I'll tell you," she informed me, heading into the kitchen to deposit her night's tips on the table for counting.

Ding, ding, and the fight began.

"We had a notice tacked on the door today, too."

I pointed to where I'd left it on the table, right next to where she was dumping her change. She let the coins trickle onto the table as quietly as possible, trying not to disturb the boys, who were already long asleep upstairs. If Terry heard her, he'd come down and whine at her about how mean I'd been to him while she was gone, or cry about being hungry or scared.

"It says they're shutting off the electric on Friday. Just in time for the weekend," I added, to be glib. Glib always pissed her off.

"I'll take care of it," she snapped, snatching the notice and stuffing it into her purse.

Damn, she's trying to win round one, I thought. *The nerve of some people!*

That was the problem with getting rid of a Leon. Who was going to pay the rent and utilities? She'd done pretty well, profiting from the bruises Leon had given her, but that game had ended once the bruising faded. The heat was on, and Betty was sweating. She wasn't too worried about the rent yet. It took a month or two to evict a family, even out of a dump like this. But the power could be shut off by the simple flick of a switch. Or disconnecting a wire, or whatever they had to do. In any case, it was going to be really dark soon.

I wanted to keep picking at her, but it was late. And I spotted something of interest just inside her purse. It looked like a checkbook. If Betty was running check scams, things were going to get intense: the end was near. She'd run up as much as she could, especially if any place would let her write checks for cash, or write them for more than her purchase, which also gave her cash.

There were still aggressive warrants out on her in at least two states that I knew of. We'd run out of Indiana some years back, and Florida most recently. Betty was afraid of Florida, since they'd already jailed her for passing bad checks before. But Betty was addicted to the gullibility of stupid people, be they landlords, bankers, or storekeepers. If you were dumb enough to hand her cash or credit, my mother couldn't resist taking it from you.

I decided to throw this fight, and told her I was going to bed. She glanced at me suspiciously, but relented, thankful to be rid of me, if only for the moment. Betty looked tired. Her job as a waitress forced her to be on her feet a lot, and fighting all the time with me when she came home didn't allow for much rest. Add the burden of hunting for Leons and occasionally feeding her brats, dodging cops and creditors, and not rolling over and crushing little Tiki to death when she was sleeping, and my mother had it kind of rough.

She looked a mess. Her eye makeup was smudged, and her cheeks were pale and drawn. Her eyes had a haunted, almost hunted look to them, as if she was always waiting for someone to jump out at her from every blind corner. Her hair was tangled and hanging in her eyes. Sometimes, I'd feel sorry for her. But then I'd have to deal with some asshole she dragged home, or find out about some scam she was running, and I'd start to hate her all over again. I didn't feel bad about it, either. She hated me more than I was ever going to learn to hate anything in this sorry world, and I knew it.

I sat in my room and worked on a drawing of Thor in the weak glow of my desk lamp, hunched over my makeshift desk in concentration, my tongue sticking out of my mouth and moving more than my pen. I loved drawing the heroic figures in my collection of comics almost more than reading them, and was always dreaming about being an artist or writer for Marvel. I even told lies about how I'd sent in some samples of my work and Stan Lee had written me back, promising me a job when I was old enough.

Although I was lying about corresponding with Stan, my work was pretty good. I would sneak my art into the library at school, run off as many copies as I could on the Xerox while no one was watching, and sell them for a nickel apiece to my classmates. I'd even had teachers buy copies from me. A touchy endeavor, since the school was providing the paper, and I usually crafted my creations during class time when I was supposed to be paying attention to real school work.

I continued to labor away while my mother thumped up the stairs, shut the door to her room, and got ready for bed. I waited a while, clicking off my light and getting into my own bed, listening to the occasional traffic outside, allowing Betty enough time to fall deeply asleep. She normally slept soundly, but the best time to risk creeping around in her room was the first hour or so after she crashed. I really wanted a look at that checkbook, so I gave her plenty of time to go under.

From the top of the stairwell I could hear my mother's snores through the door to her bedroom, louder than my brothers' heavy breathing even though their room was closer and their door wide open. I made the four strides to the end of the hall, just outside her door, the floorboards' creaking sounding like screeching children in the still of the night. My heart was pounding the way it did when I was pulling a job with the guys, and that almost made me laugh out loud.

What's Betty going to do if she catches you? I asked myself. I had no reason to be afraid of my mother.

But I *was* kind of afraid of her room. Leon had put a bolt on the inside of her door, so the boys wouldn't barge in on them to see what all the weird noises were about, but she rarely used it when she wasn't entertaining. Fortunately for me, she hadn't used it tonight either. Her door groaned at my intrusion, though not loud enough to wake Betty. The light she'd left on in the bathroom cast just enough brightness for me to see by.

Tiki's glowing eyes reflected that light. She glared at me in the dimness, as if she knew I was up to no good. The little bitch let out a growl from where she lay beside my mother, and for a moment I thought she might actually start barking loud enough to wake Betty. "Shush," I whispered, and the stupid thing dropped her head and settled down, still eyeing me warily as I continued deeper into the very bowels of Hell.

I could see her purse sitting on a heap of old clothes, not more than a few steps away. She'd left it near the head of her mattress, but the change from her tips would be hidden in a plastic bag behind her box of ceramic frogs, along with an old leather wallet that she used to store whatever folding money she had. Normally, I wouldn't steal from Betty, but I did pilfer some change now and then if I needed lunch money, never enough so that she'd notice. (I didn't want her changing up her hiding place, just in case I ever did need to rip her off.)

As I moved nearer the purse, I dropped down to my hands and knees, now just an arm's reach from Tiki. She continued to glare at me with her glowing eyes, and I could hear her tiny chest rumbling between my mother's snores. The smell of fresh cat piss assailed my nose. Fluffy was none too concerned when her cat box, lined with torn magazine and newspaper, became too soiled for her delicate nature. *Especially when Betty keeps shutting the stupid thing up in her room at night,* I had to concede. My mother's room always had that eye watering reek of cat piss, moldy clothing, and now and again, Tiki droppings.

My hand froze just inches from the purse as Betty rolled toward me and coughed, sending Tiki scrambling for a safer resting place. The little bitch was nimble. I had to give her that. She stood in place for a moment, trembling and eyeing me suspiciously, but eventually snuggled back down against my mother, still watching me. I glanced at Betty, assuring myself she hadn't been disturbed, then snatched up the purse and made my escape.

Safely back in my room with the door closed and locked, I dumped the contents of Betty's purse on my bed and was actually stunned to find not one but three checkbooks. One of them was older, and from a bank back in Florida, and the other two were newer, one in her current name of Williams and the other using her maiden name of Royce. All three showed recent activity. At least there were checks missing from them. Betty didn't bother to keep the registers in any of them completely up to date.

I knew enough about how checks were supposed to work from a class in school, but Betty had taught me the finer skills of running checks. Her lessons went well beyond the knowledge of my teacher or the instruction in any textbook. Anyone could write checks against a balance of money they'd already deposited in the bank; my mother could turn a two hundred dollar deposit into two or three thousand bucks worth of running money and unnecessary junk.

I noticed she'd written checks at the Kroger for cash and groceries, and a couple at the Shell station. At least a few were written at some dive called The Blitz, and a couple of others were made out directly to another person. Many of the missing checks weren't even recorded. *Why bother keeping a record of checks written when there's no money to cover them?* I asked myself with a silent laugh. *And never will be.* Yep, Betty was back to her old tricks, and running in high gear, from the looks of things.

There were other things of interest lying on my bed. A little flip note-book contained the numbers of people she'd probably scratched down while running around. Most of them were men's names. She had two bottles of prescription drugs that had other people's names on the labels, and a baggie of little white pills I'd never seen her taking before. There were three drivers' licenses—the one from Florida had the last name of Royce again—and two Social Security cards, one with a name I'd never known her to use.

Benji kept sniffing at the stuff I'd spilled out on the bed, but he lost inter-est as I started putting all the crap back. I'd seen enough. *Here we go again,* I told myself. I crept back into her room and put the purse back, not even bothering to crawl, thinking about moving again, and how tough it was going to be to make new friends in another bad neighborhood. Tommy and Rupe would be hard to replace. They were about the closest friends I'd ever had, but moving from place to place was something I'd grown accustomed to, and rather expected after living in the same area for more than a few months.

Betty employed a different tactic during this bout of trouble. That Wednes-day night, she stayed after church for a meeting with the pastor, a man named Grady. I wandered around the church until I found Bess. She was with Holly's twin sisters, Ally and April, hanging around in one of the base-ment rooms with some other young people. I didn't dare talk to the twins. Most of the time there were rich guys hanging around, paying them a lot of attention, but that didn't stop me from checking them out.

They weren't as pretty as Holly, but they were close. I liked them both. (At least I liked the way they looked.) Ally was good friends with Bess, and talked as much and as fast as she did. With Bess and Ally around, April didn't get the chance to say much, but that just made her the most appeal-ing of the three, if you asked me. Not that I felt I had a chance with either of the twins. What would they want with a shabbily-dressed kid off the bus from the poor side of town?

I slipped away before Bess noticed I was around and tried to include me in their conversation. I decided to climb the narrow steps up to the balcony and wait, watching the few people still milling around below me with disinterest, wishing Betty would hurry up so we could get back home. Mama Z. had brought us to church tonight, and she was sitting in the front pew nearest the pastor's office, also waiting for my mother.

Lynn sat with her mom, the pair of them chatting quietly with Mrs. Grady. I figured they were probably talking about whatever Betty was spinning on the pastor. I almost wished I could hear what they were saying, but only almost. I often felt that sitting idly by while Betty ripped people off and lied through her teeth implicated me in her schemes. That feeling was becoming more pronounced the older I got. I was starting to detest the way people looked at me, almost as if Betty and I were one and the same.

I guess what scared me most was the thought that maybe we were. I couldn't think about that for very long without feeling sick. I thought about running off almost every day, but where to go? I didn't know my father. From what I *did* know about the man, I doubted life would be any easier living with him. But could there actually be a life worse than the one I was enduring with Betty?

My father's wife had sent me pictures of them from Indiana once. I had two half-brothers and a half-sister, all with different-colored hair. They'd looked happy enough in the photos, riding horses and picnicking and smiling all the while. They lived on a farm. Each kid had their own horse or pony, and rode in competitions of some kind. Betty had been jealous as hell over how pretty his new wife—an Italian lady named Grace with long black hair—looked in the pictures. All I got out of the whole thing was a brand-new set of lies to keep track of.

No, running off to find my father wasn't an option. Truth was, I didn't have *any* options. What would I do out on my own? I was stuck with Betty. But I swore I wasn't going to live like she did. My mother hated when I'd start running on at the mouth about how big my house was going to be and how much money I was going to have. Betty loved to tell me I was going to end up a loser just like my father, but it sure looked like he was doing a hell of a lot better than she was.

I wasn't above pointing that little fact out to her, either. I let her know about almost every shortcoming she had. It was no wonder she hated me. I was making her little scams more difficult to run, giving her less room to operate as I got old enough to understand what was going down. I hated people thinking I was like her or worse yet, a part of her. *And I'll prove it, too,* I promised.

The more I waited, the more I wanted to know what Betty was telling that pastor. I knew he was already trying to help her by promising to pay off some other checks she'd written earlier in the year. He'd gone to court with her, and convinced some creditors to drop charges if he started handling her finances and got them their money a little at a time. What choice did they have? Putting my mother in jail didn't get them a red cent.

When Betty finally came out of the office, her face was all red and her eyes were puffy. *Wow, the pastor got a private performance,* I thought, shaking my head as I headed down to finally get back home. My mother didn't even glance at me as I walked up. Lynn left to gather the boys while Mama Z. pretended to give a shit about my mother's choked-up condition. Lynn and Bess's mother knew full well what Betty was pulling. Even so, she led her to a pew and assisted Betty into a seated position before heaving her bulk down beside her.

"I would like a word with you some time in the near future, young man," the pastor told me, his tone mild but holding something back.

I saw something behind his eyes I didn't like. "Sure," I returned with a shrug, anticipating a lecture concerning how mean and disrespectful I was to my mother.

The mood on the ride home was quiet, almost somber. Bess had gone home with some church people she stayed with a lot, so Lynn and I were holding the boys in the smallish back-seat of the hatchback. Both of them were asleep not long after we left the church. I tried to listen to my mother and Mama chatting up front, listening for clues as to what sort of scheme she was pulling on the pastor. They kept their voices low, and the noisy little car made eavesdropping difficult.

Including me in her plot had been a mistake. I wasn't taking anything off that pastor. I was going to answer any question he asked with utter and complete honesty, no matter what subject he brought up. If I had to, I'd play my ace in the hole and tell the man about the checkbooks and fake IDs, running with Ruby, the food stamp scams, the pills, and anything else that came to mind. *I'll show him I'm nothing like you, Betty.*

As much as I wanted to listen in as long as I could, I soon fell under the spell of the droning of the car. My eyes grew heavy, and I rested my head back and shifted beneath the baby's weight until I found as comfortable a position as possible. Chip's rhythmic breathing and soft breath on my neck kept luring me away from the chatter in the front seat. (If it hadn't been for the puddle of drool the baby was depositing down my neck, I would've been asleep already.) Just before I closed my eyes, Betty turned her head and looked at me. It was a brief glance, but I saw some emotion in her face I didn't recognize.

I wasn't positive, but I was almost sure what I'd seen in her face was fear. Fear of me, or of whatever she was pulling on the pastor? *Probably both.* I fell asleep with that eerie look of hers in my mind, her face accusing me for our sorry state of existence. It didn't bother me much, and I slept until Mama dropped us off. I was used to her blaming me for everything.

Our battle was heading toward a whole new front, escalating into a constant war instead of sporadic fights.

A week or so later, Betty decided it was time to kick the theatrics into high gear. Only the play didn't go quite the way she wanted it directed. The lights had been turned off, but the pastor got them turned back on, and he'd tried to help her with some of the creditors. Problem was, Betty hadn't told him about all of them. Kroger kept calling. A mean lady from the drug store who didn't mind cursing at kids had called twice yesterday alone. Just a few days past, I'd had a wonderful and exhilarating conversation with a lawyer who was threatening to haul us into court again—and there were others who wouldn't say who they were.

Some were looking for Leon, too. I kept telling them all Leon and my mother had shot each other while fighting over a doughnut, but none of them were buying it. The lawyer called me a smart ass and asked how old I was, so I told him I was twenty. *I wish I was twenty, dammit!* I'd thought at the time. *I'd be long gone from here.* The lawyer had promised he was going to sue me right along with Betty. I thought that was pretty funny.

I told Betty she ought to let them turn off the phone, but she just mumbled something about me always thinking everything was a joke. She said we were probably going to be moving soon. I acted surprised and said that was a shock. Then we fought again. Without a Leon around, my mother was really struggling. She'd even gotten so desperate she called her father in Florida and tried to beg money out of him, but I hadn't heard how that ploy worked out.

I hadn't gone back to the church since the night the pastor said he wanted to talk to me. Brazen as I pretended to be, I was afraid of the man. Whether Betty had spun a yarn about me or not, I wasn't sure I wanted to face that stern old man alone in his office. Those church people used God like a hammer. Everything I did was going to send me to Hell, where I was going to burn forever. How did you argue with people like that? They had God. All I had was Betty.

Dave Jones was still sniffing around all the time. He wanted me to get saved. He was always trying to convince me to walk down to the altar after church services and pray with him, asking God to forgive me for my sins so that I could go to Heaven, where I'd live forever and where nothing ever went wrong. There was no way I was doing anything of the sort in front of all those people. That was Betty's game, wailing and weeping for the audience. Not me.

So there I was one night, my eyes snapping open as if someone had pinched me hard on the end of my nose. I lay there listening, and I heard my mother moving around upstairs. I could tell she was trying to be quiet by the way the floorboards were creaking. I stood up and untangled myself from my brothers. The three of us had fallen asleep in front of the TV, watching some stupid old black-and-white thriller about a mummy, who was obviously just some tall dude wrapped in bandages. I started to turn the tube off and stopped, my hand pausing just before touching the knob as some instinct I couldn't name caused the tiny hairs on the back of my neck to stand up and tingle.

Betty was on the stairs now, still creeping. I headed toward the kitchen, moving slowly, and trying to time my movements with hers. Benji started to follow, but I pointed firmly at him and gestured for him to stay. He was a good dog, and obeyed. I had a feeling I knew what was going on. If I was correct, this was going to be good. I continued into the kitchen with a shit-eating grin plastered across my face, listening to my mother's movements in the stairwell.

As I entered, I saw Betty on her hands and knees near the bottom of the steps. I stood frozen in place. She popped the top off a pill bottle and placed it carefully on the last stair, letting the lid roll down onto the dirty kitchen floor. I stepped back just before she peered into the kitchen, moving out of her line of sight in the nick of time. I listened as she arranged herself, peeking in long enough to see her lay her head on the floor near the bottom of the steps, with her legs trailing out and up behind her.

When she screamed out loud and started pounding on the floor, I almost jumped out of my skin. After her initial outburst, she lay there moaning while I tried not to piss myself, one hand covering my mouth to keep from laughing, hopping quietly from foot to foot. Benji came scrambling across the kitchen to stand near Betty, whining and sniffing at her head of splayed hair while my mother continued to moan and wait for the cavalry.

Of course, the cavalry was supposed to be me, but I wasn't about to let her off just yet. This was way too good. Whenever her shit got real messy, Betty would fake a suicide attempt. She'd go all the way, too. The ambulance ride, police reports, stomach pumping, suicide watch, any and all attention she could get out of her performance. My brothers would be wailing away the whole time, scared to death. *Like you used to be,* I reminded myself. But I wasn't about to fall for this crap any longer.

Betty could fake a rape, too. Her last episode had been in Florida a couple of years ago. But I'd not bought that performance, and had pretty much figured her out since then. Her story had been that a man broke in through the sliding door downstairs after she fell asleep on the couch. He'd supposedly raped her while the kids and I slept soundly upstairs. She told the police that Benji had started barking just before the man ran away, but that my bedroom door had been shut and he couldn't get out.

Problem was, my bedroom door didn't have a knob. Even if it had been shut, Benji would've reached under and pulled it open at the first sign anything was amiss. And my dog heard everything. I mean *everything.* Nothing escaped a lift of his ears, especially at night. He was always slipping off to investigate a sound outside, peering out the window until he was satisfied that what he'd heard required no further inspection. I slept so well mainly because my little buddy didn't.

And there was more damning evidence that Betty was pulling a fast one. She'd woken me to get the neighbors to call the police, since we didn't have a phone at the time. Benji had followed me downstairs and to the neighbors without even bothering to sniff around the floor or that open sliding door. I'd never heard him barking because he never had. If he'd wanted out, his nose would've been all over that couch and room, and his butt would've been out that door, searching for the intruder.

I'd called Betty on that particular lie. But I was only about ten at the time and was still afraid of her, too small to fight back when she hit me. She told me to shut up, and I did. But it wasn't long after that we were loading up a car she stole from her father and fleeing Florida, the cops and jail time for mommy right on our heels. What a trip that was. She was more worried about her ceramics and plants than her children's clothes. I rode all the way to Ohio sitting on a stupid portable kiln that was now buried under a pile of cat-pissed-on clothes up in her bedroom.

Betty waited a good while, but eventually decided I hadn't heard her and yelled again, louder this time, and banged even harder on the steps. Benji looked at her like she was crazy—which she was, of course—and started running around in circles, barking at her and acting like he was going to spring a leak quicker than I was. All of this almost did me in. I really *did* have to pee, and I was barely able to hold back my laughter.

I moved as close to her as I dared, squatting down and waiting for her to lift her head again. I didn't know what I was going to say. *Say, Boo!* I told myself. But did I dare? I'd never had a chance to pull off something like this. Betty was going to flip. For a second, I almost wanted to act like I'd just woke up and play out the scenario with her, but only for a second. I was so done with all this shit.

Eventually my mother said, "What the fuck…?" with quiet vehemence.

She rose up on one elbow and threw her hair back, but a lot of it stayed clumped up and in her face, so she still hadn't seen me. Betty had thick, unruly hair. She gathered herself for another scream and made a fist to bang on the floor with.

And then she saw me.

The look on her face scared me, and all my mirth drained away as fast as my smile faded. On her face was a mixture of rage, pain, and what I can only describe as insanity. She lowered her fist slowly, and I was sure she was measuring the distance between us, preparing to rise and attack. Instead she picked up her empty pill bottle and sat on that bottom step. I saw a tear run down her cheek, and I felt so ashamed.

"I fucking hate you," she said with calm conviction, and capped off her bottle before turning and climbing the steps.

I felt numb inside. What had been so hilarious a mere few moments ago now felt sickening and surreal. I wished I had just gone along with her theatrics. Benji was still sitting there with a perplexed tilt of his head, gazing at me and waiting for direction. I noticed he was trembling too. I guess he was picking up on my own dread and fear. For all I knew, Betty might leave me behind the next time she ran. *She might try to kill you,* I warned myself.

I carried my brothers up to bed and spent the rest of that night in my room, deep in thought and worrying over these latest developments. I was still worrying and wide awake when the sun came up.

Saturday morning, I was sitting on my front step, rapping with Rupe. He'd wanted me to roll down to the skateboard lot, but I talked him into playing chess instead. I was a multicultural kind of guy. I could be a nerdy, scrawny Caucasian kid who collected comic books and played chess (only without the black horn-rimmed glasses with the tape holding them together), or I could hang out with a larger, tougher, older Negro kid, and talk and act as if I was just bad as hell (as long as I was ripping you off while you were asleep).

Not that I didn't feel like boarding, but Betty was working a breakfast shift and Lynn wasn't around. That meant I was stuck watching the boys. Sometimes I'd drag them along, but it was hard to watch them, especially Terry, and concentrate on what I was doing. I loved doing tricks on my board almost as much as playing football, but this was when riding a board was just a pastime like any other, when you could tell who rode by the scabs on their arms and legs and not their weird clothes, colored hair, or arrogant attitudes.

I beat Rupe again, winning my third game in a row. Rupe hardly ever beat me in chess, which drove him bonkers, since he thought he was so much smarter than I was, but he kept coming back for more. He was better at checkers and Chinese checkers, but anyone could play those simple games. Terry was only six, and he could already play checkers. Hell, if my dog had thumbs, I could probably teach *him* to play.

"You lose again," I told him smugly, setting up my pieces again.

"So what? Let's play checkers," suggested Rupe.

"Nope."

"Why not?" he whined, but he was already putting his own pieces back in place.

"Because we're playing chess."

"One game you can beat me in, and it's all you want to play."

"Betty bought some Pampers this week. You need one?" He adjusted the Yankees cap on his head. It was a habit he had when he was getting pissed.

"Try once more. After I whip you this time, I'll let you beat me at checkers, or any other toddler game you want to play."

"Checkers is not a toddler game, and I could beat you at chess if I wanted to work at it." He was getting really miffed. Riling him would make him want to try harder to beat me, and keep him playing. For such a smart kid, he really didn't have a clue when someone was pulling his strings. "You play chess more than me, is all."

"Rupe, you're the only person I play with," I reminded him. "Face it, I'm just smarter than you."

He laughed and made a move. The same opening move he always made. "Yeah, you get such better grades than me in school."

It was always the grades. It was the only thing he had over me. "My grades would be better if I never skipped and sucked up to every teacher in every class, *including* that insane afterschool science club bullshit you do. I don't need grades to be as smart as you."

"Who was the second president?" he asked.

I was going to lose this gambit if I took the bait, but I knew this one and couldn't resist answering. "Adams," I told him.

"Third?"

"Jefferson?" I hoped.

Rupe nodded and slid a knight out into the open. I was going to beat him again. "Who was fourth?" he kept on.

I kept meaning to memorize the presidents, just to teach him a lesson, but even if I did the smart ass would just pick some other list of meaningless crap to torture me with. "The other Adams, Quincy whatever," I guessed.

"Nope," he denied me. Rupe enjoyed hanging his perceived smarts over me way too much. *Like I care who the fourth president was,* I told myself. "Give up?"

"Benjamin Franklin?"

That set Rupe to cackling. "Franklin was never president," he told me after he'd managed to control his laughing. Benji nudged open our ripped-up screen door and trotted out onto the porch to see what all the commotion was about. "James Madison was the fourth president."

"I was going to say Madison," I lied.

"Sure you were."

"Fuck you *and* Benjamin Franklin," was the smartest comeback I could think of.

"You're so manly when you cuss." Rupe was giggling like a girl, gloating over my dumb guess. "You probably don't even know Franklin invented electricity."

"Quit giggling. You sound like a faggot."

"You don't even know what the word faggot means," he shot back, but at least he wasn't snickering any more.

"It means Thomas Rupe."

"A faggot is a bundle of sticks, you idiot," he informed me.

I was getting a bit riled up now, myself. "Your mom keeps a bundle of sticks under her bed to hit all the guys who try to leave without paying her a nickel," I said casually. *That was a good one,* I praised myself. *And made up on the fly.* The best mom cracks were always the ones improvised during a heated battle of words.

"At least my mom has a man. Your mom runs around with that lesbo cow Ruby. They getting married anytime soon?"

I'd never thought about my mom getting busy with other women. I guessed it was possible, although I'd yet to see any evidence. But Rupe was barking up the wrong tree. One of the reasons I was so good at mom jokes was because I didn't care what you said about my mother. Just about anything you could think to slam Betty for was close to the truth, at one time in her life or another.

"Don't pick on my mom 'cause she's ugly. That's not fair. Your mom is hot, and I told her that last night when she crawled in my bedroom window."

Rupe's mom *was* pretty, too. She was thin and always dressed sharp. She worked in a doctor's office somewhere downtown. She was good to Rupe and polite to me when I was allowed over at his house, which wasn't that often. She didn't like Rupe hanging out with Tommy or me. His parents talked about moving out of the city all the time, but his dad was always being laid off from some factory.

"My mom found your mom's panties in my room today, but she thought they were a bedspread, so I didn't get in trouble," he sent back.

I grimaced and held up my hands. "Damn, Rupe. You let Betty in your room? That's just gross."

"You know, cracking on your own mother kind of takes the fun out of this."

I slid my queen into his back row and pinned his king. "Checkmate. Again. Besides, Betty doesn't wear panties. She has to stay ready in case some wino finds a dollar and has a weak moment when he wants a whore instead of a bottle."

Rupe started cackling again. "Oh, man, that's good. You don't care if I use that one?"

"Not as long as you play another game."

"Deal," he agreed. "You don't seem yourself. What's up?"

"Nothing much," I said.

"Fighting with your mom again?" Unlike Tommy, Rupe was really good at picking up on my moods. I knew he often felt sorry for me, but I didn't want his pity. "Is that Leon guy still hanging around?"

"No, he's long gone, I think," I answered. "Betty's not talking to me right now. She hasn't said hardly a word to me in days." And she hadn't. Not since the night I'd busted her trying to pretend she took the pills and fell down the stairs. "I think we might be skipping out of here soon."

"She won't even talk to you?" Rupe didn't really get Betty. He kind of understood that she was different than his own mother, but you had to really know my mother to appreciate her. *That's okay, pal, I don't get her either,* I thought to myself. "What'd you do?"

I thought about telling him about the whole suicide thing, but decided not to. For some inexplicable reason I still felt kind of ashamed of the whole episode, although I couldn't for the life of me figure out what I'd done wrong. I could tell I was really stressing my mother out. Betty didn't like having someone old enough around to see the inner workings of her pathetic life, especially if that someone had a smart mouth and a tendency to blab too much.

"Nothing much, we just don't get along," was all I decided to tell him.

"She won't talk to you?"

"Hardly a word," I admitted. "It's okay. Weird, but okay. I don't have much to say to her either. She's running a scam on some preacher and his church, and bouncing bad checks all over the place. It won't be long before we have to run again."

"Run where?"

He was so naive it was cute. "To some other state, dummy. If the cops catch her she could go to jail." Rupe's eyes widened at that, and he started adjusting his cap again. He was worried for me. I really liked Rupe for that. "Once she gets in too deep, she's got no choice but to run."

"What would happen to you if she got put in jail?" he asked. "And your brothers?"

That was a good question, but one I never thought about much. I couldn't imagine Betty ever being caught and jailed for any extended period of time. I'd spent a few months living with my aunt in Indiana when I was around eight or nine, while Betty was supposed to have been visiting friends. I'd known all along that she'd been in jail serving a sentence for passing bad checks. I also had vague memories of staying with other foster families when I was really young, but I couldn't really remember those times with any clarity.

I didn't blame Rupe for asking such dumb questions. The worst thing Rupe's parents got into was smoking a lot of weed. I knew this because Tommy was always talking Rupe into pinching him a little every time his dad filled up the sugar canister they stored the marijuana in. Rupe didn't really know what it was like to live with a full-fledged criminal.

"I don't know. I guess the state would nab us, or maybe someone out at that church would put us up for a while," I murmured, wondering just what might happen to us if Betty did slip up and get caught.

"How's it going with that Dave guy?" Rupe asked, delicately changing the subject.

"I haven't gone back there in a little while. He's always hounding me to go down to the altar and pray for salvation or something. He says if I do this it will change my whole life, and says I'll live in eternity."

We sat in silence on the steps for a while, the chess game forgotten. I could hear my brothers fighting over something in the house, probably making a mess. I didn't care. The baby hadn't been changed for some time. I didn't care about that, either. Mrs. Lorret was sweeping her walk, and she lifted her hand, so I waved back. Rupe waved too. We watched the traffic race by and said nothing, not even when a pack of the Harley guys roared out of the alley and swept down the avenue like a storm on wheels.

I was sad, but I couldn't say why exactly. Maybe it was thinking about Betty, or wondering about the church stuff with Dave. Maybe it was thinking about running again, and losing the few friends I had. Benji came up and put his head in my lap. I scratched behind his ears and felt like crying, but I wouldn't. Not in front of Rupe. I cried by myself sometimes, clutching my dog and soaking his fur, sobbing like a baby. It had been quite a while since I'd given in to one of those outbursts.

I realized I was tired. I was tired of fighting with my mother, and wondering about the future; of caring for my brothers, and worrying about who she was bringing around and what they might do to the boys. I'd had enough of lugging laundry and sleeping on smelly mattresses and dirt and walking around piles of old junk. Kids my age weren't supposed to be stressed out by rent notices and bad checks, light bills and food stamp scams. *You're letting Betty's silent treatment get to you*, I told myself. Maybe that old bird was smarter than I thought.

Rupe could tell I was down. I heard him putting the plastic chess pieces back into the taped-up box, including the pair of green plastic army men we used for two of the black pawns that were lost. I still blamed Terry for that, even though he swore he hadn't gotten into my stuff. It smelled like rain might be coming in, and a gust of wind skirled dirt and trash along the curbs, moving like an invisible street sweeper. Only the debris wouldn't be gone, merely dropped somewhere else, just trash moving from place to place.

Just like Betty and her children.

I looked up, searching for rain clouds, and spotted a bird riding the air currents. It just hovered in place, catching enough air to stay aloft but not really going anywhere, looking down at our filthy neighborhood like it needed someplace cleaner to land. I imagined my life was like that bird: still, and going nowhere. Benji sighed and made a small, whining huff, asking me to perk up, or feeling depressed himself.

"I did the salvation thing with my mom," Rupe admitted.

"How was it?" I asked, truly curious. "I mean, did you feel something happen?"

"I guess... kind of," he answered. "But it wasn't that bad. At least I'm not going to Hell now."

"That's always a good thing," I said, and we both chuckled.

Rupe reached over and patted my dog. Benji stiffened and growled, letting my friend know to take away his hand. I guess we were both feeling bad. Whenever I was sad or quiet, Benji got protective. I could see his eyes looking up at me through the tangles of hair covering his face, worried. He was so intelligent. No kid ever had a better best friend. From Lassie to Rin Tin Tin, I'd take my mutt over all of them.

"I wish you could stay with me," Rupe offered. And he meant it. That he actually cared made me feel better.

"Wow. That's the same thing your mom told me last night," I said out of reflex.

CHAPTER 8

It was a wicked smile. I'd never seen her smile quite like that, a mixture of girlish nerves and pride over her control of the situation. Bess was quite pleased with herself. But I'd never been kissed before, at least not for real, and right on the lips, in my own bedroom, when I hadn't even expected it. *Get a grip, kid, you probably look like an idiot,* I told myself. *No wonder she's looking at you like that.* I closed my mouth and ran a hand through my greasy hair, trying to control my heartbeat and settle my nerves.

"How was that?" she asked, beaming.

"Fine," I answered quickly. I couldn't really remember it, but the thing she'd done with her tongue told me this sure wasn't *her* first real kiss. I wasn't about to let on that it had been mine. "It was okay."

"Want to do it again?"

And there went my heart again. "Sure," I said, trying to act casual. *Did your voice just squeak?* I was sure it had. I was sweating, too. "I guess so, if you want."

I turned toward her so awkwardly she giggled, and I felt my face and ears heating up. I could hear Tommy's voice in my head; *you got to take care of business, man.* We kissed again, and I tried to do better, but I still felt like such an amateur. The tongue stuff was a lot harder than I'd thought it was going to be. I bumped her nose with mine, and she giggled again, causing me to pull away and start raking at my hair in aggravation.

"What's wrong?" she asked.

"Nothing."

"I'm sorry I laughed," she said, trying to be sweet. Her cheeks were flushed, actually brightening the smattering of light freckles beneath her eyes, and her long, strawberry hair framed her face. I'd never realized how big her eyes were. Somehow, a simple moment of swapping spit had made her a lot prettier. "Was that your first kiss?"

"No," I said back, and way too quickly. Somewhere, Tommy was rolling around ready to bust his gut. The only business I was taking care of was the business of looking and acting like a little kid. "I've kissed lots of girls."

"Who?" she asked.

Pretty or not, I was going to bop her one if she kept at me. "Enough," was all I could think of to say.

"Name one," she persisted.

"No. Who are you, the kissing police? I suppose you've kissed so many guys?"

"A couple," she sent back smugly. Her eyes had that wicked look in them again. Why did I care about this at all? "Does that make you mad? Are you jealous?"

"Who'd you kiss? That Gordie or Gordo fag out at that church?" *Please don't say Rupe. Please don't say Rupe.* "I saw him. He looks like a girl with short hair."

"His name is Gordon," she snapped. "But he's older than you, and more mature." She was mad now. Our little kissing session was probably over. I wasn't sure if I wanted to continue berating Gordo, or try to apologize so that she might pucker up again. "What would you know about him, anyway?"

"I know—"

"Donny!" Betty screeched, cutting off a great one-liner and probably saving me from being slapped. I heard her thump into the kitchen and move to the bottom of the stairs. "Donny, get down here! I can't find your brother!"

I didn't have to ask which brother was gone. Terry was always getting into trouble, wandering off or going into some other kid's house without telling anyone where he was. I took the steps two at a time, with Bess and Benji trailing behind me. Betty glared at me like *I'd* lost the little shit. I ignored her and checked out back, looking to see if his Big Wheel was gone. The baby was playing with the pile of junk parts I had stacked next to the shed, peddling away on a bike frame with no back wheels and the oversized front wheel spinning away where it hung a few inches off the ground.

"He probably rode down to the apartment playground," I informed my mother. I smiled at Chip, and he grinned back. The baby never left the yard. He pretty much hung out where you left him, amusing himself with what was available and rarely complaining. "I'll go find him."

"You do that," my mother snapped, slamming the kitchen door.

"Bitch," I muttered. "You stay here," I told the baby, heading into the alley and toward the apartments.

Chip kept racing away, gyrating those peddles for all he was worth. He was dirty and probably needed changing. I noticed he had on the same clothes he'd worn yesterday, and remembered the laundry was really piling up. I didn't have to worry. He'd be in the yard when I got back.

"You shouldn't say things like that about your mother," Bess scolded. "The Bible says to honor thy father and mother."

"The Bible don't say nothing about Betty, believe me."

"Your mother has it hard." I hated when she stuck up for Betty. "You should have seen her Wednesday night after church, crying for you and your brothers."

That made me chuckle. "I've seen her cry before, but those tears weren't for us."

"The Fullers are going to pay your electric bill and most of your rent. And the congregation took up a collection to help with your mom's other bills." Bess was laying this out for me like it supported her argument instead of mine. "Pastor Grady is going to meet with some people to talk them into accepting payments instead of pressing charges."

I stopped and looked at her, snorting. "Now *that's* why she was dropping tears. Don't you get it? She's conning them, conning them all."

"You're horrible," she told me. "Only God is allowed to judge people like that."

"Yeah?" *I wonder what God thinks about kissing boys in the basement of His church?* I asked myself. I knew the teens snuck down there to make out. I was pretty sure that was where Bess and Gordo fooled around. "I'm not judging anybody."

We stopped to let a car roar by. There was so much stinking smoke left by the exhaust that we hurried through the noxious cloud and to the other side of the street. Benji jerked his head and sneezed, the smell was so bad. We cut through an abandoned lot and ducked under a ripped-out fence. I held the loose chain links up so Bess could get under them. We were close enough to hear kids playing on the playground, yelling and laughing, but I didn't hear my brother yet.

It wasn't much of a playground, just a few swings and one long metal slide. But there was a wide expanse of concrete surrounding the lot to ride bikes or Big Wheels on, and huge piles of dirt some construction crew had left behind for the kids to climb on or excavate. My brother liked to drive his trucks and cars around in that dirt, and ride on the lot. He wasn't much for playing alone, and was generally a real pain in the ass unless he had something to do that occupied his mind. I saw him sitting atop one of those mounds, letting his cars fall down, and making screaming and crashing sounds while they tumbled. It was actually kind of cute.

He saw me coming and knew he was in trouble, but I didn't feel like yelling at him. All I said was, "Come on, let's go. Your mother is pitching a hissy fit."

"She's your mommy, too," Terry insisted. He always reminded me about that little fact. I'd almost had him convinced that I'd been adopted and wasn't really Betty's kid when he was around four or so, but that lie didn't fly anymore. "James won't give me back my bike."

I looked to where Terry was pointing and saw a dark-skinned kid with a mean face tooling around on the Big Wheel I'd so painstakingly pieced together from junk parts; parts I'd found (and stolen) from around the neighborhood. He saw me walking toward him and rode over toward a couple of black guys a little older than I was who were tossing a football back and forth. Bess hung back, staying with Terry, while I ambled on over to retrieve the bike.

"What's up?" I said neutrally as I approached. They both looked at me and said nothing. "Hey, that's my brother's bike, and we need to be going."

"So?" the larger of the two said.

He had a combed-out afro and a wide nose. The pick was still jutting out of the frizzy mop of his wiry hair. He was looking for trouble, hoping I'd make a big deal over the bike, wanting to play the tough guy for his buddy. The other dude was skinny as me, but taller. He had thick glasses and didn't look like he really wanted to fight about some stupid kid's toy. It didn't matter though. Big Nose was the one calling the shots.

At least he thought he was.

I heard Benji trotting over to inspect the situation, his quick little steps making sharp clicks as his nails struck concrete, and watched the two guys in front of me tense and change demeanor. Big Nose actually stepped back a bit. The kid on Terry's bike tried to pedal away, but I grabbed the handlebars. He jumped off and put some distance between himself and my dog, now eager to be cordial. Benji wasn't even aware that anything was amiss, or near to being so. He was just checking things out, seeing who I was talking to and so forth, but for reasons I didn't then understand, most black people were just plain afraid of dogs in general. I was always using that mysterious little fact to my benefit.

"Thanks," I said pleasantly, dragging the Big Wheel back to where my brother and Bess waited. Big Nose muttered something under his breath, but I ignored him and continued on, glad to have escaped the encounter without any real problem. If I started mouthing off or acting bad about this, they'd hold a grudge and settle with me later. Chances were this was nothing they'd care to remember, as long as I played it loose and casual.

"Thanks," Terry said, climbing aboard after stowing his cars and trucks in the little compartment behind the seat. He turned back toward the kid who'd been riding his bike and made a face, sticking out his tongue. *So much for loose and casual.* After that he laughed and pedaled toward home. I couldn't really do anything but follow after him.

Bess glanced over her shoulder. "They're still looking at you," she told me.

"Great," I mumbled. "Stop staring at them, would you?"

"Are they mad?"

"No, Bess, everyone just loves having a tongue stuck out at them after they've been embarrassed by a kid with a savage dog."

"Benji? They think Benji's savage?"

I had to find a different kissing partner, whether I needed the practice or not.

"He didn't even bark at them."

I decided not to reply, hoping she'd drop the whole thing. She did, but decided to ramble on about the upcoming church picnic—that I was definitely *not* going to—and all the peachy keen activities they were going to have.

I was catching a lot of flack over not going back to church. Holly was always asking, and Dave was relentless. Even Betty was constantly pestering me about going, but I was sure she had some evil motive behind her requests. It wasn't that I didn't like church, or the attention I received from some of the nicer people I'd see there. (I especially liked attention from the twins.) But Betty made looking folks in the eye kind of tough. She'd found a pot of gold at Pastor Grady's church, and I was ashamed to be associated with her.

Betty was fleecing them like sheep, and the fools kept lining up to have themselves shaved clean. It was hard for me to understand how intelligent people couldn't see her for what she was. How many times would they see her blubbering before they realized it was all an act? *She doesn't even fake crying all that well,* I told myself. She could scrunch up her face and look downright god-awful, wailing and moaning and flapping her arms all over the place, but if you were observant enough you'd notice she didn't actually shed many tears.

"Dave really wants you to come to the picnic," Bess was saying as we made it back to my place. The baby wasn't outside any longer, but I found him in the kitchen eating a cheese and bread sandwich. "You know the picnic's this Saturday, right?"

I knew, but I didn't care. What I *did* care about were the two boxes of albums my mother had set on the kitchen table. I couldn't help but flip through them, noticing that Elvis and Engelbert, Tom Jones, The Carpenters, and even my latest favorite Dr. Hook album were in there. But it wasn't until I found my own albums in the other box that I started getting really annoyed. Betty had been in my room, and in my stuff. I hated anybody getting into my stuff.

"What's going on?" I asked Betty, walking into the living room.

She was laid out on the couch, watching some stupid soap opera and snacking on a bag of chips. "The church is burning all rock-and-roll albums at the picnic," my mother said without a shred of emotion. "Everyone has to contribute, so don't give me any crap about it. Those people are doing a lot for us. It's the least we can do."

"It's the least *you* can do," I said. "Nobody's burning *my* records."

I went back in the kitchen and picked up the box containing my albums. As an afterthought, I snatched the Dr. Hook and the Medicine Show album as well. I loved "Sylvia's Mother" and "The Cover of the Rolling Stone." Bess followed me upstairs, citing Bible verses and explaining to me how evil rock music was, telling me it was the Devil's music and how it destroyed your mind. I ignored her, and she started to cry. *What is it with girls using tears to get what they want?* I shut the door to my room and left her sobbing in the hall.

There wasn't going to be anymore kissing today, but at least Dr. Hook was safe and sound.

The battle over those records wasn't over. Saturday morning, I was rudely awakened by Dave Jones and another guy I didn't know. Benji was huffing and puffing, showing teeth and keeping them far enough away so that they couldn't touch me, but my mother was standing with them, so my dog knew he couldn't really bite anybody without getting into trouble. I sat up, rubbing at the smoke still in my eyes from Pops' the night before, wondering what the hell was going on and why they'd roused me so early.

Then I watched helplessly as Betty dug the box of albums out of my closet and handed them to the guy I didn't know. He looked at me as if he felt sorry for me and then left, carrying my music downstairs and off to a certain and fiery doom. I saw Terry peek at me from around the corner of my doorway, his eyes wide and curious, but heard him follow my mother downstairs. She left Dave and me alone, except for Benji, who was still not at all sure he was comfortable with this intrusion.

"Get up and get dressed," Dave said without ceremony.

Say no! I told myself as I stood up and started looking for my jeans. But he was a man, and I was just a kid. *Tell him to piss* off *and go get your albums!* I continued to silently rant. But I knew I would do no such thing. Acting the man in front of Betty was easy; doing so in front of Dave was an act I didn't have the nerve to attempt. *You know he's going to make you go to the stupid picnic!* I further warned myself. But what was I to do?

"It's time for you to start doing as you're told," Dave said, his tone soft but stern. "Your mother is the head of this house. Not you. She says you give up rock music, you do so. She says you come to the picnic, you come."

"Who died and made you the boss over me?" I muttered. I sounded so childish that I winced, wishing I'd said nothing at all.

He stepped toward me, and Benji growled for real, stiffening up and hopping off the bed to position his little hairy body between us.

"Go lay down, boy," I told him, nudging him gently with my foot.

I had no choice. Betty had let these people into our lives, into our house. I wasn't old enough to do anything but what I was told.

Dave put his hand on my shoulder once Benji was out of the way. "This is for your own good," he informed me. And he believed that. He truly did. "If you would give people a chance, you might find life a little easier."

He lectured me while I found a T-shirt and my sneaks, quoting Scriptures and telling me how he was my friend and all while we descended the steps. I let my dog out to do his business and made sure he had some food and water, wishing I could bring him along. Terry and Chip were all ready to go. Betty was wearing some ridiculously oversized blue jean skirt she'd found at some secondhand store or borrowed. Women weren't allowed to wear pants at this church or its functions.

My records were tossed in the trunk, adding to a few more crates of stuff destined to be burned at the stake. I was practically forced into the backseat of the car with Betty and the boys, where I sat silently listening to Dave plead his case all the way to the site of the picnic somewhere out in richville. Betty was so pleased with herself, playing the part of the helpless mother with the disrespectful and uncontrollable son. She acted so pious and attentive the whole way there, hanging on every word Dave and the other guy—a way too friendly dude named Darrin—uttered. All I had to comfort me was the thought of the Dr. Hook album I'd stashed behind my desk that was all I had left in the way of decent music.

"You're not saying much," Dave said as we neared the picnic, trying to get me to join in their conversation. "Are you still mad about the records?"

Actually, I hadn't said a word.

"He's always mad about something," Betty couldn't help but pitch in.

"Sometimes you just have to trust that adults are better qualified to make certain decisions than children," explained Dave. *Yeah, but who's the adult and who's the child?* I wanted to ask. "You have to believe we know what's best for you. God has a plan for you. Those records don't. The people who profit from that lewd music don't care about you one little bit."

"Rock and roll is the lure of Satan," Darrin squawked like a parrot repeating something he'd been told over and over.

"Really?" I said, finally breaking my silence. "That's why you're burning up all these perfectly good and expensive records, because the Devil made them?"

"Not just records… 8-tracks, too," Darrin recited.

"Oh, that makes me feel better."

I decided I didn't like Darrin very much. He reminded me of a store window mannequin with a tape recorder jammed in its mouth, playing the same stupid shit every few minutes.

Dave glanced at me over his shoulder, warning me to watch my tone. "In a way the Devil *did* make them, Donny. That music promotes drugs and drinking alcohol and… Well, it causes people to often make poor judgments."

"You mean sex?" I had to ask.

My frankly posed question didn't faze Dave in the slightest. "Yes, that's exactly what I mean," he said, nodding agreement.

116

"So you're telling me Donny Osmond is evil? Donny Osmond?" I asked again, just so they might clearly understand who I was referring to. "Tom Jones, maybe, but Donny Osmond can't be evil."

Tom Jones was almost as cool as Elvis, and I guess he did promote a little bit of what had the church all lathered up and burning everything they could get their hands on. Women took off their underwear and threw them at Tom Jones when he sang and thrust his hips at the screaming bimbos. I wasn't exactly clear on why that was so cool, but I was pretty sure it was.

"Aren't the Osmonds Mormons or something? Are Mormons evil?" I continued.

"No, I wouldn't say Mormons are evil," Dave said carefully. He thought a moment. "I would say Mormons are misguided."

When it came to religion, all I had to base my experience on were Betty's attempts at conning different churches. I was kind of afraid of the Jehovah's Witnesses. They clawed at your door like the undead in a zombie movie. I still had no clue what those people really wanted, although I'd gotten caught chucking rocks at them a few years back. But my information was skewed. All I knew about the different churches we'd visited was who was susceptible to giving up cash, and who wasn't.

So far, Baptists were the nicest and most gullible folks I'd ever met. I guess it was because they believed there was good in all people, if you could just convince them to be "born again" and "live for God." What they believed was fairly simple and seemed sound to me, whenever I thought about it. Betty knew they were the easiest marks. She'd been born again so many times her saved souls were going to need their own apartment in Heaven.

Methodists, Protestants, and Lutherans were okay folks, too, but not nearly so generous with their aid. I think it had something to do with the salvation thing. Baptists put a lot of stock in getting you on your knees at their altar—almost as if they were getting paid for every soul they sent God's way. Just like Dave kept doing with me, always asking me to take God as my savior and pray with him. I wondered sometimes if Dave would stop coming around if I did as he asked, if he'd lose interest in me once he'd bagged my soul.

The Catholics were the coldest, or the smartest, depending on whose point of view you took. They told Betty they had clothes for sale at bargain prices in the basement and kicked her broke and hungry ass straight to the curb, right along with her dirty-faced children. Those robed priests made me uneasy, and their services were downright creepy. We sat through one once, listening to everyone recite the same words and stand up and sit down a lot. I was more interested in the church itself than the people in it. I'd never seen such an awesome building.

We'd even tried a Holy Roller's church once. A couple of women had jumped up not long after the service started and began howling like fighting cats, running and rolling around like they were having seizures, spouting gibberish and then spitting like rabid dogs. Everyone else just kept right along like this crazy shit was nothing out of the ordinary, but I grabbed the baby and ran for the hills, deciding I'd wait for my mother outside. It turned out some deranged Holy Roller next to my mother started frothing at the mouth right after I left, and she and Terry bolted, too. We actually laughed about that one, whenever we were talking to one another and bothered to reminisce.

Betty stunned me when we climbed out of the car, hugging me without warning. "Don't worry about the records. We can always replace records," she whispered in my ear. "Now be good, and don't blow this for me," she added.

I didn't say anything back, and stood stiffly until she released me. She smelled like cheap perfume poured over the musty odor of her bedroom. I didn't like when she touched me. I really didn't much like to be touched by anybody.

After piling out of the car, I tried to wander off, but Dave made me help him unload the trunk. *You're actually carrying your own stuff to be destroyed,* I chided myself. But I had no choice. The pile of records and 8-tracks they'd amassed to destroy was huge! I couldn't believe there were so many people willing to destroy perfectly good music. This stuff must've been worth a fortune. I almost wanted to break down and cry, thinking what Tommy and I might be able to sell all this for if we had our hands on it. And they were going to burn it all! And on purpose! It was just too much to accept.

There was more than music in the pile. They were burning girls' pants and jeans, short skirts, and even some shoes and tops deemed inappropriate by the church. I saw posters of singers and bands, and other memorabilia. It was mind-boggling, the amount of stuff they were going to destroy. Some-one had even pitched a TV into the heap, but it looked old. *Probably doesn't even work,* I told myself.

I slipped away when Dave got himself caught up in a conversation with the pastor—who almost looked like a normal guy in his jeans and short-sleeve shirt—and found myself a quiet spot to pout. I sat on a log beneath a tree that looked ready to topple over as soon as a good gust of wind came along. But the tree was big, and felt solid enough when I leaned back against it. I sat there watching everyone unpack and prepare food, sulking over my records and hating my mother for dragging me into this.

More people showed up, and I watched as they set up tables to lay out the food upon. I realized I was hungry. That was going to make my continued sulking difficult. My brothers were running around with a growing group of kids, hanging out by the swings. Terry was fighting with some other boy over a teeter-totter, while Chip kicked at the sand with his toe. The baby spotted me and wasted no time heading in my direction.

"Does your brother Terry have a different father?" a girl's voice asked from behind me as I helped my brother climb up onto my lap.

I glanced back and found one of the twins standing behind me. I wasn't positive, but I thought she was Ally, the talky one. "For all I know, we *all* have different fathers," I admitted. I didn't care to lie, and I didn't care if what I said offended her.

"But you and Chip look so much alike," she observed.

"That's what they keep telling us," I said.

She walked around in front of me, and I could see she was wearing tennis shoes beneath her long plaid skirt. They looked new, and that reminded me that my own shoes must look ridiculous to her. Her yellow hair was tied back, the pigtail wrapped in red bows. When she smiled, I could see she had Holly's perfect white teeth. She was working on a sucker of some kind, watching me with those dancing blue eyes that left you wondering if she was making fun of you or not.

"I hear you kissed Bess," she said from around that sucker.

Yep, this was Ally. I felt my face growing hot and wanted to check my ears to see if they might have ignited. She kept looking down at me, those eyes now most definitely mocking me, that lollipop-stained grin growing wider. I couldn't think of a single thing to say. It made sense, though. Of course Bess would talk about our little moment. Bess talked about everything, and could no more keep a secret than stop breathing.

"She kisses Gordon, too," Ally needlessly informed me.

"So what?" I finally said.

Ally would have said more, but I was saved from further humiliation by Dave as he approached. There was a football game starting up, and he wanted me to play. I pretended I wasn't interested, but only for a minute. Saying no to eating was one thing. Saying no to a game of football was quite another. On that field, I was equal to or greater than most guys my age. It didn't matter who had the nicer clothes or newer shoes. There was no Betty during a football game, and no welfare or free lunch coupons. There were no Leons or hunger or fear. It was just me and the other guy who was about to lose and didn't know it yet.

I wound up being picked fourth, after Dave and a guy named Jim Burr picked a few teenage guys first. It was kind of an honor, being picked so soon, but I knew Jim had seen me messing around at a couple of teen functions and knew I was pretty fast. As the game started, a lot of people meandered over to watch, but I forgot them as soon as the ball was kicked off. I was like a dog in that respect. If there was a ball around, my eye was on it.

The game started kind of slow, as the two teams figured out who was fast enough to go out for passes and who was going to be stuck on the line. Dave was quarterback for the other side. Jim was our quarterback. Their team scored twice before we really knew what was going on, but it didn't take long before Jim figured out that he should've picked me even sooner. Randy and I were the only decent receivers he could throw to. The rest of our team couldn't catch a cold running naked in the dead of winter.

Dave's team was driving again, when I stepped in front of one of his teens and picked off a pass. I heard the intended receiver trip and fall as I made one move to get by Dave and outran him to our end zone. My team celebrated our first score, slapping me high fives and whooping it up. Even Dave gave me a grin and rubbed my head. The guy I'd tripped was staring at me, all pissed and what not, so I flipped him the ball and gave him my sweetest smile.

"Hey, none of that," Jim told me. "Just beat him on the field."

We soon mounted a comeback. Jim really leaned on Randy and me. Every now and then he'd toss an easy pass to some other dude out of pity, but we became the team, more or less. The folks watching started clapping and cheering when we caught passes or made tackles, and that made me want to dominate all the more. The guy I'd embarrassed said he wanted to cover me and began hand-fighting me on the line, grabbing and holding to keep me from getting a clean break out into the open.

"Stop holding," I told him after a particularly intense bout of grabbing and shoving. He was a couple of years older than me, but nothing much of a threat. He wasn't even strong enough to keep a grip on me at the line, but he was scratching me and really getting on my nerves. "Play ball, man."

He curled his lip in my direction. "Nice shoes," he said, laughing with one of his buddies as we walked back from a long out pattern.

I grinned. *Oh, no, you didn't just go there, pal,* I thought happily. I noticed the bozo had actually brought real cleats to play in. Not that the special equipment was doing him any good. "Yours, too," I told him. "Too bad mommy wasted the money. She should have bought your ass a training bra."

I heard his buddy crack up at that, but I didn't give my adversary the satisfaction of hanging around so he could try to think of a comeback.

A couple of plays later, Jim called a bomb for me. I grinned and said, "Touchdown," before breaking the huddle. The guy guarding me tried to hold again, grabbing my arm as I made my move to get by him. I shot him an elbow to break free and found myself racing down the sideline, running easily under Jim's pass and into our end zone. I dropped the ball and waited to be praised, ready to exult in the adulation of my teammates and the crowd.

Instead I was greeted with silence, and an angry glare from Dave. "Bobby's nose is bleeding," he told me. "You elbowed him on purpose."

"*Bobby* was holding me," I said, as if that explained everything.

I thought it did. But Bobby was surrounded by his mommy and daddy, and his parents and some other church people were giving me looks that suggested holding me didn't explain anything at all. Bobby's nose *was* bleeding, but not all that bad. It sure wasn't worth all this commotion. It was a wound that didn't even stop the game in my neighborhood. You sat out a play or two until the blood stopped, and then you got back on the field and went after the guy who'd gotten you. That was football. Hell, that was life.

Dave didn't see it that way. "Why don't you sit this one out," he suggested.

"*Bobby was* getting a little rough with him, Dave," Jim said, trying to stick up for me.

"That's no excuse," Dave refuted. "You know you didn't have to hit him," he said directly to me. "You could have kept beating him without that elbow, and you know it. Now go sit down. I'll talk to you later."

I left the field under the scrutiny of the spectators and the glares of Bobby's friends, feeling embarrassed and angry, but not ashamed. Bobby had that coming. If I'd been holding some guy and got wracked for it, I sure wouldn't have stood around crying about it. *What a chump!* I thought. If some guy I knew ran to his mommy during a football game, he might not survive the next week or two of his life. The fellas would come down on him so hard he might never leave his house again. But I guessed shit was different in richville. Real different.

My hunger got the best of me, and I snuck over to the food and grabbed some chicken, baked beans, chips, and watermelon. They didn't have Pepsi, so I settled for a paper cup of lemonade instead. I managed to avoid Dave the rest of the day. I managed to avoid Bobby and his buddies, too. In fact, I managed to avoid everyone the rest of that day.

Just before dusk, the pastor gave a sermon, revving everyone up for the burning. He talked about right and wrong, and was pretty convincing that rock music was coming right out of the very bowels of Hell. He backed up everything he said with Scriptures and stories, but I just wasn't buying what he was saying. The church wasn't only against women wearing jeans, but also didn't want men wearing shorts. How were you supposed to play basketball or run track in long pants? That was too much. We didn't have air conditioning in my house. I was damn sure wearing shorts in the heat of summer, church scams or not.

They prayed when the pastor was done, and everyone eagerly surrounded the huge hole they'd dug, now filled with most of the stuff they'd brought to be burned. Some men poured gas over the pile and lit it, and the flames shot skyward with a loud *whoosh!* and were soon crackling and popping in the falling darkness. Some of the stuff had been held back, so that each person could throw something into the inferno, symbolizing their commitment to turn their back on the evil of the world and embrace God.

I stayed far enough away not to be noticed, watching the proceedings with a pall of stupefied numbness falling over me. There was no way I was taking part in this. It didn't feel right. In fact, I felt kind of scared, and sad. I remembered stories one of my teachers had told about people burning books to stop the advancement of religion and education. The premise behind that story had been how doing something like that violated the rights of people to read and learn what they wanted. This fire and these people reminded me of that same lesson.

My mother did her part, chucking some records into the flames. I could see her face in the light of the fire. Unlike most of the others, I saw no emotion there. Others were solemn and serious, while a few seemed scared or awed. Some of the women were crying. The kids who took part in this ridiculous exercise were just having fun, flinging whatever they were handed and then trying to sneak back in line to throw something else. Betty was just going through the motions, not believing in what they were doing but playing out her charade. I wondered if my mother believed in anything.

Not long after everything had been tossed in, they made a wide circle around the fire, holding hands and singing hymns. My brothers found me and sat down. Terry laid his head on my leg, and the baby crawled up into my lap. They were tired. I was tired, too. We all wanted to go home. But the singing was nice. It was a soothing way to end a weird and trying day. I knew it wouldn't be long before they were asleep.

And then someone screamed, and the circle broke up. I stood up as some of the people ran in our direction. They were women and girls mostly, and a few kids, but before long even a few men began moving away from the fire, acting nervous and unsure. Chip was clinging to my neck, and Terry was clutching my leg, staring up at me with wide eyes and scared half to death. Some of the ladies stopped near us, out of breath and gasping. I was about to ask them what was going on when a high-pitched wheeze emanated from the fire, and they started screaming again.

My brothers were terrified, but I inched a little closer to the fire with them stuck up against me like leeches. There were a lot of noises in those flames. The fire popped and hissed as vinyl melted and 8-tracks imploded. Something underneath the mass of burning clothing was making the most noise. I figured it was the TV or something else one of these fools had thrown in. The fire was settling in on itself as the pile began to collapse, and when it did this it made a lot of weird sounds.

I walked back to where I'd been standing. The blazing heap moved, and the fire hissed. Of course, the women screamed again. "Sweet Jesus!" one old broad moaned aloud.

"Father be with us," another said.

"Mommy, is it the Devil?" a little girl asked fearfully.

"Yes, dear," came the insane answer. "But don't you be afraid, the Lord is with us."

There was another collapse. Flames roared for a moment, and embers floated in the night sky. "Ooooohh," moaned the throng. *This is too much.*

Terry was really scared. He looked up at me and asked, "Is it the Devil, Donny?"

The baby was getting ready to cry. I'd had more than enough of this. I laughed and told Terry, "No, it's not the Devil."

I lifted my baby brother up and tickled his ribs, causing him to smile and drool. Terry let go of my leg and looked at the fire, then back to me. He looked at the women around us and up at me again, trying to figure out what was going on.

"What's those noises then?" he asked, but I could hear the fear fading from his little voice. My brothers trusted me. Seeing me so at ease had them feeling safe, but I could tell I was pissing off the church ladies standing near us.

"It's just the fire caving in, melting records and tapes and stuff, or maybe a tube in that old TV set," I told him.

The little girl who'd been lied to looked up at her mom. "Is that true, Mommy?" she asked.

Her mother didn't hear the child because she was so intent on staring at me. I looked back at her and stood my ground, daring her to call me a liar. The fire spoke again, and people screamed and moaned. Somewhere a man's voice rose up in prayer. But I heard someone laugh, and I realized more than one of the screams I'd heard had been feigned terror. Off in the distance I heard someone running and giggling. I guessed I wasn't the only one here who was aware how silly these people were acting.

"You are an evil young man," the lady told me.

CHAPTER 9

"Excuse me, Ma'am, but could I have a dime or a quarter?" I asked the young mother pushing her stroller. "I lost my money, and I need bus fare to get home."

"Oh, you poor thing," she said, smiling sweetly.

I checked out the baby while she dug into her purse. It was just days old at best, all pink and squiggly, its little hands flailing around, and its eyes looking up at me but not really seeing anything. It was wrapped in a blue blanket, which meant it was boy. I thought it looked more like a piglet than a boy, but I wasn't going to say anything mean to a lady about to fork over money.

"Here you go, honey," she said, handing over a dollar bill.

I smiled for real. "Thank you. Your baby's pretty," I lied. After all, she'd given up folding cash.

"He won't like being called pretty by the time he's big as you," she told me, smiling again. I could tell she was especially proud of her baby. "But I guess you can call him pretty right now. Well, you be careful, hon."

I thanked her again as she left, and waited until I was sure she wasn't going to look back before pulling out the other bills from my rear jeans pocket and adding this one to the stash. I had six ones and at least four or five dollars' worth of change in my front pockets. If Rupe and Tommy were doing as well, it was going to be a productive day. *As long as Tommy doesn't hold out too much of his money,* I reminded myself.

Tommy always held out a little, but Rupe and I weren't really in any position to call him on it.

Wandering down the mall, I continued to watch for prospects to beg from. Moms with kids were always good pickings, or elderly women who gave you a smile as you approached, thinking of their own grandchildren. Men were hard to judge, and teens weren't worth the trouble to ask. They couldn't care less if you got home or not. Most of the time, you just had to try and judge each person by their appearance, but that didn't always work. I'd been handed cash by old men with the severest of faces and told to fuck off by young women with the loveliest of smiles. That was fine, though. Begging had its hazards.

Rupe was running the same line I was over at the strip mall across the street, while Tommy ran the, "Hey, man, have you seen anybody dragging a blue ten speed? No? Damn, I ain't got no way to get home. Could you spare a little change for the bus?"

The trick was to get people to feel sorry for you, to get them involved in your problem. Usually, folks were eager to help out, just to feel a little better before hurrying on with their own lives. I'd learned these tactics from Betty.

We conned people out of change, and rarely had to alter our lies. Rupe usually did the best. I guess he was better at looking helpless and pitiful than we were. Sometimes, people—mostly middle-aged men—would offer to give him a ride home, which always shattered his nerve and set him to stuttering and stammering. Tommy claimed Rupe was an *old fag magnet,* like every dude who offered to drive him home was only trying to get in his pants.

I tried a couple more times and got a "no" response, then a quarter from a lady in a business suit who acted like she was going to go broke if she gave me anything more. I thanked her and caught some guy in a shirt and tie staring at me from the entrance to a Radio Shack across the commons. *Probably the store owner,* I cautioned myself. One of the secrets of success when it came to running scams was to never stay in the same place very long. I'd probably pushed my luck a little already. I decided to vacate the area.

I found Tommy out in the parking lot, and together we went and picked up Rupe. Our buddy was more than ready to go, and Tommy quickly picked up on his eagerness. "What's up?" he asked, grinning at me behind Rupe's back.

Rupe looked over his shoulder and then glared at Tommy. "Nothing. Some freak in a white Volkswagen Bug has been sitting in his car staring at me for a while," he muttered. "Dude gives you a dollar and he acts like you're best friends."

Tommy looked back, saw the Bug and waved. He ended the friendly pantomime by flipping the guy off. We heard the car start by way of response.

"What the fuck are you doing?" Rupe squawked. "What if he comes after us?"

I'd already checked. The VW was puttering away in the other direction, but Tommy hadn't even bothered to look back. "So? Dude goes sniffing 'round for boys to get busy with, and we supposed to be afraid of him?" Tommy stuck his middle finger up again, just in case the fleeing driver might still be looking our way. "Shit, I wish that motherfucker would come over here. We could beat his ass and drive that Bug home, baby."

I thought about pointing out that none of us could drive, but Tommy would only say he *had* driven before. As a matter of fact, I was pretty sure I'd told a few lies about driving a car myself. *How hard could it be?* I wondered. I *was* going to drive a car one day. I was going to drive a flashy sports car, and I was going to drive as fast and as far as I wished. But I didn't want to steal that car, I wanted to own it.

"You sure you didn't say nothin' to turn that dude on?" Tommy asked.

"C'mon, cut it out, Tommy," Rupe whined. "I hate that shit."

Tommy and I were cracking up, and eventually we got a half-hearted grin out of Rupe. "What is it with white dudes and little kids?" Tommy asked, shaking his head. "Especially boys!" he added derisively. "My Gran says you can't trust white men. She says they stick it to animals and rubber dolls, and even their own kids. She also says only white men go crazy and kill all kinds of people for no good reason. If a black man kills you, it's 'cause you had it coming, messing 'round with his woman or stealing from him, or some other good reason."

"That's not true," Rupe returned. We checked the traffic and trotted across a four-lane road, hopped the median divider, and continued toward the Schottenstein's store. "Is it?"

Tommy cocked his head and pursed his lips, looking at us like he was letting us in on a family secret. "Tell me the name of the last nigger you saw arrested for raping kids or sneaking 'round killing people." He waited for us to think up anything. I couldn't. It seemed to me Tommy's Gran had it right. "I thought so. Nothin'. I'll go you one better... You tell me, Rupe, all those times you had some fruit sniffing 'round you for a ride home... How many of those dudes were black?"

Rupe thought a while. "None," he finally had to admit.

"There you have it. Gran knows her shit. White men are freaky."

"Not all white men," I said defensively.

"Don't get touchy, Donny," Tommy returned. "How many times has your mom brought home some sick dude you have to watch around your brothers?" *Too many,* I admitted to myself, but I didn't say anything aloud.

"I thought so. If she was knocking knees with the brothers, you wouldn't have to worry 'bout shit like that. And your mom would be a lot easier to get along with, since she wouldn't be so frustrated all the time."

"Yeah, but my little brothers would have fucked-up, frizzy afros and big lips," I pointed out.

Tommy wasn't laughing as much, but he was still grinning when he told me, "I'll give *you* a big lip."

"Your brother Terry does have big lips, and I *have* seen your mom hanging out with black guys," Rupe added.

"I'm not saying Betty wouldn't do a black guy," I told them, peeking in the store window. "Or that she hasn't. It's just that she usually wants money, and she won't give it up for food stamps or the promise that she'll get paid when they finally get a job."

"Shit, a brother don't pay for nothin'. That's another white man problem," Tommy explained, ignoring my great job joke.

"You got the receipt?" Rupe asked.

I nodded, and he went on in while Tommy and I kept at each other, trading racial insults like we were the worst of enemies. After a minute or two, Tommy went in and took up his position over by a rack of pricey suede coats, acting openly suspicious and drawing the attention of the nearest clerk. I suppose we were guilty of racial profiling, using the black guy to make the store worker worry about theft, but the color of Tommy's skin drew more attention than my own, and that was just a plain simple fact. As soon as the clerk wasn't watching the door, I slipped in and made my way unseen down the nearest aisle.

The shoes were right where Rupe was supposed to leave them, partially hidden behind a stack of pillowcases in house wares: black Keds, size six. We'd bought the first pair last week, but Tommy had demanded his shoes first. Tommy always got his way, but Rupe and I knew that going in. No matter what scam we were running, our larger, older friend had a way of taking the least amount of risk and garnering as much or more reward than we did. I pushed those thoughts out of my mind, scooped up the sneaks, and put them in the bag—a bag from this very store—and kept walking toward the rear of the building and the returns counter.

"Can I help you?" a girl behind the counter asked as I approached.

She didn't look old enough to be out of high school yet. She had pimples on her cheeks and chin, and was chewing and popping a wad of gum so hard it sounded like a cap gun going off inside her mouth. She looked none too pleased that I'd interrupted her perusal of the celebrity magazine she'd been flipping through. *Impatient and part-time,* I figured. *Perfect.* I couldn't have chosen a better target if I'd been allowed to pick out someone to be sitting here.

"My aunt bought me these for my birthday, but they're too small, so she gave me this receipt to exchange them," I explained.

"Yeah?" She glanced at the shoes, the tag still right where it should be, and then matched it against the receipt dated approximately a week ago, a little suspicious but finding everything in order. "You got the pair you're wanting?" she asked. *Pop!* went the gum as she tossed the shoes into a cart behind her, her eyes and fingers again finding the magazine with all its allure of glamour and glitz. Her jaw started working that wad of gum with renewed vigor. I stood there all but forgotten, a nuisance she wanted out of her face.

"No, ma'am, I came here first, like my aunt said to," I explained, all innocence, playing to utter perfection the part of the child who had no notion how something like this was done.

"Well, go get your size and bring them back here," she instructed without looking up from her magazine.

I left to do as she said. I noticed Tommy was gone when I passed the coats, and knew he'd be outside with Rupe, waiting for me so we could grab the bus home. I sorted through the Keds until I found a black pair of sevens, checked to make sure they were both the same size and a right and left shoe, and headed back to the ditz waiting for me at returns.

A pretty lady with glasses behind the makeup counter lowered the specs to the end of her nose, watching me carefully as I swerved through her department, but I didn't need to pay her any mind. This con was all but done. People were willing to believe what they saw, if you portrayed yourself properly. Act nervous and you drew more attention. Hesitate too much and you were better off waiting for a day when your nerve was steady. Go into something unprepared and you were done, caught before you ever got started.

Act like you belonged, and walk like you knew where you were going. Keep your eyes front and feet moving. Never dawdle. Never hesitate. Never stutter or search for words. Always be prepared. Shoplifters get caught because they're greedy. They want something for nothing. My mother had taught me the finer arts of conning. I was better at this one than she was.

The shoes in my hand had already been mine last week when we paid for Tommy's.

"Here you go," I told the clerk, interrupting another lady trying to return some dishes.

The harried mother and her bawling brat had drawn the aggravated brainiac away from the pages of Hollywood yet again, and she was clearly not happy about it. She looked at me and wracked her brain to recall what I wanted, somehow remembered me, and tossed me the now empty bag I'd brought in. I pointed at the receipt, and she flicked that back to me as well.

"Thanks," I said, dropping my shoes in the bag and glancing at the receipt before putting it away. The fact that she hadn't initialed or marked the receipt with a color or code that told the store it had been used for a return was good fortune for me. It meant that I could wait a few days to a week until there was a different clerk, and we could run the same con, actually getting the money back if we wanted to. *Or maybe a red pair,* I told myself. This was always a two-for-the-price-of-one job, and often three, if we were careful and pulled it on a big enough store. But getting your money back at the end of the con was sweeter still. That took real skill, and a little luck.

Before I'd come along, Tommy had been a real amateur, strictly a snatch-and-grab kind of thief. But I'd passed along what I'd learned from Betty, and refined him. Although he was still a bit impatient at times, he'd learned to trust me when it came to laying out instructions like the ones we employed to reuse a receipt for shoes, baseball gloves, jackets, or basically whatever we wanted. As long as we were careful, and had the money on hand to make the initial purchase, we never got caught.

I'd also taught him how to swap price tags on similar items, and use the gender of clerks to his advantage. For instance, a woman had no clue that a twenty-dollar Rawlings first baseman's mitt was any different from a cheap seven-dollar cloth glove. Again, a lesson I'd learned from Betty but modified to my own needs and motives. *You're one smart little shit,* Tommy had told me after I'd shown him how to get a new mitt, bat, and cleats for summer baseball without spending a dime. (Our illegal activities added to my own baseball equipment as well.) And if stealing without getting caught was a measure of intelligence, I guess I *was* smart.

We yukked it up outside; I hadn't even raised an eyebrow on my way out of the store. But the euphoria left behind by successful thievery was a feeling we were long used to, and we were soon throwing mom jokes back and forth, and cracking on one another with a fervor known only to boys with too much energy and not nearly enough sense. I put my new Keds on at the bus stop and hummed a funeral dirge as I slowly carried my old, ripped-out sneaks to the nearest garbage can and tossed them. Tommy wanted to tie the laces together and throw them at a power line until he managed to tangle them around it, but there were adults around and I talked him out of it.

The bus ride home that day was one of those times that still stand out in my mind. We took our usual seats in the back and acted up, making real asses of ourselves and probably bothering everyone else on the bus. Tommy flipped off some guy driving a bread truck, and the driver lost it, screaming at us and jabbing his middle finger repeatedly and with great enthusiasm. The old dude was bald, and his head got so red you could see the sweat glistening and running down his face. The higher his anger mounted, the harder we laughed, especially when Rupe started imitating him. When he almost rear-ended the car in front of his truck, we fell out of our seats, in pain and tears from laughing so hard. We were so disappointed when the irate driver made a turn and traffic pulled him away.

Two older girls took a seat just a few down from ours. Tommy tried to talk to them, but they weren't having anything to do with us, acting like real uptown bitches. We found a piece of paper on the floor and tore off little pieces, rolling them into tightly wadded balls and tossing them at the back of their heads. They glared at us, and we pointed at an elderly guy who was dozing in a seat across from them, acting like we wouldn't possibly do such a thing as wing trash at their heads. But even the girls giggled when Rupe bounced a wad off the old guy's cranium and he woke up, all startled and bewildered, trying to figure out what was going on.

A teenage couple started making out across the aisle as we neared our stop, their faces glued together and the guy crawling all over the girl. We thought he was going to start feeling her up right there in front of us. I made a kissing sound, and the guy spun around and scowled at us. We all pointed at each other, passing the blame and trying like hell not to bust out laughing. The guy wasn't much, barely bigger than Tommy, skinny, fuzzy-lipped, white, and making out with a girl who looked not much older than we were.

He tried to turn back to his girl, and I made the kissing sound again. This time it made the girl crack up, and that set us to dying. Rupe pointed at me and I pointed at Rupe, but Tommy was pointing at himself, and the poor guy didn't know what to make of that. When Tommy winked at his girl and asked her if she wanted to sit with us, she laughed again, and Fuzz Lip had to decide whether he wanted to test our Negro or take it. He grabbed her by the arm and moved up to the front of the bus, but their necking was over.

"Don't go away mad," Tommy said to his back as they moved away, but the dude didn't react to his comment.

We were cracking up again. We laughed a lot that day.

Was it childhood innocence? It seems more accurate to say that we were a blight on society, wandering where we would and doing whatever we desired. Unsupervised and unrestrained, we were free to make our own rules and suffer no judgments. Unless we were physically afraid of you, you had absolutely no power over us. We said what we wanted and respected little. We were byproducts of an existence that expected little of its progeny.

But bruised as they were, these childhood days were mine, and I embraced them, not yet understanding our paths would soon diverge. The road we were on led to destruction and waste, for with age came a lesser degree of tolerance by society. Life had a way of setting you up… of letting you think you had a hand in your fate… as if you were in control. Very soon, we would be held accountable for our actions, and reality didn't care if those actions were the result of a lack of guidance.

Today we were laughing, and pain and tears were far from our thoughts. We jumped off that bus to the relief of the driver and passengers, and headed toward our neighborhood with light hearts and nimble steps. We ducked into a McDonald's and bought burgers and fries, and sat at a table divvying up our day's proceeds—minus what Tommy held out—while we ate. I didn't care about the money Tommy was hiding; those new sneaks felt good on my feet.

"Who was the guy who dropped you off tonight?" I asked.

He'd looked like a real loser. The car had been a rusted-out Caddy, with a hood and quarter panel colored differently than the rest of the auto's body. Behind the wheel had been a dark-skinned guy with greasy, slicked-back hair and a thick gold chain around his neck. I'd noticed a tattoo on his shoulder and how white his sleeveless T-shirt was, but he didn't look to be anything special. He was probably some customer from the diner, or some bum who worked there.

"Just a guy I work with," she returned casually.

Bingo! Ten bucks says he's a dishwasher. Betty was digging through her purse. She didn't say what she was searching for, and I didn't care.

"Have you seen my little notebook of phone numbers?"

I'd seen and read it, but I wasn't about to tell her so.

"You mean the one Leon was waving around when you guys had the brawl?" I asked.

Betty sucked in those dentures, but she didn't flare up like I'd expected.

"Yeah, that's the one," she said quietly.

Her soft tone told me she was trying to avoid a fight, and that made me feel a little bad for picking at her.

"What's his name?"

My mother put her purse down, trying to think where she might have left her notebook. I'd thrown it away, but I didn't feel bad about that.

"What? Whose name?" she asked, once she realized I'd posed another question.

I sighed. "The guy who gave you the lift."

"Tony? He's nobody you need to worry about." My mother chuckled. Her laugh was deep and throaty. Most people who heard her talk or laugh assumed she was a heavy smoker, but she wasn't. "He's just a dishwasher at the diner. I needed a ride, and he offered." Betty shrugged. "That's it."

"He won't be coming around?"

My mother laughed and shook her head. "Let's not fight tonight, okay?"

Not fighting was tricky. What Betty meant by that was more complicated than it sounded. Not fighting meant avoiding all subjects that were touchy or sources of aggravation. No asking about bills or creditors, bad checks or people who were calling. No asking about the lack of food or other essentials for the boys or inquiring about the needs of even the near future. Not fighting meant pretending everything was just hunky dory.

Not fighting especially meant avoiding topics like Leon or other men who had made our lives worse. My mother didn't understand other people's obsession with dredging up her bad habits. She figured that just because she'd done those things in the past, it didn't mean she was going to do them again. If you tried to point out that she was on the verge of repeating the same mistakes, you were picking on her. You were being mean, and she'd cry on your ass to prove it.

My mother was fond of saying *the past is the past, why keep bringing it up?* But the fact was the past was always looming just days ahead of us, the next point in a vicious circle. Betty didn't want to hear about her faults because she didn't recognize her faults for what they were. Bouncing checks wasn't that big a deal. Skipping out on the rent or utilities wasn't so bad. Sleeping with men she hardly knew just happened, it wasn't planned.

Fault and blame were tough concepts for my mother. I truly believe she couldn't grasp them. At least not in a way that would allow her to see the changes she needed to make. The fact that I *could* understand why bad things kept happening to us was making our cohabitation difficult. But tonight she wanted to pretend, and I decided to try and go along. Maybe the past *was* the past. Fighting all the time was really getting old.

"Come sit with me," she urged, patting the sofa next to her. I complied, but it felt kind of like being sent to the principal's office. "You know I'm proud of you, right?" she asked, throwing her arms around me and pulling me up against her.

"Sure," I replied.

There was that perfume-over-must smell again. My mother bathed as infrequently as her children. *Maybe you could do something about that*, I told myself. After all, I was twelve and not a baby. *Maybe you could do something about your teeth, too?*

"You know I love you, don't you?" Betty asked, hugging me tightly again. I hated when she got like this. I hated to be touched. I hated to be touched by her most of all. "Can't you tell me you love me?"

This was an ordeal I suffered periodically. It was as if she had room for me during the times she didn't want other men around. She wanted to be all touchy-feely and express emotions she wasn't really capable of. The worst part was, she wanted me to do the same, and got really hurt if I didn't go along with the game and say the words.

"I love you," I said, the words as dead as I could possibly make them.

Unfortunately, Betty didn't hear the tone of my response, and playing along only made her worse. "Now hug me back," she purred, trying to kiss my cheek.

Lying was one thing, and being touched was worse, but touching back just wasn't going to happen. "Hug Terry," I told her, disentangling myself. "He's ready to cry 'cause you're hugging me and not him, anyway."

The moment her arms were free, Terry filled them, flinging his pudgy body into her lap. "You love me, don't you, baby," she told Terry, who clung to her like he was the baby in the family instead of Chip.

That boy loved to be close to our mother, and often emulated her habits and characteristics. *The little shit's probably doomed,* I thought, seeing how he was so drawn to Betty. He stared at me as I looked at them, the little jerk thinking he was somehow getting one over on me. *Yeah, kid, you got me. Keep on getting me as long as you like.*

My baby brother's reaction to motherly affection was worse than mine. He screamed his ass off if Betty held him too long, and would get so worked up he'd puke all over her if she insisted on clutching at him. The way he carried on was so embarrassing for Betty that she rarely tried to push herself on Chip. The baby loved for me to carry him around—especially on my shoulders—and didn't mind being held by Lynn for extended periods of time, but shunned my mother's touch even more openly than I did. One of my greatest fears was that the kid would manage to get away from her before I figured out an angle to get out of here myself.

Hamburger Helper mixed with ground beef was simmering on the stove. This represented the extent of Betty's cooking skills. My favorite dish was her baked beans mixed with fried hamburger, but she rarely cooked. We usually ate lunch meats and bags of chips, bowls of potato salad from the deli, cereal, cheese-and-bread sandwiches, and warmed gravy over biscuits or day-old bread from the bakery.

But Betty was in one of her going-to-show-she-loved-us moods, and had decided to cook a little bit to prove it. I wasn't about to turn down food, even though I was already done with the whole hugging-and-touching, I-love-you-do-you-love-me shit. I checked the stove to make sure she wasn't burning our dinner. Betty had water boiling to make macaroni and cheese, another of her culinary masterpieces. *Damn, she must be feeling really guilty,* I decided.

Chip was under the kitchen table playing with Benji. My mutt was a great babysitter. The baby would grab a handful of fur and tug, and Benji would growl and snarl like he was going to tear a chunk out of his hide. Only he wouldn't. The dog would grab at his hand and shirt or snap his teeth on empty air, play-fighting and rolling from side to side, causing my brother to giggle and try to keep his grip. When my dog managed to wriggle loose, he'd move a foot or two away, and the game would start all over again.

My brother had his back to me, so I snuck up behind him and poked him in the ribs. "Boo!" I said, making him jump. I lifted him up, and he held out his hands, wanting to play airplane. "You want to be an airplane?"

135

I asked him. He only nodded, so I urged him to talk. The kid was way too quiet. "Say airplane."

He grinned, but only managed, "Plane."

Drool pooled around the pair of little teeth he had jutting up out of his lower gums, and it spilled out of his mouth and hit me in the face as I spun him around. I didn't mind. He made what he thought were plane engine noises while we did this. It sounded more like a sheep imitation to me, and that always made me laugh. We dive-bombed Benji, and Chip shot him. My smart little buddy obligingly fell over like he'd been killed, his antics causing the baby to crack up and spray me with another burst of spittle.

"Donny, be a dear and go over and see Mrs. Lorret. Ask her if we can borrow a big glass of milk for the baby and some slices of bread," Betty told me as she came into the kitchen and approached the stove. "Make sure you tell her the milk is for the baby," she added as I landed my brother.

I knew the drill. I hated the drill. If I told that kind old lady the baby was out of milk, she was more apt to give up a whole gallon if she had it, and Betty knew that. Betty would often send me to one neighbor for a little of this and another neighbor for a little of that, thinking that if we spread our begging around, they might think better of us.

Betty's definition of the word *borrow* was not exactly how the rest of the modern world viewed the term. As far as I knew, we'd never returned anything to a single one of our neighbors, so I doubted we were *borrowing* jack shit. And none of them had ever asked us for a damn thing, which made me feel that much worse every time I came sniveling to their door. Asking for money was the worst, though. My mom would instruct me to ask for a few dollars, even five. I'd flat-out refused to perform that trick the last couple of times she'd asked me, throwing us into a big fight.

I wanted to tell Betty to go ask herself, but even though we were getting along okay at the moment, there was still a strong undercurrent of tension bubbling just below the surface, pulsing, waiting to explode. We were never far from a fight. An angry outburst was just a word or a look away. I knew if I gave her any guff over begging for her, this happy little television-like dinner evening would end, so I decided to carry out her request.

Benji tried to follow me out, but I told him to stay. Mrs. Lorret had a crazed Pekinese that tried to hump anything in the vicinity when it got excited. Benji always made the hairy little thing act bonkers, and I wasn't in the mood for that nonsense. I'd wanted to boot the pesky pooch a time or two, but never did. Like I said, Mrs. Lorret was a stand-up lady in my book. She'd paid me to shovel her walk the previous winter, and let me use her shovel to go door to door and make a few bucks. I didn't mind if her little psycho dog got off on my leg every now and again.

Her porch was enclosed and the storm door was locked, so I rang the bell and was rewarded by the shrill yapping of the hairball sex fiend. The porch light blazed to life, even though it wasn't really dark yet, and she came out and let me in, smiling briefly but obviously irritated to be bothered so late. It was nearing eight o'clock. I didn't know exactly when old people went to bed, but I knew they went to sleep pretty early.

"What is it, honey?" she asked.

Mrs. Lorret was wearing an ankle-length robe, and had a crocheted shawl wrapped around her thin shoulders, even though it was a warm night. I wondered if elderly people got cold more easily, too. She looked older without the heavy makeup she usually wore. Her cheeks and chin hung limp, as if her skin needed sleep too, and the bags hanging under her eyes were more pronounced in the yellowish glow of the porch bulb. She looked tired.

The fur ball was busy sniffing at my pants, whining and circling. I pretended not to notice when the little shit climbed up on my new Keds and started humping away at my ankle. She poked him with the toe of her slipper and kept waiting for me to answer, but the little bastard was determined to have its way with my leg and hopped over to climb up on my other shoe. This time I shook him off, remembering I was wearing brand-new sneaks.

"My mom was wondering if you could spare a glass of milk..." *Say it's for the baby*, I heard Betty tell me. "For the baby." This was so humiliating, and becoming more so each time I asked for something. "And a few slices of bread, if you can spare them."

She kept silent a moment, and for a split-second I thought she was going to send me packing. But then she said, "Step in."

She left me on the porch with the humping ball of hair and went back inside her house, as if being sexually assaulted was my punishment for bothering her this late in the evening. The floor of her porch was carpeted with that hard green stuff that felt like brittle grass, and everything appeared extremely clean and neat. *Damn, her porch is cleaner than our kitchen*, I realized.

I went down on one knee and patted the Pekinese. He lapped at my fingers, still scenting Benji and whining. The little dog's fur felt clean and smooth, and there was a pleasant, fresh smell coming off him as I ruffled his shiny coat. That made me smile to myself. *Her dog is cleaner than Betty's kids, too,* I inwardly joked. But my smile didn't hang around long. Maybe that wasn't so funny.

"Tell that mother of yours to get that baby off the bottle," she said as she came back out the interior door. "How old is he now?"

"Two," I answered, accepting a half-gallon of milk and most of a loaf of Wonder bread.

Mrs. Lorret frowned at me. "That baby's got to be going on three by now. He's too old to be sucking a bottle, or wearing diapers either." She shook her head, and the skin under her chin wagged like a turkey's in a cartoon. "I had all three of my boys eating at the table and potty trained by two. It's just plain laziness."

Oh, no, it's a lot more than that, I wanted to tell her. My birthday was in October, just a few months away, and the baby had been born ten years and one week after me. I guessed he *was* closer to three than two, now that I thought about it. But if Mrs. Lorret was waiting on my mother to get that kid weaned and dropping bombs in the pot instead of his pants, she was wasting her breath, and we both knew it.

I wanted out of here. Begging from folks who knew you was kind of like getting caught peeing in the bushes. "Thanks a lot, Mrs. Lorret," I murmured, moving away after dislodging Sir Humpalot again.

"You're welcome, honey," she sent back, giving me a forced smile as she bent down to scoop up her dog.

I felt her watching me as I slipped away, and I wondered what she thought of me, of my mother and our family. I didn't like thinking about that. She probably felt pity for us. Why else would she keep forking over food she knew would never be paid back?

I was never going to borrow anything from anybody when I got older. I promised myself that as I heard Mrs. Lorret close the door. Her porch light blinked off a second later. I saw the brightness fade away in the reflection of a Ford pickup's windshield. I didn't look back to see if she was still watching me, but I thought about that kind old lady's immaculate porch as I re-entered Betty's filthy lair.

CHAPTER 10

Bruce Banner was just about to go green when my mother screamed, "Donny!" I ignored her. Then she howled my name again. I was going to turn the page and keep reading, but then she let out a "*Donnnneeee!*" that was a real howl for help, and got my narrow ass moving. I leapt from the top stair, landed halfway down the steps, and made the landing on the run, Benji scrabbling down right on my heels.

"In here!" she screamed, stopping me from running through the kitchen and into the living room.

Betty was standing in the doorway of the little bathroom behind our rickety dining table. We didn't use that bathroom because the toilet always overflowed. When it rained real hard, the commode still backed up and stunk something awful, even if we didn't touch the stupid thing. "Hurry up!" my mother shrieked.

Something was really wrong. Betty was in a full-blown panic. My brother Terry was beside her, one hand clutching her sagging sweat pants and the other hand shoving his thumb in his mouth. He was sucking so hard I could see his cheeks caving in. *What the hell?* I wondered. There was nothing in that bathroom but some boxes of ceramic crap and Tupperware Betty had stored away, and an old toolbox full of shit Leon hadn't bothered to take with him upon departure.

"Is the toilet overflowing?" I asked, trying to see past my mother's bulk.

Betty stepped aside and pointed into the little room, screaming at the top of her lungs and directly into my face: "Do something!"

I looked in, and my heart lurched so hard I'll swear to this day I felt it beating on the back of my tongue. The baby was standing there with one tiny hand pressed against the toilet tank, looking up at us. His other hand was tearing at his throat, and his mouth was working for air like he was pretending to be a goldfish dumped out of a bowl of water.

I dropped to my knees with my ears ringing from Betty's hysterics, trying to see into Chip's mouth. His writhing and twisting made doing so almost impossible, and I was afraid he'd bite me if I jammed my fingers in between his teeth.

"Breathe, baby," I coaxed, trying to will him to take a breath. Then he began failing, his eyes half-lidded and rolling, his movements becoming jerky and sporadic. "C'mon, breathe, baby!" I begged, and I heard real terror in my own voice.

My mother bolted out of the house, howling for help. Terry was right behind her, his shrill screams barely audible in the cacophony. The baby's lips turned a sickening shade of blue, and he went limp in my arms.

Everything happened quickly after my mother's departure and the baby's collapse. I hoisted that child up by the ankle with just one hand (due to this experience I've always believed in stories about mighty surges of strength in moments of crisis), and held him up in the air. I brought the flat of my hand down on his back with more force than I'd intended. The *whump!* sounded more like child abuse than a lifesaving maneuver.

But when he didn't start breathing, I drew my hand back and hit him harder. *Please!* I begged the heavens. I started crying when even that blow didn't seem to affect him; the baby remained still, his dangling little hands barely jerking. *Please! Please! Please!* His face was so red his head looked like a Christmas bulb, and I could see bright pink shining through the thin strands of his yellow hair. Sobbing now, I made a fist and raised it, the arm holding my brother up beginning to ache with the strain of keeping his inert body aloft. I felt lightheaded and was afraid I was going to faint. *Please, God! Please help!*

Then Chip made a sound like a quiet hiccup, and something fell out of his mouth and *pinged* off the floor. I didn't look to see what that something was. His chest was rising and falling, so I laid him down as carefully as I could. The room was spinning. I was so dizzy I felt like I was going to heave. I sat and hung my head over the reeking toilet, not caring that I wouldn't be able to flush my vomit.

Nothing came up, but I kept my head draped there while the wave of nausea passed. It wasn't until the baby thrust a screw in my face that I looked up. Chip was grinning at me, displaying the tiny pointed piece of metal which had nearly killed him. *And me too!* After showing it to me, he threw it into the bowl. I watched it swirl down into the rusty deep and saw other nails and screws the baby had been pitching in.

I stared into his smiling, beautiful face and wanted to knock out what few teeth he had, but there was too much relief and joy swimming through me. I couldn't get truly angry. My baby brother was alive. That was all that mattered. He had a tiny bit of blood on his lower lip that I hoped had come from the screw, but he wasn't acting like he was in any pain. I lifted his dirty shirt, found a bruise already forming on his back and winced, but I guessed a bruise was a hell of a lot better than a coffin.

There were other screws dotting the floor, and I picked one up and examined it, thinking how something so small could do so much damage. Relief washed through me again, and I picked Chip up and hugged him. He laughed and actually hugged me back. I think I would have started crying again, but I could hear movement outside.

Instead I held my brother up and said with as much sternness as I could muster, "Do not put these in your mouth!" I set him down and put the screw up in front of his clear blue eyes, shaking it for emphasis. "No! Do not put these in your mouth!"

He looked up at me, a little stunned to have me coming down on him. He was getting ready to cry, so I knelt down and smiled, shaking my head and trying to calm him. I touched the blood on his lip with my finger and showed it to him. He reached up and touched it for himself, staring in wonder at the crimson wetness on his own fingers. Chip's eyes widened, and he looked worried, his brow creasing as he tried to figure out how he'd hurt himself.

"Hey," I said, getting his attention. I held up the screw and showed it to him again, then put my finger in his mouth and said, "No." I jabbed the screw at him repeatedly, emphasizing my demand.

The baby looked at the screw and the blood on his own fingers, and understood. *By George, I think he's got it,* I told myself. *Now if only he'll remember it.* My brothers had a way of forgetting what they were supposed to do, and not do. Come to think of it, I suffered from the same condition.

The baby toddled on into the living room, Benji trailing after him, sniffing away and licking the blood off his fingers. I was thinking about how to rig up some kind of lock to keep my brothers out of this goddamn room, digging through the toolbox for anything that might suffice, when what sounded like a whole herd of cattle came barging into the living room from off the porch. The house literally shook from the weight of them, and my mother's howl of joy upon seeing the baby alive and kicking rattled the windows.

"Thank God!" she wailed.

God had nothing to do with it, Betty, I wanted to say as I walked out of the bathroom.

But I didn't. I kept my mouth shut and let her bawl. She scared the baby, and he started crying, too. In fact, just about everyone in our living room was dropping tears. Mrs. Lorret was there, and crying, as was Mrs. Simmons and her sister, whose name I didn't know. Even Terry was looking around, perplexed and joining in on the tears, even though he didn't have a clue what everyone was going on about.

"Praise Jesus," Mrs. Simmons murmured, pressing both hands against her ample breasts and swaying back and forth.

She had an apron around her waist, and her hands were covered in flour, as were her sister's. Both were hefty women who obviously sampled a lot of what they cooked, but I liked them both. They were always sharing cookies or slices of pie with us, and boy, could they bake. The year before, Mrs. Simmons had baked me a scrumptious German chocolate cake on my birthday. I ate so much in one sitting I almost made myself heave.

Chip began squirming around, doing his best to get free of Betty's hysterical embrace, but my mother was in a frenzy and wouldn't let him loose, squeezing him so tightly I thought she might accidentally finish what the damn screw had started. The baby was staring at me for help, and Benji was hopping around, yapping at everybody. The poor dog wasn't sure what was going on, but had decided to join in on the commotion.

"Thank the Lord," Mrs. Lorret chimed in, touching Chip's wet face.

What is it with everyone thanking God? I wondered. Had God saved him and not me? After all, I *had* been doing an awful lot of begging. But I'd left the bruise between his shoulder blades, not some God. *Yeah, you're awful brave now,* I told myself. I hadn't been so confident a few moments earlier. I'd been praying for help from above without even thinking about it. Beseeching someone I wasn't even sure I believed in for assistance. And I'd done so out of pure instinct, without thought. I pushed those thoughts away for later assessment. Maybe that church was just messing with my mind.

All the women seemed to follow my baby brother's earnest gaze at the same time, and I suddenly found myself uneasy under their scrutiny. I swallowed uncomfortably. "He had one of these lodged in his throat," I said, holding up the screw I'd used for the baby's lesson. They looked at me like I was standing there peeing on the floor, none of them changing expression. I felt like they were going to blame me for Chip almost choking to death. "I held him upside down and hit him on the back and the screw came out." I swallowed again. "Honest."

They all jumped me. For a second, I thought I was a goner. Mrs. Simmons hugged me so tightly my face was buried between the massive mounds of her breasts. She lifted me off my feet and swayed me back and forth, bragging on how great a kid I was. I felt like I was being mauled by Aunt Jemimah. My mouth was full of flour when she let me go, and her sister hugged me too, but at least she let me breathe while she did so. Mrs. Lorret just pinched my cheek and told me I was a good boy.

Betty finally put the baby down and hugged me after they were done. "I'm so proud of you," she said. And I believed her. "How'd you know what to do? I was so scared." *Oh, yeah? Well, I wasn't exactly Mr. Cool myself,* I wanted to say. But I kept silent. This was kind of nice, having everybody think I was so great. "Isn't he the smartest little man?" Betty asked my throng of adoring fans, and they all agreed.

"Whoa, what's all the commotion?" a man's voice asked from the front door before I could begin signing autographs and posing for pictures.

"Tony!" my mother exclaimed. *Oh, great, the dishwasher.* "Donny just saved the baby from choking to death!"

Tony sauntered in like he owned the place. He was wearing another bright white sleeveless T-shirt, proudly displaying his tattoo of a heart with an arrow through it and two names I couldn't make out. His dark hair was slicked back, and he wore thick sideburns. He was skinny, but tried to walk tough. I didn't think he was too bright. The cigarette hanging out of the corner of his mouth was way too close to all the grease he had in his ridiculous hair.

"Way to go, kid," Tony said, making his way through our neighbors. The Simmons sisters watched him like he was a loose dog, and Mrs. Lorret actually turned up her lip. "You know, the Chinese believe when you save a life, you're responsible for that person forever."

"Not if they save yours back," I told him. I couldn't have some guy who washed dishes thinking he was smarter than me.

Tony smiled. At least his face split, and he flashed some crooked teeth. But his brown eyes stayed hard and calculating, measuring me. "What was he choking on?" he asked. His tone had grown cautious.

"A screw out of my mom's boyfriend's toolbox," I returned without flinching. And *that* had the visiting ladies heading for the door.

"*Old* boyfriend's toolbox," Betty shrilled quickly. I shared a glance with Mrs. Lorret. I saw pity on her face, and that pissed me off. "He's been gone for months now," my mother added.

"Yeah, at least one whole month," I said dryly.

Tony reached out and touched my face, showing me the flour on the tip of his finger much the same way I'd recently showed the baby his blood. "Your face is dirty," he said, no longer caring to pretend to be friendly.

He walked past me, as did Betty. My mother shot me a hateful glare as she followed Tony to the bathroom where the dreadful event had taken place. *What happened to me being the smartest little man?* I wondered. It seemed Betty forgot trivial little things like lifesaving pretty easily. If a man was around, that was.

"I'll put a lock on this door for you," Tony promised my mother.

"Would you?" she cooed back.

This was making me sick. "I'll take care of the lock," I told them.

Tony laughed. It was a short barking sound I would come to loathe. "If you'd already taken care of that, your little brother might not have almost choked to death." *Great, now I'm being blamed for almost killing the baby. And by a Dago who washes dishes for a living!* "Don't worry, kid. I'll take care of it."

"I don't need any taking care of."

"Donny, don't be rude," my mother scolded me.

"I thought you said I wasn't going to have to worry about this guy, Betty," I returned. She knew I was really sore when I started using her first name on her. "What was it you told me…?"

"Shut your mouth," Betty warned.

She stepped toward me, meaning to slap me if I kept on. She knew I was going to say something to embarrass the guy, but I wasn't about to let her stop me.

"Oh, yeah, now I remember," I said, dodging her advance. "You said, *Who, Tony? He's just some prick who washes dishes at the diner.*" Of course, I imitated her with my best Betty voice, a mixture of dumb blonde and Elmer Fudd on good grass.

"I never called him a prick!" Betty screeched.

"But you did call him *just a dishwasher?*"

"Not the way you're implying!"

Her dentures slipped, and I heard her suck them up. Clamping in those falsies made her quiet down, but I knew she'd really want to get me back for that. Betty hated messing with her fake choppers in front of possible studs.

Tony was leaning on the doorjamb, fingering an Italian horn he wore on a gold chain and giving me his best look of intimidation. I wasn't impressed. He walked around the table, and I stood my ground. I didn't have anything to fear from him. This was no different than the school yard, only he was an adult and not allowed to whack me like another kid could. Benji's nails clicked on the dirty linoleum of our kitchen floor as my wary buddy came to stand beside me, eyeing our guest with interest.

I didn't like what I saw in Tony's olive face. For some reason the hair on my neck was standing up, and I heard my dog's chest rumbling with a warning growl. I could smell alcohol on his breath even though it was still afternoon. Benji could feel something, too. Tony flicked his gaze from me to my dog and back, then gave me that fake lifting of a lip that was supposed to be a smile.

"Niggers are afraid of dogs, and I ain't no nigger," he told me.

"My, aren't you lucky," I said.

Dammit! You sound scared. Cut it out! Tony lifted his hand and started toying with his chain again. Benji let out a serious huff that meant back off.

Tony looked at my dog again. "That dog bites me, and I'll kick it clear across the room," he informed me as casually as if he'd asked for a glass of water.

"That dog lives here and your ass don't," I returned just as pleasantly.

"Never mind him, Tony," Betty said, trying to intervene. "He's always been a wise ass, and he just keeps getting worse. For your information, Tony's just working at the diner while he's laid off from the box factory," my mother informed me. *Wow!* I wanted to say. "He also works as a painter on the weekends." *A regular genius.* "And it's none of your damn business who I bring around here! So stop acting like you pay the bills!"

"It's not the *who* paying the bills concerns me, Betty," I drawled, unable to hold any more remarks back. "It's the *how.*" She was sucking on those dentures again. "How much can you pump out of a dishwasher-painter guy? Do they make more than mechanics or plumbers?"

"You *do* have a smart mouth, kid," Tony told me.

I could tell he wanted to do more, to jab me with his finger or try and prove how tough he was some other way, but he didn't dare. Benji was all fired up, his hackles standing on end and his teeth exposed, eyes bulging and body tense, poised for action right at my feet.

"But we can talk about that later."

And he turned and walked away, letting everything drop. I tried to slip upstairs, wanting away from the dude, and away from Betty. But they weren't done with me.

"Tony's taking us to the drive-in tonight," my mother said, as if that would smooth everything over.

My back was to them. I'd reached the first of the two steps to the landing and the stairs leading to the safety and seclusion of my room. "Not me he's not," I let her know, and took another step.

"I'm buying dogs and root beer," Tony added. "You stop acting up and I might throw in some ice cream."

The mention of ice cream had Terry jumping and squealing, but this ploy wasn't going to work on me. I had over thirty-two bucks hidden behind my desk. By kid-money standards, I was a wealthy guy. If I wanted ice cream, I could buy it myself. I wanted to pull a Tommy and flip our intruder the bird over my shoulder, but I wasn't that brave.

"Why don't you be a good little boy and listen to your mother."

That *little boy* shit lent me some courage. "Why don't you mosey over to our sink and wash those dishes," I said as I continued to ascend the stairs.

Tony tried to play my comment off, but I heard a threat in that mean bark of a laugh he let fly. "Have it your way, kid."

There was no way I could know that was just the first salvo in what would grow into a real war between my mother's dishwashing beau and her scrawny, mouthy firstborn.

"So your mom's getting nasty with a dishwasher?" Tommy asked again, not even bothering to hold his voice down. He was wet, and not happy about it. The whole rain thing had been my idea, and it had sounded good at the time. But Tommy was blaming me for his misery. "You calling him Daddy yet?"

"Would you hold it down?" I said through clenched teeth. "What the fuck are you trying to do, get us killed?"

Tommy laughed at me. All I could really see were his white teeth gleaming in the darkness. I wanted to punch him, but I was nervous, not suicidal.

"*I* won't be getting killed," he explained needlessly. "I'm out here and can run for it. But *you*... I doubt you could get out this window before one of them biker dudes had your white ass."

We were waiting on Rupe to get back with another cart. Tommy removed a couple of bottles from the one we had loaded and waiting and clanked them together. The *tink* sounded louder than thunder, and really pissed me off.

"Cut it out, you fucking eunuch!" I whispered with real vehemence.

"Why you calling me a horse with a spike on my head? They like to play in rain or somethin'?"

"You're thinking of a unicorn. I called you a eunuch," I patiently, although very quietly, explained.

"What's a eunuch?"

"A dude with his dick cut off."

"Who cut some dude's dick off?" he asked, totally ruining yet another great one-liner.

"Kings would cut the dicks off the men who guarded all their women," I explained. "That way they didn't have to worry about them fooling around."

"If you think I'm one of them eunuchs, you better talk to your mom," he said, laughing like we were in the cafeteria instead of stealing from a bunch of guys who could rip our heads off and eat them like peanuts.

"You ain't doing my mom. You hate to wait in lines," I explained. That was true. Tommy was always cutting in the lines at school, especially at lunch.

"You read too much," he said way too loudly. "You going to cut mine off, you better have one of those saws two big tree-chopping dudes pull back and forth, and they better want to work overtime."

"Or a pair of nail clippers," I said before I really thought about it.

"A pair of what?" Tommy asked, practically yelling, and startling me so badly I went scrambling for the window. He was cracking up, giggling like an idiot, and pushing me back when I tried to get out. "Calm the fuck down." He was trying to stop cackling, but with difficulty. "They can't hear shit." He checked the rear of the house, where the bikes were parked. No lights came on. "See?"

"Don't do that!" I hissed.

Rupe came rattling back with an empty cart. It sounded to me like he was just pushing the damn thing along as if he didn't care who heard him coming or going, but I knew he would be trying his best to be quiet. Rupe was a bigger coward than I was. That Rupe was scared shitless was a certainty, like the sun rising and the world turning. Why he kept doing dangerous things like this with Tommy and I was way beyond me. *Maybe he likes slumming,* I thought. I'd never thought much about our bond with Rupe. Truth was, I couldn't have explained it if I wanted to, then or now.

They loaded up the next cart while I waited. When the first cart was loaded, Rupe took off, and Tommy loaded the other one and covered it with tarp. I cursed myself again for forgetting to steal another cart or two. *Or four!* It was taking forever to empty out all these bottles with just the two we had available.

Lightning flashed, but not near. The following thunder was distant as well. But the wind was picking up as the storm moved closer. It was a warm night, even in the rain. Still, I found myself shivering. *Probably from fear, you coward!* I scolded myself. Tommy reached in, and I began filling his greedy hands. We repeated this procedure until he had the narrow lane between the detached garages too cluttered to continue. He had to leave enough room for himself and Rupe to work around the carts.

"How much more?" Tommy asked.

I thought about lying, but didn't. "At least two more loads," I told him.

"Didn't I tell you this was the fucking mother lode?" he repeated for about the tenth time. "This's going to bring in... how much?"

He waited, knowing I had a pretty good idea what we were going to rake in. "Around twenty-five bucks, give or take," I informed him.

The wind blew harder yet, and the night cursed again. I was cold, and it wasn't just from fear. *Jesus, this was a lot of bottles,* I thought. Most of them were 7UP bottles, which I knew from a couple of Betty's more refined suitors were popular for mixing with alcohol. There had also been Pepsi and Coke, as well as some ginger ale. But if I'd known it was going to take so long to get them all out, I might not have ever crawled in this dank, dark garage in the first place.

Tommy whistled, but at least he did so quietly. "Mother fucking lode," he grunted. "Hey, you okay in there?"

No, I'm freezing. I think I might be catching a cold, and I'm scared to death I'm going to get caught and dragged behind some Harley dude's bike until all the flesh is scraped from my bloody bones. "Yeah, I'm fine."

My knees were sore from kneeling, and my jeans were wet from the damp concrete floor. I'd leaned against the wall while resting between loads and soaked my shirt, and my nerves were frazzled. I didn't like being enclosed. My feet were my greatest asset when and if it became necessary to escape. I didn't like my chances of getting away if we were discovered. It just took way too long to squirm through that window, and more than one of the bikers I'd seen going in and out of that house were young enough to run a kid down.

"Hey, Donny," Tommy called softly.

"Yeah?"

"That dishwasher fucking with you much?" Tommy asked. "I mean, he pushing you around or anything?"

Relations between Tony and me *were* getting pretty hairy, but he hadn't laid a hand on me as of yet. "I can handle him." It was a guy thing. You never admitted if you were afraid of another dude. "He probably won't be around much longer. Betty's starting to ask him for money to help with the rent and food. That's usually when they come around less and less."

"You just let me know," Tommy said, grinning at me through the window. Lightning crashed behind him, near enough to get him studying the sky, and the thunder boomed more quickly, and more closely. "You and me, baby. If his skinny ass gets out of line, we'll whip it for him."

"Speaking of skinny asses, I'd like to get mine out of this wet garage," I told him. "Any sign of our gimpy friend?"

Tommy's face disappeared, but when he came back he had good news. "I can hear him coming back. He's about a block off. He takes this load, and we'll go ahead and drag all of 'em out, even if we got to put 'em out in the alley."

"You got enough tarp to cover them?" It wouldn't do to have the cardboard cartons getting sloppy and falling apart. Half of them were weak on the underside already, due to the dank concrete. "I mean, for the extras?"

"Yeah, I think so," he told me after checking. "What you going to do with your money?"

"I don't know." I was thinking about buying an art kit, complete with inks and pastels, but I wasn't about to tell Tommy that. "You?"

"Lucy Perez," he answered without hesitation. "She wants me to take her to the mall and buy her this jacket she's had her eye on."

"What are you getting out of that deal?" I asked, setting myself up.

But we only laughed together. All I remembered about Lucy was that she had a pretty face and a butt I wasn't sure I could wrap my arms around. For Tommy, it seemed, the bigger the better, and he especially favored the Spanish girls. I was still equally afraid of every nationality.

"You got any money now?" he asked.

"A few bucks is all," I said. My lie echoed quietly in the hollow darkness, but I was pretty sure Tommy was in trouble with Candy again. He hadn't paid me back for the last couple of times I'd floated him money. And he wasn't going to. But he was my friend, so I asked, "Why?"

He didn't respond right away. "No reason," he finally said. I knew he was lying. Tommy's smoking habit was getting expensive. Add in the occasional Lucy Perez and grass or a drink now and then, and Tommy needed money he didn't have and couldn't easily get. And Candy was not the guy to be borrowing from. *Especially without his permission,* I added. I was starting to think Tommy was getting in over his head with our neighborhood's dark overlord. Candy had already smacked him around for pinching. The next level of punishment would be worse. But I couldn't really tell Tommy this. He didn't like being preached at, especially when it came to acquiring the funds for doing the things he loved most.

We finished up, and Rupe and I said our brief good-byes to Tommy when he left us to push the last two carts off to hide in the garage. We watched him walk away, a blur in the rain distinguishable only by the glow of the cigarette hanging out of his mouth. Soaked and miserable, we made our way in silence, but I could tell Rupe had something on his mind. I waited until we were out of the rain, unloading in his garage. "What's up?"

"Nothing."

I snorted and looked at him, wondering if I was as big a mess as he was. His wet clothes clung to the bones of his thin frame, hair hanging in his eyes and dripping rain. There was even water dripping from the end of that pointed nose. I noticed he was shivering. *At least I'm not the only one who's cold.* I figured Rupe was shaking from fear as well. It had been a stressful, tense operation, but it was over now and I was feeling pretty good.

"C'mon, give it up," I urged.

Rupe sighed and wiped rain out of his eyes. "I'm going to stop doing this shit," he told me flatly. I just stared at him. "You should stop, too."

"What are you talking about?"

"Donny, it wasn't a big deal when we were taking a few cartons of bottles off the back of some old lady's porch, or even tricking stores with receipts for shit we'd actually bought… But it's starting to get heavy." He waved his hand over our mound of stolen goods. The large amount of bottles looked better to me in Rupe's garage than they had in the biker's place. "This is too much. And Tommy's talking about stealing hubcaps and car radios, and breaking into garages and stealing power tools."

"He's just talking." But he'd been pushing me about that shit as well, and pushing hard. "Just tell him you don't want to."

"No, Donny, Tommy's not talking. That's Candy talking," Rupe explained, watching me absorb his point.

"What do you mean?"

"For a smart kid, you can sure be stupid," Rupe said, pissing me off. "It's Candy. Tommy can sell anything he steals to him. That mean black bastard runs so much shit out of the back of that pool hall, he sells more than Sears. Tommy needs more money, so he wants to steal better stuff, and Candy and his crew are the ones talking him into it. Where do you think Tommy gets the grass he sells in school?"

"From Candy. I knew that." And I had. But Rupe was talking sense. I shook water out of my hair. "I need to get home, man. We can talk about this later."

"Donny," Rupe said as I turned to go. I looked at him and noticed how serious he was. "I mean it." He pointed at the bottles again. "This is it for me. I'm done. No more. And you should think about slowing down, too. You're going to get busted."

"That's an easy decision for you, Rupe." I was getting mad again. I pointed in the direction of his nice clean house. "You go on in to Mommy and Daddy's nice safe house. You want something and you get it. I'm not so lucky as you."

"It's not like that!" he shot back. He was getting riled up right along with me, and that surprised me. What did he have to be sore about? "I don't get anything I want. We have problems too. All families do. Don't accuse me of being lucky just because I have two parents. That's bullshit, and you know it."

I spread out my hands and shrugged. "There's no problem," I told him. "You don't want to do something, you don't have to. All you have to do is say no."

"Yeah, right," he spat. "I'm telling you, Donny. I'm out of this, and you should think hard on cutting this kind of stuff out, too. You keep on doing what Tommy tells you and you're going to go down with him."

"Don't worry about me. I can take care of myself. If I don't want to do something, I don't have to either." I turned to go again, tired of pissing and moaning with Rupe. "Jesus, you act like you're my dad or something."

"Yeah, sure," Rupe muttered.

I paused at the door, standing in the rain. "What do you mean by that?"

Rupe looked me dead in the eye. "When's the last time you told Tommy no about anything?"

CHAPTER 11

Rupe had been right on the money about Tommy. But he still wasn't smarter than I was. Just because he figured out where we were heading before I did didn't mean squat. Chalk that fact up to fear. He'd wanted out because he couldn't handle the pressure, and because he was afraid of getting busted. And why should he take the risks? He had a great family and a dad who just might knock his block off if he got caught stealing from people.

As our thievery escalated, the arguing between Tommy and me intensified. He was pressuring me to do more and more. So far I'd relented to popping some hubcaps and ripping off a few unlocked ten speeds left on porches or outside a store. He sold those to Candy, but I wasn't allowed to come along when the sale was made. I was pretty sure he wasn't giving me anything close to half of the proceeds, but it was better than the piddly amount of money we got by scrounging and lifting pop bottles.

One day, we were scouring cars in the parking lot of the mall, checking to see if they were locked. If they weren't, one of us raided the open automobile for anything of value while the other kept watch. (I was the one inside the car almost every time.) *You never tell Tommy no,* Rupe said in my head. Most people left loose change in the ashtrays if they weren't smokers, and often left money in the console. We had done pretty well, but we'd been at it long enough that my instincts told me we should be getting along.

Then Tommy saw the purse lying on the seat of a Ford pickup. The doors were locked, but I could tell he had his mind set on getting that purse. "Move over a row, and let me know when the coast is clear," he told me.

"The doors are locked, Tommy," I told him needlessly.

"No shit. I'm going to bust the window with one of those bricks out of the back. I'll grab the purse, and we can scram."

"Hell no, man!" I sounded like a scared little kid. *You are a scared little kid.* "You're out of your damn mind. Someone's going to hear that window breaking."

"So?" he said with a shrug, glancing around. I was afraid he was going to bust it while I was standing right there. "Quit being such a pussy. Who's going to catch us?"

A car with a man behind the wheel rolled by, searching for a parking space. There wasn't much traffic, but there were a few shoppers walking to or from their cars, close enough to hear us arguing. None of them paid us any mind. For the first and only time I could recall, I wished one of them actually would. Maybe if somebody got curious, Tommy would give this insane idea up and agree to go home. *Where's a cop car when you need one?* I asked myself. Just the sight of the fuzz might get Tommy to quit this.

But nothing happened, and Tommy was looking at me like I was Rupe whining about ripping off bottles. *This is different,* I told myself. *Isn't it?* If it wasn't, it sure felt that way. My heart was racing like I'd just run five blocks, and I felt trapped. Usually Tommy let me make the calls when it came to what we stole, and how we did it. I didn't like not being in control of the risks.

"I don't know, man, this is plain crazy," I squeaked. Tommy just laughed and reached into the back of the truck for a brick. "Waitaminute!" I whispered harshly before scooting over to the next row of cars and checking for traffic, wheeled or afoot.

Before Tommy could make his move, one of the people walking near us turned and approached the truck he was standing next to. It was a lady in jeans and a flannel shirt, with long gray hair and work boots like a man would wear on a construction site. She looked like a farmer's wife. She had keys in her hand, but when she saw Tommy standing there holding the brick, she dropped them and stood very still. I could see that she was startled and afraid.

For a second, Tommy just stood there. Neither of them moved nor spoke for a few seconds. Then Tommy laughed, a coarse chuckle, evil, and tossed the brick back into her truck. She flinched when he brushed past her, and she followed his progress with wide eyes while he walked toward me.

Our eyes met. I realized she was afraid of me, too. I was ashamed of that. I'd never heard Tommy laugh this way. The sound of it reminded me of Tony, the way he barked like a whacked-out hyena. *You never tell Tommy no,*

Rupe chimed again. Maybe Rupe was right. If so, that still left me with the problem of dealing with Tommy and his constant pressuring to take greater and greater risks.

I glanced over my shoulder once we started moving away. The poor lady was still standing there. She hadn't even bent down to pick up her keys yet.

"We should get out of here. She might go back in the mall and call the cops."

"Fuck her," Tommy said, and then spit on the nearest car. He was really angry over missing out on that purse. "I should have picked up her keys and opened that truck myself," he murmured, almost to himself.

I'm not sure where or how I'd devised my line when it came to theft, but I drew a clear distinction between *stealing* stuff while its owners slept and physically *taking* something from somebody. I thought of myself as a thief, not a criminal.

I checked once more. The woman had gotten into her truck and was roaring out of the parking lot. Tommy tried not to let me notice, but he looked too, to see which way she was heading.

"We should still get out of here," I insisted. "She might find a cop."

"And tell him what? What'd I do? I just stood there and then tossed her brick back into her truck." Tommy shrugged. "You can't arrest a brother for that. Fuck the man." I wished I was as confident about our situation as he was. "You need to grow a pair, white boy."

I thought about a comeback, but kept silent, checking behind us every now and then, never feeling safe, even after we made it way past the mall and were hanging out at the bus stop. Tommy was rapping with some older black dude with a large boom box, asking him where he bought it and how much it was. They gave each other five when "Killing Me Softly" came on, singing along with Roberta and sliding around. People cast irritated glances when the dude cranked it up so loud it hurt your ears.

Tommy's new friend wore a black power T-shirt, adorned with the raised fist. He swayed back and forth in his bell-bottoms and long 'fro, laughing with Tommy. I found myself on the outside looking in, feeling sorry for the people they were bothering, and embarrassed to be seen as one of the kids causing the disturbance.

The dude checked me out as I walked up to tell Tommy our bus was approaching. He nodded toward me and asked who I was. Tommy told him I was with him, but that wasn't good enough for Mr. Cool. He told Tommy he'd check him later, and warned him against hanging with whitey, twisting his lips at me in distaste as he strutted away. *Hey, I'm not whitey!* I wanted to tell the dude. *I'm from the same neighborhood as he is.* But lately I was feeling a distance forming between my friend and me, and not just over our escalating criminal activities.

"What's all that whitey shit?" I asked Tommy when we'd found seats on the bus.

Tommy was still watching the guy out the window. "I have *got* to get me one of those boom boxes, man," he said. Then he gave me a gentle elbow. "Don't worry 'bout that shit, baby. You can't help it you white."

"What's being white have to do with anything? That dude sneered at me like I was some faggot trying to ask him out."

"He can't help it. A brother has it harder than any white dude. That's just the way it is. He don't really hate you." Tommy pinched my arm. "It's your skin, man. You white, so you don't know how bad shit really is. But don't worry. I got your back. You my nigger, you know that."

I didn't get it. As far as I knew, being white-skinned hadn't done jack shit to assist me in life. I was worse off than most of the black kids I knew. Betty was white, as were most of the losers she slept around with. Hell, I'd have traded the lot of my mother's bed buddies for one intelligent black guy with a real job.

"Check this out," Tommy told me in his best conspiratorial voice. I forgot all about our skin tone discussion when he slid a switchblade out of his jeans pocket and clicked the blade free. "Is that a beauty or what?"

I looked around the bus, worried that we'd get instantly arrested or something, then I bent in close and whispered, "Where did you get that?"

"What? The knife?" he asked real loud. He laughed at me when I jumped and started looking around again. "You such a pussy. I got it from Candy."

"What are you going to do with it?"

He shrugged and pushed the blade back into its shiny polished casing. "You know. Use it if I have to." He put it away. *Thank God.* "Candy says if I just flash it at a dude, he'll back way off."

"That, or shove it right up your ass," I said with a laugh.

Tommy didn't think I was funny. "What the fuck would you know about a blade?" he asked, glaring at me. "You afraid of an old bitch in army boots."

"Take it easy, man. I was just messing with you. Why are you so touchy all of a sudden?"

155

"You been pissing me off. We could be jacking car radios or getting tools worth money out of garages, but you too chickenshit. Then we go scouting cars, and you get all pussy on me as soon as it gets a little heavy."

"What? Did you want to mug that lady?" He was really getting under my skin. "I suppose you were going to use your new knife on her? You're taking some crazy chances."

"Then keep us sharp. You the brainy one." He grinned at me like the Tommy I knew. "Let's go out tonight, and I'll show you some new tricks I've learned, baby."

"I can't. Betty's working the next two nights," I explained, relieved that I had an honest out. *Tricks?* I wondered. If they were tricks he'd picked up from Candy and his crew, I wanted no part of them. "I have to watch my brothers."

"Shit, they'll be asleep."

"We're hauling those bottles to the Kroger Friday morning. How about we go that night? Betty's going out with the dishwasher, and Lynn's sitting with the boys." Tommy didn't like being put off, but he sighed and started writing something nasty on the grimy window.

You never tell Tommy no, Rupe mocked again.

Walking home after parting ways with Tommy, I found myself thinking more and more about Rupe's warning, and the other stuff he'd said. The kid made sense. I didn't think badly of him for getting out of our risky schemes. Truth was, I didn't much like stealing either. But it was an easy way to get money, and the quickest and cheapest way to collect comics, baseball cards, or sporting equipment. Getting something for nothing was a hard lure to resist.

My way home took me past Bess's apartment, so I cut over a block to see if she might be home. I hadn't seen much of her lately, since I'd been ditching church and she never missed. There was talk going around that she might go to their Christian school out at the church, and live with some people out in the suburbs who were church members. I wondered if Lynn would go too. Dave was still pestering me about salvation and whatnot, but I had bigger things on my mind lately and kept avoiding him.

They lived in a seedy row of two-bedroom apartments. Mama Z.'s car was gone when I walked into the parking lot, but that didn't necessarily mean Bess wouldn't be there. I knocked on the door and waited, knowing someone was home by the sound of movement on the other side of the door. Bess had three creepy older brothers who were all living in the apartment at one time or another. *When they aren't in jail,* I thought, chuckling. They reminded me of a trio of trolls.

One of them answered the door. He was the small one with the crazy hair and scraggly beard. *Okay, you just described them all,* I corrected myself. The tallest and oldest was named David. He was the only one I could actually talk to or look at without getting the willies. The short chubby one was named Bob. Bob never talked. He reminded me of a badger who'd lost its hole in the ground and was pissed at everybody for not telling it how to get home. And there was the aptly named Charles—who did look a lot like Charlie Manson—standing in front of me.

I didn't know who was the youngest, Charles or Bob, but I *did* know Charles wasn't currently wearing anything besides his yellowed, tattered underpants. *Dave, Bob, and Chuck... someone put a lot of thought into naming those three,* I suddenly thought. That struck me funny. And then I remembered my own name was Donald, and that made me laugh out loud. Charles, who'd obviously been asleep, opened one eye wider and gave me a suspicious stare, trying to figure out what I might be laughing at.

"What you want?" he asked, acting very gruff for a hundred-pound hairy dude wearing briefs that had probably been handed down from one of his larger brothers.

I found myself choking back laughter. "Bess here?" I managed. He just shook his head. "Lynn?" There was another shake of his ratty head. *Damn, he's already falling back asleep,* I realized as he started closing the door.

I started for home, but had only taken a few steps when Mama's hatchback puttered into the parking lot. They beeped at me, waving. Bess and Lynn were both with their mom, and I walked up and said hello as they piled out. There were groceries in the back, so I grabbed a couple of bags and helped carry them in. I told Mama to leave what was left after the girls loaded up (Lynn picked up as much as I had), and she thankfully obliged me.

One of the trolls let Mama's pug out of the apartment, and the ugly little dog came hopping and grunting across the parking lot, hurrying to greet her. She made over the wriggling dog for a moment, stooping down to pick it up.

"Did you miss mama, Puggy?" she asked it.

Puggy. *What is it with this family and the lack of effort they put into names?* I wondered. But then again, I'd named my own dog after a movie. That hadn't taken an awful lot of ingenuity either.

The inside of their place might have actually been worse than ours. The smell was, for sure. That apartment reeked like my gym locker at the end of the school year, only the gross smells were animated and had names. Bob was squatting on a recliner over in the corner, his sullen eyes peering at us while we dropped the bags on their kitchen table. *Still haven't found that hole, have you, bub?* I could feel those mean beady orbs on my back as I left to go get the last of Mama's groceries, but when I came back, both Bob the Badger and Charlie Manson were gone. I figured Mama had probably ordered them to get dressed.

"We haven't seen you at church lately," Bess told me, unpacking the bags with her sister.

"I haven't been."

"I'm going to the bathroom," Mama said, waddling away. *Okay, I could have gotten along fine without that information.* "Tell your mother I said hello," she added from the little hallway before the bathroom door slammed.

Puggy had followed Mama down the hall and into the bathroom, imitating its owner's walk. We could hear her peeing, and I grimaced, making both girls laugh.

"Dave's really worried about you," Bess announced. "He asks about you all the time."

"Yeah? Well, I've got things to do besides answering to Dave."

Mama Z.'s family rarely threw anything away. There were two stacks of old newspapers next to the door, sort of leaning against their refrigerator, and I took a seat on one of them. The papers smelled like Puggy had been using them as a fire hydrant. *That or the trolls pee on them if Mama takes too long in the bathroom.*

"Did you know the preacher's helping your mom?" Bess asked. "And some other members of the church are, too."

"What's he doing for her, printing up some better fake checks? Betty will drag your whole church down if that preacher don't watch himself."

"You shouldn't say things like that," Bess scolded.

"What, the truth? Don't you church people believe the truth will set you free or something like that?" I asked, even though I knew who'd said that famous line.

"That was Martin Luther King," Bess informed me.

"I know that, Bess. That was a joke."

Bess pointed a loaf of bread at me, wielding it like a sword, and said, "You shouldn't joke around about God."

"I wasn't making fun of God. I was making fun of your church."

I wasn't exactly sure that church and God were on the same page, or even close to walking hand in hand. In many ways, those people were no better than the folks living in this neighborhood. *And maybe worse,* I added. Pastor Grady had even done a sermon on that subject one Wednesday night, reading passages from the Bible that warned against using God falsely.

"Bess got caught kissing Gordon in the basement," Lynn blurted, like the words had been beating against the back of her teeth.

"We weren't kissing!" Bess snapped, blushing. "You don't know what you're talking about!" Lynn was pleased with herself.

The girls kept bickering while Bob and Charles came shuffling in, digging through the groceries. Charles found a bag of pretzels, and the Badger snuffled up some powdered doughnuts. Mama heard their foraging and came scurrying out of the bathroom, screaming at them to keep their filthy hands out of the food. I decided my visit wasn't such a grand idea and slipped out the door, sharing a wave and a mouthed "later" with Bess before leaving.

She caught up to me outside and grabbed my arm. "You aren't mad about Gordon, are you?" I could tell she was hoping I would be. I guess in a way I was, but I wasn't going to tell or show her that. "It wasn't like Lynn said."

I shrugged. "I need to get home." I didn't like the baggy, ankle-length skirt she was wearing, but her face was as pretty as ever. Her face had me thinking about that kiss again.

"Sure you're not mad?" I just shook my head without looking back and kept going.

I wasn't prepared to deal with Bess at the moment. I always felt like she was teasing me, toying with me. I was fairly sure interacting with girls was going to get worse as I grew older.

It turned out that going home wasn't such a grand idea, either. I knew something was wrong when I walked in the front door and saw the baby sitting between the couch and the end table supporting our only working lamp.

Chip always huddled in that spot when he was scared or pouting, and the tears streaming down his face told me he wasn't pouting. Benji was pacing between where I stood at the door and where the baby was hiding, whining until I crossed the room and picked my brother up.

"What's wrong?" I asked him. He wrapped his little arms around my neck and held on like a drowning rat, still crying. "It's okay," I told him, patting his back. "Let's go find Mommy and that silly brother of yours." I could smell shit in the baby's diaper, and there was crusted snot all over his dirty face.

I didn't have to find Betty; I heard her before taking two steps. Terry I discovered sitting on the stairs, listening to my mother and Tony going at it in her bedroom. "Get your ass down here!" I ordered him. The little pervert practically flew down the steps. The noise of his rapid descent went unnoticed, or ignored, by Betty and her grunting companion.

You've never been sick, and I mean really, really sick to your stomach unless you've endured the sounds of your own mother having sex with some dude she hardly knows. Not that this was even close to the first time I'd been so privileged. But it pissed me off to see the baby so scared. Tony was getting raw with Betty, making her say nasty things. I told the baby not to be scared and set him on the couch. The smack of Tony's hand on my mother's ass echoed down the stairwell.

I winked at the baby. "You'll like this," I told him. It made me feel good when he grinned at me and started sucking on his grimy fingers.

"What you going to do?" Terry asked.

"Shut up!"

I was still pissed at him for sneaking around on the stairs and listening to that shit. It was almost as if he was old enough to get off on it. *He's only six,* I reminded myself. This was Betty's fault.

"Go sit with Chip," I ordered, and he wisely obeyed, scrambling up onto the couch next to the baby, where he sat in eager anticipation of my next move. Terry was old enough to remember me doing funny things to my mother and her odd assortment of friends.

With no preamble, I slammed the front door as hard as I could. The reverberation of that assault sent a shudder through the foundation of the house and brought about a pause of the mating of pigs upstairs. For a second everything was silent, and then I heard arguing. Tony's voice raised in anger and my mother's in some semblance of concern.

Betty opened her bedroom door and called out, "Terry?" He started to answer, but I sternly pointed at him and then pressed that same finger to my lips, telling him to keep silent. He finally grasped the concept of the game and smiled up at me, nodding his understanding and keeping his mouth shut. "Terry, what was that loud bang?" She came down a couple of steps. "Terry, answer me!"

"They probably slammed the door going outside," Tony said. He was still in her bedroom but somewhere near the door. "Come on. Get back in here."

"You think so?" Betty asked, but all I heard was *Mooo! Mooo!*

"Yeah, sure, they're fine."

"Maybe I should check on them," my mother offered halfheartedly.

Mooo!

I grinned at my brothers and held up both hands, letting them know this was the grand finale. I carefully and quietly opened the door again, and then slammed that door so hard the vibration cracked the glass in the nearest window. My mother screamed, and Tony let out a "What the fuck?" But they both came running down into the kitchen while I hurried over to sit next to my brothers on the couch. Betty had the common courtesy to show up wrapped in a sheet, but Tony came trotting in wearing nothing but his stupid Italian horn and a glistening sheen of sweat.

Betty froze at the sight of me. "What are you doing home?" she asked in a small voice, pulling her sheet more tightly up around her neck.

"I'm sorry, is this a bad time?"

"What was all that fucking noise?" Tony asked, not at all concerned about standing bare-ass naked in front of three kids he hardly knew.

"I could ask you the same question."

He started toward me. Benji was growling and the baby began wailing and pressing his face against my chest, shoving himself under my arm, hiding his eyes and clutching at me. Tony kept coming. I couldn't believe it, but I was fairly sure he meant to hit me. *If* he got past my dog, but true to his word, he didn't look at all concerned about the snarling mutt attempting to bar his way.

"Tony!" Betty yelled, and Tony paused. "For Christ's sake, you're walking around naked and upsetting my kids! You could at least put your pants on."

Tony swung away from me and back toward Betty, his penis flapping around like a little arm between his skinny legs. Considering the way he'd been abusing Betty, he looked like the kind of guy she'd let hang around as long as he wished. *Unless some other bum with a little money comes along.* If that happened, Betty would make them share, and sneak around until the lid blew off her steaming pot of loser stew.

He walked right up to my mother. Chip looked up and then hid his face again, still crying. I had slobber and snot all over me. Terry just kept staring at Betty and Tony like they were a Saturday morning cartoon.

"You weren't complaining a little bit ago, bitch," Tony said, giving Betty's thinly covered chest a jab with his finger.

My mother floundered. "Don't be mad. I didn't mean anything by it."

He continued to glare at her, then flicked his eyes toward us kids and nodded his head at me. "I'm going to shut that mouth of yours for you," he promised. A dozen comebacks flooded my brain. "Mouth off one more time," he told me. *That's a pretty safe bet there, moron.* But I wasn't brave enough to say that out loud. "And don't you ever raise your fucking voice to me again," he warned my mother, letting his gaze linger on her a moment before heading into the kitchen and back up the stairs.

Betty's eyes welled up with tears. "Now look what you've done!" she yelled at me.

"Me?" I was taking Tony's shit, keeping quiet since he was on the edge, but I wasn't about to be lectured by Betty. "Do you see the baby? Do you see him crying and dirty and sitting in his own shit? Do you know what he was doing while you were upstairs ranting and raving for the whole fucking neighborhood to hear?" At least Chip wasn't crying anymore. He was used to her and me screaming at one another. It had been Tony's naked presence that had upset him.

"Don't tell me what I can and can't do!" she screeched. "I keep telling you you're the kid and I'm the mother!"

That was it. I lost my cool. "You're no mother!" I screamed back, bolting to my feet.

"I wish I wasn't your mother!"

Duh, that's a shock. "So do I," I said with flat conviction, dropping my voice as I heard Tony pounding down the steps.

Betty panicked when she saw him. He was completely dressed, with a freshly lit stick hanging out of his mouth and every greasy hair in place. "I'm out of here," he spat at my mother, like that was a bad thing.

"Tony, wait!" she cried. *Don't go outside like that,* I pleaded. But she did. My mother followed him out onto the porch as he made for his Caddy, clothed in nothing but that faded, Tony-stained sheet. "Are you coming back tonight?" Betty yelled for the whole neighborhood to hear.

"No," he shot back. I peeked out the window. Mrs. Lorret was peeking out of hers too. Some black kids on bikes were pointing at Betty and laughing as they rode by. Fortunately for me, they were younger guys I didn't know. "I may not come back at all," Tony added before climbing into his rust bucket and slamming the door.

"Promises, promises," I muttered.

He'd be back. They always came back. The Caddy roared to life, blue smoke billowing out into the street as he roared away from the curb and down our street. Betty's sobs drifted after him like the forlorn mating call of a lovesick whale. I thought about locking the door and teaching her a lesson, but she came barging in before I had time to act on that thought.

"Goddamn you!" she shrieked, coming right at me.

She could only swing with one hand, using her strong right while the left kept clutching at the sheet. I kept dodging and grabbing her hand, afraid only of the fact that she might lose her grip on what covered her up and temporarily blind me. I'd seen my mother naked on a few occasions, none of them pleasant.

"See what you've done?" she screamed, her swings growing feeble as she tired. "*I've* done?"

After all these years, she still stupefied me. The girls at school all huddled together and acted like the sky was falling every time one of them broke up with Johnny Nobody, but were fine a few days later when Billy Somebody gave them a little smile. Betty was still doing the same thing, only her Johnny was usually a dishwasher with a penchant for violence, and her Billy was normally a dude with a hankering for little boys.

"Yes, you. I'll never have a man in my life because you'll keep driving them away." The sheet slipped, and my heart skipped a beat. "Nobody's good enough for you."

"You'll never have a man because you keep climbing on every guy who stands still long enough for you to get your pants off," I said, risking her dropping that sheet while she swung at me again. I grabbed her hand and shoved it away, holding my ground. "Why don't you date the Three Stooges? They'll make less noise in your bedroom." *That was a good one,* I praised myself. "Hey, maybe some of the baby's first words will be *lift your ass up higher* or *tell me to spank you, bitch.*"

Here it comes. "I hate you," she snarled at me.

She got real ugly when she was this far gone. Her face twisted up, and her eyes bulged. "I wish I could get rid of you."

Her teeth slipped, and she didn't bother sucking them up tighter. Chip sensed something beyond the norm and started crying again. Terry turned on the television. Benji was fairly sure Tony was gone for a while and curled up under the end table, one eye watching me through the tangle of fur.

"You need a new line," I told her. "That one's getting old."

"Does the truth hurt?"

That particular curse had lost whatever sting it might have possessed long ago. "Do Tony's smacks hurt? You getting paid by the blow?" *Wow, a comeback within a veiled comeback,* I realized, awed by my verbal barb. I ducked another swipe. "You're going to hurt yourself." *Or lose that sheet and kill all of your sons with a single blow.* The baby was sensitive. I didn't think he'd survive the sight of an enraged, naked Betty without building up some kind of immunity first.

"I'll throw you out! I swear I will! You just keep your shit up." She was raving now, completely gone. Spit was flying, and dentures were flapping. "I'll have them put you in a home. I swear to God I will." I kept my mouth shut. She swung wild and slipped through my guard, landing a solid blow on the side of my face. I stumbled but kept my balance, sidestepping her next advance and heading for the kitchen. "Get out! Get the fuck out!" Betty wailed, running after me.

I bolted for the back door and managed to get it open, but I had to stand there warding off blows until Benji scampered out with me. Betty missed and hit her hand on the door, and that had her speaking in tongues, the flesh of her cheeks and neck vibrating with the power of her unintelligible screams. She got me again on the back of the head before I jumped off the porch and ran, dodging dog shit and lifting my knees like Archie Griffin breaking into the secondary. Benji followed.

My mother slammed the door, still ranting. "And stay out!" was the last thing I heard.

We slowed and walked down the alley, avoiding a speeding dump truck before we reached the relative safety of a sidewalk. Most of my money was still hidden behind my desk, but I had the change we'd stolen in the parking lot of the mall today. That would buy us food at the Dog 'n' Suds. The thought of a chili dog and hot, crispy fries smothered in salt and ketchup had me walking a little more quickly. I hadn't eaten since breakfast.

I always felt bad after fighting with Betty, even when I was in the right. I had to wonder if I was pushing her too hard. *Could* she get me thrown out? Our mutual existence couldn't last much longer under the current circumstances. It wouldn't take my mother long to figure out she needed some sort of weapon in order to cause me any damage. She'd tried using belts, but I just grabbed them away from her. She'd thrown glasses and plates, but she didn't have much of an arm, and I easily dodged those projectiles. I wasn't sure what would be next. *A hammer maybe,* I warned myself. *And she just might be crazy enough to kill you, boy.* I would have to watch my back. It would really suck if she murdered me and I had to spend the rest of eternity being mocked for letting a lunatic like Betty take me out.

At the moment, life was good. I was away from Betty. The summer afternoon was warm and dry. I was with my best buddy, and we had money for food. What else did a kid need?

CHAPTER 12

This was a shitload of bottles. Rupe was standing guard on the first three carts we'd hauled to the back of the Kroger, and Tommy and I had barely managed to get the rest of our treasure in the last two we were trudging along with now. So far we'd dropped three bottles. Their shattered remains lay in the roads behind us as a testament of our passage, along with the echoes of Tommy's vehement cursing. Tommy told us those broken bottles had our names on them, every time one shattered against the concrete.

My Negro buddy was an extreme penny pincher until he actually had the cash in his pocket. Tommy would probably be a collector for Candy one day. He could be persuasive when it came to getting money out of you, whether you owed it to him or not. He was definitely worse if you owed him. So far, he'd never paid back a dime he'd ever borrowed from me, but never forgot to get back a single penny on the rare occasions he had to float me a quick loan. *If he'd stay in school, he could be one hell of a tax guy,* I imagined.

Crossing Second Avenue was tricky, due to traffic and the greater risk of a cop catching sight of us with stolen—we'd call them *borrowed,* if we got busted—shopping carts and more pop bottles than a... Well, than a house full of Harley bikers could go through in a month. These were more bottles than we'd ever brought in before, way more. My end of the payback was going to push my stash of hidden funds to well past fifty bucks. I was practically rich.

I was glad we'd left Rupe back at the Kroger. Tommy wouldn't stop riding him about not going out on our little missions anymore. Rupe had stayed true to his word. He was done stealing, and Tommy could pound sand. I had to admire Rupe for standing up. He wasn't talking back to Tommy, but Rupe wasn't giving in, either. He just shook his head and said he was done every time Tommy brought the subject up.

It wasn't that Rupe wasn't getting on my nerves a little, too. He'd kept on griping about getting the bottles out of his dad's garage until I'd almost lost it on him. I'd been for taking them in a little at a time, but Rupe wanted them all out as soon as possible. He was afraid his dad would find them and figure out what we'd been doing. Knowing that that was possible didn't make Rupe's constant bitching any easier to take.

But when Tommy had started pushing to exchange the bottles, too, claiming he needed the money, I gave in. I needed to keep those two apart. Rupe was a coward, but even he had his limits. I didn't want him popping off to Tommy, getting something started that he couldn't finish, and I couldn't delay. Tommy was taking our friend's decision to cut out as some kind of betrayal, making it a personal thing.

It's going to be an interesting school year, I realized. Tommy kept guys off our backs. It went without saying that he wouldn't protect Rupe any longer. In fact, I was pretty sure Tommy would probably send some grief Rupe's way, as sore as he was. I would have to do my best to help my more hapless friend any way I could. *How?* The last thing I needed was to relive those dreadful days I'd spent running home after school every day, dodging enemies, and ducking fights.

I waited for a lull in the traffic and darted off the curb. "Stay close, boy," I told Benji, but I didn't need to remind him. He kept right on my heels all the way across, with Tommy just behind him. Some asshole in a long, expensive-looking sedan beeped at us. Tommy flipped him off and told him where to go, so we were cracking up as we reached the other side of the road and the nearest parking lot of the Kroger.

Benji was with me because I was afraid to leave him alone after the row with Tony and Betty. That dude really hated me, and I couldn't depend on my mother to protect my dog if her Italian hump buddy decided to be mean to him. It was a rare thing if she actually stood up for her children, much less a dog. It was making my life more difficult, constantly worrying about that Dago, but I didn't have a good plan for dealing with him. *Yet,* I promised myself.

Thinking about Tony got me to thinking about my brothers. Dwelling on them made me feel guilty. I was old enough to take off when shit got hairy, but they weren't. *Maybe that's why Terry keeps sneaking down to the apartment playground on his Big Wheel?* I wondered. Could be the kid was learning to avoid Betty already.

The baby was taking all this especially hard, clinging to me more and crying if he spotted me trying to leave. Lately, he'd taken to sleeping on my mattress instead of in his own room. The baby was crowding me when I tried to sleep, but I didn't mind. Benji complained more than I did, grumbling and huffing during the night. Sometimes I'd wait until the little guy fell asleep and then carry him off to his own room, but lately he'd been waking up and coming right back to bed with me. Just this morning I'd woken up with one of his feet practically in my mouth and pee from his diaper leaking onto my mattress.

As we veered around to the rear of the store, the paved lot sloped downward, and we had to strain to keep the carts from getting away from us. Tommy laughed when he noticed me struggling, but I was concentrating too hard to say anything back. He would kill me if I lost control and wasted any more money. *Or take the losses out of your end,* I told myself. But I wasn't sure he'd think of something like that, or be able to calculate the deductions.

"Hey, lay off Rupe, okay?" I asked him as we reached the area where the pavement evened out.

Tommy snorted. "Fuck Rupe, that daddy he's so afraid of, *and* his sexy little mom. And fuck you, too, you start taking his side and not mine."

"I'm not taking any side," I told him. "I'm just trying to keep you two from getting into it. Just let it go. We're supposed to be friends."

"Fuck that. Friends don't cut out on one another." He wasn't just annoyed at this split. Tommy was really pissed off. *This is going to get ugly,* I realized. "I'll tell you something else. We get that money, and we cut it in half. He wants out, he's out. You like the kid so much, you give him half your shit. But it's a two-way split today, baby."

That wasn't fair. Tommy was just using his irritation over Rupe wanting out to take money from him. *And from me!* I couldn't think of anything safe to say. Tommy couldn't count very well, but he was an expert at the one-for-you-and-one-for-me dividing of money. My worst fear was that Rupe might speak up when Tommy informed him of his underhanded scheme. *Are you kidding?* I asked myself. I figured that was a pretty stupid concern; Rupe would keep his mouth shut and get this over with, relieved to let Tommy get one over on him and be rid of the guy.

Rupe was sitting against the concrete steps as we rattled up, but he stood to greet us. Benji trotted over and started sniffing at him, and he even let Rupe pet him without showing his teeth. *Maybe he feels sorry for him, too.*

"I'll go get Freddie," Rupe announced as we arrived, eager to be away from Tommy and have this deal done.

"Yeah, you do that," Tommy grumbled.

Rupe banged on the large metal door until Freddie finally opened it. Freddie was a middle-aged dude who ran shipping and receiving. He had tufts of hair above both ears and a missing front tooth. Freddie was always asking Rupe about his mom. She shopped at this store, getting the perv revved up about once a week or so.

"That's a load," Freddie mumbled around his tooth, leaning on the rail and surveying our goods from the top step.

"Yeah, it is," I agreed.

I wasn't about to offer anything more. One of the most intricate tricks of the art of lying was not lying when you didn't have to. Until he asked where and how we'd come up with so many bottles, I wasn't about to tell him. I had a good story ready for when he did ask.

Freddie surprised me. "Totaled them up yet?" was his only question.

"You always do that," I reminded him. *And you never give us a nickel more than we bring in, and dock us for chipped bottles,* I wanted to say, but didn't. "You've never trusted us to count them before."

"Yeah, but this is a lot of bottles, and I've got a truck to unload."

He pointed at a trailer docked in one of the bays, as if we thought he might be lying. Freddie thought a moment, scratching at the wisps of hair above his right ear. I didn't think he had much longer to be scratching any hair at all. He looked like Larry from the Three Stooges.

Thinking about that reminded me of the wisecrack I'd used on Betty, and that reminded me of my brothers being home without me.

"C'mon, man," Tommy grumbled. "I got shit to do."

Freddie ignored him. "Tell you what," he finally said. "Sort them for me, and I'll count them out. Stand all the loose bottles up here divided by size." He pointed to the top of the steps. "Put all the full cartons at the bottom of the steps, also divided by size. And make sure they're full and not partials. Bang on the door when you're done, and I'll come add 'em up."

"Shit!" Tommy cursed as Freddie left, the heavy metal door thudding shut in his wake.

Bitching wasn't going to get anything done. I told Tommy to start setting aside the cartons while Rupe tossed me the loose bottles. Rupe and I got into a pretty cool rhythm. He was flipping them up as I set them down, keeping it challenging for me. We were grinning and making a game of it. I wasn't going to drop a single one. *Unless Rupe throws one too fast,* I thought, wanting him to try it. "You clowns drop shit, and it comes out your ass," Tommy told us. Rupe ignored him but slowed his pace.

I should have caught on. Later that day, I kicked myself more than once for missing the clues. There were telltale signs something was up. For one, Freddie never had us sort anything before. He'd always pushed our carts into the nearest bay and had a stock boy unload them. For another, there wasn't a peep coming out of that trailer he was supposed to be unloading. There was no forklift banging in and out of it or pallet jack bumping around. In fact, there weren't even footsteps echoing off the walls in that trailer.

And the biggest clue of all? "Hey, Rupe?" I called out as the thought occurred to me.

Rupe was bent over in the last of our carts. We were nearly finished. Tommy was already done sorting cartons and was sitting on the steps having a smoke. Benji was sitting close to him, but watching me at my work.

"Yeah?"

"Freddie didn't ask about your mom," I told him.

Rupe tossed me another bottle, and I bobbled it due to my lack of concentration. We both glanced at Tommy, who thankfully had his back to us. "Good." Rupe's response was curt. We were all tense. "I don't need that snaggle-toothed freak worrying about her anyways."

"Yeah, but he always asks about your mom," I mused.

Then we heard the Harleys, and everyone exploded into action. Everyone except me, that is. A pair of bikes came thundering at us from either side of the back of the store. Rupe ran right past the ones between us and the way toward home, his limp barely discernible as he churned for freedom, arms pumping wildly. One of the bikers spun around and gunned the throttle. Rupe wasn't going to reach the street before that dude had him.

Tommy dropped his cigarette and bolted straight across the lot, leapt as high as he could and grabbed the top of the tall concrete divider between the store and the backyards of some houses on the other side of the wall. He hooked his foot on the top of the wall and flipped himself over, leaving behind only a pick that fell out of his hair before he completely vanished. One of the bikers roared on toward the street, meaning to head him off and catch him. That dude might as well have been chasing dandelion fuzz in a tornado.

I stood in place, only moving enough to get my dog to climb the steps and stay closer to me. One of the bikers stopped right at the base of the stairs, shutting off his engine and removing his gloves. He looked up at me, but I stayed calm, thinking things through. I did pretty well under pressure, even when I was scared. Naturally, I wanted to flee, but where was I going to run? I wasn't about to risk my dog getting run over, and they were on bikes while I was on foot. I decided to stay where I was.

The guy near the steps had a receded hairline with dark curly hair, striking blue eyes, and a square jaw. He was clean-shaven, which made him look younger than he probably was. He had a deep scar near the cleft of his chin that only added to his rugged appeal. He was the kind of guy my mother swooned over but never figured out how to get noticed by. I thought the guy looked like some kind of movie star, like Marlon Brando in that biker movie.

The other dude who was still here was big as a grizzly, with bare arms so hairy you could hardly see the tattoos beneath his fur. He was bearded, but when he pulled off his German-looking spiked helmet, he was bald as a newborn baby. His bike was a chopper, with an extended rake attached to the front wheel and a real high sissy bar off the seat. The big bastard glared at me with open contempt. He flipped down his kick stand and rocked his bike backward into a balanced, parked position.

Freddie cracked open the door and peeked out, but he slammed it shut again when he saw me on his landing. I heard him turn the lock. Nobody spoke, and it wasn't long before one of the dudes came back, hauling Rupe by the back of his shirt. My friend looked like a kitten being carried by the scruff of the neck. The biker puttered along, half-carrying Rupe with one strong arm while the kid stumbled, tears in his eyes.

We still didn't say a word. In the distance, the only Harley still running faded in and out of hearing, but eventually grew loud and constant. I sat down next to my dog and waited, with my heart pounding and the guy at the base of the steps still eyeing me. He wasn't as big as the others, and he didn't look that old. He was wearing an army green bandana that he readjusted on his head, and I was positive I'd seen him before. *But where?*

Rupe was still sobbing when the last of the bikers came back empty-handed. He had shoulder-length, rust-colored hair, and a drooping mustache. He wasn't wearing any protective gear on his head or face, and he looked sheepish as he explained, "I couldn't catch him. That nigger runs like a nigger."

Then it hit me: these guys had noticed they'd been ripped off and warned the nearest stores to alert them if anyone hauled in a massive amount of bottles. Freddie must have called them. If I hadn't been so close to pissing myself, I might have screamed out loud. *You are so stupid!* I yelled in my head. I was a dunce for not recognizing this. Still, there was no reason to drag Rupe down with me.

"He didn't do anything," I told the guy holding Rupe. His parents would flip on him. All I had to worry about was Betty. *And the four bad asses surrounding you*, I reminded myself. "He's just helping us haul the bottles. You don't have any beef with him."

"I think we'll be the ones to say who we have a beef with and who we don't, you little asshole," the bear growled at me, swinging his bulk off the bike and standing. He wore a jean jacket with the sleeves cut off. Harley Davidson wings proudly covered the back of his denim vest. His arms were kind of flabby, but they were bigger around than my legs.

Maybe your waist. "You don't tell anybody shit."

"Easy, Chick," the guy nearest me warned.

Sweet Jesus! The grizzly's name is Chick! What kind of shit was that? "I'm just saying, if you're going to have the fuzz after you for beating on children, you might as well make sure you're smacking around the ones who deserve it," I offered.

The guy holding Rupe started looking around like there might be a cop nearby. "Hey, I didn't hit the kid," he muttered, letting him go. Rupe stumbled back a few steps, unsure if he should try to run again. "You ain't hurt, are you, kid? Nicky, I swear to God, man. I didn't hit the kid."

"Don't sweat it," the guy close to me told him. He tugged his bandana a bit lower on his forehead and smiled at me. He had an okay smile for a biker. "That was pretty good, kid."

"That was the truth. I stole from you, not him," I said.

"So you fucking admit it!" Chick growled.

"Why should I believe you, kid?" Nicky asked. "I already know you're a thief. Why not assume you're a liar too?"

I shrugged. "I am a liar, but I'm not lying right now. He couldn't tell you jack shit about your garage, but I can. I can tell you about the spare bike parts, the old tires, the can of Jack Daniel's bottles, the old calendar of naked chicks"—*careful with that chick word, dumbass*—"and how the floor near the back of the building stays a little wet. I can tell you this because *I* was in there and *he* wasn't. You saw the way his ass ran. You think a kid as slow as him would climb into a garage with all you dudes just a few feet away? What chance would he have of getting away? If I'd of took off when you guys showed up, you wouldn't have had a chance in hell of catching me. I'm telling you… I stole your shit, not limpy over there."

"If you could have got away, why'd you stay?" Nicky asked me, just like I'd hoped he would.

I pointed at my dog. "I couldn't climb the wall with him along, and I'm not going to risk him getting run over by one of you or getting hit by a car trying to cross these busy streets."

"That's not going to matter much when I kick the little fucker to death," said Chick. That was my biggest fear, that they'd come at me and Benji would bite. I didn't want them to hurt my dog. Chick tapped a chain he had wrapped around the back of his seat. "Or bash his head in with this."

"So you stole all this by yourself?" Nicky asked me. I didn't answer. "I asked you a question, kid," he said, his tone not mean but serious. I didn't want to throw Tommy under the bus, but Rupe's ass was on the line. I shook my head. "The black kid help you?" I nodded. He'd said black kid and not nigger. I took that as a good sign. "Anybody else?"

"Yeah, a guy named Mike Collins who lives over on Sunset," I threw in. *And I hope one of you break his legs.* God, I was good at this.

Nicky rubbed at a leather wristband, musing. I could see some kind of Japanese symbol burned into the leather, and maybe a name. But he eventually said, "Go on, kid, scram." My buddy stared at him like he'd told him to strip and dance a tango instead of leave.

Rupe looked to me, and I nodded. "Go on, I'll be all right."

And I would be. If Nicky was letting Rupe go, he'd bought my story, and would buy more. Nicky was in charge, and he wasn't stupid. If he was letting Rupe go, he wasn't going to hurt me. Rupe had seen them, and would be a witness if anything serious went down. After a last glance at me, Rupe trotted off, looking back more than once before he went around the corner and I lost sight of him. I was hoping he was smart enough not to go after any cops.

Nicky *was* smart. A lot smarter than I'd first thought. "You probably think you're going to get off free and clear, huh, kid?" Nicky asked. *Well, yeah, but you weren't supposed to know that.* "I got news for you, boy." *Oh shit.* "Just 'cause I let your friend slide doesn't mean you got away with shit. I've seen you around, and I'm going to introduce you to an underage friend of mine in the not-too-distant future." Nicky smiled again, and this time there was nothing nice about it. "Think about that on your way home."

"And I'm still going to kick your fucking dog," promised Chick.

Oh shit. Oh shit. Oh shit. Nicky pushed his bike back a little and waved his arm in an invitation for me to leave. "Be seeing ya, kid," he told me. And there was that smile again. "Real soon." *Think think think think.* Chick moved closer to the stairs, moving into position to possibly hurt my dog. He had big boots with metal studs and leather straps. It was crunch time. *Either start crying or say something,* I told myself.

"Come on, kid, get moving," Nicky said soberly.

"How about a deal?"

"You got nothing to deal with, kid," Nicky returned. "We've got the bottles, and we're going to get the money for them—and you're going to get an ass-whipping." Nicky leaned out a bit and spit on the Kroger's pavement. "End of story."

"We don't know you from Adam, boy," added Chick. "Now come on down here."

Then I remembered something.

"Your friend Harry knows my mother."

"How does your mom know Harry?" Nicky asked, taking the bait.

"He took her to some picnic you guys had out at the fairgrounds just before school let out," I explained. *Keep them talking. Get them involved in your problems,* I heard Betty telling me.

They all laughed. One of the guys sitting back said, "If she was with Harry she must be a real winner. Dirty Harry only fucks porkers."

Nicky wasn't laughing as hard as the others. "You sure your mom was with Harry, kid? Harry isn't exactly a mom kind of guy."

"Harry's not even a guy, he's more dog than man," the other biker said. They all laughed again.

I remembered Harry fairly clearly. He had a gut and bad pock marks on his cheeks and neck, with a bulbous nose full of more craters than the moon. He wasn't an easy dude to look at, and he'd scared the living shit out of my brothers.

"She's screwed around with way worse than him," I informed them.

"What's your mom's name, kid?" Nicky asked.

"Betty." Just saying it made me feel dirty. I knew they would remember her.

"Hey, yeah," Nicky said, snapping his fingers. "She was with that tub you were wrestling around with, Chick. What was her name?"

Nicky kept struggling to remember, so I filled him in: "Ruby." Saying her name was worse than uttering Betty's, but at least I wasn't related to *her*.

"Yeah! Ruby!" the redhead crowed. They were losing it now, and Chick dropped his head, chagrined. I didn't know if I was helping myself or writing my own death warrant. "You were with her in the back of that little pickup and the camper broke loose!" Even Chick cracked a grin. "You got to remember her!"

"I fucking remember!" Chick yelled at him, and that had them all laughing hysterically.

Nicky wiped tears from his eyes. Behind me, Freddie poked his head out again, but shut and locked the door after a quick look-see.

"I guess that's a little something, kid. You got a fucked-up mother. But why should I listen to your deal?"

"Because you helped me out this summer, and the Chinese believe you're responsible for someone when you save them," I explained, almost hating myself for using Tony's line.

"I helped you out? When?"

My goose was cooked if my memory had failed me. "You were jogging by when I was in a fight. Your buddy wiped my face and told me to keep my dukes up."

Nicky opened his mouth slightly and nodded. "I remember. But that wasn't a fight, kid. You got blasted, and I didn't save you from anything."

"You helped me," I pleaded.

Nicky shook his head. "Not enough. Got anything else?"

This was my last hope. I glanced at Nicky's forearm. He had an Army tattoo very similar to my stepdad's. "You were in Nam. So was my dad. Well, not my dad, but my brothers' dad. My stepdad."

"How do you know I was in Nam?" I had his attention now. I had everyone's attention.

"Your tattoo."

"Your dad had a tattoo like this?" He held out his arm and touched his ink.

"Not exactly." I explained the differences as best I could.

"Airborne," Chick pronounced, and Nicky nodded.

"What happened to your dad?" Nicky asked.

"His helicopter got shot down, and they sent him home with multiple shrapnel wounds. He had a medal shaped like a purple heart, and he was nominated for a star of some kind, but I don't know if he ever got it." All of that was true. I could tell my story fit what they knew about my stepdad's tattoo. "I have a picture and a letter he wrote me. I'll show you if you want." That was true, too.

"Where's your dad now, kid?" Nicky asked.

"He split." I swallowed.

Terrance had been good to me. I had memories of Christmas with lots of toys, of playing with him and wrestling on the bed when he'd wake me up in the morning. But those good times had been long ago and were hard to recall.

"He was hooked on drugs when he came back, and my mother had been fucking around a lot. They couldn't work it out. He split."

Nicky was rubbing that wrist band again. He got off his bike and stooped down, snapping his fingers and motioning for Benji to come down. I nearly shit myself when my dog scrambled down the concrete steps and let a stranger rub on him. "You a good mutt?" he asked my dog.

"You *were* in Nam, right?" I asked.

"We all were," Chick told me. His voice had changed. It wasn't quite as gruff. "You don't ride with us unless you were in country."

"Okay, kid, we'll listen to your deal, but no promises," Nicky said, rubbing behind my dog's ears. *Great, they'll kill me and keep my dog.* "That much we owe, but for your dad, not your stealing little ass."

I was taking anything I could get. "I was thinking I could pay you back. If you give me a break, that is."

"And how would you do that?" asked Nicky.

"I could come by once a month and haul your bottles here, only instead of keeping the money, I'll bring it back to you."

"Like we could trust you," Chick muttered.

"Test me. Count the bottles if you want. I ever short you and you can still have my ass whipped."

"Your ass already *is* whipped, junior," Chick promised.

"Hold on, Chick, I kind of like that proposition. In a way, we'd be doing our part to raise the kid right. You know, teaching him something." Nicky gave me the grin I'd seen earlier, the smile that had given me hope. "Only it'll be every two weeks, kid. And you don't miss. And you do it alone."

"You bring a nigger around our place again, and *I'll* whip your ass, fuzz or no," the redhead who'd let Rupe go told me. There was that black-and-white thing again. Maybe Tommy was right, and there was more going down against blacks than I was aware of.

"Easy, Monroe," Nicky said. "You do this alone, kid. You understand?" I nodded. "This is between you and us. Nobody else is involved, or else we end our deal and see what happens after. You in with that?" Oh, I was in. I was most definitely in. I nodded again, trying to stay cool and not let them see how relieved I was. "Good."

"What's your name, kid?" Nicky asked.

I almost lied but thought better of it. I was skating on ice that started melting an hour ago. "Donny."

"Well, Donny, I'm going to give you a free piece of advice." He pulled his gloves back on. Benji realized the petting session was over and hopped up a couple of steps closer to me. "You seem like a smart kid, so take this for what you will. When you steal from the Kroger, they have to call the police. They have to follow the law. Follow rules." He let me soak that up, watching me closely. "But when you steal from the street, there's a whole different set of laws to be leery of."

"The law of the jungle," Chick chimed in, like we were in school and he was proud to know the answer to a teacher's question.

Nicky laughed. "He's right. You steal from somebody, or step on them any old way, and you better know what they're capable of." His face hardened. "What they're willing to do in return."

I nodded because he looked like he wanted some kind of response from me. "Okay," I said. "And thanks for giving me a break."

He threw a leg over his bike, getting saddled up to leave. "Donny, the next time I go to court, you're pleading my case. Stay in school and think hard on being a lawyer. You're already a thief, so the transition should be pretty smooth."

I was thinking that I'd pulled off one of the greatest escapes in the history of mankind when Chick said, "I'm still going to slap you one and kick your dog."

I wasn't sure if he meant it or not. I looked to Nicky, and he only shrugged. "Sorry, kid. He's too big for me to tell what to do."

"Lay off, Chick," Monroe urged. "Let the kid and his dog go home."

"You need to shut up before I wipe my ass with a wad of that red hair," Chick warned.

"Sorry, buddy," Monroe told me, sighing. "Like Nicky said, he's just too big to fuck around with."

Part of me was sure Chick was only messing with me, trying to give me a good scare. *You hope.* But another part was truly terrified that he was going to hurt my dog. "I thought we had a deal," I said directly to Chick.

"Only for the bottles, boy," he said. "I still owe you for sneaking around my place."

"Just take your medicine, kid. It won't be that bad," the biker whose name I'd yet to learn said. "Take it easy, Chick. They're both kind of small. You might kill one of them."

Okay, now I was pretty sure they were fucking with me. I held up my fingers and made the play gun out of my hand. "Hey, Chick, can you do this?" I asked him.

He scowled at me. God, I was praying this wasn't a huge mistake. "Why the fuck would I want to?"

"Please, just do it. Trust me, you'll like this. If you don't, you can hit me twice as much as you were going to."

"Go on, tough guy," Monroe urged.

"What are you afraid of?" the other guy asked. "Go on. Do it."

Nicky was watching me as Chick hesitantly obliged. "Now point your gun at the dog," I instructed. Chick made a face, but slowly did as I'd asked. Benji saw him and stood expectantly, tail wagging. *Come on, old buddy. Save my ass.* "Now say bang."

Chick didn't follow instructions very well. Instead of bang, he made a noise like a shotgun going off, jerking his hand like his fingers had a recoil he could barely control. Still, Benji fell over right on cue, like he'd been laid to waste. The hair covering his eyes even made it look even better, since they could hardly see that the dog was still watching Chick.

Our act cracked them up, and as menacing as Chick tried to appear, he kind of looked like a little kid when his fat head was split by one of the biggest grins I'd ever seen.

CHAPTER 13

"You talked yourself out of it?" Rupe asked yet again. He tossed his nickel and it *pinged* off the wall and rolled about two feet back toward us. "Shit!"

That money was mine before I ever tossed my own coin. Patrick and Dorsey hadn't fared a whole lot better. I pitched my nickel, and it bounced to within about four or five inches of the base of the wall. *No use wasting any real skill on a gimme throw.* The guys were grumbling and muttering as I gathered my winnings, adding to the pocket already bulging with what they'd lost to me.

"You want me to help you with their bottles?" Rupe asked.

I shook my head, and then had to flip the hair out of my eyes. I hadn't let Betty cut it for so long I was having trouble seeing half the time, but she'd butchered me so badly the last go-round, I wasn't about to let her have another whack at my head.

"Nah, I have to do it by myself."

"Why don't you two lovebirds chat later?" Dorsey muttered. "Throw your fucking nickel, will ya?"

Rupe stooped to do just that, but I looked at Dorsey. "You know, if this is really pissing you off, you could just give me all your money and go the fuck home. That way you'd have more time to play with yourself tonight, and we wouldn't have to listen to your ass cryin' all the time."

"Yeah? I gots something you can play with," Dorsey mumbled, knowing he was making a dreadful mistake.

"No thanks, you keep her. I'm tired of your mom. She doesn't play fair. It's always about her. It's like… *Kiss me. Rub me. Spank me. Turn me over.* I'm telling you guys. That's one stingy bitch." Rupe and Patrick were dying. I acted like I had no clue what they were on about. "What? What did I say?"

"Your mom paid *me* last night," Dorsey sent back.

At least he was trying. "No way, Dors. You got to stop lying. That bitch is broke as hell." Rupe tried to stop laughing long enough to toss his nickel. It wasn't a bad shot: about an inch from the wall. It would be tough to beat, but I was way up. "Go on, Dorsey, throw your coin. Don't worry about losing all your money 'cause you won't go hungry. I gave your mom a two-buck food stamp tip for the job she did last night."

Dorsey tried to block me out and concentrate, but his nickel flipped off the wall and rolled far away. "Fuck!" I grinned at him, and he said, "Fuck you, too!" And then, "Fuck you two, too!" I thought I was going to have to sit down for a while. My sides were starting to ache from laughing so much. Dorsey reached in his pocket and checked his ammo. He only had a few nickels left in the palm of his hand.

Patrick threw but didn't come close to Rupe. I bent low, flexed my knees, and released what felt like a real good shot. My nickel tapped the wall and fell to the ground, landing on edge and rolling to a leaning stop.

"Leaner!" I exclaimed. "Double up, bitches!"

"Kiss my black ass," Dorsey muttered, handing over his extra coin. Rupe and Patrick did likewise.

Patrick never won at this, but he never ran out of change either. He had a pocket still bulging more than my own. His folks ran a vending machine operation. They owned soda and snack machines all over the city. His parents didn't let him or his sister have friends in their house because there were bags of change sitting around all over the place, and they were afraid we'd steal. *Who, us?* I liked pitching with Patrick because he sucked at this and didn't give up no matter how much he lost. It was real nice that he could shit nickels, dimes, or even quarters on command.

"Patrick, let me have some nickels, and I'll pay you back when I start winning," Dorsey demanded.

Patrick was a short, chubby kid who got picked on a lot. His face was already blotchy with pimples, and his teeth were crooked. I felt bad for him. His parents drove around in their van eating snacks all day, and they looked like circus freaks. Patrick wasn't adopted. "C'mon, man, give," Dorsey pushed, holding out his hand.

"Hold on," said Patrick, sticking out his lower lip as he painstakingly counted out a dollar's worth of nickels and handed them over. I thought that was pretty stupid. Patrick knew as well as we did that he was never going to see that money again, whether Dorsey started winning or not. "That was a dollar's worth," he reminded Dors, just to finish up his display of bravado.

"Throw your nickel," was all Dorsey told him.

"Didn't they want to know who else helped you?" Rupe asked, still a little nervous about some kind of reprisal.

I thought about telling him how I'd implicated Collins, but decided not to. I couldn't trust Patrick or Dorsey; I wasn't even going to trust Rupe with that little detail.

"At first they did, but only for a little while. By the time it was over, they seemed pretty cool with me making up for ripping them off by hauling their bottles and delivering the money."

"How long do you have to work for them?"

I shrugged. "Until I die, I guess." I pitched and came up a little short of Dorsey's toss.

"Oh, yeah!" he crowed, all excited to finally win a round. "I'd tell those motherfuckers to kiss my ass if they told me to haul shit for them," Dors told me as he came back from the wall, jangling his winnings. "Buncha fat white dudes still riding bikes like kids. Shit. They can kiss my black ass, too."

"Yeah? Well I wouldn't say anything like that too loud," I told him. "Especially around the guy that's bigger than my mom. In fact, he's bigger than all our moms rolled up together."

Dorsey whistled. "No shit?"

"He was a monster," Rupe informed him.

"Never mind. I ain't messing with no man bigger than Donny's mom, and I ain't even looking hard at some dude bigger than Patrick's mom." Dors knelt and pitched, beating out Patrick again. That was a damn shame. Taking a kid's money *and* cracking on his mom. "Oh, yeah! I am definitely on a roll now!"

"Only thing you should be rolling is grass," Tommy said as he came up behind us. "Irving told me to tell you Candy wants to see you," he told Dorsey.

"If it ain't Jesse Owens," said Dorsey, grinning at Tommy.

Dorsey was telling the whole neighborhood how Tommy had run away from a bunch of fat honkies. The two of them had fought before. If Dors wasn't careful, they'd fight again. It didn't look like he was getting to Tommy. My friend just returned Dors' grin and eyed my bulging pocket with mild interest.

"I'll catch Candy later. I gots some money to win back right now."

Tommy just chuckled. "Irving ain't but right down the alley. When he gets here why don't you tell *him* Candy can wait?"

Irving was a crazy dude who moved drugs in the high school. He was also known to carry weapons and to frequently lose his temper, especially when he was hopped up on speed or alcohol or both.

"Hold on, I'll go get him," Tommy offered.

"Wait!" Dorsey looked at the alley skeptically, but I could tell he was nervous. "Candy say what he wants?"

"Nigger, you don't ask Candy what he wants."

"Shit!" Dorsey jammed his money in his front pocket, including the dollar in nickels he'd coerced out of Patrick. "He at the pool hall?" Tommy only nodded. "All right. I gots to go. We can finish this later." He took off at a trot, avoiding the alley where Irving was supposed to be and taking an out-of-the-way route to the pool hall.

I knew Tommy pretty well. "Irving's not down the alley, is he?"

"Nah."

"Does Candy even want to see him?" Tommy shook his head, and we all laughed, especially Patrick. Maybe imagining Dorsey's face when he bothered Candy was worth a dollar's worth of nickels. "That's pretty good."

"Nigger kind of looked like Jesse Owens running away, huh?" Tommy asked us, and that had us laughing harder.

"Want to join in?" I asked.

"No, I was looking for you. I thought we might get into something tonight." Rupe stood and started acting like he was about to head for home. "You don't have to run off, bitch," Tommy snorted.

Rupe ignored the jab. "I need to get going."

He gave me a look that invoked every warning he'd ever brought up with me. Our shared glance wasn't lost on Tommy.

"C'mon, man, lay off," I urged Tommy, hoping he'd let Rupe leave without badgering him further.

"I'll do something with you guys," Patrick offered.

Thank God for the offspring of the circus freaks. Tommy turned his venom on Patrick instead of Rupe, letting my friend slip away. "All I want out of you is the keys to Mommy and Daddy's machines," he told Patrick, who visibly wilted. Tommy checked on Rupe and found him already gone, so he turned back to me. "What about it? You down or not?"

I shrugged, playing it cool. "Sure."

We headed for my place so I could get rid of my change and tell Betty I was staying at Tommy's tonight. I tried to pry out of him what he had in mind while we walked to my house, but Tommy wasn't giving much up. We cracked on each other and laughed about Dorsey. Tommy did an imitation of Candy smacking Dorsey and cussing him out that was really good, although my portrayal of Dorsey fell short. For some reason, my inability to properly imitate Dors made Tommy laugh harder than if I'd been good at it.

It was the beginning of August and hot, but the heat didn't bother us near as much as the thought of the school year lurking right around the corner. Some teenage girls in shorts and halter tops walked by, and Tommy lit up a stick, whistling and commenting on how good they looked. One of them flipped him off. He told her okay, and that made the girls giggle. They acted like he was just a mouthy kid, but I noticed one of them looking at us over her shoulder as they walked away; she sure wasn't checking *me* out.

Crossing the street, Tommy strolled slowly out and forced an old dude in a Buick to hit his brakes. The guy laid on his horn while Tommy stood in place waiting for me, and I hurried to catch up, hoping the driver would just keep going after we'd passed. He yelled something we couldn't quite make out but drove on. Tommy told me I was a pussy; he was letting me know that a lot lately. I asked him about Lucy Perez. That got him telling me all about what they'd been doing lately, which was a lot, and how he'd gotten into it with some old boyfriend of hers and scared him shitless with his new knife.

I didn't know how to respond to that. Tommy's forays into violence and girls were beyond me. *Maybe his ventures into stealing out of cars and dealing with Candy are beyond you, too.* Whatever Tommy had in mind for tonight made me nervous. It wasn't like him to keep anything to himself for long, and that made me all the more uneasy. But I forgot about Tommy's plan for our evening when I saw Tony's rusted-out Caddy sitting behind our house.

The first thing I did when I got in the kitchen was check on my brothers and my dog. Benji met me at the door, tail wagging and anxious. Both of my brothers were at the table eating food from McDonald's with Betty and Tony. My mother tried to act pleased to see me, but I could tell my arrival made her nervous. Tony just kept chomping on his burger and stuffing fries in his mouth, staring at us with grease and crumbs dripping off his lips, his dark eyes watching us with no visible emotion.

"Tony bought us McDonald's," Betty said proudly.

Great, he pays with a few dollars' worth of food for what other guys shell out cold cash, and you think he's a swell guy.

"There are a couple more burgers and some fries in that bag," Tony offered. He was in the same stupid white T-shirt and wore the same chain. I was beginning to wonder if he only owned one shirt or had a drawer full of them. "Dig in."

Nice try, asshole. "No thanks." I *was* hungry, but I wasn't about to eat a damn thing he paid for.

"Can I have his?" Tommy asked.

I shot him a glare which he ignored. You didn't get to be as big as Tommy was without eating a lot. Tony didn't say a word, but my mother filled in the silent gap before it became too awkward. "Sure, honey. Help yourself." Tommy gave Tony a big grin and snatched up the bag. Tony didn't smile back. I didn't say anything, and Tommy followed me up to my room with Benji right behind us.

"I need to talk to you!" my mother called after me.

I thought about ignoring her but answered, "I'll be right back down."

Once we were in my room and the door was safely closed, I dumped all my newly won nickels on my mattress and snatched the bag out of Tommy's hand. He had half of one of the burgers already devoured. He grinned at me around his mouthful of food while I took the other burger out of the bag and removed the wrapper. After wiping off as much of the ketchup as I could with a paper napkin—and the onions—I tore it and tossed the smaller half to my dog.

Tommy snatched the bag back. "I thought you didn't want any."

"Not where he can see me eat it." Tommy didn't say anything, understanding my predicament. He reached in the bag and pulled out a handful of fries, tossing a few to Benji before jamming the whole wad in his maw. "You're gross," I told him.

"Yeah?" He ripped the tip off a bag of ketchup and squirted it into his mouth, mixing it with the mess he was already chewing. He then opened his mouth as wide as he could, revealing the mixture of greasy potatoes and ketchup, asking, "And how gross is that?" He almost gagged as he asked his question, and that got me to chuckling at him. I grabbed a few fries before he had the chance to eat them all.

Gathering up my nickels, I dropped them into a sock and hid them under my mattress. I wasn't about to trust Tommy with the knowledge of the hiding place behind my desk, or let him know how much money I had saved. He asked how much I'd won. I told him it felt like about three bucks by the weight of it, but he didn't seem too interested in my loot other than that simple question. Benji was chewing on the ketchup wrapper Tommy had dropped. I dumped the last of the fries out of the bag and cleaned up all the excess paper while my dog avidly gobbled them up.

"Donny!" Betty called from the bottom of the stairs.

My mother's shrill cry whipped around us, a harsh, frigid wind that could strip leaves from trees. The raw edge of her howls could make your bones feel like brittle glass, as if she just might shatter you if you didn't do whatever it took to silence her.

"Donny!" she screamed again, moving up a step or two.

"Damn, that bitch can yell," Tommy whispered with vehemence, covering his ears.

"I'd better get down there before she moves any closer." Tommy quickly nodded his agreement, and we headed downstairs.

"You hear your mother calling you?" Tony asked me from where he still sat at the table, tearing into an apple pie.

"Helen Keller heard her," I told him. "I'm sorry. Helen Keller was a deaf and blind girl in a book I read."

"I know who Helen Keller was," Tony shot back, dropping crumbs. The dude was sloppier than my dog. "Got anything else smart to say?"

I placed my forefinger carefully on my chin and cocked my head. Tommy smiled in anticipation. "How about...? You eat like a pig?"

"Donny, that's enough! Don't start!" Betty warned me.

I pointed at the disaster Tony had left on the table and around his chair. He'd made twice the mess the baby had. There were splatters of mustard and ketchup, little pieces of bread, and what might have been some form of drool or slobber pooled right under his chin. Benji was feasting on the droppings. It irked me that he'd somehow managed not to get a single stain on that white T-shirt, as if the fabric was somehow immune to his slovenly eating habits.

I decided I'd had enough of Tony and turned away. "I'm going to spend the night at Tommy's," I told Betty, heading for the door.

"Oh no, you're not!" my mother shot back. "That's what I was calling you to talk about."

"Screeching," I corrected her. "You were screeching. There's a difference."

"Don't start with me." She used her tongue to push up her teeth. "I'm going out with Tony tonight, and you're watching the boys."

"What time are you coming home?"

She glanced at Tony, stammering a little as she said, "I—I'm not sure."

I shook my head. "You're not coming home, are you?"

"I'll be home in the morning, sometime before noon."

"Maybe," interjected Tony. I didn't look at him.

"Wow, such a considerate mother. She'll be back from her orgy before noon." Now I did look at Tony. "*Maybe,*" I slurred directly at him.

"You better watch your mouth," Betty warned.

I ignored her threat and asked, "I thought you had to work tomorrow?"

"We're calling off."

I never got that. We were poor. We needed money real bad. We were often low on food or couldn't keep up on the electric or pay the rent. But if some guy asked her to crawl around in bed for a while she'd call off work and even risk losing her job. *And then blame it on the guy when she gets fired.*

"If Ken calls from the Big Boy, I'm sick in bed and asleep from the medicine."

I'd almost forgotten she'd managed to get the phone turned back on.

"If Ken calls, I'll tell him his waitress and his *dishwasher*—" I looked at Tony again"—are at a slumber party. I'm tired of lying to everybody for you."

"You'll do as you're fucking well told!" Her upper plate slipped, and she clamped her mouth shut to disguise it. "I'm so sick of you and your shit!"

Tony stood up slowly, and I didn't like the tilt of his posture. I found myself unsure if he might actually hit me or not. If he did hit me, what would I do? Worst was the thought of getting smacked by one of my mother's bed buddies in front of Tommy. I'd never hear the end of that.

Fortunately, a lot of things happened at once, preventing Tony from confronting me. Terry dumped his drink (he'd removed the plastic lid from the paper cup so he could blow bubbles in the soda with the straw) all over the table. The liquid made Tony jump away from the table, and he bumped the baby's chair, toppling Chip out of his seat. The baby started wailing while Betty ran to his aid. She slipped in the soda, and Tony had to catch her. Benji began lapping up the wet mess, and Terry was howling over his lost soda. All the while, Tommy and I just stood there gawking.

Tommy looked at me and shook his head. "White people is crazy."

I sure wasn't about to argue. Tony was bitching that they had to be going, and Betty was trying to calm the baby, who was even more upset and reaching for me now that she was clutching on him.

"Everything's cool," Tommy told my mother. "I'll just stay over here tonight, if that's okay with you?"

Betty seized on the opportunity to be rid of her children and get out of here with Tony still halfway sane. "That would be great," she told Tommy as I took the baby from her. She smiled, relieved, and Tommy acted like he was just happy to help out. I knew he had some other motive behind his offer. Tommy never stayed in at night.

"Shut up, you're not hurt," I told the baby after making sure he wasn't. He did, and I set him down and told him to go in the living room. "You shut up, too," I told Terry, snatching him out of his seat and sending him after Chip. "Go find something on TV."

"You're not the boss of me," he proclaimed with his best air of belligerence.

I gave him my best I'm-going-to-kick-your-ass smile. "Tell me that in five minutes." It finally soaked in that his mommy was going to be leaving him, and Terry opened his mouth and began howling anew.

I was suddenly sick of the sight of Betty and her Dago. "Just go. I'll clean this up."

My mother handed me the filthy dishtowel she'd been about to sop up the soda with and went into the living room to find her purse. Terry trailed after, begging her not to go. Tony nudged Benji out of his way with the tip of his boot, earning a low, throaty growl from my mutt. Tony brought his foot back as if he meant to kick my dog again, but I stepped in front of him, denying him the opportunity.

Tony grinned and lowered his foot, but then he poked me in the chest with his thumb. I tried not to act like it hurt, but it did. He moved in so close I could smell the grease in his hair and see the pores on his nose.

"You and me are going to have a little talk real soon," he promised. "Capisce?"

"I'm Donny, he's capisce," I said before I'd really thought about it, jabbing a finger behind me where Tommy still stood.

"Hey, what's a capisce?" Tommy asked me.

"It's the Italian word for understand," Tony told him.

"You're Italian?" I asked him. Benji was actually snarling. Tony was really pushing his luck. "I thought you were Puerto Rican."

187

That really pissed him off, but before he could reply, Betty came back, still trying to get away from Terry, who was clawing at her leg like a drowning rat. "Donny, hold him until I'm gone," she ordered me. "Come on, let's go," she told Tony, while I pried my brother's fingers out of her flesh. Tony hesitated, but followed her to the door after another hateful glare for me.

"What a dick," Tommy said just before Tony shut our back door.

Stupid, stupid, stupid, stupid! I kept calling myself. Every instinct I'd ever counted on was bellowing alarms. I hadn't wanted to leave my brothers alone, even though they were asleep and my dog was with them. As smart as he was, Benji was just a dog. He couldn't open doors or pick up the phone. What if there was a fire? What if Betty and Tony had a fight and she came home early? That was a real possibility. If she did, I was in for it, and she'd come at me with some kind of weapon I wouldn't be able to deflect or dodge.

But Tommy wouldn't let up. He kept on promising me that we'd be back in no less than an hour, probably only thirty minutes, even though he wouldn't tell me what we were going to be doing so late and so quickly that was so fucking secret and important. I'd tried to bribe him with the offer of a pizza and Pepsi, but not even food could reduce his insistence. *You never tell Tommy no,* Rupe whispered quietly within my head.

"Where are we going?" I asked Tommy.

My words, although uttered quietly, sounded eerie and loud in the stillness. It was about an hour after midnight. The only signs of life were the headlights of passing cars, and even those were infrequent.

"Will you tell me what we're doing now?"

Tommy grinned, the glint of his teeth and the whites of his eyes floating in the darkness. "Just wait. We're almost there."

As we turned into the apartment complex off the railroad tracks, I felt a strong sensation of foreboding. The apartments had a name, but the dilapidated sign at the entrance was so faded and the paint peeling so badly I couldn't make it out in the gloom and didn't remember what was written on it. Most kids I knew just called this dump the projects, since everyone who lived here was on welfare and usually even poorer than those of us living out in the neighborhood.

All the streetlights in the parking lot were busted, having long ago fallen victim to bored kids with too many cheap rocks on hand. The parking lot wasn't but half full, and some of those cars didn't look to be running. Most of the residents rode the bus. I knew Tommy hadn't brought me here to look for anything of value in these cars. People here knew better than to leave anything worth much so accessible. It was difficult enough to keep real thieves out of your damn house, much less a car.

Tommy ducked between two of the buildings and slowed his pace, creeping along quietly but not acting too concerned. I followed his example and kept my mouth shut, even though I was about ready to burst with aggravation. At the corner he told me to stay put for a moment and slipped off, but he was back real quick, and appeared pleased. He motioned for me to follow. I took a deep breath and did so, creeping around the corner and toward an open sliding door with the sounds of a television blaring.

Once we were standing on the cracked concrete patio outside the door, Tommy moved aside and pointed, letting me know he wanted me to peek inside. There was no porch light, so we stood in relative darkness, but I was still afraid to plunge my face into the dim glow emanating from within the apartment. Tommy grinned and gave me a shove. I braced my nerve and craned my head around to see through the screen.

There was an enormous black man with his back to us, sleeping on a couch with his feet curled up. His body was longer than his makeshift bed. He wore only shorts, and the light of the TV reflected off the rolls of his bare back. He was snoring so loudly I could hear his every breath over the sounds of some old movie rolling along on the screen.

I carefully moved away and turned to Tommy. "So?" I whispered.

He shook his head and rolled his eyes. "Look on the coffee table, moron," he whispered back, shoving me again toward the opening.

I did as he ordered. Sitting there was a wallet with a watch draped over it, and a small pile of loose change. Everything fell into place as soon as I saw the wallet. Tommy must have discovered this dude's sleeping habits some time back and had been waiting for the right time to try and rip him off. These apartments were supposed to be air conditioned, but even if your unit worked, electricity cost money. Leaving the door cracked to allow the cooler night air in was cheaper than running the AC.

The only thing I was yet unclear on was why Tommy needed me. I asked him about that. "You'll see," was all he whispered.

What I saw that night wasn't the friend I'd known the past school year. The person I watched breaking into this guy's home was a future career criminal, laying groundwork for more serious crimes down the road.

Tommy clicked open his knife. He slit the screen enough so that he could reach in and unlock the latch, and then carefully slid the door open. After that he tried to open the inner glass door more, but it wouldn't budge.

My heart fluttered—I realized the opening wasn't wide enough for a man to get inside. *Or a kid as big as Tommy.* It would be a tight fit, but there was probably just enough room to allow a scrawny little guy like me to wriggle through. That was why I was here. I was Tommy's inside man. He was going to make me go in there and risk my neck just to grab a wallet that might not have more than a few bucks inside it.

You never tell Tommy no.

"No way!" I hissed as Tommy came back and put away his knife.

I started to leave, but he grabbed me by the arm and jerked me back. "Hey! I already opened the fucking door. You're wasting time. Slip in there and grab that shit, and we'll be out of here so fast this'll just be a funny memory we laugh about in the morning."

"Fuck that! I could get killed in there for a wallet that may not have any money in it at all." Tommy let me jerk my arm free. "You want that shit so bad, you go in and get it."

He patted his belly and grinned. "I won't fit." He grinned wider. "But you will. C'mon, man, don't let me down. I'll be right out here if you need me, and even if there's no money in the wallet, I know that's a nice-ass watch."

"Jesus, Tommy... I don't know."

You're just whining now. I was stalling, hoping for some kind of miracle. I would have been grateful if some old bat had noticed us prowling around and screamed out her window, just to get the hell away from here and Tommy's insane plan. But he was sending me in there, and we both knew it. There was no way around it.

"Man, if that dude wakes up...?"

"What's his fat ass going to do?" he asked, laughing softly. I couldn't believe how calmly he was acting, how sure of himself about something this dangerous. *What's he got to worry about? He's not going inside.*

"Hurry up. Let's get out of here. Don't forget your brothers are home alone."

I let him nudge me toward the opening, pausing to take a peek inside before actually sticking any part of my body into another person's home. Chubby was still snoring and still had his back to me.

Please don't fit, I prayed, but I knew I would. The sliding door hardly moved as I squirmed through. My head was the only thing that was snug, my ears brushing both sides of the opening before I was all the way inside. The difference between shoplifting from a store or lifting a few bucks from your parents, and standing in a home you don't live in with the intention of stealing while a big black dude sleeps just a few feet away…? The difference felt as wide as going from kissing your homely sister to showering with the Dallas Cowboy cheerleaders.

I had never been so alive, so aware of my surroundings. I wanted to check and make sure Tommy was still at the door, but I couldn't take my eyes off that man's back. I could feel every muscle in my skinny legs as I took my first step. I could feel the scrunch of the carpet beneath the soles of my sneakers. The hair on my arms and neck stood up between every breath and guttural snore that dude let loose.

By my next step, I could hear the humming of the picture tube in that television. The movie paused for a commercial, and I didn't move an inch until there was noise in the room again. If that big sucker would have rolled over or stretched, coughed or even scratched his ass, I would have bolted like a racehorse from the starting gate. He never moved, though. He just laid there while some stranger was but one more step away from taking his shit right out from under his nose. Or, more appropriately, from behind his back.

I could feel the blood moving in my veins, and hear the pounding of my pulse in my ears. Every sound was magnified. I felt the slightest sway of the floor beneath me, the cooler air wafting through the opening behind me caressing the back of my neck. My muscles ached with the need for flight, just waiting for any excuse to bolt for freedom. I could even hear my joints working as I moved, poised and tense, resting on nothing but the balls of my feet.

I was beginning to think this wasn't going to be so bad, although I already knew I was never going to do something even remotely like this again. *You never tell Tommy no.* I made a mental note reminding myself to punch Rupe square in the nose the next time I saw him.

I was there. The coffee table was right under me, the snoring dude so close I could feel the reverberations of his deep breathing on my goose-pimpled skin.

My hand moved toward the wallet and watch, but I caught movement out of the corner of my eye and froze, looking up but not daring to move my skull. Down a short hallway was a mirror at the base of a stairway. Reflected in that mirror was a black woman in a nightgown with some kind of cap covering the top of her head, eyes so wide they looked like light bulbs. She was clutching her chest with both hands and staring at me while I stared at her, as frozen in place as I was.

But her lungs weren't frozen. "Jerome!" she screamed.

Jerome flipped over, and we shared a moment—a skinny scared-shitless white boy coming face-to-face with a bloated and sleepy Negro. His eyes focused on me. He wasn't happy, but I already knew I wasn't a favorite cousin and was leaving a hell of a lot more quickly than I'd arrived.

That sliding door shuddered when I hit it. I felt the heavy glass move as I collided with the frame at the wrong angle, and I'm pretty sure it came off its track as I squirmed through. Tommy was nowhere to be seen. As I tasted the night air and freedom, just preparing to take my first full step toward home, a strong black hand clutched at my hair. I ducked and twisted as his fingers tore at my mane, but he didn't get a grip and I was gone. I've never thought about it before now, but the fact that my hair was always dirty and greasy might have saved my young life.

If I hadn't broken that door, my pursuer surely did. I heard him grunt and glass shatter as the door fell and smacked against the concrete. I was running so fast my feet weren't touching the ground. By the time I made the street I thought I was free and clear. I'd never moved faster, and the dude trying to chase me was as flabby as a walrus in the zoo.

Only some unnamed football intuition saved me. That or there really is some saint who watches out for stupid children. I heard the slap of his bare feet on the pavement—otherwise, he'd have snared me. Chubby's hand managed to get a grip on my hair this time, but I twisted and shoved at the same instant, just like I'd shed tackles in a zillion football games, and his own body weight and momentum carried him past me.

We played cat-and-mouse for another two blocks, me dodging around parked cars and waiting for a chance to get clear, him breathing heavier and heavier, staring at me with his eyes bugging like Mama's pug and growling and cursing. He promised all sorts of nasty ends to my life. He was going to kill me *and* my family *and* all my friends. After we'd played this game for two blocks, he was so incensed he was going to kill all white people just to be sure anybody who might be related to me paid for my transgression.

I had to give him credit: heavy as he was, the dude was agile. If he'd been twenty pounds lighter or a few years younger, I probably wouldn't be alive, and he would have been sent to prison for life. "I'm gonna get your white ass," he promised around ragged breaths, staring at me over the hood of a car. I didn't respond, only ran about a half block to another car, measuring his stamina. He didn't have much left in his tank. His rage had faded, and with it his surge of adrenaline.

I decided it was time, and I turned and bolted down the alley behind me, meaning to run all out until he broke and gave up. For just a second I thought I might have gambled too soon, as he gave chase for about a hundred yards, his feet smacking the ground and his grunts loud. But he finally stopped. I looked back one last time before turning a corner. He was standing there, his chest heaving while he rested with his hands on his knees, glaring at me. "You one fast little motherfucker," he admitted just before I was gone.

I didn't stop running until I reached home. Once there, I locked all the doors and checked on my brothers while Benji kept sniffing at me, trying to understand what I was afraid of. I had sweat dripping out of my hair and my T-shirt was soaked, but I collapsed onto our sofa and tried to collect myself, waiting on Tommy to show up. I was going to give him hell for leaving me behind after forcing me to go in that apartment.

You never tell Tommy no, Rupe said in my head for the last time. But his warning now sounded diffident and unsure. "Watch me," I told Rupe. And I meant it.

CHAPTER 14

Betty came home before noon, but not noon the next day. Ruby dragged her back the day after. My brothers and I stood and watched as she practically carried Betty into our living room and dropped her in our only comfortable chair. My mother looked at us with little comprehension, barely able to keep her eyes open. Ruby didn't look a whole hell of a lot better. Her spandex pants were ripped in the butt, her hair looked like a rat's nest, and she didn't have any shoes on.

"She drunk?" I asked Ruby before she could get away. Betty wasn't a big drinker, although she was known to get sloppy a time or two.

"Huh?" Ruby asked. I think she just realized we were standing there, not having noticed we'd been watching her haul our mother in. "Hey, Donny."

I shook my head and sighed. "Hey."

Ruby and Betty both began rubbing at their temples at the same time, as if they were sharing a pain. "You take care of her, okay? I got to go." And she did, stumbling out the door and waddling down the steps. I heard her get in her car and putter away, wondering how she was able to drive when she could barely walk.

Moving closer, I bent down and took a good look at my mother's unfocused eyes, getting a whiff of her breath at the same time. I smelled a little trace of alcohol mingled with the heavy odor of vomit. She wasn't drunk, but she was still pretty high. Betty didn't like needles. Her drug of choice was pills, usually Valium. I was pretty sure that was what she was floating around on now.

"Get out of my face," she slurred. She pushed weakly at me, but I'd already stepped back, and her hand fell helplessly into her lap. She knew who I was, though. "Help me get upstairs."

There were a lot of things I wanted to say. Rage had been building inside me for two days—really, it had been building for years. Now it screamed to be let loose. I wanted to ask her how she could live like this. How she could leave her children alone while she ran around letting men use her. How she could keep making the same mistakes over and over again, never learning, never seeing. But I was too tired, and she was too fucked-up to argue anyway.

Her blouse was buttoned askew, with one of the buttons in the middle completely missing. She'd lost her bra. Her hair hung in disarray and her skirt was stained by what smelled like beer. She'd managed to wear her shoes home, but her nylons were ripped and one of them had fallen down around her ankle. I didn't want to look at her. I didn't want to talk to her. And I sure didn't want to touch her.

"Where you going?" she asked me as I headed for the door.

Her upper plate collapsed on every word. I was surprised she'd managed to bring her teeth home. Terry was crying for her. The baby was crying for me. I had to get away. I just couldn't stay in the same house with her.

"Did you hear me tell you to help me upstairs?"

At least her anger was waking her up, clearing her head a bit. "I'm not touching you. Who knows what you've got all over you. You smell like shit." She was yelling something else and starting to cry as I slammed the door behind me.

Rupe was at some shindig down around Cincinnati, so I went looking for Tommy, even though we'd been fighting a little about the other night. My buddy saw more humor in my near-death experience than I did, and he didn't yet believe me when I told him I was through stealing. (That is, I was through stealing in situations that meant risking my neck.)

I found Tommy at Candy's. He nodded at me and waved me over. It normally cost per hour to shoot in here, but I wasn't sure what the rate was. Candy let us shoot for free if there were tables open. I was always careful with my stick and never tried any stupid trick shots or hit the balls too hard, not wanting to risk Candy's wrath. When Candy scowled, I felt like an M&M without its protective candy-coated shell. He'd eat you if he wanted to, and there was nothing you could do to stop him.

The pool hall was one of my favorite places. I loved the low-hanging dim lights and the glowing green felt of the tables. I could sit and watch the guys who were really good play for hours, and I was a pretty fair imitation of them when I chalked my cue and called my shots. I wasn't as good as I would one day be at this particular game, but I was well on my way to being above average.

"Side," I told Tommy, forming my bridge with my hand and extended thumb.

Tommy wasn't very good at forming a bridge. He always used his knuckles. He also couldn't hit bank shots and usually missed if there was too much green between the ball he was aiming for and the cue ball he was lining up. I almost always beat him at pool, even though he was in here way more than I was. Candy's place was a black hangout. Only a few white guys came to shoot in the weekend tournaments or play in the high stakes poker games in the back room.

I sank the purple four ball in the side and lined up on the yellow one ball for the far corner. "Corner," I said, cool as hell.

"Fuck you," Tommy grumbled through the cloud of smoke obscuring our vision beneath the light.

He moved over to the corner I was aiming for and leered at me, the cigarette hanging off his lip adding to the smog, hoping his childish antics might make me miss my shot.

"No—" I struck the cue ball cleanly, and it clicked off the one, sending it sharply off the table "—fuck *you*." The ivory cue ball bounced off the rail and rolled slowly out to the middle of the table, leaving me an easy shot at the eight ball on the opposite side and giving me another game. "Side," I told Tommy as I moved around to take my final shot.

"*Side,*" Tommy said, imitating me as he swept the eight ball off the table, robbing me of the thrill of actually winning. He knew I hated when he did that. "I'll rack 'em up. That's three games for you and one for me." Actually, I'd won four, but I wasn't going to piss him off by arguing. I was playing pool for free because he worked for Candy, and I was away from Betty. Life was pretty good. "You can't keep getting so lucky."

"That white boy gonna beat you all night, Washington," Irving told my friend, drifting up to our table like a specter out of the smoke. *Okay, maybe life's not so good.* "Why you bringing that honky in here, anyhow? Ain't you learned shit yet?"

Irving scared me. Everyone knew he carried a razor. He'd done time in juvie for slicing some dude up a year or so back. I thought of Irving himself as a sort of human razor. His ebony skin was stretched taut over the sharp features of his face, and his well-over-six-foot frame was all angles and length. His wide, round eyes constantly darted back and forth, looking for anything he might use as an excuse to get pissed off. I'd never said a single word to Irving, and I fully intended to continue that wise habit through tonight.

I'd only seen Irving lose it once. He'd been playing basketball at the park this summer, and the game had gotten pretty intense. Irving was fast and tall, and a lot of the older guys said he could've played ball in college, if he had been smart enough to stay in school and out of jail. Some guy who wasn't from the neighborhood had fouled Irving pretty hard, and he shoved the dude. When the unknowing dude shoved Irving back, that notorious straight razor had appeared from somewhere in his shorts. Irving punked the guy so bad, just about everybody felt sorry for him, although retarded Louie kept bouncing around, yelling, *Cut him! Cut him!*

"Donny's all right," Tommy told Irving, not looking up from the table.

Irving's long arm snaked out of the smoke and took the eight ball out of the rack Tommy was putting together. "He ain't black as this ball, motherfucker, he ain't *all right*."

Tommy took the ball Irving was shoving under his nose and dropped it among the others in the rack. "Candy said it was cool he play in here," Tommy told Irving, hoping that fact would send him on his way.

Irving leaned in and put his face closer to Tommy's. "I ain't talking to Candy, little nigger. I'm talking to *you*."

Tommy spread out his hands and stepped back. Some of the guys at the nearer tables were watching. I suddenly wanted to be anywhere else but here. "Okay, Irving, talk. Tell me what's up."

"I *am* telling you, bitch. Problem is you don't fuckin' listen." Irving pointed at me, his long fingers accusing me of sins. "He a white dude, nigger. And one day he gonna be a bigger white dude. White is white." Irving leaned in again, still pushing up on Tommy, invading his space. "And white is all the same. You best believe that."

Before Tommy could say anything else, the voice of God resonated throughout the dim pool hall, rumbling the walls and making the balls tremble. "Irving," was all God said. One word, uttered quietly but with supreme authority. God was a rotund black dude in a silk shirt and dark sunglasses. "You a preacher now, nigger?" Candy asked.

Irving melted into the smoke as quickly as he'd appeared. "Who's winning?" Candy asked.

As tall as Irving was, Candy was taller, and he was bigger than Chick the biker. I'd once heard a man at Pops' describe Candy as blacker than hell on

Halloween, and twice as mean as Satan. He was sweating down his back and under his arms, the thin shirt clinging to his skin, and his pants were tight against his massive thighs.

"He is," Tommy admitted.

"I seen you shoot pretty good," Candy told me, turning those shades toward me and revealing his gold teeth when he smiled. *Don't stare at the teeth. Don't stare at the teeth.* You couldn't see Candy's eyes behind those dark glasses, and that made everyone uneasy. I was sure Candy knew full well the effect his murky and obscured gaze had on others. "You working with Tommy?"

"A little," I squeaked. Now I knew how a mouse felt trapped by a cat. I didn't like being the mouse.

"You boys should come by and rap with me before school starts. Could be we might work something out that makes us all happy 'bout getting up in the morning."

Tommy nodded for both of us. "We'll be here."

Those shades turned in the direction Irving had slid away. "Let me know if that nigger come messin' 'round you again." Candy turned to leave. Before he left he placed a hand on Tommy's shoulder, the way a father might before heading off to work. "Don't feel too bad. You got a white dude whipping on you out here, and I got one whipping on me back there. But at least your whipping ain't costing you nothin'. Rather lose a friendly game to a dude I run with than money to some mother I hates any night."

After a last smile for us both, Candy sauntered away, moving with more grace than a man his size should possess. He reminded me of the way a lion strolled along in Africa like I'd seen on TV, so sure of himself and concerned about nothing and nobody. Like a king. It was then I spotted the handle of the pistol he had tucked along the small of his back.

I was so rattled I let Tommy win the next game. He kept going on about how Candy was going to hook us up with so many great ways to make money and how lucky I was to be allowed to deal with him. Tommy crowed that Candy must like me if I was invited into the back room, since he didn't like many white people. Problem was, I didn't feel lucky. I was petrified. The last thing I needed was for Candy the Overlord of Darkness and Irving the Razor to have a vendetta against my scrawny ass.

Fortunately, Tommy had something else going on, and I headed for home, my head full of dreadful possibilities. I'd never felt I had much control over what happened to me. It felt like I was losing what fragile grip I did have on tomorrow more and more with the passing of each day. I needed help. I needed someone to talk to. I was wondering if Dave might not be a good source for advice as I made it home, barely taking notice of Tony's Caddy parked out back.

That was a mistake. That was a *big* mistake. If I hadn't been so wrapped up in my thoughts, I would have caught on before even going in the house, but my dog and my brothers were in there, so I'd have fallen into Tony's trap anyway. The first thing I heard was Dr. Hook crooning about being on the cover of *Rolling Stone*. That record was supposed to be tucked safely away behind my desk. I bolted up the stairs straight from the kitchen door, panicked about the money I had hidden there as well.

My room was in a shambles. My comics and baseball cards were strewn all around my mattress and floor, and my desk was pulled out away from the wall. The money was gone, all fifty-four dollars of it. Even the sock full of nickels was gone. My blood was already boiling when I realized my dog hadn't come to greet me. He was lying in the corner of my room, but he wasn't as excited to see me as he usually was.

When I touched him he whimpered, and when I tried to make him stand he whined and sat down again, refusing to move. I picked him up, and he cried. I sat him on my mattress, and he managed to get off again, limping severely.

Something in me snapped.

This was my first real rage, and the first signs of an ugly temper I would have to deal with for many years to follow. I ran back down those stairs intent on...?

What I intended, I wasn't sure. If my child's mind had taken the time to consider my man-sized rage, I might have saved myself some trauma.

Tony was lying in wait for me. Dr. Hook was still wailing away when I ran into the living room. My mother and brothers were huddled on the couch, Terry wide-eyed and frightened and the baby sobbing; Tony was standing boldly next to the front door, blocking my avenue of exit. His arms were crossed over another white T-shirt, and he was swaying slightly, glaring at me.

"My dog's limping, you motherfucker!"

Tony's face hardened. He had that stiff tilt to his posture again. He stepped closer to me and said, "That's because I kicked the little shit all the way down the stairs."

I looked to my mother. "Where the fuck were you?" Betty was aware of her surroundings but still not altogether there. She couldn't meet my gaze, and turned her face away.

Tony jabbed me in the chest with his thumb knuckle again. This time I couldn't pretend it didn't hurt. "You got me fired, you little asshole," he reminded me.

Oops. I'd forgotten that their boss had called yesterday. I'd also forgotten that I'd told him they were off at some orgy getting stoned and dancing around naked. It had been real funny at the time. It wasn't quite as funny at the moment. Tony's breath reeked of alcohol, and his eyes were glassy but intense. He'd been fuming, and building up a real hard-on for me. I was thinking about running for it, but then I remembered my money and got angry again.

And brave. "You're going to give me back my money."

That made him grin. "You think so?" He did the thumb thing again, knocking me back a little. "You stole that money from your mother. I'm taking it back. You want it?" He knuckled me again, harder than before. "Why don't you come get it?"

"I didn't steal anything from her!"

He grabbed my lower jaw and squeezed. I tried to act tough and left it there, as if he couldn't hurt or frighten me. But he was doing a pretty good job on both counts. "Well, you stole it from somebody. Now I'm taking it from you. Consider it a down payment for fucking with me."

"Take it easy, Tony," my mother managed to murmur.

"Shut the fuck up!" he snapped at her. "Your mouthy little bastard got me fucking fired! He could have got you fired, too!"

My mouth has gotten me in real trouble many times over the years. This was just the first time. I shook my head out of his grasp and said, "My, Anthony, waitresses must be harder to replace than *dishwashers.*"

I saw it coming. I watched Tony cock that fist and reach back, but for some reason I couldn't move. None of Betty's studs had ever really hit me before. I'd been slapped hard once or twice, but never really cold-cocked a good one like Tony was going for. I watched that fist coming and stood there like I was deaf, dumb, and blind.

When he hit me it felt like the whole world exploded. Bright, hot light shot through my brain, and my head bounced off the door frame behind me with a loud *crack!* I don't remember hitting the floor, but I wasn't out for very long. When I came to my mother and brothers were all screaming, and I wiped blood out of my eyes just in time to see Betty get whacked right across the face, sending her scrambling back to the relative safety of the couch.

I stared at the red on my hands in disbelief while the cut above my eye continued to gush. Tony looked as dazed as I felt. I think all the blood running down the front of my face and shirt scared him more than it did me. I tried to get up, wanting to run away, but Tony grabbed my arm. I slipped in my own blood and fell while trying to jerk free of him.

"We're going upstairs to clean you up," he told me.

"The fuck we are!" I screamed.

I tried to kick at him, but he was too strong. He grabbed a handful of my bloody hair and leaned in close, his ugly face contorted in a drunken rage. "I'll fucking smack you again," he promised. "Now get your little ass up."

And then Benji bit his arm and lunged at his face, his teeth just barely missing giving the Dago a scar he'd carry the rest of his life. Tony lifted his hands to ward off my dog and fell backwards. I had all my senses again, and I was on my feet and heading for the back door in a flash. To his credit, Tony was only a step behind me, but I flipped a kitchen chair into his way. The drunken bastard tripped over it and went sliding across the dirty linoleum, crashing into the broken kitchen radiator.

He'd locked the door, but I had it open and was off the steps and across the yard before I saw the silhouette of his shadow in the doorway. He was stupid enough to come after me. Dusk had fallen on this summer day. I would use the gloom and shadows to full advantage. I took a glance over my shoulder and slowed down a bit. My dog was limping after me. Tony was stumbling along between me and Benji, but weaving erratically and hardly able to keep his balance. The Dago was no longer a threat now that we were out in the open.

And his drunken ass was mine.

I let him catch up and then took off along the row of backyards off the alley running the length of our block. Tony followed, just as I'd hoped. I knew my neighborhood pretty well, as most kids would. There wasn't an abandoned house I hadn't explored or a vacant lot I hadn't played baseball in. There wasn't a trash dump I hadn't purveyed for anything of value.

And I knew where every torn down wire fence was, just lying in wait to trip up anyone stumbling along and chasing me.

I ran that asshole right across those fences. He somehow made it over the first one, and that really pissed me off. But his encounter with the second row of rusty loose wire was a thing of pure beauty. His boot got caught in the fence and stopped him cold. I watched as Tony grunted in surprise and went over face first, his arms flailing and his skinny body twisting around. When he hit the ground I felt it in the soles of my feet, and his head sounded like a coconut bouncing off stone when it smashed into the packed earth of that dirt yard.

As he struggled to rise I was pleased to find that I wasn't the only one bleeding now. But Tony was way over the edge. He was growling and cursing in Italian. His eyes were rolling, almost bulging out of his face as he tried to wipe off the dirt and blood so that he might locate me again. He fell once more while getting himself untangled, and that made him howl like a madman. The lady who lived near the fence was peeking out her back door, her hands covering her mouth in dismay.

I wasn't taking any more chances. I ran out into the alley, scooped up my struggling dog, and ran for all I was worth. As I crossed my street, I noticed Mrs. Lorret watching me from her porch. She gasped at the sight of me. I must have looked a mess, with blood all over my face and chest, clutching my dog. I wanted to tell her I was okay, but I could hear Tony moving behind me and couldn't risk him getting his enraged hands on me again.

Three blocks later I realized I had no place to run, no safe haven in mind. I thought about going to Candy's and looking for Tommy, knowing he'd put me up for the night. But Betty would tell Tony where he lived. She'd expect me to go there. I didn't even want to risk going to Candy's. *No, go ahead, I'm sure they wouldn't mind if your mommy sent the police into that den of thieves looking for you.* My head was hurting—especially the back of it—but my brain still worked. I wasn't sending even a hint of trouble anywhere near Candy.

By the time I reached the truck stop by the highway entrance ramp, I realized I was hoping to find Leon. He might have been just a dim slob of an overweight truck driver and mechanic, but he was a *big* dim slob of an overweight truck driver and mechanic. And Leon hadn't been half bad most of the time. It was a long shot, but it was all I had. *Jesus, how low is that?* I had no reason to believe Leon would come to my rescue, or assist me in any way, but he was my only hope.

I didn't see his El Camino or his rig in the expansive parking lot behind the truck stop. I peeked inside anyway. Leon wasn't there. I turned away from the broad window, feeling woozy. My head was throbbing, and my arms were tired from carrying my dog, who by now felt like he weighed three times what he actually did. The crusted blood around my eye was drying, and I couldn't pick at it without risking dropping Benji, so I sat down on the bottom of the steps, meaning only to rest a minute or two.

I heard the clanking of two paper bags full of cans being set down beside me. "Jesus, kid, every time I see you, you're bleeding or in trouble," a familiar voice said from somewhere above me. I knew that man's voice, but I couldn't place it. I squinted up with my clear eye at the face swimming in the glow of the truck stop's neon lights, trying to recognize the speaker.

"Who did this?" he asked, kneeling down. It was Nicky the biker, with another dude I didn't recognize. I felt him lightly touching my forehead above the cut eye. "You're going to need a couple of stitches there, pal." I didn't say anything. I felt a little sick. He asked again, "Hey, who did this?"

"Tony." I wanted to cry. But I wasn't going to.

"Tony a friend of yours?"

The guy behind Nicky laughed, but not in an unfriendly way. Benji tried to move down a step closer to Nicky and whimpered, laboring to descend just the one step. The other dude stopped laughing.

"Easy, boy," Nicky told Benji, extending the back of his hand so my dog could sniff at him, trying to show my mutt he meant no harm.

"My mom's boyfriend." My voice sounded funny. "For now." I decided to get to my feet, but I was a little wobbly. "He kicked my dog," I said, as if that would explain everything.

Nicky put a hand on my shoulder to steady me. "Why don't you come with us?" he asked me. "I know just the person to fix you up."

I went along where he led me, barely aware that he'd carefully picked up my dog, and dimly surprised that Benji was allowing some stranger to carry him. Both of us were deposited into the back seat of a car, and I think I dozed off as we drove the blocks in between the truck stop and the bikers' hangout. All I really remembered about the ride was hearing "Witchy Woman" on the radio during the trip, and that the dude driving drove fast and took corners real hard.

We parked on the street in front of the house instead of in the back where the bikes usually were. I told Nicky I could carry my dog, but he kept an easy hand on my shoulder as we climbed the steps from the walk to the porch. Music blared from the house. It sounded like two stereos were competing to be heard over one another as we entered, and I found myself bathed in a slowly revolving black light, with dark purple shadows floating all over the walls and ceiling.

"About fucking time!" Chick boomed, reaching into one of the bags the other dude was carrying and ripping out a six-pack. He was shirtless and wearing a ten-gallon cowboy hat like Hoss on *Bonanza*, only with fur. He popped the top on a can and guzzled it down, spilling beer along both sides of his mouth and dripping it all over the floor. "What's with the kid?"

"Don't worry about it," Nicky told him, guiding me past the brute and on toward the other end of the room.

The heavy, sweet aroma of grass hit me harder than Tony had as soon as we got in the house. There was a ceiling fan whirring away above me, but I was sure there was reefer being pumped into the building by some kind of machine. A girl who didn't look old enough to be out of high school looked up from some kind of glass bong on a coffee table and waved at me as Nicky steered me past her. She had dark glossy hair that shimmered in the black light when her head moved. One of the bikers from the other day was asleep in a chair behind her.

"Fuck that, Nick!" Chick belched so loud it momentarily dwarfed the music. He was really drunk. "This is my house, and I'll worry over who comes in it if I want!"

He was following us as we went into a kitchen that was even worse off than Betty's. There were bags of trash and beer cans everywhere. I almost slipped on an empty wine bottle, and Nicky kicked it out of the way so hard it broke against the wall. He placed me in a chair and set the bags he was carrying on a countertop covered with empty pizza boxes.

"You hear me, Nick?" Chick asked, towering over my chair.

"Yeah, I hear you," Nicky said, moving over to the sink and looking under it for something. "Where's that peroxide we used on Jerry's new tattoo last week?" Nicky had to talk loud to be heard over the music. Benji was trembling in my lap; it took me a moment to realize it was *me* who was shaking, and not my dog. "Joey, go upstairs and get Mandy for me. Tell her to get her ass down here right away."

"Hey, ain't that the fucking kid and the little dog from the other day?" Chick asked, leveling a swaying finger in my general direction.

Joey seemed relieved to be getting away from Chick and Nicky's continuing disagreement. He ducked under Chick's extended hairy arm and slipped out of the room.

"I'm talking to you, Nick!"

I'd finally figured out what was going on. Chick was a cowboy, and the music down here was Johnny Cash. Johnny was currently wailing "Walk the Line," while somebody upstairs was cranking "Mother's Little Helper" by The Stones. We'd intruded upon some kind of country versus rock battle. The music war wasn't doing a thing to help the ringing between my ears, or the fuzziness behind my eyes.

"Nick, I'm talking—!"

Nicky was on top of Chick in two quick steps. Those bright blue eyes of his were narrowed and his otherwise good looks were marred by an ugly expression as he said directly into Chick's face, "I fucking hear your fat ass, motherfucker. And I *don't* want to hear it again. Now go turn that shit off before I throw your stereo right out the front door and you right behind it."

"Shit, Nicky," Chick whined. "I was just kidding around." He pointed to a cabinet above the sink before he left. "The peroxide's in there."

Shortly after Chick left, the country music abruptly ended, and the rock music clanging upstairs was far enough away that it didn't hurt so badly. Mick kept singing, mocking Chick as he came back into the kitchen. The big baby looked at me like I'd gotten him into trouble.

"Anything you need, Nicky?" he queried, subdued.

"How about a clean towel or dishrag?"

Chick went to a drawer and found Nicky one. He didn't look so drunk now, and the hat was gone. "What happened to the kid?"

"Mom's boyfriend," answered Nicky, bending down in front of me and soaking a tip of the rag with the peroxide. He gave me a smile that greatly relieved my quaking heart. I wanted no part of the Nicky who had just cowed Chick. "This might hurt a bit." It didn't hurt. It stung like hell. I did my best not to show the pain.

"Give me that," said a woman's voice.

And she *was* a woman. The prettiest woman I'd ever seen. She pushed Nicky out of the way and took the rag and the smelly bottle from him, stooping in front of me. She had long, straight blonde hair and green eyes, a summer-brown perfect face, and was wearing only a T-shirt with two big lips on the front of it. Without meaning to, I noticed the swell and sway of her breasts beneath that shirt while she dabbed at my eye.

"What happened to you, honey?"

Her touch was so much lighter and gentler than Nicky's that it hardly hurt while she worked, or maybe it was just that I no longer noticed the pain. She looked like she might have stepped out of one of Rupe's dad's *Playboy* magazines, except for the dreamy, unfocused daze in her eyes. I knew she'd asked me a question, but all I was aware of was the fact that her ample bosom was pressed up against my knees.

"Hey, if that boyfriend or his mom is after this kid, I can't have the cops here looking for him, Nicky," Chick whined as Joey came back in. Joey had long hair in a ponytail, and a scraggly beard. He rustled around in the bags and came out with a beer. "If we have any more trouble with the heat, my mother swears she's going to kick me out and sell this place."

"Calm down," Nicky told him. *Great, one of the baddest dudes I know is afraid of his mom.* I thought that was hilarious, but I wasn't going to tell Chick that. "I'll take him home once Mandy says he's okay and gets him put together."

"Do me a favor, hon. I want you to look at my fingertip and follow it with your eyes without moving your head. Okay?" I nodded, and she smiled. She had a smile that promised all kinds of things I didn't have a clue about. "Follow my finger. That's it. Good."

I'd have followed her anywhere. She seemed satisfied with my ability to watch her lovely finger, but when she touched the back of my head I winced, and she pulled my head gently forward and began probing my lump.

My head was right up against her chest. She smelled like reefer and suntan lotion with a hint of musky perfume. Her gentle hands were lightly running through my hair, and my nose was filled with the scent of her. I could have stayed there forever. I found myself wishing Tony had hit me five or six more times, so Mandy could have examined lumps and cuts all night.

"Well, nurse?" Nicky asked over her shoulder.

"It's not the cut over his eye that really worries me. He's got a lump back here that's really going to hurt by the morning. He could use a stitch or two, but I think the cut will lay closed if he doesn't mess with it much. Are you taking him home?" Nicky nodded. "Tell his mother to check on him during the night. If she has any trouble waking him, he should go to the hospital right away."

Chick leaned in and looked at my cut. "Shit. I've popped pimples worse than that," he told us.

"Do me another favor, honey?" I quickly nodded agreement. *Anything.* "Don't grow up to be a bloated, hairy, dumb alcoholic who eats out of the trash." She smiled, and I smiled back. I'm sure I would have smiled back no matter what she'd said. I'm also pretty sure I was getting a buzz just from breathing the air in Chick's house.

"At least I'm not named after a fucking stupid song," growled Chick.

"I'm two decades older than the song, Chick. Do the math." She stood up, but smiled at me again. "See what I mean, babe? Dumber than a buried rock."

She might not have been named after Barry's song, but as far as I was concerned she could have been the inspiration for it. I knew I would forever think of her, whenever I heard that tune.

"The dog's hurt, too," Nicky told her.

Mandy bent down and took my dog right out of my lap without hesitation. I started to warn her, but Benji let her lift him. She squatted down, placing him gently on the floor. Apparently, my mutt was as much in love as I was. I became further entranced as Mandy bent over right in front of me, revealing the most perfectly rounded and heart-shaped behind I'd ever beheld (my experiences in the beholding department were limited to women in tight jeans and Rupe's dad's collection, which I'd only perused twice) and just a peek of that special something more.

Nicky grinned and put a hand in front of my eyes. "Christ, Mandy, couldn't you throw on some shorts?"

Mandy blushed and tugged at her shirt, then giggled and sat down cross-legged next to my mutt. "You said be naked and high when you got back, killer." She puckered her lips and sent Nicky a kiss. "I keep telling you, you're the boss."

I swear I felt my heart lurch. She was the most beautiful woman in the world. I loved her looks and her sass, and because of that one brief glimpse of her I would forever be a butt man. Bess was my first real kiss, but Mandy was my first sexual experience. To quote my friend Tommy: I have just got to get me one of those!

Benji whimpered a little while she explored his rear leg. "I know. I know," she whispered. "Just a little more." He yelped, and she winced. "I think he dislocated his leg, but it's back in now. Probably sore as hell, though."

Mandy stood back up, being more careful with her shirt. (Much to my chagrin.) "I can't feel any fracture, but try to keep him off his feet for a few days," she told me. I nodded. "You guys are a couple of tough patients."

"I'm going to walk him home," Nicky told her.

They shared a long, knowing stare. "That must be one mean boyfriend," she said, but her eyes never left Nicky. "You want me to wait for you?"

Nicky was fingering that leather wristband again, but he leaned in close and gave the lovely Mandy a long, wet kiss. "Sure do," he told her, and then winked at me.

She grabbed his arm and prevented him from pulling away, glancing at me while I picked up my dog. "I would like that to be a promise," she insisted. I could hear real concern in her voice. *She's worried about Nicky going after Tony,* I realized.

"Hey, kid," Chick chimed in. "Wait 'til the bastard falls asleep and hit him with a sledgehammer. I've got a small one about your size around here somewhere."

"It's in the garage on the workbench, under the girlie calendar," I informed him. Chick raised his eyebrow, and I grinned sheepishly.

Mandy laughed. I was so pleased I'd caused that wonderful sound to come from her. "Is he *that* kid?" she asked Nicky. Nicky chortled and nodded. Chick didn't laugh at all. Mandy leaned in and stood up on her toes, hugging Nicky tightly. I couldn't help myself. I was blessed with another peek at the lower half of that glorious rear end. Nicky reached out and covered my eyes again while Mandy whispered, "You can't save the world, Nick. Promise?"

"Yeah, baby. I promise," he gave her before she let him go.

"What's going on in here?" the dark-haired girl asked, popping into the kitchen as Nicky and I started for the door.

Mandy leaned in close to me. Upstairs, Mick was bitching that he couldn't get any satisfaction while she gave me a little kiss just above my unmarred eye. "You take care, honey," she whispered.

I didn't like the pity that had crept into her voice. She touched Nicky on the shoulder and pointed upstairs, mouthing that she'd be waiting for him. I knew that if I'd been Nicky, I wouldn't be walking any brat home.

"Hey, kid," called Chick. I turned toward him and the room spun a little. I was definitely a little tipsy from the heavy air. "I wasn't going to kick your dog. You know that, right?" I nodded. Chick was feeling bad for sending me home. I was feeling bad because Mandy was gone. "You come on back when there's no heat on you, huh?"

"See ya, kid," Joey sent, wrapping his arms around the dark-haired girl and walking her out of the room.

Before we were out of the back yard, Johnny was walking another line, and Chick was yelling about something. "Want me to carry him?" Nicky asked. I told him I was all right. "What's his name?"

"Benji."

"After the movie?" I nodded. "Pretty good name, since he's so smart."

"Are you married to Mandy?"

Nicky chuckled softly in the darkness of the alley. "No. She goes to school at OSU and works at the hospital. She really is a nurse."

All I'd heard was no. I was real glad Mandy wasn't married. "Are you going to marry her?" I asked as we crossed the first street.

"I'm already married, kid, but my old lady split with my little girl last year." We walked in silence for about a half block, Nicky lost in his own thoughts. "My daughter's a couple years younger than you."

"Do you live with Chick?"

"Are you kidding?" He laughed. "I have a place south of here. I just hang out at Chick's on the weekend for… I just visit there, kid."

"For drugs and bikes and Mandy?"

"You ask a lot of questions, Donny." He remembered my name. That thrilled me. He chuckled again. "But, yeah. It's something like that." He rubbed the top of my head. "You liked Mandy, huh?" *What wasn't to like?* "Be careful with women, kid," he said more seriously. "Whoever said 'you can't live with 'em and you can't kill 'em' sure knew what he was talking about."

"Where do you work?"

"I make auto parts."

"Do you make good money?"

"Why? You thinking about dating me?"

I could tell I was asking too many questions, but couldn't resist one more; "Why do you wear that wrist band?"

"You ask too many fucking questions. How much further to your house?"

Realizing I'd pushed too much, I answered, "Not far."

We walked the rest of the way in silence. Nicky's boots crunching gravel and clacking off the pavement the only sound we shared until we were on my back walkway. I was pissed at myself for prying. Now that he was angry at me, I'd probably blown any chance I had of Nicky helping me with Tony. The lights were on, and Betty was moving around in the kitchen, but Tony's Caddy was gone. I was grateful when Nicky walked me up to my door and then followed me in.

"Where the hell have you been?" Betty said when I walked in. "Mrs. Lorret called the fucking police. Do you know—" Nicky came in and Betty said, "Oh." She touched her hair, looking like she'd just gotten caught standing outside naked in a crowd. Nicky smiled and flashed those baby blues, and that made Betty even worse. "Hello," she said in a small voice.

"How are you?" Nicky asked, reaching out and shaking her hand. "I'm Nick."

"W-well," Betty stuttered. "I'm Betty." Hearing her tell him her name actually stung me.

"I found Donny here and got him cleaned up."

"I hope he was no trouble," Betty cooed.

"*I hope he was no trouble,*" I mimicked her.

"Hey," Nicky smacked me lightly on top of my head. "Cut it."

"Sorry," I mumbled. I didn't mind Nicky correcting me. I wouldn't have minded Nicky correcting me all the time. It was too bad Betty looked like she did, when he had a girl like Mandy. My mother listened to my apology and stared at me like I was some kid she'd never met. "Where's Tony?" I asked her.

My question made Betty fidgety. She glanced at Nicky and said quickly, "He had to go."

I grinned. *Of course. He was worried about the cops and where I might have run to.* I was going to pay for that later, though.

"You need to keep an eye on him," Nicky instructed Betty. "I mean tonight. If you have any trouble waking him or if he acts crazier than normal, call a squad." Nicky tapped my head again. "But I'm pretty sure he's okay. That brain of his is working just fine, you ask me."

"I will," my mother promised. *Yeah, right.*

"I have to be going," Nicky said then. He paused before ducking out. "Maybe you can ask your boyfriend to take it easy on the kid?" Betty didn't say anything. "Let him know that sometimes what goes around might come back around, huh?" Betty nodded, wide-eyed. I didn't want Nicky to go, but he closed our kitchen door after a last nod for me.

I was on the landing heading upstairs, meaning to leave without speaking further to my mother. There was nothing to be gained with words. It was all the same shit, just repeated over and over again. It was late, and I wanted to rest.

But our door opened again. Nicky called after me, "Hey, Donny?"

I spun around, my voice cracking and hopeful. "Yeah?"

He held up his forearm and tapped that leather wristband. "My daughter made it for me. She burnt our names into it. The symbol is Japanese. It means forever." He gave me that nice grin before shutting the door again. Nicky had a great smile.

CHAPTER 15

"Reverse back to you," I told Rupe.

Of course, nobody noticed I'd thrown that yellow reverse card on a blue seven. It was a timing thing: when everyone was tossing cards real fast, you could get away with a move like that. Although it didn't look like I was going to win this hand, even with my cheating.

Rupe took a big swig of Pepsi, noisily gulping it down. "Uno!" he belched real loud, displaying the single card he had left. Bess made a face and told him he was gross while I applauded and Terry cackled.

Lynn grinned and sucked in air, then belched right back. "Good one." She didn't have Rupe's volume, but her burps were much easier to understand.

Rupe played after me, since I'd reversed the flow the last time around. I didn't have any draw cards to hit him with, so I changed a red four with a green four and hoped the color change might cause him a problem. He left us hanging while he repeatedly checked his card, acting like he was pondering a dilemma. I knew by the way he was hamming it up he was going out.

With a wide grin, he turned his card around and revealed a black wild, then flipped it arrogantly on the table. "I'm out again," he proclaimed. "And I saw you cheat, *Donald*," he added, wagging his finger and making a prune face like a teacher.

"Can I play?" Terry asked yet again.

"No," I snapped. I hated losing. I really hated losing to Rupe.

Terry sniffled like he was going to start crying. He was shirtless and had Doritos cheese all over his face, chest, and fingers. It was even in the curls of his hair. He stared up at me with those big brown eyes and asked, "Why?"

"Do you know how to play?"

He looked down, knowing I would send him away once he admitted he didn't know how to play the game. But then he grinned as he stumbled across an idea. "I could sit on your lap and play the cards you tell me to."

"No." He started to cry, hoping I'd melt like Betty always did. "Go in the other room and cry."

"Why are you so mean to him?" Lynn asked, butting in.

I could've given her about a thousand reasons, but none she hadn't heard before. The baby toddled into the kitchen gumming Doritos. He was a worse mess than Terry. Chip eyed our brother with mild curiosity, wondering what he was wailing about now. He lost interest quickly. He was used to Terry's fits. Everyone was used to Terry's fits.

"Okay, okay, he can sit on my lap and play the cards I tell him," I pretended to concede. Terry stopped crying like someone had thrown a switch. He reached up, expecting me to haul his little ass up, but I slapped him on the head and said, "Psych!"

He started blubbering anew, and louder than before. Everyone looked at me like I wasn't funny. Even Rupe seemed to be on their side. But I didn't care. "Come here, baby," Lynn said to him, reaching out to scoop him up. "You can sit with me and play my cards."

Rupe piled up all the cards we'd thrown into the center of the table. "He's not touching my cards with those sticky hands," he told Lynn. She cast him that look we knew usually meant you had a good punch coming, then sighed and got up to take my brother over to the sink to clean him up. Rupe shuffled half the deck, and I crunched the rest.

Mama Z. had given the girls money, and they'd bought pizza and Pepsi, and a big bag of both plain and barbecue chips, along with the Doritos my brothers were half eating and half wearing. Because they'd sprung for the food, Bess and Lynn had insisted we play Uno, while Rupe and I'd wanted to set up a game of Risk. Uno was okay, but I always got bored with it pretty quick. Risk gave me the opportunity to swarm all over the world as the mongrel horde, slaying anyone who dare oppose me.

Bess squealed a little as she picked up her cards. That meant she had at least a draw four card in her hand. I was glad she wasn't sitting next to me; either Lynn or Rupe was eating that card. The church people she'd been staying with had flown somewhere on vacation, and Bess was stuck back home for a week. She'd been kind of quiet all night. I was wondering if that was the reason why.

Rupe started laughing, and I followed his gaze to where my baby brother sat, next to the pillow I had Benji lying on. My dog was busy licking all the cheese off the kid's hands and face. Chip was just sitting there giggling, doing his best to push Benji's lapping jaws away but not trying to leave. I figured it was less work I'd have to do later.

"That's disgusting," Rupe stated even though he was still chuckling. "That dog licks his butt."

"So? All dogs lick their butts. If a dog's tongue is good for cuts, why is that disgusting? Dog spit makes wounds heal faster." Everyone knew that. Benji had been licking on my cuts and scrapes for years. "He's not hurting anything."

"That's not true," Lynn corrected me as she returned to the table. Terry greedily gathered up her cards, dropping them so that we could easily see what Lynn had in her hand. He gave me an arrogant little leer and stuck his tongue out. I decided I would smack him right off Lynn's lap if he kept it up. "A dog's mouth is full of germs."

"My dog doesn't have any germs."

"*You're* a germ." I started to argue further, and she cocked that strong right arm. "Don't make me do it. I still owe you for being mean to the baby."

Rupe reached out and put a hand on my shoulder. "Don't do it, man. You're young. You have a lot of years in front of you." Lynn flinched, and I pretended to be afraid while Rupe and I cracked up.

"I'll smack *you,* too," she promised my buddy, who stopped laughing right away.

Lynn had pinned Rupe once already this summer, putting him in a head-lock and throwing him down. Their wrestling match had ended with Rupe screaming for assistance and Lynn's sweating face just inches from his, gloating while she bore down on him. It was a moment Rupe wasn't soon to live down. Tommy and I kept telling him that Lynn had gotten pregnant during their melee.

"Good idea. Don't hit me. Hit him," I proposed. "I'm already hurt."

"Thanks buddy," muttered Rupe, playing a green three on Bess's green nine.

I *was* still hurting. My black and swollen eye was still puffy three days later, although the purple had now faded to a sickening yellow. I had a little blood in that eye, but not much. I thought it kind of made me look tough, but Tommy had shot down that foolish notion the first time I brought it up.

"If the other guy looks like you…? Then you're tough," Tommy had corrected me. Tommy was the only one who really knew Tony had clocked me—besides Nicky and the guys—since I'd told everyone else it was from a hard tackle during a football game.

"Okay, how about durable?" I'd countered.

Tommy had shook his head and laughed at me. "Sure, Donny, you'll make some mean drunk a great wife one day." *Touché.* Tommy was right. I didn't like getting smacked around. I liked being bullied even less. "You have got to pay that motherfucker back," Tommy had urged me. *Great advice.* But how was I going to pay Tony back? He'd only been around once since that night, and that time but briefly. Betty was doing her best to keep us apart.

"It's your play, man," Rupe said, snapping me out of my thoughts. I didn't have any wild or yellow cards, and I had to draw four cards before I could play one. I was suddenly tired of Uno. "You okay?" he asked me.

Bess was watching me as well, but saying nothing. *She's being way too quiet tonight.* Something was up with that. "Yeah, I'm fine."

Our cat darted into the kitchen and up the stairs. We had the back door wide open and a fan set on a stool in the opening, trying to draw cooler air into the house. It felt like that fan was only moving the tepid, stale air in the kitchen around, but doing little to cool anything down. Both of the girl's faces were flushed, and their hair was damp and clinging to their cheeks. They had air conditioning at their place, but they also had the trolls. I figured that was a toss-up.

"You haven't been coming out to church lately," Bess said suddenly. "Holly and Dave have been asking about you." Even though she was talking to me, she still wasn't really looking at me, which wasn't like her at all. She kept giving me quick little glances. "Other people too."

"I've been busy."

I heard Tiki on the stairs. The little dog minced over to the open door and looked outside, checked the other room for any sign of my mother, didn't find her home, and lapped a little water out of the community animal water bowl before deciding it was safer upstairs in Betty's deplorable love dungeon. Her little nails scrabbling on the wooden stairs sounded like every step was taxing.

"Busy with what?" Bess persisted. "Don't you know how important God is?" I shrugged. *Here we go.* "Dave and Holly really care about you. Without God in our lives, we're hopeless. The Bible says—"

Rupe smacked at a fly on his face and missed, but left a cool handprint on his sweating cheek. The bad thing about leaving the door open was allowing mosquitoes and flies in. I grinned at Rupe. He grinned at me. The good thing about letting flies in was that Rupe and I loved competing against each other, killing the damn things with rubber bands I had left over from my failed paper route venture. Late nights and early morning deliveries don't mesh well. *And the fact that Betty kept spending the money I collected as soon as I had it in hand.* The *Dispatch* was still after us for that money.

"Fly war?" Rupe asked me.

"Oh, no," Bess groaned.

I was up for anything that spared me another sermon. "You're on."

Bess was obviously disappointed that I didn't want to listen to her, but she let the subject drop as I pulled a bag of rubber bands out of the cabinet and grabbed a handful, as did Rupe. She was soon dodging fly guts and running into the living room, while Lynn—who didn't seem to be afraid of anything known to man—casually walked right through our war zone, leaving Terry at the table to play with the cards. My brother was trying to shuffle Rupe's new deck, but they were slick and kept sliding all over the table and falling on the floor.

Rupe killed first, wasting a fat, lazy fly on the windowsill. It wasn't long after that I plastered one right off the bare light bulb in the kitchen's ceiling. He shot one on the wall, leaving a gruesome splotch on the old paint. I picked one off the bread wrapper hanging out of the trash. Rupe missed an easy countertop shot, and I took the lead, still using the trash bin as my happy hunting ground.

We couldn't do shit like this at Rupe's place, which was one of the reasons he liked to hang out here. His mother kept a real neat and clean house, and Rupe got reamed if he did anything he couldn't easily clean up. He also had to check in periodically, and wasn't allowed out late at night. If he wasn't staying with me, he had to sneak out, and he'd get grounded or at least ripped a little if his parents caught him acting up.

Betty's house had a different set of rules. We pretty much came and went as we pleased, and did just about anything we wanted to. Of course, my house didn't have the luxuries of his place. We didn't have a big color TV and Jiffy Pop at our fingertips. There was no fridge stocked with a never-ending supply of anything and everything you might want to eat, and you never had to worry about trivial necessities like gas or electric. Rupe's house was actually kind of boring. The heat or air always worked, lights came on when you flicked the switch, and the phone had a dial tone every time you picked up the receiver.

I tried to shoot some kind of alien insect off the top of Terry's head, and the rubber band got tangled up in his Dorito-stained curls. He started snitting about that. Lynn called a temporary truce to our combat and came in to gather my brother up, letting him know they were watching *Batman* so he'd agree to leave the cards behind. She also made me adjust the aluminum foil I had wrapped around our broken antenna until I got them a clearer picture. (I was a world-renowned expert at making bunny ears out of foil by the time I was eight or nine.)

When the war resumed I made the fatal error of killing a really plump and bloody fly right on one of Rupe's blue skip cards. The dismembered carcass caused Rupe to blame me for an otherwise brilliant shot, and he decided to shoot at me instead of an intruding bug. The impact didn't hurt, but it struck me on the neck, stinging just enough to force retaliation. I caught him in the ear, and he almost got me right in my already blasted eye, and it was on then.

Our little spat quickly swelled into an all-out battle. I was much quicker at reloading, so it didn't take me long to pin him behind the table. I kept his head down with a flurry of shots that skimmed the tabletop every time he tried to sneak a peek, the whole time inching closer while using a chair for cover. Rupe was forced to take ineffective shots at my exposed legs from under the table while I moved in for the kill.

Unfortunately, my baby brother came waddling into the line of fire. Rupe wasted no time in grabbing the helpless child and using him as a human shield. I wasn't sure about the unwritten rules of rubber band warfare, but taking hostages just didn't seem right. Chip wasn't helping; the baby kept laughing at me, acting like this was still just some kind of game while I tried to maneuver into position for a clear shot at my cowardly adversary.

"Back off or the baby gets it," warned Rupe. I was pretty sure he meant it, but in my line of work there were often innocent casualties. "I mean it," he continued to threaten when I kept trying to get an angle on him.

I'd just about given up on saving the kid and decided to take my shot when Betty walked in the door. That was bad, but then Tony came in right behind her, and that was worse. My mother just stood there tapping her foot on the linoleum, looking around at the catastrophe. There were rubber bands and fly guts everywhere. The table was scooted clear against the wall, and two of the chairs had been flipped over to provide cover. Uno cards were everywhere. The plastic trash can beside the door had fallen over—*when did that happen?*—and a milk carton had leaked a little on the floor.

It took a moment for me to realize I was in trouble, so strong was my bloodlust, but soon I joined Rupe, who was already setting the table and chairs back in place and scrambling to gather his new cards and all our loose bullets. Lynn came in the kitchen and laughed at us, while Betty finally stopped tapping and sat a bucket of KFC on the counter. Tony didn't say anything, but he shot my dog a dark glare when Benji sent a few low grumbles in the Dago's general direction.

Nobody said anything while we cleaned up. Tony wandered on into the living room; I heard Terry complaining as our visitor rudely switched channels. The girls decided it was time to head back to their place, and Rupe used the excuse of walking them home to get out of wiping the gore off the counters and walls. I didn't blame him for cutting out on me. I'd have done the same to him, given the opportunity.

We said our good-byes quietly. Bess acted like she wanted to say something more, but didn't. Again, she wasn't acting like herself.

"You going to be okay?" Rupe asked just before leaving. I knew he suspected something was going on between Tony and me, but I shrugged and nodded, actually wishing he was staying overnight. "See you tomorrow," he said. *Promise?* I wanted to say. But I just stood there as he left, staring at the empty doorway.

I could feel Tony behind me. "How's that eye?"

"How's that unemployment?" I returned before thinking about it.

I expected him to shove me or something, but he didn't say anything and stepped past me as Benji got off his pillow and stood, hackles up and growling. I snapped my fingers and pointed at the pillow, and he dropped his ears and head before reluctantly lying back down. I would have sent him upstairs to the relative safety of my room, but I knew he wouldn't go. This conflict with Tony was something he wouldn't readily agree to let me handle alone. I wasn't sure I wanted to handle it alone.

"I bought some chicken," he offered.

Betty tiptoed into the kitchen behind me. I could tell they were about to discuss something with me. My mother had tried to convince the boys to stay out of this room with earnest whispers.

"Congratulations."

I was pushing it, but that was who I was. My mouth ran whenever I was afraid or intimidated. Speaking before thinking would be a problem for me pretty much the rest of my life. *You need to calm down.* My heart was beating fast, and my breath was coming too quickly. I didn't want to be afraid of this guy, but I didn't want to be hit again. Or have my dog kicked.

We were both still smarting from our last encounter with this dude. *At least he's not drunk this time.*

"Sit down a minute," Tony said, pointing at our table.

Betty sat. I wasn't going to. "I'll stand," I said, but even I heard the nervousness in my tone.

"You don't let anything go easy, do you, kid?" asked Tony. He stared at me for just a second, considering, but then took a seat across from my mother. "Suit yourself."

"Honey, we need to get past this. Tony didn't mean for things to get so out of hand." Just listening to her talk was worse than dealing with Tony. At least he was a stranger and an asshole I wasn't supposed to succumb to. But my mother was supposed to be my mother. "Come on. Sit down. Tony wants to put this behind us."

I didn't move while Tony said, "Come on. What'll it take to patch things up with you?"

"Fifty-four dollars and distance," I told him. And I meant it. Tony wasn't going to apologize for real. He just wanted to get on and off my mom with as little aggravation as possible. I was just something in his way he was trying to smooth over, but I sure wasn't going to make that easy for him. I held out my hand. "You got my money?"

"Why you have to be such a hard ass, kid?" Tony stiffened a little in his chair. He glanced at my hand like he wanted to spit in it.

"You kicked my dog."

Tony was just about done talking. I could see the hatred in his eyes, and he had that angry tilt to his upper body I'd noticed before as he leaned forward on the table. "You keep running your mouth and I'll kick that little shit again. Maybe I'll kick you both right out that door."

"Tony, you promised," Betty mewed.

No matter what happened tonight, I drew some satisfaction from the abrasions still marring Tony's forehead. He caught me checking out his scratches and reached up to touch the wound, his dark eyes narrowing further. This encounter felt more like I was facing some older kid in high school than a grown man, but I was still more afraid of Tony. High school kids couldn't come right into my house to kick my ass while my mother watched.

"Tony…" Betty whined. She could tell he was getting pissed. "You promised we'd work this out. Don't forget, I got you your job back."

"I'm trying to *work it out.* It's your little asshole here making this hard." *Don't say anything,* I warned myself. Tony began drumming his fingers on the table. I was praying he'd catch some fatal disease from the fly juice I hadn't wiped off yet. "Can't you make him sit the fuck down? I hate looking up at him while I'm talking."

My mother glared at me. "Donny, do as he says and sit down."

I pulled a chair out away from the table and fell into it like a dying man, crossing my arms and wagging my knees back and forth like this was just killing me. I glanced at my mother. "There. Happy?"

"Donny, listen to me. Mrs. Lorret called the police the other night. A cop called me here yesterday asking questions about what happened. There's a chance they might come back around even though I told them everything was fine." Betty swallowed uneasily when I didn't change expression. "They especially might come back around if that nosy old bitch calls them again."

"She's not an old bitch when you want to borrow shit from her all the time," I told Betty, but she wasn't about to be deflected from the case at hand. She sat there waiting to see which direction I was going to go with her latest bit of news. "Is that what this is about? You're afraid I'll say something to the cops that'll get Sonny Bono here tossed into jail?"

Tony sat up and leveled a finger at me.

"Stop it!" my mother hissed.

But my mouth was running, and I couldn't find the brake. "What?" I asked Tony, pointing right back at him. "You going to belt me again? Fuck you." I spun back to Betty, fighting tears. "What could I tell the police? You'd just lie for him. And do you think I'm stupid? Do you think I want this motherfucker smacking me around? Kicking my dog? Worse, maybe going after the boys next?"

"He would *never* hurt the boys!" Betty bellowed, all affronted.

She was trying to pretend she had limits. Isn't it funny how the oddest little things said at the strangest moments hurt the worst, and stick in your brain forever?

"Don't you even try to say I'd let anyone hurt my babies!"

Tony's anger was way deflated. He leaned back in his chair and took out a cigarette, watching me and Betty go at it while he calmly lit up. I pointed at my eye and asked her, "Stick up for them and fuck me, right?" *Don't you fucking cry!* "So it's okay to pound on me, just don't hurt the little guys?

What are you going to do when *they're* old enough to understand that you're a criminal and a goddamn whore, too?"

She slapped me a good one, her hand lashing out so fast I didn't have time to deflect or dodge the blow. I didn't care. I kept my face right where it was in case she wanted to hit me again, actually kind of wishing she'd keep on smacking me. I felt like hitting myself, like I could punch myself in the head until there was nothing left on my shoulders but a bloody mess.

Betty was seething. So was I. "Look, kid," Tony said, breaking the tension. "I won't hit you again if you'll just quit breaking my balls. Why don't we eat some chicken and drop this shit? Your mom and I were thinking about going fishing with my brother this weekend. How's that sound? You ever been fishing? What do you say?"

I looked that bastard right in the eye and said, "Fifty-four dollars and distance."

Tony's lips twisted up like he'd just swallowed a bucket of lemons. Betty gasped aloud. "You just don't get it, do you, kid?" Tony said softly, but with an audible strain.

I was spared trying to figure out what it was I didn't get by a knock at our front door. Betty screeched at Terry to stay where he was, stopping my little brother from greeting our visitor. She scrambled to shut and lock the back door, knocking over the fan and the stool in the process. Tony was a little nervous as well. I already knew that whoever was at our door, it wasn't the fuzz. The rap had been sharp but not pushy, almost polite. It was probably a neighbor or some guy looking for me.

It wound up being neither. "It's a guy from my church," Betty whispered at Tony after cautiously peeking out the window. Then she looked at me, concerned again. "It's Dave."

I looked at them both. "Jesus Christ, are you going to let him in or not?" I asked my mother.

"I don't know," she whispered, still looking to Tony for direction.

I stood up, shaking my head at her. "I'll go out and talk to him if you're so worried."

"Sit down." Something in Tony's voice had me obeying without hesitation. He exhaled smoke slowly, watching me. "We'll all visit together." He nodded toward the door and told my mother to let him in, then leaned closer to me and said, "Be smart, kid. I'm the last guy you want to have for an enemy."

"What are we now, best friends?"

Tony wanted to say something back, but Dave was already stepping in. The Dago clenched his jaw and snuffed out his cigarette in an empty bowl, rising to greet Dave as Betty led him into the kitchen. I stayed seated while they shook hands and were introduced, Dave a bit stiff and reserved, Tony all smiles and grease and T-shirt and gold chain. The two of them looked like men from different planets.

I'd never been a stupid kid. Everything fell into place. Bess had a pretty clear picture of what was going on in this house, and she wasn't a girl who kept much to herself. She'd told Dave what was going on. That was why he was here now. But I wasn't sure what he could do for me. I wasn't sure I *wanted* him to do anything for me. The last thing I needed was for the people from the church Betty was conning to start pissing off her paying customers.

"How are you, sport?" Dave asked me, taking the seat Betty had vacated. "You haven't been to church for a couple weeks now. I've been worried about you." I gave him a weak grin and shrugged. Dave was looking at my face. I looked down. "What happened to your eye?"

Dave Jones was a simple and direct man, one of those guys who gave you the plain truth whether you wanted to hear it or not. He also wasn't afraid to ask tough questions. I'd always liked that about him, but that frankness wasn't going to do me any good in this situation. I looked at Dave, and he gave me a nod of encouragement. Behind me, Betty's breathing grew louder.

"Football," I said. I hated lying to Dave, especially after the deal we'd made. But no pact was worth keeping if it meant getting smacked around.

"That doesn't look like a football injury," he said softly. "Are you sure there's nothing you want to tell me?"

"He told you already."

Dave looked across the table as Tony also seated himself. "Tony, right?"

Tony lit up, staring right back at Dave. "That's my name," he admitted, trying to act tough and cool for Betty. *Or maybe he's puffing himself up?*

Dave was a little bigger than Tony. He wore a short-sleeved shirt and a tie, with dress pants and a fresh, neat haircut. I could smell aftershave and see the creases in his ironed clothes. Dave was a little intimidated. He'd probably not counted on finding Tony here during this visit. Tony sensed Dave's insecurity as well, and he was wasting no time in playing on it.

"Exactly what is it you want?" Tony asked, propping himself on his elbows and blowing smoke out above the table.

"I visit this home about every week," Dave said without hesitation.

Tony's smirk didn't appear to impress Dave very much. "That right?"

I didn't want Dave to get hurt. Tony wasn't a street threat by any means, but Dave couldn't have been more white bread if he'd been swaddled in Wonder Bread wrappers as a newborn. If Dave thought he could take on Tony, he needed to understand the rules: there were no rules. Tony would probably bite and kick and use whatever was lying around if a fight started, and then call up his buddies to go after Dave again no matter who won or lost. I didn't think Dave and his wife Jewel needed a problem like Tony, and I knew they weren't prepared to deal with shit like him. Good people had no way to conceive of lowlifes like Tony.

I cleared my throat and leaned in between the two men. Betty was huffing and puffing like she was halfway through a marathon. "Really, Dave, it's nothing. I've popped pimples worse than this." (I often stole good lines from other people, and I still do.) "Why don't you let me walk you out?"

I managed to get Dave on his feet. "Nice to meet you," he told Tony. It sounded like he was talking to a pile of dog crap as he wiped it off the bottom of his shoe.

"Sure," was all Tony drawled back, flashing his fake smile and then blowing smoke, not caring where it wafted or who had to breathe its stench.

I couldn't get Dave out of the house fast enough. Neither could Betty, but she wasn't about to let me talk to our visitor alone. My mother followed us through the front door and out onto the porch.

"Why don't you ride the bus this Sunday?" Dave offered hopefully.

I'd already broken our little deal, so, "Sure. Maybe. We'll see." *Stop yammering, jackass!* "I got to go, Dave. See ya." I turned my back on the man, heading inside.

But he stopped me. "Donny." I couldn't turn around. My mother was staring at us like we were a horror movie she couldn't turn off. I couldn't face him. I don't know if it was fear or shame. I just wanted him rid of me and Betty and all our shitty problems. I wanted him to go home to Jewel and take a shower and be clean. "I'm here for you. You trust me, and I can help you."

I swallowed. "I'm fine, Dave." I managed to turn around and give him a cheesy grin. "See you Sunday." And I went on in. Behind me, Betty murmured a good-bye and he said something back, but I couldn't hear him clearly. She was already closing the door before I reached the kitchen. Dave had driven a long way just to be turned away. He was a nice man, too nice to help me with Tony.

I tried to go on up to my room, but Tony wasn't done yet. "Kid, there's one more thing."

I sighed and picked up my dog, then turned around and said, "Yeah?"

"Who's Nick?"

So Betty told you about old blue eyes. I'll bet she didn't tell you how hot and bothered she got when Nicky was standing in her kitchen. "Just some crazy biker who rides around with a bunch of mean dudes. You've seen them around the neighborhood. He did some time for killing a couple guys." That was pretty good. Maybe not really knowing who and where Nicky was might get Tony to cut me a little slack.

"How the fuck you know a guy like that?"

I shrugged, but then I came up with a stroke of genius. "Last time I got in a fight, he broke it up." *That's enough. Let his imagination do the rest.* I hadn't seen Nicky since he'd helped me out. *Or Mandy.* I'd stopped by there once, but been turned away by some gruff dude I'd never seen before. "He throws the ball around with us from time to time is all. Why? You want me to tell him something for you?"

Tony blew smoke and didn't say anything, but he didn't look quite so cool. I carried my dog on upstairs, and Tony left me alone the rest of the night.

CHAPTER 16

Even at age twelve, I'd heard somewhere that all good things must come to an end. My friendship with Thomas Washington came to an abrupt end on a summer afternoon near the end of August.

We were at the park, and the city workers had come through with their bush hogs and mowed down a ton of thick weeds along the creek. We'd made a huge pile of the dried brush and were jumping our bikes off the bridge where the handrail was busted, soaring as high as we could before landing in the massive mound of dead grass.

Tommy's best trick was doing a black flip. I didn't have the guts to try anything so dangerous. My only daring move was to stand on my seat and jump off my bike as I sailed through the air. To gain speed, we'd pedal our asses off all the way down the hill and hit that bridge, as close as we could get to the speed of sound. That first moment I was airborne always gave me such a rush. The most difficult part of all this was dragging your bike out of the tangle of grass without getting gouged or scratched to death.

I felt bad doing this without Rupe. This was probably his favorite of all our activities. But Tommy and Rupe had gone their separate ways. *That's putting it mildly.* Their split left me juggling time with both of them, and watching what I said about Rupe around Tommy. We'd been jumping all morning, going faster and farther, competing with each other on height and distance. People kept stopping to watch us jump, clapping and cheering. We were like a ghetto X Games.

I had a chipped front tooth and a scar inside my upper lip from doing something very similar to this when I was younger, only we'd been using a ripped-down slide as a ramp. My front tire had slipped out from under me. I'd bitten the nasty edge of the upturned metal slide, and the slide had bitten back. That was a bloody mess, but not my first or last rush to the emergency room. I had my scars, and even though I was an excessive bleeder and screamed like a little girl when I was hurt, I never stayed down long, or was afraid to come back for more.

I checked the sky as I hauled on my bike, trying to get a stubborn branch out of my rear tire's spokes. It had to be getting well past noon. I was hot and thirsty, and hoping Tommy would agree to take a break when I heard the thrum of rubber tires kissing wooden planks. I dove for cover as his shadow fell upon me. He slammed into the debris just beside my bike, howling at the top of his lungs.

"You crazy fucking Negro!" I screamed at him, spitting dead grass probably coated with poisonous pesticides and God knew what else. "Are you trying to kill me?"

Tommy was rolling, but he stopped cackling long enough to say, "Negro?"

That had me laughing as well, plus the fact that he had a little branch poking out of his wiry afro. He looked like a black My Favorite Martian missing one antenna. I decided to keep that little tidbit to myself and see how long he walked around with it wiggling above his head for everyone to stare at.

I fell back into the brush, squinting in the sunlight and relieved to still be breathing. "I can't believe you did that."

Tommy was laughing so hard he couldn't talk, but he controlled his hilarity long enough to gasp, "Why you still on the landing pad, man!"

I pointed at my rear tire. "I was stuck!"

I don't know why he thought that was so funny. I also didn't know why I was laughing with him instead of snatching up a pointy stick and trying to poke out his eye. But we kept on cackling the whole time he dragged his bike out of the mound and helped me untangle my own. Both of us were filthy and drenched with sweat. I had scratches all over me and a fairly deep scrape on the small of my back. Tommy looked just as bad. I pointed out a bleeding cut just beneath his nose, and he probed it and waved off my concern.

"I need a break," I announced.

Tommy nodded. "Me too."

I'd made about fifteen bucks last weekend at Pops', but blown it all during the past few days, spending more than half of it on my brothers. We'd raided the ice cream truck three days in a row. The rest I'd wasted bowling with Rupe yesterday. *Yeah, because he wouldn't agree to sneak out without paying like we used to.* But I didn't hold that against Rupe. In fact, he'd slid me a couple ones to help me pay my half the bill as we were settling up.

"I need to run home," I told Tommy. "You want to meet back here later?"

"Nah, let's just clean up in the bathroom, and I'll buy hot dogs and root beer."

I stopped pushing my bike up the hill and stared at Tommy like he *was* a black My Favorite Martian. He still had his lonely little wooden antenna. "Okay, who are you, and what did you do with my friend?"

Tommy tried to act hurt, but he wasn't disguising his sly grin very well. "What do you mean?"

"You know damn well what I mean."

"What?"

I made a face like I'd just eaten toe jam. "You never pay for shit."

He kept going toward the squat concrete building that was the bathroom, and I had to follow. But I could tell he was smiling even though he'd turned his back on me. His chubby cheeks gave away his grin, even from behind. "Let me see if I have this straight. You're going to buy the dogs and root beer—for both of us?" He gave me the famous bird over the shoulder.

Money didn't seem to be a concern for Tommy lately. He was spending more and more time with the older guys from Candy's place, and was always pushing on me to come along. He kept on talking about us packing reefer into the school, and running the numbers over to the factories and gas stations. He said picking up the payoffs early in the week was the easiest money we'd ever make. Candy encouraged underage kids to work for him, and paid them well.

On our way to the bathroom, I noticed a lady with two little kids trying to get a kite out of a tree. Tommy groaned as I decided to help them, and he stood there holding our bikes and bitching while I climbed up to free the kite. It wasn't too high, but I had to break the string with my teeth since it was so tangled. The mother couldn't speak English, but she kept nodding at me and smiling while I handed it over. She had squinty eyes and big teeth, but she seemed nice enough.

"*Fank u, fank u,*" Tommy teased after we were back on our way, nodding at me and jutting out his teeth. His teeth were bigger than the lady's he was mocking, but I wasn't going to point that out. "Does that make you feel good? You like wasting our time to help people with stupid shit like that?"

I tried to ignore him, but I answered, "Yeah, I guess so." Tommy just shook his head at me while we wheeled our bikes into the bathroom.

The interior of the shabby facility was cooler than cooking in the hot sun, but other than that it wasn't a very pleasant experience. Spray paint covered the walls and trash was all over the floor, since there wasn't even a garbage can. The toilets didn't work, but that didn't stop people from using them. The light was busted, the mirrors were cracked, and the urinals were full of cigarette butts, but the tepid water in the sinks ran, so we could at least wash our faces and hands.

We leaned our bikes against the wall under the missing paper towel dispenser and bent over the sinks. We knew better than to leave our wheels unguarded. I'd had a bike ripped off late last summer while playing football, and if there's anything a professional thief hates, it's being ripped off. If anyone should know better than to leave anything of value lying around, it's us. I still got really pissed off whenever I thought about that bike.

I suppose with the water running and all the splashing and scrubbing going on, we really didn't have much chance of overhearing the four guys who snuck up behind us. Even if we had, there wouldn't have been much we could have done about it. They'd been really careful and waited for the right opportunity. If we'd have caught a whiff of them lurking around the park, or noticed them watching us outside, things would have turned out differently, at least on this particular day.

But we knew we were had the moment they spun us around. The biggest dude put me in a headlock and drew me away from the sinks, squeezing my throat so tightly when I tried to resist I thought the fat bastard was going to break my neck. The other three jumped Tommy and pinned him face down on the filthy concrete floor after a brief and violent struggle. For just a moment I thought I was going to die right there in that murky concrete bunker, with the smell of shit in my nose and some gang of perverts doing whatever gangs of perverts do to skinny kids like me.

"Remember me, nigger?" one guy asked Tommy, leaning down over him and speaking right into his ear. Tommy just growled and resisted while the dude rifled through his pockets, producing a small wad of cash, half a pack of Marlboro's, and the switchblade Candy had given him. "Well, looky, looky here." He clicked open the knife and put the exposed blade right in front of Tommy's struggling face. "Remember this?"

I thought about crying out for help, but the dude holding me had his forearm pressed right up under my chin with my toes barely touching the floor. These guys were still in high school, but every one of them was muscular and bigger than Tommy. They looked like football players from a school in the suburbs. They were all dressed in jeans and sweatshirts, and they were all white. I was pretty sure this had something to do with Tommy pulling his knife on Lucy Perez's boyfriend. *Just your luck to be in the way of this train wreck.*

The guy doing the talking grabbed a handful of Tommy's hair, jerking his head up and twisting it around. "What was it you told me outside the skating rink? I remember now. I think you kept asking me if I was scared. And you kept thrusting this little knife at me, grinning and laughing, and having a good old time."

If I had the whole story, the guy doing the talking hadn't been alone when he'd caught Tommy behind the roller rink with his hand up Lucy's skirt and his tongue down her throat. Supposedly, Tommy had held the jilted boyfriend and another guy off until a few of his black friends showed up to even the odds, and then he'd offered to fight it out without the knife. I'd heard from more than one source that the dude had decided he wanted no part of Tommy and left while everyone outside—including Lucy—had laughed at him. Nobody was laughing now.

This was Tony's fault. If he hadn't kicked my dog, Benji would have been here with me instead of laid up, recuperating. My angry mutt might not have saved us from this pack of pretty boys, but he sure would have kept us from getting ambushed and more than evened up the odds. That was another one I owed Betty's Dago. *If you survive.*

"I fucking told you to stay away from Lucy, motherfucker," the dude continued. "Didn't I tell you that?" he asked, jerking savagely on my friend's head.

Tommy made a noise like a madman. I'll never forget the wild look in his round, white eyes. With one guy laying on his back and restraining his hands and another sitting on his legs and pinning his feet, Tommy continued to tremble with rage and glare at our attackers, while I hoped I wasn't going to piss all over myself or get hurt. *He's right. You are a pussy.* I tried to move, and Lurch shook me a little, but only enough to remind me I was a helpless little bitch.

"I asked you a question, nigger," he said again, and leaned in even closer. Tommy spit right in his face. "You fucker!" the dude screamed.

He raised his fist and slammed it into the side of Tommy's head. I heard the initial blow, and the echoing thud of my friend's head colliding with the concrete. I was afraid he'd sliced Tommy with the knife, but I could see the blade lying beside the guy's shoe and was relieved to find he'd only used his fist. Tommy jerked his bleeding face back up and spit again, growling a mixture of pain and rage known only to those people who have endured years of racism at the hands of white people.

"Leave him alone," I squeaked. Lurch squeezed. I shut up and prayed for air.

"Easy, Chris," the guy holding Tommy's arms urged as the dude who'd punched Tommy picked up the knife again, wiping spit out of his eyes. But Chris closed the blade and put the knife in his pocket, along with Tommy's money. He left the crumpled pack of cigarettes on the floor. "Is that enough?" the nervous kid asked. He kept glancing over his shoulder, checking the door.

"Fuck no, it's not enough!" spat Chris.

He had hair the color of mine, only shorter and neatly cut, with acne on his cheeks visible even in the dim light. Now that he had Tommy, he wasn't quite sure what to do with him. I found hope in that. Maybe they would let us go without too much more damage.

"Come on, man, it fucking stinks in here," Lurch said. His deep voice didn't sound like any high school kid's. He sounded even stronger than he felt. "That nigger's friends catch us down here, and we're fucked. Let's go."

"Hold on." Chris was panicking. Obviously, the big sucker holding me was kind of in charge. *Probably the driver.* Chris jumped up and kicked open one of the stalls, his pimpled face splitting into a wide, mean grin even as he waved his hand repeatedly beneath his nose in a vain effort to escape the noxious odor. "Yeah, it *does* stink in here. It smells like nigger shit."

"What are you going to do?" the other guy holding Tommy's legs asked.

Chris motioned for them to haul Tommy up on his feet. "Not *me*, fellas; *we*. We're going to jam his fucking frizzy head right in that toilet full of shit." Tommy began jerking against them, kicking at their legs with his feet and trying to bite their hands. Chris stepped in close and drove a fist into Tommy's gut, ending his resistance. He then turned toward Lurch. "Him, too," he said.

Him? Me? And there went that hope I was clinging to. All of a sudden getting my ass beat didn't seem so bad. The thought of having my face pushed into one of the putrid bowls had my mind racing, searching for any idea to break free. My only option was trying to kick Lurch in the balls and run for it. Of course, that meant running the risk of pissing Lurch off and having my face *permanently* shoved into one of the toilets, if the big bastard didn't drop me. I decided that was a risk I was going to have to take.

"Why the kid?" Lurch asked Chris, hefting me up like someone might have forgotten who he was asking about.

"Because he should pick better friends. What's the matter, David? You afraid to give some white trash little punk a shit whirly?" So now I knew Lurch's name was really David. Knowing his name didn't make me feel a bit better about this whole thing.

I felt David shrug. "Let's get this over with and get the fuck out of here. My car's probably stripped down to its frame by now." *God, I hope so, you big shithead.*

The big ox took a step toward the stalls as the other three guys struggled with Tommy. I was gathering strength for my daring maneuver when some screaming kid ran into the bathroom and startled our attackers. Lurch spun around, and I took advantage of his momentary lack of concentration to wrench myself free. I hit the ground running, jumped over the surprised kid, and sidestepped another running little boy, barging through the entry with Lurch stumbling along after me.

Once outside, I threw a glance over my shoulder and stole a peek at the dude chasing me. He was huge, ponderously muscle-bound and slow, probably a lineman. I almost had to stop and ask him if he was kidding—and if he'd have chased me further than a few more yards I might have done just that. But I'd already spotted what I was hoping for, and I was pretty sure I looked like Gilligan running away from the Skipper as I tore a path through the grass and directly toward the first two black guys I spotted.

"There are four white guys beating a black kid in the bathroom!" I spouted around ragged breaths as I reached them.

They were older dudes in their twenties, and they were walking with a couple of black girls who both gasped aloud at my proclamation, their hands covering their mouths while their eyes searched the field behind me.

"What you talking about, kid?" one of the men asked, but both of them were already staring over my shoulder.

They were heading the way I pointed before I even got my hand up, and I raced after them with the two young women running in my wake. I could see Chris and his boys running out of the bathroom as we crossed the field, but Tommy didn't come out and I remembered their threat of the toilet.

That scared me. Then I remembered the knife, and that scared me worse. *They didn't have time enough to dunk him. Did they?* I wasn't sure just how long it had taken me to find help. I kept assuring myself that was what I'd done. I hadn't run away and left Tommy. I'd gone for help. I sure hoped that was the way Tommy would see it.

We found my friend with his head in one of the sinks, rinsing out his hair. None of us said anything while he washed. It looked like Chris and his boys might have gotten Tommy's 'fro into one of the toilets, no more than that. I saw Tommy wince as he straightened up, but he ignored the pain in his ribs and ran a finger over his teeth in an unbroken section of the mirror. When he'd made certain he had still had everything in place he ran his tongue across his lips, licking blood.

"You gonna be okay, young blood?" one of the black men asked quietly. Tommy nodded, but said nothing. The other black guy came jogging back into the bathroom. I hadn't noticed him leaving. "They split?"

"Uh huh," he answered.

Tommy looked different. I could see that he was fighting back tears, but I wasn't sure they were the same tears I was familiar with. He had a grip on the sides of the sink he was leaning on, and his long fingers were tightly clutching and releasing the dirty porcelain. He was staring at himself in the broken mirror, but I didn't think he was looking at his refracted reflection. Whatever was on Tommy's mind was beyond me. I didn't understand it, but I had the feeling the rest of the people in the dim bathroom did.

I was suddenly an outcast, caught up in the space between being one of the black people standing in this foul enclosure and one of those white fools who had assaulted Tommy. It would become a common feeling.

The two men stepped up and spoke quietly with my friend, and both of the girls whispered words of encouragement. I felt more like an intruder than ever, although I *knew* Tommy and none of them had ever met him before. I didn't get this at all. Tommy was black. Lucy was Puerto Rican. Chris, Lurch, and his friends were white. It just didn't make sense. *Then why did you look for the nearest black men when you escaped the bathroom?* Maybe I knew more than I wanted to admit.

We walked our bikes out after Tommy retrieved his cigarettes, and the others went on their way after another look around to make sure we were safe. They warned us to watch out in case our new friends might still be lurking near the park, but Tommy didn't seem too worried about that. He straddled his bike and spit on the sidewalk. I could see that he was still bleeding. I just sat on my bike while he lit up, not knowing what I should say or if I should say anything at all.

Neither of us spoke while he inhaled and exhaled deliberately for a few minutes. He was thinking, and I was pretty sure I knew what his next move was going to be. "I'm sorry about your money, and your knife," I said, breaking the silence. (I never was too good at keeping my mouth shut and just letting things alone.) "I'm sorry I ran, but I thought if I could find—"

"It's cool," he said, looking back and lifting his lip, granting me a brief and bloody smile of encouragement. "I'll get that shit back." He looked forward again, chuckling. Even his laugh had changed. He looked like a man sitting on a kid's bike. "*That* and a little more," he added, but it sounded like he was making a promise to himself and not really talking to me.

"What do you mean?" I asked. *You know what he means.* I sounded like a little kid.

He rubbed his jaw and blew smoke at the sun. "That fool will show up at the rink, or over at the drive-in. If I don't catch up with him there, I know where he goes to school." Tommy flicked the stick away. "Besides, Lucy knows another girl his ass is chasing." He gave me another bloody grin, licking blood off his teeth. I knew the taste too well. "I'll get him. Don't you worry 'bout that. Him *and* his fucking brave-ass gang of friends."

He kept looking at me. I didn't know what to say. "That's good," was all I could offer, nodding encouragement. The new Tommy was looking at me with different eyes, probably seeing what I was feeling. I was just a scrawny kid. What was I going to do to help him get back what was stolen, or assist him in exacting the pound of flesh he so badly wanted and needed?

"I got to go see Irving and Jo Jo," he told me.

That made sense. Jo Jo had a car. And Irving had a razor. Irving was the means by which Tommy was going to strike back. Even though I understood, I wasn't so sure Tommy was doing the smart thing. But I wasn't about to say a word against his plans. He kept spitting blood like it was going to leak out of him forever. In a way, maybe it would.

He started to ride off but stopped. He kept his back to me as he asked, "You want to come along?" I didn't answer. He hadn't really wanted me to. That simply phrased question was a courtesy. "Later," was all he said before taking off.

"You coming to Pops' tonight?" I called after him, but he didn't answer.

233

I watched him ride away, his bike kicking up dry grass on the paved path. He never looked back. Just for a second or two, I considered going after him. Part of me wanted to help him. Another part of me wanted to try and talk him out of his schemes for revenge. Instead, I just sat there watching him leave, until he crested the hill we'd just been racing down and was gone. Then I remembered I was alone, and Chris and his buddies might still be roaming around. So I started leaning on those bike pedals for all I was worth.

He slapped her again, but she kept right on. "You're not going to keep waltzing in and out of here whenever you want! Either you're with me, or you can go stay with *her!*" my mother screamed. There was yet another slap. I wasn't sure if I was hearing Tony smacking her, or Betty taking shots at him. *Who cares?* That was a good point. Those two deserved each other.

"I fucking told you already!" Something fell over. It sounded like a box of ceramics. "She's an old girlfriend I borrowed some money from! I was just paying her back!" This time there was a series of smacks. That was Betty. The old bitch could put together a pretty serious combination if you got her really riled. "Cut it out!" I heard a solid slap. That had to be Tony giving her a good one.

This was just another Friday night at Betty's. My brothers were huddled up next to me on the couch while our mother and Tony sparred in her bedroom. *I'd rather hear this than the other noises they like to make.* Tony drank more than normal from Friday morning on through Sunday night—way more. Weekends around here weren't something to be looked forward to any longer. In fact, they could be downright dangerous if you didn't watch your step and keep your mouth shut.

"Oh, right! Pay her and forget what you owe me! I have rent due the first of the month and you promised to help out!" As far as I knew, Tony had never given up a dime. He just bought food now and then and jumped on Betty like she was a penny carousel that took fast food in the slot instead of coins. "You owe *me* money! Where the fuck is *my* money?"

"You'll get paid, bitch!" There was a loud thud and some thrashing around. The baby looked up at the ceiling like it was going to cave in. I wondered how many kids had ever died because their bloated-ass mother fell through a ceiling and squashed them. "Use your fucking welfare check to pay your rent! That's why they give you the damn thing!"

Tony, Tony, Tony, what are you thinking? I guess the stupid Dago hadn't figured it out yet. Betty's check didn't pay any bills unless she had to hand it over to the pastor who was trying to dig her out from under her mound of past due notices. Tony really didn't get it. Betty was humping him so *he'd* pay her rent, and if Tony didn't catch on pretty quick, he was soon going to have company in her turnstile of a bed. *And the sooner the better.*

Benji whined at my feet. The weekends were probably the worst for my dog. He could never relax while Tony was around. I checked the clock and saw that it was only about half past six. I usually didn't head out to Pops' for another hour or so. But the drama upstairs was quieting down, and I didn't have the stomach for a makeup session. I listened closely and still heard nothing. *Maybe they killed each other.*

Terry was asleep next to me. One of the few cool things about growing up in a madhouse is developing the ability to sleep through a rock concert if you have to. I stood up and positioned him more comfortably on one end of the couch.

"Don't start with that again!" Tony erupted.

There goes your double homicide theory.

"I'll say whatever I want in this fucking house! I pay the bills here!"

She uses that one on me too, Tony.

"You don't pay anything! You trick dumb fucking Bible thumpers into paying them for you or you throw the goddamn things away!"

That's a good one.

"You sure don't help!"

That's true.

"Fuck you, whore!"

You do, and way too often, if you ask me.

"What did you call me?" my mother asked him.

Like you didn't hear him clearly the first time.

"You heard me!"

Here it comes!

"Get out! Get the fuck out!"

Chip and Benji were both staring at me as if they were terrified I was going to desert them. I didn't want to, but I didn't want to miss the money I was going to make at Pops' either. Upstairs, the argument waged on, but I was tuning them out. I picked up the baby and went out onto the porch,

Benji following me closely. He still had a limp, but his hip was doing much better. Outside, I set the baby down on the porch, where he immediately began climbing on the railing.

Mrs. Lorret was sitting on her porch across the street. She lifted her hand, and I returned the gesture, knowing she was eavesdropping on my mother's little spat. Chip swung out and began carefully negotiating the outside of the wobbly railing, sliding along hand over hand and grinning at me through the spaces in between the slats. It was a good two-foot drop if he fell, but it was grass below. I figured there was no use trying to talk him out of doing the things he needed to learn for himself.

"You're going to fall," I told his grinning mug. As if to mock me, he started bobbing up and down, hanging his butt as far out over the edge as he could. "Okay, don't say I didn't warn you." He tried to keep going and did fall. Benji barked and scrambled down the steps after him, but the stubborn kid was back up on the porch and traversing that railing again without shedding a tear. I laughed at him. "Don't come crying to me when you fall on your head."

I heard a motorcycle, but it didn't come down my street. The bike wasn't a Harley in any case. I'd stopped by Nicky's place yesterday, but nobody had been home. *Chick's place,* I corrected myself. *Actually, Chick's mom's place,* I further corrected. That memory made me smile. Any hope I'd had of Nicky helping me out with Tony had long since faded. I hadn't even seen any of those guys since the night they'd patched me up and Mandy had become the love of my life.

The baby fell again. Benji yipped and dove after him. Chip lost interest in the porch railing and started walking the cinder block retaining wall that kept our little raised patch of grass and dirt from spilling out onto the sidewalk. All the kid had on was a diaper and a pair of shorts, so there was a real good chance he'd get skinned up if he fell onto the concrete. I sighed and got up off the steps, walking along beside him just in case he tried to take a tumble.

Having me there to catch him if he fell took all the fun out of his daring adventure, so the kid went wandering off into the yard and picked up a stick. It was against Benji's law for anyone to hold a ball or stick without sharing it with him, and my greedy mutt went after the baby in earnest. Chip did his best to keep his prize but lost it quickly. And then it was Benji's turn to keep dropping the stick and teasing the baby. My dog kept letting Chip almost touch the stick before snatching it up and proudly prancing a few steps away, where he would again drop the branch to lure the baby into another attempt.

"You're not going to get it," I informed my brother as I fell back onto the steps.

He stuck a finger to his lips and shushed me as he crept slowly forward, all grins and slobber and dirt from his previous failed attempts at retrieving his stolen stick. Benji was lying down and acting like he wasn't paying attention. But he was, and he was feeling a lot better. My dog waited until Chip was right on top of the prize before snatching it up and trotting away. The poor kid ate dirt again, but he was still grinning.

"I told you so."

Their game carried on toward the rear of the house, where Tony's Caddy was parked, and I followed them back there, hoping to keep my brother from stepping in the dog shit I was supposed to have cleaned up. "Watch the dog shit!" I warned him as he trotted right past a fairly fresh pile.

Chip looked at me, trying to see what I was on about. I pointed at the mess near his bare feet. "Dog shit," I said again.

My little brother cracked me up by pointing at the topic of our instruction and proclaiming, "Da sit!" I was laughing so hard the kid got all proud of himself. He began searching the yard and pointing out my many neglected responsibilities. "Da sit! Da sit! Da sit!" He kept on and on. He was still trying to find and label more piles when I darted in and scooped him up, tickling his ribs and throwing the kid into a seizure of wriggling giggles.

Benji growled. I turned and had Tony in my face.

The baby buried his head in my shoulder and his little body tensed. Tony just leaned in and breathed on me. His breath was a familiar reek by now. He reached up and grabbed my lower jaw, pulling me along until we stood right above a pile of what had just seconds ago been so funny.

"See that?" he asked. I tried to nod, but he had to do that for me. His fingers were digging into my skin. "I step in dog shit just one more time and you know what's going to happen, right?" This time he let me nod. "Capisce?" I would detest that word for the rest of my life. *Don't get smart. Don't get smart.*

He wanted me to pop off. I could see it in his drunken face. "Yes, I get it," was all I told him, mumbling around his firm grip. "I'll clean it up."

"You leave him alone!" Betty screamed from the back door. "I told you to get the fuck out of here!" I knew better than to take any stock in her defense of me. Once they made up, I was back to being cannon fodder. *Probably by tomorrow.* "Get out! Go see your new fucking girlfriend!"

"What's the matter, kid, nothing wise to say?" He leaned in and let me breathe the aroma of cheap beer and stale cigarettes, bumping my forehead with his own. "Say something."

Okay. "Your nose is bleeding onto your shirt."

He checked to see if I was telling the truth; I was. I'd finally seen him foul one of his before now impervious T-shirts. *Now if he'd only lose that stupid chain.*

Tony reached up and wiped at the blood on his upper lip, smearing it across his face. "What the fuck?" Betty had gotten in a good one. He had a scratch next to one of his eyes, too. "The stupid fucking whore busted my nose."

I wanted to tell him his nose wasn't actually busted. Another *guy* would bust your nose. In reality, his nose was bleeding from a bitch slap. But I couldn't really point that out while he had such a tight grip on my jaw.

"I said let him go and get the fuck out of here!" Betty screamed.

Mrs. Lorret and the rest of the neighbors were getting a really good show. *Yeah, but it's a rerun.*

Tony gave my mother a dark glare and my jaw a vigorous jerk before releasing me. "Fucking bitch," was all he had to say. But he smacked me on the ear hard enough to set it to ringing before turning away.

I thought he might decide to go another round or two with Betty, but he wobbled to his car and climbed in, slamming the squeaky door and tearing out of our yard, leaving ruts all the way to the alley. His tires were still squealing when he made the corner, and I sent a prayer to anyone who might want to listen that he'd kiss a tree and kill himself. Leon always said God smiled on children and drunks. I thought that must have been true, even if it was an odd combination.

Chip was looking up at me, relaxed now that Tony was gone but still hanging around my neck. "Now *that* was a pile of dog shit," I told him. I knew he wouldn't understand, but the baby grinned at me anyway, a few more teeth trying to peek through his wet, sloppy gums.

"Da sit?" he asked.

"What did he say?" Betty asked as she approached.

"I don't know."

"What did you say, baby?" she asked Chip, reaching for him. The kid decided he couldn't trust me to protect him and let go of my neck, sliding down my body and heading for the house as quickly as his stubby, nearly three-year-old legs could carry him. "Are you okay?" my mother asked as we watched my brother make his escape.

I gave her my best are-you-kidding-me look. Betty wasn't bleeding, but her eyes were all puffy from crying and her face was red and swollen from playing patty cake with the backs of Tony's hands. Her lower lip had a blood blister on it, but it wasn't split. I noticed Mrs. Lorret sweeping her walk so she could see us better. Why the old lady was so interested in the pathetic drama of our lives was way beyond me, but at least my mother was clothed in this week's sorry episode.

Betty followed me into the house. I had to put Benji up and get to Pops'. My mother got all woe-is-me and clingy whenever she was fighting with her boyfriends. There was always the risk of her hugging on you or crying on your shoulder, the whole time sobbing about how sorry she was that things were so bad and trying to convince you how much she really cared. I'd nearly lapsed into a coma after one of those sessions when I was ten and we lived in Florida.

But the worst part was getting away without having her turn on you. Anything you said could get you snared. Agreeing with her might come off as sarcasm. *Who, me?* If you agreed with her and ran the dude down, she'd make up with him hours later and rat on you, turning his venom on you. Under no circumstances was it okay to point out her obvious faults or suggest she dump the guy and try to hold out for a better choice of men. That was considered kicking her while she was down.

No, the only safe play was maintaining as close as possible to absolute silence and hitting the road. Anywhere was safer than here. A needy Betty was more dangerous than an angry Betty. In a way, my mother was like three or four different people, depending on who was around and what her circumstances were. Even I wasn't quite sure who the real her was. *And I'm not sure I want to know.* Right now, I just needed to get away.

I put my dog up and gave him a good rub before closing the door to my room; I left it cracked in case he wanted out, but he knew he had to stay put because I was leaving. Betty was waiting for me in the kitchen, like a vulture swooping in on a dead carcass. She hugged me against her and dripped tears into my hair. I shuddered as the wetness of her Tony grief tried to permeate my shield of cold indifference.

"You know I love you. Don't you, honey?"

Oh shit! She called you honey! I just nodded when she pulled back to look at me. *For Christ's sake, don't say anything.* "Can't you tell me you love me, too?" *You're dead.* She hugged me again. "I'm sorry Tony hit you. I won't let that happen again." *He can hit me! Just let me go! Please let me go!* She pulled back again. "Come on, tell me."

There was a ringing sound. For a second I thought it was my ear again, but Tony hadn't slapped me all that hard. Betty let me go to answer it. *It's the phone!* "Bye Mom I gotta go to Pops'. I'll see you later tonight or in the morning when I get home; maybe I'll have a few extra bucks see ya then," I said in a rush as I practically flew out the door.

Adrenaline and the sweet air of freedom had me skipping like a girl with a brand-new jump rope. I couldn't believe I'd gotten out of there without suffering too badly. *Talk about being saved by the bell.* My only worry at the moment was wondering if Tommy would show or not. Rupe hadn't been coming to Pops' since he and Tommy weren't getting along, and if I had to work alone it was going to be one long ass-busting night.

It was a tough night. Tommy never showed up at Pops'. In fact, my friend never worked at Pops' ever again.

CHAPTER 17

We sang "Amazing Grace" and some other hymn I didn't know. I just mumbled along, inventing my own words while Bess jabbed me in the ribs with her sharp elbow. Some kid behind me sounded like a dog I'd once heard dying on the side of the road after being hit by a car. The girl sitting right in front of us sang so shrill I was sure she'd sat on something and it was still jammed up her butt. I snickered, and she spun around and glared at me right in the middle of the song, then lifted her chin and belligerently crooned even louder while Bess tried to crack my ribs.

Now the youth pastor was rambling on and on about something or other. He'd quote a scripture, and Bess would flip her Bible to the correct page with unerring accuracy. All that I had memorized was John 3:16 and the first few books of the Bible. *Genesis, Exodus, and L something,* I recited to myself. Bess jabbed me again and pointed to her Bible, wanting me to read along with her.

I kept catching her buddy Gordon sneaking peeks at us from a few pews up. Bess had purposely brought me to this special youth group meeting just to piss the guy off. I'd agreed to come along due to the tension in our place. Tony and Betty were fighting almost every day. *And night.* The constant stress was starting to get to me. Although now that I was here, I wished I'd stayed home. I hadn't counted on all the stupid singing and the drawn-out boring sermon.

Everybody murmured *Amen!* as the pastor ranted on about something he must have really meant. All I heard was, *Blah, blah, blah.*

I disliked the youth pastor—a younger, smooth-talking, and good-looking man named Kim—even more than I hated prissy-ass Gordo. There were whispers going around the church that Kim was sleeping with a teenage girl he and his wife were supposed to be helping out. (A rumor that might have turned out to be true, since he later slipped away to build cars in a factory instead of ranting behind a pulpit.) *Who names their little boy Kim, anyway?* I wondered if he was actually a pretty tough guy, like in the Johnny Cash song where the kid's name was Sue.

I didn't think so. In fact, I'd seen him playing basketball last summer. He'd been guarding the pastor's son, a really cool older kid named Jeffrey, and he'd been sorely overmatched. In fact, I was pretty sure he'd faked an injury to get out of playing after competing in only one game. He'd told me once I was disruptive and disrespectful. *Yeah, and you told him he forgot disliked, disparaging, discontented, disgusting, and disoriented.*

Why he needed to fool around with some other girl was something I didn't get. Kim had a really hot wife and two cute little kids. He drove a shiny new car and walked around the church like he owned the place, bossing all the younger people like he was their dad. He wasn't as nice to the bus kids as the people who worked on the busses were. Sometimes he made you feel like you were intruding into his territory, and he hated it if we made any noise while he was trying to preach.

Once, while riding the bus home, I'd voiced my *dis*like of Pastor Kim. Holly had defended him, although she'd agreed that the guy wasn't the best choice to talk to children. She told me Kim was just running the youth church and preaching the Wednesday night services until he took over for Pastor Grady full-time, since the older man was considering retiring soon.

When the sermon was over, Mrs. Grady started softly playing the organ while Pastor Kim tried to talk anyone who was having problems into coming down to the altar and praying with him. They especially leaned on those who hadn't yet asked Christ to be their Savior. The message was forthright: accept Christ and live forever in Heaven, or don't and burn in Hell for even longer.

I had a hard time believing it was that simple. Dave and Holly kept telling me salvation was the greatest gift in the world, and could only be granted through the blood of Jesus Christ, who had been nailed to a cross and died for all our sins. Dave insisted that once you were saved nothing could take it away from you, and that accepting Christ would change your life forever. But Betty had walked the aisle and knelt and said the words more times than I could remember, and I hadn't seen any changes in her.

Yet something about this always nagged at me. There was no way I was walking down the middle aisle in front of all these staring people and praying with some dude named Kim to a God I'd never met and didn't understand.

But something about this always got to me. The soft music and the heartfelt words of encouragement pulled at something inside. If it was a con, it was a damn good one.

"You want me to walk down with you?" Bess asked me.

There was no use acting like I hadn't been thinking about it. "No thanks."

She reached out and took my hand, urging me toward the aisle. "Come on. It's easy. You'll be glad you did it once it's all over."

"I know it's easy," I said, pulling my hand away. "'Cause I ain't going nowhere except home." She looked hurt, which made me feel bad, so I added, "Don't worry about me. I'm fine." She didn't look like she believed me. "I'm just waiting for a pastor named Bill or Chuck. I don't want to kneel down in front of a guy named Mary or Kim."

"You're horrible." But I'd gotten her to smile, and that eased my guilt.

And my guilt over not giving in to the salvation thing faded before I was on the bus to take us home. Gordo followed us around after the service, but Bess ignored him and he kept his distance. After we were seated I looked out the window and spotted him sulking around in the parking lot, staring at us through the window. I pressed my lips against the glass and left him a big wet smooch smear. Gordo tucked his hand against his belly and flipped me a real quick but demonstrative bird. I guess Gordon wasn't such a good Christian after all, but I always did have a way of bringing out the worst in people.

"What did he do?" whispered Bess, as if her sad little friend might hear her if she talked too loud.

"He flipped me off," I said, loud enough to make her jump. The kids sitting near us all turned and peered in our direction, curious. I was laughing and warding off another of her underhanded elbow shots.

"He did not!" she hissed, but I could tell she was thrilled that he would do something so unlike him. I didn't know why I was playing along with this, letting her use me to make another guy jealous. *Because this is better than Tony and Betty?* "What's he doing now?"

I looked and said, "Oh my God! He's making out with Pastor Kim over in the corner!" I tried to block an elbow and missed. Her blow wasn't playful. It knocked the wind out of me for a second. I doubled over while she came in for the kill, punching me in the back and slapping me on my exposed neck. I *oofed!* and *owed!* while she beat me, trying to breathe and hoping old Gordo could see her jumping all over me.

"You *are* awful! Gordon does *not* kiss boys."

I sat up and took a peek. Gordon was long gone. "I think you ruptured my spleen," I informed Bess as our bus started pulling out of the parking lot.

She pouted and leaned across me, trying to see if Gordon was anywhere in sight. "You don't have a heart or a spleen. You're just full of mean." I was sorry when she pulled her lithe frame off of me. Having Bess pressed against me hadn't been quite as thrilling as my date with Mandy, but it had been nice all the same. "I thought he would try to talk to me," she admitted sadly.

Okay, this is awkward. Was I supposed to commiserate? I sure didn't want to. As far as I was concerned, Gordon could pound sand. "Well, he *was* staring in the window," I offered, hoping that would be enough sympathy.

Bess shook her head and groaned. "You *kissed* the window! Why did you do that?"

"I was lonely." I blocked that elbow. *Missed me, bitch,* I crowed silently, all proud of my quick reflexes and anticipation. "What did you want him to do, storm the bus and carry you away?"

"Who's going to storm the bus?" Dave asked, taking the empty seat in front of us.

Thank God. "Gordon," I informed him. I had to block another elbow.

"Nobody," snapped Bess, glaring at me.

Dave just chuckled. "Never mind." He reached out and touched my eye, probing the scar left by the now completely healed wound. "I see that closed up all right. How are you and your mom's friend doing lately?"

"Just great. He wants to adopt me." *Take it easy. Dave doesn't deserve sarcasm.* I sighed and shrugged. "Not too bad. We try to stay out of each other's way."

There was an uncomfortable pause. "That's good," said Dave. He pursed his lips and eyed me frankly. "I see you still won't give God a chance."

"A chance for what?"

He made a fist. "I'll open that eye back up," he threatened playfully. "You know what I mean. You won't accept Christ into your heart and trust God to help you." He lowered his hand and gave me the stern, serious face I was used to. "You really need His help, Donny. Without God none of us have a chance."

I couldn't help myself. "A chance for what, Dave?" I repeated more seriously. Bess and Dave shared a look, and she slipped off to sit somewhere else, leaving me alone to suffer beneath the intensity of his scrutiny.

He started to say something and then thought better of it. I was being mean. *Again.* But that was what I did. He wouldn't stop gazing at me, though. I broke off our stare and watched out the window. It was dusk, and the reflection of the passing headlights glimmered in the murky window glass, blinking on and off as the faster cars raced by our plodding bus. I suddenly wished I was in one of those cars.

Dave made some sort of decision. I could hear it in his voice: "This is getting old, Donny. You're a smart kid." He swallowed, a bit nervous. "You can do anything you want with your life. One day you'll be old enough to strike out on your own, and when that day comes you are going to have to leave this life and all the baggage you're carrying behind." I opened my mouth to speak, but he lifted a finger and silenced me, wanting to make a last point. "And you must *also* leave behind all your excuses."

"Excuses?"

He nodded. "Excuses. You may not like hearing this, but just because your mother hasn't done so well and you've had to do without a few things, doesn't give you an excuse to fail. I expect you to succeed, and so does God. I know you've had it rough, but I'm not going to sit here and tell you how terrible that is, or allow you to convince yourself that it's okay if you don't expect much from yourself."

He was talking crazy. "What am I supposed to do, Dave?" *Answer that.* He had me in a corner, but I was prepared to fight my way out.

"I don't know," he admitted. A smile died before my lips could form it, as he held up that finger again. "But I *do* know where it starts." *Oops.* "Because God *does* know. He has a plan for you, but you'll never achieve His grace or know His plan unless you stop being so stubborn and ask for it."

I was going to be a wise-ass again. I could feel the mean coming before I even started spitting words. "So if God has this great plan, what the hell am I living now?" *Why are you so defensive? Don't let him get you going.* But he already *had* me going. "What did I do to deserve this shit?"

"I told you already. I don't know." There was that finger again. "And don't you curse on this bus."

I hadn't meant to do that. "I'm sorry." He lowered the finger.

Cursing, cussing, or swearing, no matter what you wanted to call it, I definitely had the habit. And I always would. I was a kid going nowhere, riding a church bus back to a home I detested. Betty and Tony were waiting for me. Dave didn't get that, just like I didn't get his God. How could I tell this nice man I wasn't sure I believed in something he'd built his whole world around? I didn't want to hurt any of the few people who were taking time out of their own lives to come into our shitty neighborhoods and cart us back and forth to church and other activities we were otherwise deprived of.

"Okay, Dave. I'll think about what you said. I promise." And I would, whether I wanted to or not.

"You need to think about it *real* hard," he said, still pushing. I just nodded and said nothing, wishing I'd told Bess no when she'd talked me into this trip, and hoping Dave would back off. He motioned for Bess, letting her know she could have her seat back. "Okay. I'll see you Saturday." Gently lifting my chin, he said, "I care about you. And I'm going to see you accept Christ, young man. You can count on that."

Bess put her hand on my arm as she sat down. "Wow, that was serious," she whispered, watching Dave carefully negotiate the moving bus, heading back to his seat up front. I didn't respond, no longer interested in banter or fooling around. Instead, I just watched the cars as they swept by us, dreading the evening ahead of me.

Cartoons chattered on the tube, mesmerizing my brothers. *And Tony, too.* My mother's Dago was hogging the couch, bleary-eyed and hung over from a hard Friday night. Tom was chasing Jerry around. Lately, I was feeling a lot like that mouse. Tony hadn't belted me again, but he was poking and pushing on me every time the opportunity presented itself, getting freer with his hands.

I was sitting at the kitchen table with Rupe. We had baseball cards stacked up all over the place, trading and bartering like old people at the flea market. Rupe was a big Yankees fan, and one of my best sources for Cincinnati Reds cards. It didn't really matter how the value of our trading went. I always came out ahead, since he'd bought and paid for his collection while I hadn't spent a red cent.

We were in some serious negotiations over a Johnny Bench when Terry interrupted me again. "Donny, can I have some more cereal?"

I didn't even look at him. "You ate all the cereal."

He thought about that, standing there and irritating me. I'd already told him that little bit of info twice this very morning. "Did you buy any doughnuts?"

We had another week or so until Betty got her blessed welfare check, so food was in short supply at the moment. "Hold that thought," I told Rupe. "Jesus Christ, Terry!" I got up and walked over to the cabinet where I'd hidden the stuff I'd bought for them after working Pops' last night. I'd wanted to save it for tomorrow morning, but Terry wasn't going to leave me alone until I gave him something to stuff in his mouth.

"What else is in there?" he asked while I tore open the two packs of chocolate doughnuts I'd actually paid for and plunked them into the cleanest plastic bowls I could find.

"Never mind," I told him while he followed me back into the living room. *Don't forget to hide that shit, or the little rat will devour the whole stash*, I told myself, making a mental note to do that right after Rupe and I finished up. "Here." I gave Chip his bowl and Terry the other as he sat back in front of the TV. "Now leave me the hell alone."

"I'll take Munson and Alomar," Rupe informed me.

"Munson and Alomar my—" Chip's screaming killed my comeback. I darted back into the living room to find my brothers fighting over a single bowl of doughnuts. They'd spilled some of them already. "What the fuck? Cut it out!" I pulled them apart and snatched the bowl, picking up the crumbling cakes off the floor before they smashed them. "Where's the other bowl?"

Terry was so upset he couldn't speak. His mouth was hanging open, and he was doing that silent crying thing, his face turning red because he wasn't breathing. But he could point. I followed his trembling finger as he finally sucked in a big gulp of air and wailed, "Tony took mine!"

The Dago was lying back on the couch, the bowl on his bare chest as he licked the tips of his fingers and grinned at me. "You're blocking the TV, asshole. Move."

"That's fucked up, man, stealing food from little kids."

He laughed. "What? I left the little shits a bowl. Say something else, and I'll eat those too." I didn't doubt that he would. "And you better get that look off your face."

I turned my back on Tony. "Here." I gave Terry Chip's bowl, and the baby began crying again, thinking he was going to be the one to lose out. "Shut up," I snapped, picking him up. "You want some Cracker Jacks?"

The crying stopped, and I was rewarded with a sloppy grin. "Jack jacks?"

"Yeah, jack jacks." I set him down. "Stay here."

"Can I have something else, too?" asked Terry before I even moved.

I gave him the best warning glare I could muster. "You're going to get something you don't want if you keep messing with me."

I took a step but was stopped again. "Bring me a beer before you feed the rug rat," Tony said. Every fiber of my being wanted to tell him to get stuffed, but I didn't dare. Even if he didn't jack me up with Rupe here, he'd surely get me later. "You got a problem with that?"

There were only three cans of PBR left in the fridge, but I yanked one free of the plastic strapping. Rupe was watching me as I did Tony's bidding. I hated that he was seeing me dancing for my mother's dishwasher, but I really didn't have much of a choice. I dug under the counter for a box of Cracker Jacks and opened them up, handing the popcorn to Chip as I passed back through the living room. "Open the toy for him," I told Terry.

I held out the beer to Tony, who was now sitting on the edge of the couch. He wouldn't take it. "I thought I told you to get my beer first?"

"I did."

"Yeah? Then why is the little bastard eating while you're holding my beer?"

"He's not a little bastard."

Tony was in a playful mood. "Open it." I did. "What? No service with a smile? Your mother's a good waitress. One day you'll make a good waitress too." His face hardened. "Now smile." Tight-lipped, I did as he instructed, still extending his PBR can with my ears burning. Rupe could hear this. Tony knew that as well as I did.

Tony finally accepted his beer, taking it from me almost begrudgingly. "Hold up," he said, stopping me from leaving again. Obviously, Tony wasn't done with this round of make Donny dance and sing. "I said the kid was a little bastard."

That was going too far. "I said he wasn't."

"I say he is," Tony persisted.

"Tell you what. Their dad makes a habit of stopping by every now and again. He ever shows up, just have this argument with him." *Please, God. Let Terrance show sometime soon.*

If my onetime stepfather ever made an appearance, Tony would end up hospitalized. I'd seen my brothers' dad fight more than once, and he wasn't a man to talk or argue. He'd beaten a truck driver to a bloody pulp on the side of the road one rainy, windy night, with Betty circling the combatants and screaming for Terrance to stop and me staring at the bloodshed, all wide-eyed and awed. It was a pleasant vision to imagine Tony taking the surprised driver's place in that memory.

"I wish he *would* show up," said Tony.

"Me too."

"Say it."

"Say what?"

"Say he's a little bastard."

"No."

"You will."

"I won't." My heart was thumping away. I could tell Tony was going to smack me. "He's my brother."

"I don't care if he's—"

"Donny, you want me to go get your mom?" Rupe asked from the opening between the two rooms.

He was standing there watching us, but I was somewhat strengthened by how calm he appeared. He leaned against the doorjamb, one hand holding the Bench card I was after and the other hand tucked into his front jeans pocket.

"No, I'm fine," I told him. Benji came clicking into the living room from where he'd been dozing under the table, one eye on Tony and the other searching for crumbs left by the boys. "Really, it's okay."

Betty wouldn't have been of any assistance, anyway. She was drinking more because of Tony, and popping her favorite pills with dangerous regularity. Tony had her missing work and church, and was borrowing money at an alarming rate. Our mother was home less and less on the weekends, and when she was she was usually sick and high, or sleeping off being sick and high. *Like she is now.*

"Who's your sweet little friend?" Tony asked with a chuckle.

"I may be sweet, but I don't have soft little man boobs," Rupe sent back.

Tony didn't know what to say to that. That had been a comeback worthy of me before Tony had busted my eye and made me his bitch. He just sat there stunned, staring at the relaxed and casual Thomas Rupe while I stood there with the same look on my own face. Rupe broke the most beautiful smile of sarcasm I'd ever seen.

I turned stiffly away from Tony and gathered Rupe up as we went back to the kitchen. I could feel Tony's glare between my shoulder blades. "What are you doing?" I hissed at Rupe, gathering my cards and throwing them back in the shoe boxes I stored them in. I was hoping to get our shit together and get him upstairs to my room. *Or maybe out of the house.* I knew Tony was going to come sauntering into the kitchen any second, looking to start up with us.

"What are you doing?" Rupe asked. "I thought we were going to do some trading?"

Benji's ears lifted. My dog was staring at the other room, letting me know Tony was moving around and probably coming. I gave Rupe the Thurmon Munson and Sandy Alomar cards he'd been wanting.

"Here. They're yours. Now come on. Pack up your shit and let's go upstairs."

"Why?"

"Fuck, Rupe! Would you just do it?" *Here he comes!* I didn't think Tony would be stupid enough to hit Rupe. He was mean when he was hung over, but he was sane. *Kind of.* "Come on. Would you just do it?"

Tony was standing in the doorway with nothing on but the sweat pants he'd slept in and that stupid chain, leaning on the jamb much the same way Rupe had. My friend didn't see him as he asked again, "Why?"

"Because he's a scared little pussy, that's why," Tony told us with a laugh. "You both are."

Rupe just snorted, not even bothering to look at Tony. "You're calling *us* little? I've got a sixteen-year-old cousin bigger than you. And she has *nice* breasts."

I fell into my seat, dropping my cards onto the table. *Why bother with them? Dead kids don't need baseball cards.* The cartoons kept going in the other room. I was wondering if the boys would remember me after I was buried. Of all the times Rupe could have chosen to find a big set of brass balls, why now? Why with Tony? Even if the Dago just kicked Rupe out, I was a goner. *Here lies Donny, maybe Davis but the dude wasn't sure, beaten to death because his friend told a crazy Dago he had boobies.*

"You have a smart mouth, you little punk," Tony said, crossing to the table and leaning in on Rupe, trying to cow him.

"I've got one word for you…" Rupe was waving his hand, trying to clear the stench of Tony's rancid breath. "Mouthwash," he told him. Tony's face looked like Rupe had kicked him right in the crotch. Rupe glanced over at me. "Is mouthwash one word or two?" he asked me.

"Don't ask me, I'm dead," I mumbled. This was great. I had one friend running around with Irving trying to kill some rich guys from out in the suburbs, and another who was losing his marbles right in my kitchen. The world was going crazy. "What are you doing?" I asked Rupe, my voice cracking.

"He's getting ready to get my foot in his ass." I knew that tone. Tony meant it. I wanted to warn Rupe not to say anything else, if not for his own safety, then for mine. "You hear me, kid?"

Rupe didn't flinch. He snorted again. "You won't touch me, pal."

I looked at Tony and saw uncertainty. "That what you think, kid?"

"That's what I know." I was pretty sure I was going to faint real soon. But something was wrong. Tony wasn't sure what to do, and Benji crawled under my chair and plopped down, like he already knew there wasn't going to be any reason to keep an eye on the Dago. "You look curious, *Anthony*. Don't you want to know how I know you aren't going to even touch me? This is what you do, right? You scare kids and smack them around, right?"

Tony was furious. He was fingering that horn around his neck and sweating. "I'm going to tear up all your little cards and throw you the fuck out of here, punk. Right on your ass." Tony cocked that thumb and prepared to poke Rupe with it. My friend just stood there like a retard, all smiles and confidence.

But Tony flinched like he'd stuck that thumb into an electrical socket when Rupe said, "Frank Rupe."

"What'd you say," Tony asked quietly.

Rupe began picking up his stacks of cards and placing them in his own shoe boxes. "I said Frank Rupe. That's my dad's name. You know him. He worked with you at the box factory." Rupe looked Tony right in the eye and gave him the sweetest smirk. "Before you got canned, that is. My dad was there the night you got your ass whipped by old man Hugh." Rupe leaned toward me and whispered, "They call him old man Hugh 'cause he's in his sixties."

"You need to go, kid," Tony ordered feebly.

But Rupe was on a roll. "Don't you want to hear what else I know, Anthony?" He did the neat lean-and-whisper thing again. "They didn't call him Tony at the factory. They called him Anthony." He kept cleaning up his cards while Tony stood there like a shirtless mannequin in a store window. *With soft man boobs.* "I know you got fired for drinking on the job. And I know you live in your mother's basement. And I know you've been

251

arrested for beating on your elderly mother. And I know you've been in jail for hitting women and selling drugs. And I know my mommy knows your mommy. And that means my mommy knows where your mommy lives. And I know my dad—" Rupe gave Tony the smirk again "—you remember him…? Frank Rupe? Well, he would beat the living shit out of you if you even breathed on me too hard, which you kind of already did. So I'd back off if I were you."

"I never touched you, kid."

And wonder of wonders, but that was fear I heard in Tony's voice. Rupe was going to walk out of here like John Wayne after a gun duel, even though I was dead as a doornail. *Dead as a doornail? Who made that up?* Isn't it strange the things that go through your mind right before you die?

"I never touched you," Tony repeated, stepping away from Rupe.

All packed up, my smug friend headed for the door. I was proud of him as I watched him go. Of course, using a protective father wasn't an option I had at my disposal, but Rupe had backed Tony down like a seasoned pro. Maybe one day he wouldn't be such a coward after all. *And if he comes to visit me in the hospital, I'll even tell him so.* Although I doubted I was going to survive. Once Rupe was gone, I would pay for the way my friend had so thoroughly ridiculed Tony.

Thank every angel in the heavens Rupe had thought of that as well.

He turned to me after opening our back door. "I know this asshole's been hitting you, Donny. Mrs. Lorret told my mom at the store last week." Rupe glared at Tony, no longer looking at me while he talked. "Know what would happen if this guy hit you and you went out and fell over in the street? I'll bet old lady Lorret would call the police and the FBI and maybe even the White House. She'd tell them how *Anthony* here had been beating on you."

Rupe turned back to me. "Know what happens to a dude with a record of hitting on women and using drugs when he decides to start abusing children? Especially if that kid says the crazy bastard had been sneaking into his bedroom or trying to watch him take baths? And the cops have a witness like Mrs. Lorret and cuts and bruises on the kid as evidence?" Rupe shook his head, faking sorrow. "I sure wouldn't want to be *that* guy." My friend gave me a little nod of encouragement. "Thanks for Munson and Alomar. I left the Bench card on the table."

Bewildered, I sat there while he shut the door and headed home. I was having a gay moment: I loved Tommy Rupe. In my mind I rushed out the back door, and he turned in the yard and ran toward me, our arms all out-stretched while we raced toward each other in slow motion, just like in those sappy lovey-dovey movies. I would have kissed him too, probably right on the lips. *Just once,* I told myself, hoping that thinking about smooching another dude didn't make you officially a fag.

But I never moved. I just sat there looking at Tony while he looked at me. I think the Dago could probably see the light bulb above my head, glowing there just like in one of those cartoons my brothers were watching. If he couldn't see it, I could sure feel it there. It was like Rupe had reached out and pulled on the little chain.

"What the fuck are you looking at?" Tony growled, reaching for that cocksure attitude I'd once feared.

So many comebacks flashed across my brain pan I almost shorted out, but there was time for them later. All of them and then some. I grinned, and Tony saw it. He looked smaller to me now, so skinny and stupid I could scarcely believe I'd once lost sleep and avoided coming home because of him. *He kicked your dog.* That was going to cost him more than fifty-four dollars. *Oh, yeah, the money.* I couldn't forget the money.

"I said, what the fuck are you looking at?" he asked again.

My grin was just burning right through his hangover. I had to wait a moment before speaking; all those awesome one-liners were trying to jump right off my tongue. But all I said was, "Son of a bitch, he *is* smarter than me."

CHAPTER 18

Ever try to slice a tire with a steak knife? Believe me, it doesn't work. If you press too hard, the cheap flimsy wooden handle will break, and you're lucky if you don't cut off one or two of your fingers. Maybe God does smile on drunks and children, because I'd been blessed and allowed to keep all my extremities after having a go at Tony's worn Goodyears with one of Betty's supposedly good knives. The thing snapped in two, the handle still in my hand as I fell, trying to carve at the stubborn rubber. The blade barely missed the ends of my fingers and whirled right past my face before whistling off into the yard.

But the screwdriver-and-hammer method worked. A love tap or two, and every one of those tires hissed and cursed at me while the life drained out of them. I stood back and surveyed my work when I was through, my hands black and my heart full of joy. All the fear I'd bottled up inside gushed out of me much like those deflating tires. It was time for us to lay down some new ground rules.

I went inside after hiding my tools of destruction. It was a satisfying feeling, tearing the Dago down. Of course, flattening his tires was going to delay Tony's departure. But it was his return I was striving to prevent. I didn't know what I would do to his car if he called my bluff. *Throw something through the windshield?* As I entered the kitchen, I was wondering whether the Caddy would explode if I poured gas all over it and set it ablaze.

Tony was sitting with my mother at our kitchen table. They ceased their hushed conversation as I entered. "Donny, we'd like to talk to you," Betty requested, her tone neutral.

I no longer cared about trivial little things like tone or intent, or even drunken tempers. "Your tires are all flat," I told Tony, washing my hands in the sink.

He sat bolt upright. "What?"

"How?" Betty asked, as the havoc I'd wrought began to dawn on her.

I was drying my hands. "I tried to slice them, but I didn't have a good enough knife." I shrugged and grinned at Tony, who was standing in the doorway, staring at his car to make sure I wasn't fibbing. "But I managed to pound a screwdriver right through them with hardly no problem at all."

"You better not have!" my mother warned, her shriek making even Tony wince as she went to the doorway to see for herself.

"I'm going to whip your fucking little ass," Tony growled.

It was so weird. Just a few days ago I'd been scared shitless of the guy. But now he just looked like a dishwasher again. His chain and his shirt and his tattoo and his greasy hair and his scraggly sideburns looked completely ridiculous. I was ashamed of myself for letting him torture me for so long. But that was over now. *Thanks to Rupe.* That was the only part of my good fortune that irked me a little. Only a little.

I tossed the towel back on the sink, shaking my head. "I don't think so. But if you do...? Make sure it's worth your while. Rupe's dad says—you remember Rupe's dad? Frank? The guy who can snap you like a twig?" Tony's face went blank. It was priceless. "*Anyways,* he told me to make sure to point out my old scars to the detective if and when you give me any new ones. I already showed them to Mrs. Lorret, and told her I would try to crawl across the street for help if you beat me or tried to molest me again."

"Tony never tried to molest you!" screeched Betty.

I just kept grinning. I couldn't help it. "Yeah? Well, for all I know he's been sniffing my underwear every chance he gets. I say we tell the cops the whole story and let them sort out the charges." It felt so good to be me again.

"You know what it's going to cost me to get those tires plugged?" Tony asked. His voice was so constrained with pent rage I almost had to hug myself with glee.

"Don't bitch to me, pal. I told you to pay me back the fifty-four bucks you owe and keep your damn distance." I dropped my smile and stepped toward him, placing my skinny carcass within striking distance. "You come back here, and I'll throw something right through your fucking windshield."

He wanted to hit me so badly. He had that stiff tilt to his shoulders. Benji was sitting near the steps, watching us. Tony nodded toward my dog. "Maybe I can't hit you, but I can still kick that fucking mutt of yours."

Now we were getting right down to it. "That's the spirit, asshole. Look for a way out." I stepped right up to him. I must have grown a bit over the summer; Tony didn't seem all that much taller than I was. "You touch that dog again, and I'll bust open my own face and still lie out in the street. And I'll still tell the cops you've been grabbing at my ass and my pee-pee every time my mommy left the house. And guess what else?" This was fun! I loved being in control and having a solid plan of action. "I'll wait a while and then find your car at the diner, or maybe where you park it at your mom's, and fuck it up again."

Tony didn't know what to do. *How's it feel, asshole?* The biggest problem with being a dumb loser is having only those resources available to those who are dumb losers. No longer being able to punch or threaten left Tony hapless. He stood there all confused, and I could tell he was embarrassed. He didn't like being talked down to in front of Betty. But I think he knew I'd follow through with my threat to plead my case to the cops. What could he really do?

"Donny, we were going to talk to you about calming things down around here," Betty said. Her face was full of panic. She was afraid if Tony left he might stay gone.

I was afraid if Tony left he might come back. I decided to give him another little push toward the door. "Nope. Fifty-four dollars and distance, that's the only deal he gets."

"You don't give me rules!" she yelled at me.

I shook my head, feigning exasperation. "I'm not giving *you* any rules. I'm giving *him* rules." I spread my hands and confronted Tony.

"So? Are you going to smack me one or get out? What's it going to be?"

"Keep pushing me, kid," he mumbled.

I grinned. He didn't grin back. "I just wanted to make sure everything was clear between us," I explained. "What was it you like to say to me all the time?" I scratched my head and gazed up at the ceiling, pretending to search for his favorite catch phrase. *You should go into acting,* I told myself. "Wait. I remember now." I had been looking forward to this. "Capisce?"

Tony looked like he had something caught in his throat. I could almost hear his brain working. "You hurt my dog. One day, maybe I'm going to be big enough to pay you back for that." I felt like spitting in his face, but I didn't want to push my luck. "Until then I'll just have to lie in the street and cry to the fuzz, but don't you ever forget me 'cause I'm not going to forget you."

He didn't have the slightest notion what to do with me. Instead of speaking he pushed past me and crossed to our phone, where he dialed a number and began muttering and bitching in a quiet voice with someone on the other end. Betty kept staring at me with a mixture of contempt and fear. My brothers were standing just in the living room, watching our little play.

"Jones is coming over to help me haul those tires to be plugged," Tony told my mother after he hung up. "I'm going to jack up the car and get one ready to go." Tony paused in the doorway, ignoring me altogether and looking only at Betty. *The nerve of some people.* "Keep your fucking kid away from me and my car until I can get out of here." That said, he drifted on out to the yard, leaving me alone with an incensed Betty. I almost wanted to offer my assistance to Tony just to get away from my mother.

Betty was nearly too stunned to move. "Why'd you do this?" she hissed at me, her head swaying like a cobra preparing to strike. But she darted out after Tony before saying anything more, sparing me from having to respond.

Tony and his buddy Jones spent a couple of hours running tires back and forth from the gas station. I hadn't known it was so easy to patch a simple hole in the tread of a tire. If I'd have managed to slice them the damn things would've been ruined, and that would have cost the bastard a lot more. *I think you made your point,* I conceded to myself. He still got all dirty and was extremely pissed off, which was a hell of a lot better than nothing.

Still, as I watched Betty, stealing peeks through the smeared up kitchen window, I felt awash in guilt. It seemed like every time I got one over on her or one of her screwed-up friends, I couldn't truly enjoy my victory. My cow of a mother followed Tony around all the while he worked, fetching him beers and weeping in his ear about how sorry she was because of what I'd done. Tony kept giving her the business, answering with short, harsh responses and abusive language, taking what I'd done out on her since he couldn't strike back at me.

I hated her for giving him that power, for submitting to his will. Tony wasn't worth the time it took to flush a toilet, but there was no telling Betty this. Whenever one of her boyfriends decided it was time to head for greener pastures, he suddenly became Mr. Right. She somehow managed to forget all his faults and sins, no matter how severe they'd been or who'd been hurt by his actions.

And there was nothing I could do to rid myself of the guilt and shame I felt. I felt sorry for my mother, watching her stumbling around in circles, following after Tony. She'd been alone before he'd come along, and she would still be alone after he was a memory. What Betty couldn't understand was that she'd actually been alone while Tony was here, too. Leon, Tony, all of her sporadic live-ins, not one of them had ever intended to stay long. I seriously doubted any man ever would.

Betty was a desperate woman searching for a man who didn't exist. What guy in his right mind wanted to throw in with a broke, rundown, slightly heavy thirty-year-old woman with no teeth and three troublesome brats? Especially when the oldest was a pain in the ass like me? *She'll be discussing that very thing with you as soon as Tony rolls out. And she'll be using her loudest and highest pitched shrieks. She'll probably scream at you for the rest of the day and into the night and maybe for the rest of your life.*

Surely she wasn't going to take his side after he busted my eye? She was. I knew that. Hell, I'd known that long before flattening Tony's tires and calling the dude out. But just as I was aware of her despair, I was also aware of my own. She was floundering about looking for help, dragging me and my brothers like an anchor as she tried to pretend she was free and available. I was floundering as well. But my anchor was my life.

So I watched as Betty made a fool of herself. She traipsed along behind Tony like a loyal hound dog, her head down and her demeanor sorrowful. She tried to be helpful, offering to fetch tools or clean up, but Tony just kept brushing past her or barking at her. I even caught Tony and his buddy laughing at her when she wasn't looking, and that was more than I could take.

I made Benji stay inside as I went out. The boys were eating cereal and watching TV. Betty and I both used the tube as a baby-sitter as often as possible. Tony and Jones stopped chuckling when they saw me hopping off the steps. Betty whirled around and glared at me, her hands all dirty from rolling one of Tony's tires and carrying tools.

"Ain't you done yet?" I asked Tony.

"I told you to keep that fucking kid away from me," he told my mother.

She had tears in her eyes. "Haven't you done enough?" All of a sudden I wished I hadn't even come outside. "What do you want from me? What? Do you hate me so much?"

I pointed at Tony and his buddy. "They were laughing at you when you weren't looking," I said. But it sounded lame. Why would the kid who'd caused the uproar suddenly give a shit if the people he'd hurt were laughing at one another? *That's a good question.*

My mother choked back a sob. "So?"

"So?" And here came that familiar rage. "So? What's wrong with you? Why do you let him treat you like that? He's a piece of shit! He never gave you any money or treated you nice! All he did was buy food now and then! Fuck him! Bring Leon back or find another trucker! Anyone would be better than his ass!"

"Go back in the house!" she screamed at me.

"No!" I screamed back. "Why are you doing this? Why are you following him around like he's worth something?"

My mother turned away from me. "I'm sorry," she sobbed at Tony, who just stood there enjoying himself while Betty and I went at it.

"*You're* sorry? Sorry for what?" I was trying to get her to look at me. "What did you do to be sorry to him for?"

"I'll make him stop," she told Tony. "He won't mess with your car again, and I'll get him to stop talking back." Betty was crying and pleading. I was afraid she was going to drop to her knees and start begging. "Just tell me you'll give me a chance."

"He split my eye open!" I yelled. There were tears in my own eyes now. "He smacked you around too! And he stole my money! And he hurt my dog! And he scares my brothers! He's the one should be sorry!"

"I don't care if he hurt your eye!" Betty shrieked, spinning on me. "I wish he'd broken your fucking neck!" Spit was flying as my mother screamed. "Why won't you leave me alone? Get the fuck away from me!"

I heard Jones mumble something and head for his car. The guy must've been somewhat normal and wanted away from our sick fiasco. He was about my mom's age, but dressed decently in jeans now dirty from swapping tires and a short-sleeved buttoned shirt. He wore a wedding ring and a Reds cap. Tony looked a bit uncomfortable all of a sudden; maybe he didn't want his buddies knowing he smacked women and children around. Jones hopped into his pickup after a last doleful glance in my direction and thundered down the alley, leaving us to continue our insanity in private.

Betty was ready to burst. Tony bent to resume tightening up the last of his tires. My mother stumbled over to him, blubbering openly. The Dago continued to ignore her, spinning the lug wrench in his hands as he worked. I wished the heavy steel tool would break loose and bash him in the teeth. I couldn't stay outside and watch my mother fawn over him, so I headed back inside.

The phone was ringing when I entered the kitchen. "Hello?" I said, expecting some bill collector or maybe one of my mother's managers from the Big Boy.

"Betty?" a man asked.

God, I was going to be so glad when my voice changed. "No. This is her son."

I was getting ready to feed the dude a load of shit when he said, "Donny?"

That threw me. Betty's creditors didn't normally know my name. "Yeah."

"It's your grandfather. Your mother's father." I detected the remorse in that admission, through his deep southern drawl. It was a pain I knew all too well. "Are you still there?"

"Yeah."

"How are you?" I could tell he was only being polite. He sounded mad, and anxious to speak to Betty. She was probably pulling some kind of fast one on him again. "Donny?"

"I'm fighting with one of Betty's asshole boyfriends right now."

What the hell. He asked.

He chuckled. "Who's winning?"

I couldn't lie. "I thought I was, but now I'm not so sure."

"Are you joking? He hasn't hit you, has he?"

It was sweet of him to pretend to care. "Not today."

He swallowed uneasily on the phone. I wasn't being fair. What could he do from Florida? He'd helped us out more times than anyone should have. He didn't deserve a daughter like Betty. "I'm doing okay though," I said, letting him off the hook.

"That's good," he hurriedly sent back. "Is that mother of yours there?"

"Yeah. She's out back with the asshole, crying 'cause he's leaving."

"Why's she crying?"

"Beats me."

"Why's he leaving?"

My grandfather asked the best questions. "He's upset 'cause I punched holes in all his tires."

He chuckled again. His laugh was bass-sounding, like Fat Albert's. But I couldn't tell my grandfather that, since he hated black people. "Why'd you do that?"

"He hit me."

I heard him sigh. "Would you put your mother on the line?"

"Sure." I laid the receiver on the table, but then picked it up and added, "Bye."

"Donny?"

"Yeah?"

"If that Yankee puts his hands on you again, just…" He paused, searching for words. Grandpa was a tough old cuss who'd retired from the Navy. I was pretty sure what kind of advice he wanted to give me. "Never mind. Good-bye, son."

Outside, I found Tony behind the wheel and Betty leaning into his car, practically hysterical. She was promising to pay for what I'd done. It seemed Tony would still be getting at me, only he'd be doing it through my mother in the way of money she didn't have to spare. I wasn't sure if I hadn't been better off when the dude was smacking me around. The money Betty would be giving him would mean less food for me and my brothers.

"Phone for you," I called out. They both ignored me. "It's long distance."

"Who is it?" she snapped. Tony started the Caddy. Betty panicked and tried to keep him from shutting the door, heaving her bulk in his way. "Wait a minute! Don't leave!"

"It's your dad," I told her.

Tony was rolling forward and trying to get his door closed, pushing at my mother to get her clear. I don't think it was until this moment that I truly understood what it meant to hate another person. I believed I would have killed Tony if I thought I could pull it off and get away with it. She kept scrambling after him, getting jostled by the car and shoved by the Dago. I was afraid she might slip and get run over.

"Tell him I'm not home," she quickly instructed me, still pawing at Tony, frantic and sobbing.

"I already told him you *were* home."

"Then tell him I left!"

I couldn't watch her anymore. I felt sick. All of this clamor would be blamed on me. I would defend myself by using Tony's abuse as justification. Betty would say none of that mattered and claim I had it coming. Maybe I did. Perhaps our lives would roll along a lot more easily if I just accepted whatever happened and didn't try to stick up for myself. But that was how Betty lived. I may have been feeling guilty and confused at the moment, but I didn't want to be like my mother.

Terry was prattling on the phone when I got back inside. I snatched the receiver away from him. He made a face at me and scampered back into the other room. "Betty says to tell you she left," I abruptly informed my grandfather.

"What? Is she still there?"

"Yeah, she's out back. But she's not going to talk to you."

"Did you tell her it was me?"

"Yes."

"Tell her it's important."

I guess he didn't know his daughter quite as well as I did. "That won't matter. She's not coming to the phone." There was silence for a while. "She using your name in a check scam again?"

"Something like that," he muttered. I could tell my frank question made him uncomfortable. "Your brother said he was hungry," he informed me, trying to change the subject.

"He's always hungry." He was thinking. I heard a woman's voice questioning him in the background. "If you have a message for her, I can make sure she gets it. You don't have to hide anything from me. I know what she does." *And how she does it.* But I didn't want him to know just how well I understood her illegal activities. *Guilt by association.* "I think we're going to have to run again pretty soon. There's a lot of pissed-off people calling and looking for her right now."

He stayed silent for a few more moments, trying to make some kind of decision. "Donny, you tell your mother I'm not going to lie for her. And you tell her to call me." He tried to subdue the anger in his voice. "You tell her if I don't hear from her soon, I'll be calling the police myself."

"What'd she do?"

"Never you mind. Just give her my message. Okay?"

"Okay."

"You take care, son," he murmured.

I heard Tony roar out of the yard, and Betty wailing in the fumes of his exhaust. I didn't want my grandfather to hang up. "I will," was all I said. And then he did hang up. I listened to the dial tone for a while. When my mother came storming into the kitchen, I pretended he was still on the line so she couldn't jump me. Betty checked her rage and went upstairs to repair her ravaged face. The look she gave me promised it was going to be a grueling night.

Ever the opportunist, I waited until I heard her clumping around in the bathroom and fled. Benji was getting around with only a hint of a limp, so I let him trail after me. I was halfway down the alley before I heard my mother bellowing out my name, but I sure as hell wasn't going to go back or even answer her. Our fight could wait. It wasn't like her anger was going anywhere. *You're just afraid she's so far gone she's going to attack you.* Hopefully, she'd calm down if I stayed away for a few hours. *Or a year.*

Rupe was out of town again. He and his parents had been spending a lot of time down around Cincinnati. I kept meaning to ask him what was going on. Bess was back with her new church family, and hanging out with Lynn wasn't worth putting up with the trolls. That left Tommy, so I headed for his place. I hadn't talked to him much since the day at the park.

It was getting on in the afternoon. I was pretty sure he'd be up and around. *And his mom will be heading out.* Tommy's mom tended bar at a dance club, although how she handled bottles and glasses with her long, hooked fingernails was beyond me. She wore a lot of makeup and tight clothes, but she still looked good enough to make a hell of a lot more money than Betty managed. She usually wore a wig that made her look like Tina Turner.

Her car was gone when I arrived, the back door wide open save for the screen, and it wasn't locked, so I went on in. There were a couple of older black dudes I'd seen around but didn't know sitting at Tommy's kitchen table, one rolling joints and the other smoking one of the finished products. The house reeked of grass, but that wasn't anything new. Tommy's mom and her friends smoked the stuff like regular cigarettes. She sold grass for Candy out of the club where she worked.

"Who the fuck are you?" the guy doing the rolling asked, his long, nimble fingers pausing like he was considering getting up from the table.

"I'm Donny, a friend of Tommy's," I explained.

"You ever heard of knocking, motherfucker?" the other dude asked. And he *did* get up.

"I usually just walk on in," I squeaked. "I'm over here all the time," I added as he loomed over me.

"Yeah? You pack for Candy?" He exhaled, blowing smoke right in my face. Like a child, I began hacking. "I can see you don't toke." They both laughed.

"Not exactly." He pushed me back into the screen, forcing the door open and shoving me out onto the porch. "Hey, wait—"

Benji sat, anxiously awaiting my return. My dog saw the dude with his hands on his beloved master and responded accordingly. Within a few seconds there were two Negroes on top of the table, rolled joints falling onto the floor, and a spilled baggie of grass being trampled. I was trying to catch my snarling mutt and at the same time reassure the two guys who were probably going to kill me later.

"What the fuck is going on?" Tommy yelled, running into the kitchen. I finally had a hold on my dog, but the two guys on top of the table didn't trust me to contain him. Neither of them was too eager to climb down. "Donny? Why is Benji after my boys?"

"I'm sorry... I... I mean... They..." I didn't know what to say. I didn't want to blame anything on them and maybe be tortured *before* they killed me, but they *had* started with me first. Benji was only protecting me. I stood there stammering until Tommy led me to the door and safely outside. "Thanks," I murmured.

"You keep that white boy and his crazy dog out of here!" one of the guys yelled at us once the door was closed.

"Just get off my table and pick that shit up, you scared bitch!" Tommy barked right back.

"What'd you say?"

Tommy grinned at me. "You want this killer back in there?" he asked, opening the screen and holding the door ajar while he stuck his head inside. Benji cocked his head and looked at me, not even thinking about trying to wriggle free and get back inside. But the cowards in Tommy's kitchen didn't know that.

"Hey, man!"

"Close the door!"

Tommy laughed at them. "I thought so. You better shut the fuck up then." He let the door slam closed and sat down on the step. Benji was still worked up, but I set him down and he stayed put, one eye on the door and a perked ear listening to the movements within the kitchen. "What you doing here?"

"I was just coming over to see what's up," I said. We didn't say anything for a moment. Tommy looked tired. "Who are those dudes?"

"We're rolling some shit for my mom to deliver Friday night," he explained. "I guess the stupid bitches over at the roller rink can't roll their own. Candy says they buy by the stick."

More silence. Dusk delivered a cool breeze. September was days away. I sat down a step beneath him. "Won't be long until school starts," I said.

"Yeah," he responded. There was a lot of woe in that single word.

I glanced up at him. He was lost in his own thoughts. He didn't look hurt, but something was really on his mind. "Get your knife back?"

He looked at me. Some emotion wafted behind his deep brown eyes. It was something older than me, something beyond me. I was pretty sure it was something I didn't want to know or understand. He gave me a slow nod.

"How'd that go?" I asked, and then wished I hadn't. Tommy probably felt like I should've backed him up on that one. *What could you have done?* I asked myself. "I mean… You didn't get hurt or anything?"

No laughter. No arrogance. He just shook his head again and lit a cigarette.

"Hey, nigger, you rolling this shit or not?" one of the guys inside called out.

Tommy sighed. "Just a minute!" he barked.

"Hey, I'll get going. I can see you've got stuff going on." I stood and called Benji, who was sniffing the fence line between Tommy's place and the next yard. "Maybe I'll see you tomorrow?"

"Maybe."

"See ya."

I felt weird, turning to leave. It was like we'd had a fight or something. Tommy was normally so talkative, he told me more than I wanted to know about everything going on in his life. It wasn't like him to hold shit back. But curious or not, I wasn't about to press him. Especially with the two thugs he had hanging around, wanting him to get back to work.

"Donny," Tommy called quietly, stopping me at the edge of the yard.

"Yeah?" He opened his mouth and closed it. I could tell he wasn't sure how to say what was on his mind. I laughed nervously, but then shook the hair out of my eyes and said, "What is it? Go ahead and say it."

"You probably shouldn't be coming around here no more," he finally blurted out. "I'm gonna be running more shit for Candy, and some of the brothers don't like…"

"White people?" I finished for him.

Tommy only nodded and stood up, flicking his cigarette into the falling gloom. "You start carrying for Candy when school starts, and maybe they'll get to know you." That wasn't happening, but I didn't tell him so. We both knew it already. "I'll see you at school. And I'll come over to your place sometimes."

"Sure."

CHAPTER 19

"Hey, laundry lady, you hear about your boy?"

I was unloading my last dryer in a hurry. It was drizzling outside, and the skies were threatening to turn the falling rain into an outright deluge. I didn't want to be stuck at the 'mat with the Blue-Wisped Witch. She sat behind her little desk, her black-and-white TV crackling, watching me with jaundiced eyes and wringing veined hands. I'd had nightmares about being locked in this place with the old hag. I wasn't about to find out if she really *did* have a cook pot hidden behind a sliding door, where she boiled kids alive before devouring their flesh.

Dorsey had been jogging by and noticed me in the Laundromat. He was wearing a cut-up sweatshirt and sweat pants sawed into shorts, with a 'do rag wrapped around his head. He'd grown over the summer, putting on pounds and a couple of inches. It looked to me like he might have outgrown Tommy. The ebony skin stretched tight over the muscle he'd added to his frame glistened with a mixture of rain and sweat.

"Why you running in the rain?" I asked him, ignoring his lame greeting and dumping my final load on the folding table.

His face split into a wide grin. He flexed both arms and posed. "I'm going out for football. Coach says I might play varsity. I busted my ass all summer. Can you tell?" I could, and I told him as much. "Football's my ticket out of here, baby."

I didn't think so. Dorsey was strong, but not so quick or coordinated. Tommy ate him alive when we played football. When we picked teams, Dorsey was never picked before Tommy or me.

I wasn't going to say anything to curb Dorsey's enthusiasm. "That's great, man. Maybe I'll come to some of your games."

That wasn't happening. People got beat to bloody pulps before, during, and especially after Central's games. I'd heard a kid had gotten himself killed

266

during a brawl a couple of years before we'd moved here. Attending that high school wasn't something I was looking forward to. They were bussing kids in and out of different areas, and the friction was only causing more riots and other violence. The stories of drugs and brutality couldn't be too exaggerated. They'd shut the school down and raided it at least three times last year alone. I'd even heard a teacher had been raped in her own car one evening after school.

I moved the clothes I'd already haphazardly folded into my shopping cart to make room on the table. Dorsey was in my way, and I almost tripped. "Look out, man." I moved another armload over.

"What's your hurry?"

Dorsey might have gotten bigger, but he hadn't gotten any smarter. I pointed outside. "The rain?" I pointed to my freshly washed and dried clothes. "The clothes?"

He figured it out. "Oh, yeah." He checked nature's progress and shook his head woefully. On cue, the heavens opened up and began a heavier stream of life-granting and Donny-soaking moisture. *Shit!* "I'd say you screwed," Dors informed me.

I was either going to have to wait out the rain here and risk being eaten, or push the clothes home as fast as I could and lay them out all over the kitchen table and chairs to dry before putting them away. Problem was, Betty was there and in a foul mood; we'd been fighting hot and heavy for days. I was sure to hear about it if I wasted her money drying the clothes and then got them all wet again. *Eaten by a witch or nagged by a bitch? Hey, that rhymes.* I decided I'd risk being devoured.

"Did you hear what I axed you?" Dorsey said

"No, what did you *axe* me?"

He didn't even notice my jest. "Your boy Tommy got busted last night."

I stopped folding. "What do you mean busted?"

"The fuzz nabbed him and Irving at Candy's. I hear they still locked up. Word is some white dude got sliced at the skating rink." Dorsey ran a finger along his jaw line. "Like ten or twenty stitches along here. Fuzz is looking for Jo Jo, too."

All of a sudden I forgot the rain. "Did you hear if Tommy cut the guy?"

He shook his head. *Thank God.* "Nah, dude said Irving did the cuttin'. Tommy *was* holding the white boy, though. He'll go down for the shit same as if he held the blade." Dorsey clicked his teeth. "That dumb nigger ought to know better than to hang with Irving. That crazy motherfucker slice his own mama she woke him up wrong."

I stood there, dumbfounded. The thought of Tommy being jailed scared me. If he was locked up, *I* could be locked up. We both did the same stupid shit. *You didn't cut anybody,* I tried to convince myself, but the notion still hit close to home. How many times had we stolen or trespassed, risking trouble with the cops?

They still locked up, Dorsey had said. How long would they hold Tommy? Would he be in school at the start of the semester? But why did I care? Tommy had made it clear we were going our separate ways. As far as I was concerned, the trouble he was currently in only made my decision to stay clear of Candy and his little errands easier to live with.

"I hear them white boys jumped you and Tommy."

Dorsey surprised me with his knowledge of that little piece of information. I almost asked him what else he knew, but decided to swallow my question. If Dors knew about the toilet-dunking, he'd say so. Something like that was too juicy to hold back. I was also more than a little concerned about how Tommy might have narrated my role in that sorry escapade. I'd never live it down should Tommy or the other guys label me a coward and say I'd run off and left a guy from the neighborhood to hang.

"Why wasn't you there for the payback?" he asked.

I realized he didn't know very much. He surely didn't know about the toilet or my running for help. "I guess I *do* know better than to hang with Irving," was all I replied. Dorsey chuckled, knowing exactly what I meant. "Hey, will you tell me if you hear anything about Tommy?"

He nodded, but I'd aroused suspicion. "Sure." He pushed water out of the wiry hairs sprouting above his lip, eyeing me. "You and Tommy have a fight?" I shook my head, resuming my folding. "Why you need me for info? He's *your* boy. You over at his place all the time, ain't you? Why don't you just check with his mom?"

"You're right. I'll just do that." *Why'd you say anything?* I scolded myself.

Dorsey's damp face scrunched up as a thought intruded upon his otherwise impenetrable brain. "Tommy's running more for Candy, and you ain't down." I kept folding. *Great, the dude fails health, but he can figure out your deepest secrets.* I moved another armload of clothing to my waiting cart. "You met Lonny and Hops yet?"

"The dudes he's rolling grass with?"

Dorsey grinned. "Yeah."

"I met them." I checked the rain. Outside, everything was a dull gray. I couldn't quite make out the buildings across the street through the haze of rain. "They didn't like me much."

"Lonny ain't bad, but Hops hates white boys." Mercifully, Dorsey turned away and acted like he was going to leave. "You keep away from Hops. That brother almost bad as Irving, only he don't need no razor."

"See ya," I sent as Dorsey stuck his head out the open door, looking up at the dreary sky.

"Damn," he muttered. But before he left he gave me a little more advice. "You stay away from Hops, Donny. And you smart to duck Candy. 'Tween you and me, that's one greedy-ass nigger. Once I make varsity and get some colleges wantin' me to play ball for them…?" He posed again, displaying his biceps and trying to flex the muscles in his neck. "Soon as that day rolls around I'm done runnin' for Candy's black ass myself."

That made me sad. Dorsey wasn't a bad kid. As big as he was, he could have pushed on smaller guys a lot more than he did. But he rarely tried to intimidate anyone. *Except to take change from Patrick, but so what.* Patrick had a never-ending supply of coins. Dors had even helped me out of a scrape in the lunch room last year, backing down an older guy who'd tried to take something off my tray.

But I didn't think Candy was someone you could so easily shed. I couldn't imagine waltzing into the pool hall and telling that big bastard anything he didn't want to hear. What could you do if you tried to quit and he said you couldn't? Who would dare to talk back? I could envision Candy turning on you with those malevolent shades and reaching behind him for that all-too-accessible pistol, while you stood helplessly waiting to be gunned down.

Dorsey stepped out into the rain, gave me a brief Heisman pose in the doorway, and darted off, just a purpled shadow in the blur of indistinguishable gray until he crossed the street and left my line of sight. I finished my folding, lost in thought, wondering about Tommy and worrying that my involvement in the conflict wasn't over. This really sucked. Now I was afraid of catching flack from both sides of a fight I'd run away from. *And living with Betty.* Sometimes it felt like you couldn't win, no matter what you tried to stay out of.

Finished, I shoved my loaded cart closer to the door and took a seat, hoping for a break in the rain. The witch was watching me from behind her desk. She was always watching. *Why bother bringing in the TV?* It seemed to me she paid more attention to the customers than her flickering tube. There wasn't anyone else in the 'mat, and that had me nervous. I twisted in my seat and faced outside, trying to ignore the old hag as I waited out the weather, wondering if I should risk leaving my cart here and run home to get something to cover the clothes with.

Thinking about home brought to mind my mother's latest batch of accusations. She was constantly blaming me for Tony's departure. Even though I would gladly have taken the credit for his absence, I was trying to be nice, calmly reminding her that he'd never helped her out at all. She defended him by pointing out that his lack of assistance was only because he was laid off from his *good* job right now, and he didn't currently have any extra cash. By about the second or third time she said something as stupid as that, she actually began believing it.

Eventually dialogue always broke down. I couldn't resist logic, and she couldn't resist her hatred and contempt for me. I pointed out how much he spent on liquor and cigarettes, and she got angry. I pointed out how he was so free with his hands, and she took up for him. I pointed out how he was always dragging her away from home and her kids, and she told me to mind my own business. When I grew angry enough, I told Betty the dude was a straight-up lowlife loser, and she informed me that she hated me and wished I would go live somewhere else.

Fighting with Betty wasn't fair. You couldn't win. No matter how right you were or what undeniable facts you pointed out, she could just hate you and ignore your logic. And the more you pressed her with solid arguments, the louder and more out of control she became. Eventually the sheer volume and venom of her outbursts drove you to madness, and you fell into the chasm her yowling created, where you resorted to cursing and yelling right back at her. (I was pretty sure this was the point at which many of her boyfriends belted her.)

My mother lived by her mantra—that nothing was her fault—and nothing was going to convince her otherwise. She believed the world was mean to her. There were many times when I truly believed Betty was insane. I'm sure at times she was. And she was never worse than when she was without a man. I was the root cause of why my mother didn't currently have a man. I felt like a target for a Robin Hood versus William Tell archery competition. Sooner or later I was going to suffer an arrow.

With my back to her and deep in thought, I didn't hear the old girl moving around behind me, and when she laid a wrinkled, bony hand on my shoulder I nearly jumped up and ran screaming out into the rain. As it was, I bolted to my feet and spun around, scared half to death. I could see myself bound and gagged, bobbing around in a cook pot with a raging fire licking up the sides, slowly boiling to death while the hag watched on, licking her toothless lips.

Instead of trying to eat me, the old lady handed me a few oversize trash bags she must have dug up. "Here you go, baby. These should cover your laundry and keep it dry until you make it home." I took them from her, and she smiled. It looked to me like she pretty much had all her teeth, even if the sparse strands of her thinning hair *were* blue. "You be careful going home, hon," she told me before heading back to her desk.

Ashamed, I croaked, "Thanks." But she only lifted her hand. Feeling stupid, I wrapped up my clothes, tucking the plastic bags tightly around the folded stacks to protect them from the rain, and trundled on home.

Donny's log: eleven p.m. on Friday night. The Christian interlopers have followed me home and refuse to leave. Nothing I say seems to have any effect on them. Although passive in nature, their dogged determination to take possession of my soul has left me little room to safely maneuver. Nothing will deter them. As a last, desperate measure, I intend to try lying and extreme procrastination. But I fear these tactics may fail and all will be lost.

Dave had given me a ride home after a teen get-together at church. (Yeah, Bess talked me into another make-Gordo-jealous adventure. Sue me. She was pretty.) I'd gotten more than a little suspicious when Dave and his wife had parked out on my street and decided to walk me in. But I'd known something was definitely up when Lynn and Bess followed us inside, all packing Bibles and wearing grim, determined faces.

"I'm not leaving until you pray with me," Dave said again. He sounded serious, but I doubted he was going to stay much longer. We'd been at this for almost two hours already. "Come on. A few words and a few minutes, and your life will be changed forever." His tone was earnest. Dave fervently believed everything he was saying.

"Can't I think on this and talk about it Sunday?" I asked yet again.

Dave shook his head. "Absolutely not. This is it. Now. This night. I'm not leaving until you accept Jesus as your Lord and Savior."

"You should push drugs, Dave," I told him. The poor man flinched like I'd slapped him. I heard his wife stifle a giggle. "I mean, is this how we're supposed to do this? Shouldn't I be the one to decide when and if to ask God for help or whatever?"

Dave shook his head yet again. "If I keep waiting on you, this might never happen."

My brothers were asleep upstairs. Lynn, Betty, and Dave's wife were all perched on the couch, watching my battle of wills with Dave. Betty kept shooting me piercing glances that said to just do it so they'd leave and we could turn the TV on. I sat on the floor next to the dormant tube, resting against the wall, Bess hovering beside me and watching closely for any sign of a crack in my resolve. Dave sat in our only chair leaning toward me, his face avid and his gaze as intense as ever.

Benji was hunkered down between Dave and me, at ease for the moment but ready to leap into action if necessary. Every now and then he rose and paced, nuzzling me and whining a bit, wondering what the hell was going on. Lynn tried to persuade him to come and lie down near her, even scratching and rubbing on him to keep him calm, but my dog didn't like the abnormal hours we were keeping, or the tension he was sensing.

"I know you've been thinking about it," Bess piped in.

Dave kept staring at me, waiting. His constant gaze wasn't physically threatening, but it promised a long and militant siege. The man was determined to have my soul, or at least deliver it to his God. "I'll bet you never lost the blinking game when you were in school," I told Dave. He gave me a wry smile and shook his head.

Bess punched me in the shoulder. "Stop trying to change the subject," she scolded.

"Want to watch some TV?" I asked.

"No," Dave answered. "No TV tonight."

I sighed. "Want something to eat? We've got some moldy cheese and curdled milk in the fridge." Dave didn't respond but I heard Jewel giggle again. I shrugged. "Sorry. I was just thinking that if you got sick you might have to leave."

Dave crossed his arms and cracked his shoulders, stretching. "No, I could be sick right here just as well as anyplace else." His eyes never left me. "I'm not going anywhere until we do this. You might as well believe that."

"Don't you have visiting tomorrow? You always visit the bus kids' homes on Saturday. Think about all those poor little waifs just standing around looking for you, their innocent eyes brimming with tears as they search up and down the street, hoping for you…" I paused for effect. "Waiting for you… longing for guidance… but no Dave."

Jewel and Lynn laughed, and that caused even Dave to chuckle. "You should be a writer when you grow up."

"Or a comedian," Jewel proposed.

I gave her my Charlie Chaplin grin and bobbed my head back and forth. She held up her hand and pretended she was holding a cigar. Jewel was smart and extremely witty. The more I got to know her, the easier it was to see why Dave had married her, although I was still leaning toward acquiring a girl more like my Mandy.

"Joke around all you want. I'll stay here all night and all day tomorrow," he promised.

And I was beginning to believe him. I was kicking myself again. If I'd have just worked at Pops' and not gone with Bess to the church, I wouldn't be in this predicament. *And you'd be ten to fifteen bucks richer.* There was a part of me that was always thrilled by the attention Dave cast in my direction, but this was different. He was intent on having his way, and I wasn't sure I could give him what he wanted of me. So I settled in and prepared to have my mettle tested.

Donny's log: midnight on Friday night. Is midnight Friday or Saturday? The Christian interlopers have weakened, with the exception of their stringent leader, a reaper of souls marked by a pale swatch of hair just above his fierce eyes. The man will not be deterred from his mission. He means to have my immortal soul. For the first time in my storied career, I find myself doubting if I possess the means to thwart this uncompromising adversary.

"I have to pee," Betty mumbled before shuffling upstairs.

To her credit, she did pee. We all heard her, since she neglected to fully close the bathroom door. Dave tried to ignore the sounds of her urinating, but I made a face and was rewarded by a very brief smile from Jewel. She was done giggling. It was late, and we were all tired. Betty had glared openly at me before leaving, pissed that I wouldn't just play along. She'd kept on griping about how she had to work tomorrow. *Today,* I'd corrected her. My mother was gone for some time. I seriously doubted she would be coming back.

"Really, Dave, let's talk about this later," I insisted.

"Let's talk about it now."

Nothing about him had changed. He still sat on the edge of the chair, leaning forward and waiting for me to weaken. His hands rested on his knees. His body was relaxed, his manner composed and patient. But his eyes were fervent as ever. They threatened to bore right into me, to shatter my defiance and reduce my trembling wall of will to rubble.

Lynn was asleep, her head back and her mouth hanging open, snoring softly. Bess had taken my mother's vacated spot next to her. *It won't be long until she's sawing logs with her sister.* Benji had decided Dave and I were involved in something well beyond him and curled up next to Lynn. Even Jewel was dozing off now and then, and had finally decided to rest her head on the arm of our couch. They would all be in never-never land in no time at all.

But Dave wasn't going to sleep any time soon. He was like one of those statues outside the buildings downtown, holding its pose forever, immune to wind and rain and bird droppings, oblivious to all the petty problems of the living. Only my Dave sculpture had penetrating eyes and a purpose, and was oblivious to everything except me.

"Can I ask you a question, Donny?" the statue asked.

He'd startled me. I realized I'd been falling asleep myself. "Sure." I adjusted my tired frame against the wall, trying in vain to find a more comfortable position on the unyielding floor. This was getting old.

"Are you ever afraid?"

What kind of a question was that? "Sure," I admitted. I glanced at the girls. They were all dozing. *Or pretending.* Jewel was a smart lady. She might have been faking just so I might feel better about talking with Dave.

"What are you afraid of?"

We were speaking softly, almost whispering as we tried not to disturb the others. But it felt weird, almost as if we were conspirators in some plot, passing secrets in the dead of the night.

I thought a moment. "All sorts of stuff. You know, getting beat up or pushed around." I decided to be honest with him. "Mostly I'm afraid of how I'm going to get by. Know what I mean? I worry about how I'm going to make money and stuff. I want to make a lot of money."

"Why?"

Okay, now he was just being stupid. *Maybe he's tired too.* "Why? If you have money you have everything, houses and cars and stuff."

Dave shook his head. "I don't have a lot of money, and I have a house and a car. I know people with big houses and two or three cars who don't have a lot of money."

"I don't get it. What are you trying to say?"

"You don't need a lot of money to have those things. You just need a job and to be willing to work to have them." Dave pointed at me, his face sober. "There's no big secret to getting ahead in this world. Just be willing to work, and you'll do fine."

"That's easy to say." It couldn't be that easy. If what he was saying was true, how could he explain Betty and Ruby and Leon and Tony? "You've seen the losers I have to deal with."

Dave held up his hand. "I don't want to talk about them. I'm talking about you. Have I ever lied to you?" I shook my head. "Then trust me. If you keep your nose clean and work hard, you'll go a lot farther than most." I opened my mouth, and he waved off my unasked question. "Just forget that for now. Believe me. I have no doubt you're going to do well in life." He smiled. "Probably *real* well, but what I'm trying to give you is much more important than any house or car. This life goes by like that." He snapped his fingers. "It seems like just yesterday I was your age. I'm trying to give you peace of mind, a gift so fulfilling and eternal you never have to be afraid again, of anything."

"That sounds real nice, but—"

"No buts, Donny. Once you accept Christ, you are given the gift of eternal life. Whether you get hit by a car and die tomorrow or live to be the richest man in the world and a hundred years old, that gift can't be lost. It will always be waiting for you." He leaned closer. "Doesn't that sound like something you should accept? Especially since it's free?"

Dave made it tempting, but this was his gig and he was good at it. "So you're saying no matter who we are or what we've done, all we have to do is ask and we're going to Heaven?" I pointed upstairs. "My mom's going to Heaven? If some murderer or drug dealer or child molester kneels and begs, that's all they have to do to go to Heaven?"

"You are such a stubborn kid," groaned Dave, rubbing at his temples. "Donny, every experience is different, and only God knows our hearts. If one of those people you mentioned is truly repentant...? Then yes. The Bible tells us God's mercy is there for everyone."

"You ever hear that saying about something being too good to be true?"

275

"Yes, I've heard that one."

"This sure sounds like what they were talking about."

"Those are man's words. What I'm trying to give you is God's promise. You shouldn't confuse the two." Dave was showing the first signs of strain. "Will you pray with me?"

I didn't want to. I was only a kid, but his happy-ever-after theory had more holes in it than my gym socks. Why would God want lowlifes in Heaven with Him? And why make it so easy? *If it's so easy, why haven't you done it yet?* That was a good question. The truth was, I wanted to believe in something, especially God. My mother wanted me to just pray with Dave and see him on out the door, but that was her way of doing things. I owed Dave more than that. And I wasn't about to start fooling around with God, even if I was unsure about my position with Him. I had enough to deal with already. There was no sense in making an enemy out of someone all-powerful, even if I wasn't sure I believed in Him.

"I just don't want to right now," I told Dave.

For just a moment I thought he was preparing to get out of the chair and maybe leave, but I was wrong. He fell back into the chair and made himself comfortable. "Fine, I'll wait."

Donny's log: one a.m. Saturday morning. All resistance has proven futile. The Christian interloper will not be swayed. Nothing but the surrender of my soul will satisfy him. He has refused all other treaties or offers of compromise. I fear this may be my last log entry. (At least as a heathen.) If I don't survive salvation, tell Spock he's to assume command of the ship.

Somewhere between one and two in the morning, I gave in. Once I agreed, Dave had me on my knees and praying with him so fast it felt more like I was being arrested than saved. As we began walking what Dave called the Romans Road, I felt Jewel place a gentle hand on the back of my head and heard her whispering, praising Jesus. *I knew she was faking.* That or she sensed a submissive soul and was just as greedy as her husband, only nicer about it.

"Romans 3:23; For all have sinned, and come short of the glory of God," Dave began. I repeated his words, feeling self-conscious and embarrassed while he explained the meaning of what I thought had been a pretty self-explanatory phrase. Dave barged on, his voice serious but soft and melodious; "Romans 6:23; For the wages of sin is death; but the gift of God is eternal life through Jesus Christ our Lord." Dave explained how every person born was doomed to eternal damnation. I thought that was a pretty dirty trick. Then I remembered I was praying and hoped I wasn't in trouble for thinking something like that.

Bess and Lynn were awake. I could hear them praying together. Bess was crying. I thought that was sweet of her. *She should be crying, it's her fault I got forced into this,* I remembered. *Oops. Sorry about that, God.* Dave was rolling now. "Romans 5:8 says; But God demonstrates His own love toward us, in that while we were still sinners, Christ died for us." He went on to explain how Jesus died on the cross for all our sins, but I'd heard about that every time I'd visited the church.

"…confess with your mouth Jesus as Lord, and believe in your heart that God raised Him from the dead, you will be saved."

I so confessed. And I wasn't worrying over what anyone near me thought about it. I wanted help. I needed help. I was hoping God could work a miracle and do something for me. That became the overriding hope in my fragile psyche as I continued to repeat every word Dave asked of me. He'd been right. This was easy once you got going. Dropping my pride had been the hard part.

"Do you accept Jesus Christ as your Lord and Savior, Donny?" asked Dave.

"Yes."

"Praise Jesus," murmured Jewel. Lynn mumbled something. Bess just kept on crying.

"Do you believe His blood can wash away all your sins?"

"I do." And I did. I really believed.

"Amen," said Jewel.

I followed Dave down the rest of the Romans Road, repeating everything he said and listening closely. Somewhere along the way I forgot my unease and every trace of chagrin, caught up in the moment. I felt something. To this day I cannot honestly say what that something was. My head spun. Something stirred within me. I swear my very bones quivered before I was through with that prayer. The people and voices around me faded. I believed *something* was happening to me. But from that moment to the present, I was never sure exactly what to believe in. God has remained an abstract concept.

Dave was all smiles when we were finished. He obviously had more faith in what we'd just done than I did. Jewel kissed me. Bess hugged me, all weepy but happy. Lynn gave me a way-to-go-pal punch in the shoulder. My dog was staring at me with his head cocked, all confused. I knew how he felt. The girls had to be home, so Dave promised to see me later that day to talk about when I was going to be baptized. *Baptized? What? Does he mean the dunking thing they do up in that booth?* Before I could ask about that, he left. I sat in the chair after they were gone, my head still spinning, wondering what I was supposed to do now.

After listening to a couple of cars roll by, I thought about turning on the tube, but then decided to catch some sleep.

"About fucking time," my mother grumbled from beyond her bedroom door as I made the top of the steps. There was nothing like her growl to remind a kid how feeble a thing like salvation was going to be in her house. "You do it?"

"Yeah."

She laughed. Her mirth was a coarse, ugly sound. For some reason it was meaner than I remembered, and actually stung a bit.

"I knew you would. Was that so damn hard?"

I decided not to give her an answer. She didn't really want one.

"You could've done it hours ago and they'd have left, but not you. Don't think I'm going to let you sleep in when I leave for work in the morning. Your ass better get up when I call you." She sounded unreal, like maybe I was dreaming. "You hear me?"

She was real. "I hear," was all I said before going on into my own room.

CHAPTER 20

This had to be a record, even for me. *Only you can get called down to the principal's office before school even starts.* But here I was. And I wasn't alone. My brothers sat behind me. There was a guidance counselor, a caseworker, and a woman lawyer whom the principal had introduced as a public defender. Principle Davenport's bulbous nose was even bigger and a brighter red than last year. All the kids and teachers knew he drank himself into a stupor almost every day.

"Will your mother be attending?" the public defender asked me.

She wore a slick business suit and expensive nylons, her auburn hair pulled up into a tight bun and pinned. When old Davenport had introduced her as Mrs. McConnell, she'd corrected him, pronouncing her name as *Mizz* McConnell, as if that was somehow very important. She'd been digging around in her briefcase, making everyone wait while she pulled files and a notebook out and positioned them carefully in front of her. Even though she dressed sharp and acted high and mighty, I found myself doubting her intelligence. *Seriously, lady, would I have drug my brothers all the way down here if I didn't have to?* I wanted to ask her. But all I said was no.

The school had called yesterday, informing me that my presence was required at this little meeting. Even though they assured me I wasn't in any trouble, they made it clear that if I didn't cooperate, there would be repercussions when school started next week. I hadn't expected this many people to be in attendance, although I was pretty sure all the hubbub had to do with Tommy and the cutting of the guy at the roller-skating rink.

"Is she working?" She was really getting on my nerves. She clipped every syllable, and she wasn't bothering to look at me as she tossed out her questions. "I asked if she was working." At least she glanced up as she repeated her question.

"No, she's sleeping off a few Valiums."

Her hands paused in the briefcase. I'd pronounced my answer as properly as possible, attempting to imitate her lofty phraseology. *You sounded English*, I told myself. My mockery, although not exactly perfect, had managed to get the attention of everyone in the room except my brothers. Terry was banging a couple of Hot Wheels together, and Chip was investigating the underside of his chair. Davenport cleared his throat and raised an eyebrow in my direction. I pretended I hadn't a clue what they might be on about.

"Do you realize we've called your home several times and had a detective actually come to your door?" asked the arrogant lady, continuing a bit more cautiously.

"Who's we?"

She lifted her head and looked at me like I was daft. "I'm referring to the police, Donald." She was flipping through some files. One of them had my name on it.

"My mother doesn't take calls from the police at our house," I explained.

She gave me a tight smile. "Why is that?"

"Are public defenders the lawyers who have to take all the crappy cases, like when people don't have any money?" *Call me, Donald, will you?* Davenport cleared his throat again, and scowled at me. "I saw a Perry Mason show once where he had to step in and save a guy because some public defender had really botched up the case. Are you handling Tommy's case?"

Her fake smile was gone. "The court has appointed me to represent your friends in this matter, yes." She flipped through some other files. I couldn't see any names on those, but they looked more official than my school file had. "Tommy? I suppose he would be Thomas Washington?" I nodded. "Are Irving Franklin and John Johnson also friends of yours?"

"John Johnson must be Jo Jo, but we aren't friends. And Irving doesn't have any friends." I figured that much was safe to admit.

Mrs. Ferris, one of the school's guidance counselors, pointed at the baby, who'd managed to dislodge an old, hardened wad of gum from beneath his chair and was examining it like he was thinking about popping in into his mouth. I jumped up and snatched it out of his hand, tossing the rock into Davenport's trash can. The hard ball bounced around the empty metal container, making quite a racket. Chip gave me a look and went back to exploring for more treasures under his chair.

"I'll get these files back to you when we've finished," Davenport told Mrs. Ferris. "Would you buy Donny's brothers something out of the snack machines and entertain them until we're through here?"

Mrs. Ferris wasn't old, but she was getting there. She wore glasses with a thin chain around her neck. Her dark hair was streaked with gray, and she wore baggy clothes to disguise her shapeless body. The guidance counselor nodded at the principal and rose to leave, giving my baby brother a smile and extending her hand. (Terry was already at the door the very second a snack machine had been mentioned.) Eager to oblige, Chip grinned right on back and accepted her hand, showing off yet another wad of petrified gum in his other grimy paw.

"I'll be needing copies of some of these files," *Mizz* McConnell announced while I hurried to relieve my brother of his prize and make another jump shot.

It was Mrs. Ferris's turn to flash a fake smile. "Of course, just let me know," she said before closing the door behind her.

I shared a glance with the caseworker, a middle-aged guy in a pair of jeans and a corduroy jacket who was just sitting off to the side, his legs crossed, watching everyone. He lowered his glasses and gave me a nod and a smile. I returned his nod but reserved my smile. He seemed cool enough. I was going to wait and see whose side he was on before getting chummy. He had a file, too, but his was on the chair next to him, closed. He had a mustache and looked unshaven. His shirt was a bit wrinkled and not tucked in. He was quite the contrast to the pristine lady questioning me. But he had an air of confidence that belied his shabby appearance. I was hoping the smile he'd flashed meant he was on my side.

"I see you struggle with your classes, Donald," the lawyer noted.

"Yeah? Take a look at those finals." She glanced briefly at the column on the right hand side of the page she was holding. "How's that for grades?"

"He prefers to be called Donny," Davenport mumbled.

There wasn't enough alcohol in the state to help the poor guy forget *my* name. I was in here on pretty much a weekly basis. I didn't get in all that much trouble, though. *If you exclude attendance issues, that is.* But I didn't have any problem with Mr. Davenport. He was a fair man, just cranky.

"His file says Donald," she informed my principal. *Okay, it's on.*

"By no means must we ever divert from the files, Mr. Davenport," the caseworker finally chimed in. I liked him more already. "Nothing's pertinent until it's all typed up and official."

She ignored his verbal barb. "How well do you know Mr. Washington?" she asked me.

Our librarian always called us Mr. whoever and Miss so and so, but she was the only one I'd ever heard call Tommy Mr. Washington. She made my friend sound like a grown man. "You mean Tommy?"

She sighed. "Yes."

I decided she was going to be sighing a great deal more. *And maybe some cussing.* "We're not in love or anything. But we hang around a lot together."

"Were you hanging around with him the night of August 25th?"

"Was that the night the guy got cut at the skating rink?" I wasn't sure about the date. The whole summer was a blur.

"Yes."

"Nope."

She didn't like that answer. "Were you even at the skating rink that night?"

"Nope."

"Are you sure?"

"I can't skate, and I'm white as Casper. If I ever do get brave enough to skate there on a Friday or Saturday night, I'm pretty sure I'll remember it." She was scratching on a pad as I answered, keeping notes. For some reason I didn't like that. "Believe me. I wasn't there."

"Were you with him the day of the 23rd?"

"Huh?"

"August 23rd. Were you with Mr. Washington on that day?" she repeated, as if adding in the month again would help me remember.

"The day at the park," the caseworker piped in.

"I don't need your assistance, Mr. Sutton." She clipped her words even more sharply when she was angry.

"Maybe you don't, but the kid does. Why don't you ask the questions so he can understand what the hell you want to know?"

"I'll ask the questions how I see fit!"

"That's enough," Mr. Davenport said quietly. "This is not a courtroom. I agreed to have Donny in here so you could talk to him about Tommy's case. This is not what I had in mind. If we can't get this done calmly and with professionalism, I'll just send him home, and you can gather your details on your own time."

"This is *my* case, Mr. Davenport."

"This is *my* office and *my* school, Ms. McConnell."

All of a sudden Davenport was the principal and the lawyer looked like an out-of-line student. I was proud of the old drunk. *Way to go, Cranky!* "Of course," murmured Mr. Sutton, but prissy *Mizz* prim and proper was too full of hot air to actually give voice to an apology and only nodded stiffly before turning her attention back on me.

"Tell me about the day of August 23rd."

"The day at the park?"

"Yes." She was beginning to seethe. "The day at the park."

I balked. I suddenly realized Tommy hadn't asked me for any help at all. For all I knew, everything I said might get him in even more trouble. What if he was denying the whole thing? If I told about the ordeal in the bathroom with Chris and Lurch, it might give them a motive, a reason to pin the attack at the skating rink on Tommy. *You watch too many crime dramas,* I told myself. But my caution had merit. The biggest no-no in my neighborhood—and in this school—was running your mouth when something didn't concern you. Hell, you were taking a risk when what you talked about *did* concern you.

"Well?" she persisted. "Were you even with him at the park?"

Unable to decide whether or not to speak up, I just sat there. "We're wasting our time." Obviously, public defenders had very little patience. She began tossing files into her leather briefcase like she was done with me. "I told you this was a foolish idea."

"Just wait a minute," said Sutton. He leaned in closer to me. "Listen to me, Donny. Your friend Tommy told me everything. How else would we even know about the park?" That was a good point. "But I need your help. So does Tommy. If your story corroborates Tommy's—"

He paused. "Go ahead. I know what *corroborates* means."

He grinned at me. "Smart kid. Like I was saying… if your story matches Tommy's, I hope to convince our good attorney here to plead this case. If we can prove both sides were attacking and provoking one another, the judge will be more prone to reducing charges, at least with those who didn't use a weapon. But I have a ways to go to get there." He sounded sincere. "I really need your help with this. What do you say?"

"Can you promise him nothing he says will leave this room?" Davenport asked them, cutting right to the heart of the problem. I had to admit the old boy had learned a few things running this fine institution of learning.

Sutton removed his glasses and shook his head at me while he cleaned the lenses with the hem of his shirt. "I'm not going to lie to you, Donny. There's a chance you might have to testify in court. What I *can* promise you is that Tommy needs you to tell the truth about this."

"I wish it was that easy," I muttered.

"What does that mean?" Sutton asked.

"It means that when he talks about Tommy, he's also talking about Mr. Johnson and, more importantly, Mr. Franklin," Davenport informed them. I was just going to have to raise my opinion of my principal, wino or not. *Just how in the know is the old sot?*

"Mr. Franklin would be the cutter?" Sutton asked him.

"Irving did his first cutting while roaming these very halls. He was a constant and grave threat in the high school until they managed to kick him out last year. He's cut before."

"We have his file," the defender informed Davenport, her tone casual but with that ever-present hint of arrogance. "We know full well how many times he's been arrested for attacking citizens."

My principal laughed at her like she was a naive schoolgirl. "Pardon me, Ms. McConnell, but it's the cutting Irving's done that's *not* in your file that makes the kids around here afraid of him." She didn't know what to do with information she couldn't read in her files. "It might be best for Donny here to stay out of this whole mess, especially in light of the fact that he didn't even witness the assault."

"But all I want to know about is the park," Sutton insisted. "The other two older boys weren't even involved in the altercation at the park."

"Alleged altercation," the defender reminded us.

I knew what alleged meant, too. Sutton had made a good point. Only Tommy and I had been in that bathroom. I sure hadn't done any talking about it. That meant Tommy had. I decided to trust the caseworker and tell him what had happened. I wasn't sure I was doing the right thing, but I knew I disliked this public defender more than I feared a reprisal from Irving.

"They jumped us in the bathroom."

"You'll have to be more specific than that," she shot at me.

Sutton didn't like her either. "Let him talk, would you?" They glared at each other, but then he gave me a reassuring nod, encouraging me to go on. "Just tell us what happened."

I did, narrating every detail to the best of my vivid and overactive imagination. I added an embellishment here and there to make us look a little better, but there was nothing I could do to portray myself as other than the helpless little shit who ran away and brought back the cavalry. Such was life. I also left out the part about looking for black guys when I escaped the bathroom. If pressed, I intended to call that coincidental and circumstantial evidence.

"I'm not sure that's assault," the defender murmured. She'd been scribbling furiously while I'd told my tale of thrilling derring-do.

"What? Having four young rash men jam your face in a bowl of waste and foul water is better than being cut?" asked Sutton. He'd been writing as well. "The kid could have suffocated. I have no problem calling that assault."

She spun back on me. "You don't know any of the people who helped you after the alleged attack?"

Her constant use of the word alleged was getting on my nerves. But I couldn't deny I'd not seen those people before or since that day. "No."

She shook her head. "No witnesses."

Sutton wasn't having that. "*He's* a witness," he refuted, pointing at me.

"You didn't actually see them force your friend's head into the toilet," she told me.

She was good. "No, but I saw him rinsing the shit out of his hair. I doubt he put his own face into that shitty bowl."

"Language," murmured Davenport. I'd thought he'd fallen asleep.

"And taking the money adds robbery." Sutton sounded almost ecstatic. "More than one witness at the scene claimed the knife used in the assault was taken from the victim. And the victim claims the knife isn't his." Sutton beamed and closed his file. "I'm more than convinced we have enough to plead this."

The defender wasn't as sure. "You're positive there were four?"

"I can count."

"How much money was allegedly stolen?"

"Tommy never said. It was a small wad of bills."

"For somebody who was supposed to have been there, you don't know a whole lot."

"I know the guy who took Tommy's knife and money was called Chris, and that the big guy who was holding me was called David. And I know David did the driving, because he was worried about his car." Sutton had his file open again, writing the names down. "Why don't you ask *them* how much money Tommy had?"

"Why were they after Tommy in the first place?" Sutton asked me, almost as an afterthought.

"Because Chris caught him making out with Lucy behind the skating rink."

"That's it?"

"Well, he *was* feeling her up." Davenport cleared his throat. "I heard Tommy punked him real bad, and everybody, including Lucy, was laughing at him. Chris didn't like Lucy fooling around with other guys, especially *black* guys." From what I knew of Lucy, she was heading down the road to Bettyism.

"Hearsay," the defender muttered.

Sutton was pleased. He shut his file and gave me a contented sigh. "Donny, you were great. I seriously doubt if you'll even have to testify at any hearing."

"I disagree," the defender informed him. *That's a big surprise.* She was packing her stuff up, too, carefully sliding files into her briefcase. "Could I have a copy of these?" she asked Davenport, setting a few pieces of paper aside. Sutton stood up. "We need to talk about this," she told him.

"Look. I can prove those kids were lying about motive, and I can lay out a credible trail of circumstances proving what Donny's told us, even without his testimony. I've got a racially motivated attack over a girl with a stolen weapon passing hands between assailants. Not to mention strong-arm robbery. No judge I know is going to drag all this into a courtroom." He nodded at the principal. "Thank you." Sutton patted my shoulder and headed for the door. "Thank you, too."

But the defender wasn't done. "What you have is conjectures and theories, while the prosecutor has a brutal assault with a dozen witnesses."

"*Alleged* brutal assault," I corrected her. *Sorry, lady, but you had that coming.*

She looked kind of cute with a prune face. Davenport couldn't hide his smile, and we all heard Sutton chuckling out in the hall as he left.

I was bent over my desk, working on my new idea for a comic strip when the phone rang. Betty and the boys were out with Tony getting something to eat, so there wasn't anybody downstairs. (Their breakup hadn't lasted as long as I'd hoped.) I just let it ring. *Probably a bill collector.* We were getting more calls all the time. Betty's scams were running in overdrive, and the engine was real close to overheating. I'd heard her talking to my Aunt Kathy about us maybe moving back to Indiana. It wouldn't be long until we were hitting the road.

Then it started ringing again. And it kept ringing and ringing. Finally, after listening to it blaring time and again as long as I could stand to, I threw down my pen and rumbled down the stairs. "Yeah?"

"Donny?"

Hey, somebody didn't think you were Betty! I was thrilled. "Yeah."

"It's Leon."

Uh oh. "Yeah?" *Stop saying yeah.*

"Your mother around?"

"No."

"Where is she?" he asked sullenly.

This was a dilemma. Betty had met Leon over at the truck stop a couple nights past. I was hoping the big guy was going to horn in on Tony, but I couldn't tell him about Betty being out with Tony at the moment, since that might drive him off. *Wow, I guess even slobs like Leon have standards.* I'd never thought too much about handling something like this. I sure wasn't going to do or say anything to push Leon away.

I had no choice but to lie. "She and the boys are out. She's trying to find Terry some clothes for school." That was good. Sometimes I amazed even myself.

"Oh." He thought a moment. "What about you? You all ready for school?"

Wow. He's taking the time to chitchat with you. The poor man was really desperate. "Sure," I answered, smiling to myself.

My mother had raided two local church basements. After that humiliation, we'd gone to a Goodwill outlet, sizing ratty jeans and shirts she thought I would wear to school. I hadn't agreed to wear much of what she found. I had two sets of sneaks and a few pairs of jeans that still fit, all thinning badly in the knees and grass-stained. I'd given Betty so much trouble, she'd actually broken down and spent real cash on a new pair of Levi's and two T-shirts, just to shut me up.

"Tell her to call me when she gets home, wouldya?"

"I will."

"I'm at my mom's. She's got the number."

If I was still living with Betty when I was half Leon's age, I was going to throw myself in front of a bus. "Okay."

He hung up, and I headed back upstairs, my mind still on my story line. But the phone started ringing again. I figured Leon forgot to tell me something important. *Like he bought some new underwear, and he promises to keep his pecker where it belongs from now on.* "Yeah?" *Stop saying yeah!*

But it wasn't Leon. "Donny?"

"Oh, hey, Rupe."

"Can you come over for a minute?"

He sounded funny. "I'm working on something. Does it have to be right away?"

I heard him swallow. "Yeah. Please?"

"I'll be there in ten minutes."

"Okay. Good."

And he hung up. I stared at the phone for a second, wondering what might be wrong with him. *He's heard something about you and Tommy,* I figured. *Or Irving.* That thought sent a chill up my spine. I ran upstairs and pulled on my shoes. My bike had a flat so I was going to have to run, but that was no big deal. Benji followed after me, and we shot down the alley out back, already sweating in the afternoon sun.

About halfway there I rounded a corner and was nearly wiped out by two little kids flying at me on bikes. "Shit!" I yelped, barely managing to dodge them. Benji evaded them more easily than I had. *Oops. Sorry about that, God,* I apologized silently. I'd been really self-conscious about cussing ever since praying with Dave. But it was a war I was losing more every day, and a habit I couldn't seem to break.

They said the Lord moved in mysterious ways. In my case He was not only moving mysteriously, but invisibly as well. Nothing in my life had changed at all. Dave insisted I shouldn't challenge God. He said I might not reap the rewards of my decision until later in life. But I needed to do some reaping now. Salvation left me feeling bitter and dealing with a load of remorse. It felt like I'd simply followed my mother's example and knelt and prayed without changing a bit, almost as if I'd not meant a word I'd prayed. But I had meant what I'd said. At least I kept telling myself I had.

We dodged traffic and cut through a yard behind the gas station. The same lady yelled out her window. I ignored her outcry the same way I had a hundred times before. Even though it was hot, the air had that fall smell I would always love. September through November would always be my favorite time of year. I would be fond of saying *it smells like football in the air* when I was older.

Some guys I knew tried to talk me into throwing a baseball around, but I resisted the urge. Benji was moving pretty well, though he still had a discernible limp. I was beginning to believe he always would. I fully intended to make Tony pay for that one day. Neither Dave nor God would approve of my plan to exact vengeance, but I figured that was a debt from before I'd prayed, so maybe that wouldn't count against me.

I swung by Pops' place and found the old guy sweeping out the tavern, all the chairs setting atop the tables. He moved through the beams of light streaking through the windows, disturbing the motes of dust I could see floating. He moved like he was in pain, his steps stiff and slow. He didn't hear me when I walked in; I was pretty sure the old man's hearing was following after his failing eyesight.

Even when nobody was in the joint, it still reeked of cigarette smoke. I coughed but he didn't hear me. "Hey, Pops!" I called out.

"What? Who's that?" he mumbled around the cigarette he was currently working on. He was looking right at me, just four or five steps away. "Who's that?"

I moved closer. Pops squinted, straining to recognize me through the shadows and hazy rays of light. When he realized who I was, he grinned and exhaled, loosing a trail of vapor that wafted slowly toward the ceiling. Ash fell from his cigarette, falling down his shirt and striking the dingy apron he wore around his waist. I could see traces of burn marks and ash skids all along the front of his ragged clothing. *Jeez, it's a wonder he hasn't burned the place down, and himself right along with it.*

"Where was you this weekend?"

He resumed his sweeping. It didn't look like his efforts were having much effect on the perpetually dirty floor. It seemed to me all the old guy managed to do was urge some of the clutter and debris close enough to the door to propel it out into the alley. Most of the bottle tops and cigarette butts littering the floor were only moved from here to there and left behind. I figured some of them were as old as Pops himself.

"Yeah, sorry about that. Something came up. I wanted to stop by and let you know I'll be here this weekend."

289

I felt bad about missing. Friday hadn't been my fault, since Dave had parked his holy butt in my living room and outlasted me in the battle of wills for my soul. But I'd slept little and stayed up all of Saturday, and I'd fallen asleep in front of the TV and slept like the dead that next night. And Dave had made me go to church Sunday morning, explaining about how getting baptized was the next step in the process of me changing my life. *I knew there was going to be more to this whole salvation thing.* Getting dunked in front of the whole church congregation was going to be tougher for me than the praying part.

"You going be here both days?" the old guy asked me, sending another ember tumbling down the front of his dingy unbuttoned shirt.

"I promise." I would be. I needed the money.

He grunted, accepting my apology and my promise. "Hear anything about Washington?"

"Not really. But I did hear he was supposed to come home yesterday or today." Even if he was home, I doubted I'd be hearing from Tommy.

"I warned that boy. He going to follow right after his no-good daddy."

"Okay, I got to go. See you Friday night," I told him. Pops just kept on preaching to shadows and sunbeams while I slipped away. He was still grouching and raising dust when I leapt off the steps and beat feet for Rupe's, Benji trotting along in my wake.

There was a big truck in front of Rupe's place. As I neared, it became clear that the truck was one of those big moving trucks. And the stuff the men were lugging up the ramp was coming out of Rupe's front door. The truck was nearly full. Stunned, I stopped a few houses away and watched for a moment. Rupe's dad was one of the men helping with some boxes. His mom was putting a lamp in the trunk of her car, placing it carefully among some other glassware she already had stored in there.

"I didn't know how to tell you," Rupe said. He was standing in front of me, but I hadn't been aware of him approaching. "My dad got a good job down around Cincinnati. He won't be getting laid off anymore. My mom's transferring to a hospital down there. She's always wanted to live closer to her family in Kentucky."

"You're leaving tonight?"

He looked down. "We were going to wait another week, but Dad found us a house to rent, so he decided we'd move before school starts." He took off his stupid Yankees cap and ran a hand through his freshly cut hair. That reminded me how shaggy my own mane was looking. "I'll call and give you my new phone number when we get it."

I was getting mad. "What was the big deal about telling me?" I'd been through so many schools and so many friends over the years, I wasn't sure why his abrupt leaving was causing me any difficulty at all.

A lot of things were bothering me more as I got older. "Why all the fucking secrecy?" I didn't even bother to apologize for cussing.

"Well. You know."

"No. I don't know. Why don't you fill me in." I flipped the hair out of my eyes. "Don't forget how stupid I am. You might have to speak slow and use small words."

"C'mon, man. Don't be like that." He swallowed uneasily and checked to see if anyone was close enough to hear us bickering. I felt like punching him right in his pointy nose. "You know, you've been dealing with a lot lately. That Tony asshole, and Tommy. I guess I kind of felt like I was running out on you."

"I'm doing fine." My chest felt constricted. I wanted to tell him I didn't need anybody, but I didn't trust myself to say the words. *Get a hold of yourself!* I was just surprised. That was all.

Rupe's mom walked up. "Hello, Donny." She looked at us and realized our good-bye wasn't going so smoothly. "Did Tommy tell you all the great news?" I didn't say anything. "We were hoping you would come down for a couple of weeks next summer. How's that sound?"

I smiled at her, but it wasn't a very good smile. Rupe looked uncomfortable. He was tapping his fingers on his thighs and kept looking down like he was searching for something. My face felt hot, and I was breathing too hard.

"I have to go." I couldn't think of anything else to say. I turned to leave.

"Donny," Rupe called after me. I paused long enough to look back. "I'll call you." I only managed a nod. His mom had a hand over her mouth and his dad was watching us from the porch. "See ya."

I didn't say anything.

CHAPTER 21

I was aware of a commotion outside the house. There was screaming and hollering. *Just stay asleep.* I was so tired. The light from the window was trying to infiltrate my closed lids, so I rolled away from the window and threw an arm over my face. The smoke from Pops' the night before was stinging my eyes, and they were leaking at the corners. My pillow was slick with sweat, and I had to adjust my head. There was drool dripping down my chin. My lower lip felt numb and heavy.

I'd been having a dream about Christmas and Terrance. There'd been presents. I had been waddling around with some toy guns pulling down my pajama bottoms, threatening to blow a hole in my stepdad's newspaper if he didn't stick his hands up and pay more attention to me. As my breathing slowed, the light faded, and the yelling outside grew dim. I sought and reclaimed my desired dream with little effort.

I could almost feel the weight of my new pistols. The cold plastic handles felt deadly in my nimble little hands. I called Terrance out again, but he only mumbled and turned the page, ignoring my threat. *Go ahead and blast him,* I told myself. I knew what came next. This was an enjoyable re-run. He would jump up and chase me around, growling and grunting like a wounded bear. I would flee to no avail. I would be caught and tickled mercilessly for my intrusion.

"Donny," Betty called from somewhere far away before I could draw my gun. *No! Not now!* I tried to shut her out. Terrance contorted in my dream, threatening to blur and slip away. I focused all my energy and pulled him back. "Donny!" Her shriek pierced my festive Christmas vision and Terrance was gone. *Dammit!* I opened my eyes. It wasn't Christmas, and I wasn't a little kid. There were just the same old water marks on my ceiling from the leaky roof, the same peeling paint along the bowing molding around the closed entrance to the unfinished attic area.

"Shit," I muttered, sitting up.

"Donny!" Betty wailed again.

It dawned on me that my mother was calling for me from somewhere outside. *Is she hollering from out in the street?* I rose and looked out my open window. Betty was standing in the street with Mrs. Lorret and one of the Simmons sisters. She saw me and waved frantically for me to come down. *Now what?* I slipped on my shoes, noticing the absence of my loyal dog. On my way through the kitchen, I checked the clock. It was barely past eleven. I'd worked late at Pops' and wouldn't normally be up until well past noon.

I almost ran into Ruby on the porch. "Shit, Ruby."

Oops, sorry about that. I had to jump the railing just to avoid her wide ass. She was wearing curlers in her hair and smelled like talcum powder. She wore so much of the stuff you could see it caking in the sweat along the loose flaps of skin under her chin and armpits. The sleeveless shift she wore couldn't contain her mass. It bulged dangerously beneath her arms and around her waist.

"Aren't you supposed to be afraid of direct sunlight?"

"Good morning to you, too," she spat. "Your brother's lost."

Betty spotted me and charged. "I can't find Terry!"

In the distance, I could hear somebody calling out my brother's name. It sounded like Lynn. *All this commotion because Terry snuck off again?* "Take it easy," I said, backing up a step and warding her off. "Is his Big Wheel out back?"

"No, but we already checked the park, and he wasn't there."

My mother began to cry real tears of concern. Mrs. Simmons laid a reassuring hand on her shoulder and murmured words of comfort. I wasn't about to panic yet. There were a couple of other places my brother liked to sneak off to.

"You check Ricky's house?"

"Yes. They haven't seen him all day."

She was crying now. The baby was sitting on the front steps with Benji. Chip saw Betty crying and began bawling with her. *Jesus Christ.* I sent a quick apology to Heaven for that thought, even though I hadn't cursed aloud. I knew taking the Lord's name in vain was even worse than actually saying the regular old foul words.

"He was here when Ruby picked me up to go get our checks, but I couldn't find him when I got back," my mother said around sobs.

Okay, I was ready to panic just a little. "You check down the alley where they dumped all that old furniture?"

Terry had decided to construct a fort out of a three-legged table and a couple of chairs last week. He'd lobbed a rock at me when I'd come after him. *Almost hit you, too.* The little shit had planned an ambush. If his first throw had been a trifle more accurate, he'd have got me a good one.

"Ruby looked there," said Betty. "You have to find him. You always find him."

Now I was ready to panic a lot. "Did you look under the table?" I asked Ruby.

"He wasn't there," she muttered. Chip's crying was getting on my nerves. I told him to shut up, and he did, his lower lip sticking out as he sputtered more quietly.

"You didn't see his bike anywhere?"

She sighed. "He wasn't there."

"Don't bust your spandex," I snapped at her.

"Bite me."

"Go turn a trick."

"Donny, you need to find your brother," Mrs. Lorret urged me softly but firmly, reminding me of the important task at hand.

"Yes, ma'am." She was right. "How long have you been looking for him?" I asked my mom.

Betty tried to answer and couldn't. She kept looking around, searching for some sign of my wayward brother. The baby began wailing again. Even Ruby was starting to cry.

"Well over an hour now," Mrs. Lorret finally informed me.

"What?" *What?* Too many things to imagine skipped through my brain. An hour was an eternity in this neighborhood. *An hour?* Where would he stay for an hour? Worse than that, Mrs. Lorret had said *well* over an hour. Just how long had Terry been missing?

"I'm calling the police," Mrs. Simmons stated defiantly. When nobody spoke up to deny her notion, she trotted toward her place, spouting "Oh my Lord" with every step.

I had to move or risk suffering a complete meltdown. "Come on, boy," I said to Benji, taking off.

But where was I to look first? The pile of furniture was just down the alley, so I went ahead and checked around there, not trusting Ruby. I found no sign of my brother. From there I simply followed instinct and habit. Terry always rode his Big Wheel to the park, and the bike was gone. It was as good a place as any to search. *Maybe he was behind one of the mounds of dirt,* I told myself hopefully. *Maybe.* I didn't want to think about maybes.

Along the way I asked anyone I knew if they'd seen the twerp. No one had. I heard a siren in the distance, and that quickened my steps. I was convinced I'd find him hiding at the park, proud of himself for evading us for so long. By the time I made the playground I had my dialogue all prepared, complete with a counter for every excuse the little shit was going to throw at me. I was getting sick of always having to run him down every time Betty lost him. This wasn't my job.

The park was deserted. I checked behind the dirt, found only more dirt, and turned to go. But then I paused. And I *knew.* I swear to God I *knew* where my brother was. I was as certain as if he'd called out my name. With the hair on the nape of my neck standing on end, I searched the expanse of high grass standing between the blacktop and a few deserted houses. My gaze settled on one of them and my feet moved with a mind of their own, leading me toward the rundown building I'd chosen.

Halfway through the brake I stumbled upon Terry's Big Wheel, although I never really looked at it. My eyes were trained on the house. My heart was pumping blood too fast for my veins to contain it. I felt like I was going to burst, like if I didn't start running to accommodate my surging pulse, my body might just explode. I could hear my breath coming and going as I forced myself to continue toward the supposedly deserted and suddenly terrifying structure before me.

A teenage girl stepped out of the building and set my brother down. I froze. She'd had her hand over Terry's mouth, but when she removed it he began screaming, reaching for me and running towards me, tripping repeatedly in the dense brush. I couldn't understand the words as he cried. The intensity of his misery and his haste to reach me converted his howls into gibberish. His shuffling little steps were awkward. I knew he was hurt. Worse, I knew *how* he'd been hurt.

But I still couldn't move. I'm ashamed to say I just stood there while my brother struggled and strained to reach me, crying out my name. The girl looked at me. I looked at her. Something about her wasn't altogether there. She had that cross-eyed look that came from living in her own demented world. Only there was no innocence in that face. She was evil. I could *feel* her in the dimpling of my skin. But when Benji ran toward Terry she bolted for the hills, racing towards a beat-up and rusted-out Chevy van.

I could hear Terry now. His words were clear enough to understand. But I wouldn't let them in, couldn't let them reach me. Not yet. The retarded-looking bitch had an older brother. He had the same crossed eyes and thick forehead. He was staring at me out of a window with no glass, really nothing more than a hole in a leaning wall. I could tell he was dressing himself by the way his hands were moving below my line of vision. I wanted to move, to charge or run. But I couldn't seem to do either. I couldn't move. I just stood there while the son of a bitch finished dressing and ran after his sister, carrying his shoes in his hands. He fired up his van and drove off, his spinning tires spitting gravel as he gunned the engine.

If I could relive any single moment of my life, any, it would be this one. I wish I could just say what I would do under the same circumstances today and alter time, but I can't. I stood there while they escaped, doing nothing. Fear stayed my hand. They cast my little brother away like a used condom right in my face, and I didn't have the guts to say boo. Nothing in my life had prepared me for a moment like this, and nothing since has ever taught me how to deal with the memories of it.

"Donny, he put his pee-pee in my butt!" Terry's screech finally shattered the benumbing spell of terror I was under, allowing me to move. I knelt to scoop him up. "They hurt me!"

Through my own tears, I had no choice but to witness the carnage they'd wrought upon my brother's helpless body. His sneakers were on the wrong feet, the laces catching burrs as he'd dragged himself through the brush. Scratches marred his sweating, flushed face, and his chin was scraped from having his head jammed against the floor while they'd raped him. Some of his hair had been torn out, and the loose strands hung oddly above one ear, dripping dark blood. There was blood lining the rims of his nostrils, and he'd bitten his tongue. His brown eyes were wide and wild, and he kept looking at me as if I could fix everything, as if I was going to make everything all better.

I clutched him against me and dashed for home. He felt clammy, and his little hands were like claws tearing into my back. He was terrified that I might put him back down again. Even though I was holding him, my brother wouldn't stop screaming, wouldn't lower his voice. He kept yelling as if the field still stood between us, yelling and yelling. And narrating. He told me a tale of promised candy and abduction, of rape and tears, of being restrained afterwards even though he begged to be released, of having his mouth covered when he screamed too loud, and of being raped again.

Details a six-year-old little boy should never comprehend kept flowing out of his mouth. He told me the boy stayed in him forever the second time, the weight of his attacker so oppressive he could hardly breathe. He told me the boy kept trying to make him say he liked it. "But I didn't, Donny! I didn't tell him that!" *Shut up! Shut up!* He told me the girl got mad when he wouldn't say what they wanted. "She pulled my hair! She banged my face on the floor, Donny!" *Please shut up! Please!* He told me the girl kept asking the boy if he liked that ass while the boy was hurting him. "He smacked me and said I was his bitch, Donny!" *No more. Please.* "They said they were going to kill me!" *Please.* "The boy put his pee-pee in my face!" *It was just an hour.* "The girl peed on me!" *No, it was well over an hour.* I could smell piss on him, now that he'd filled me in on that gory detail. "They were kissing each other!" *Shut up!* "He hurt me two times!" *Stop it!* "She was mean to me!" *Please stop. I'm sorry.* "Donny, I was screaming for you! I was screaming for you!"

Running along like a drunkard, I felt something wet and hot on my hand. I peered over my brother's head and saw that there was blood leaking through his shorts. I had to change my grip on Terry as I studied the warm liquid dripping through my fingers, like I didn't already know where it had come from and what had caused it. Terry shrieked, thinking I meant to put him down, clutching at me like I was trying to throw him over a cliff.

"It's okay, Terry. It's okay."

His face went slack. My brother's skin was cold and pale. I could feel him shivering. He looked right at me and loosed the fattest tears you can imagine. My heart broke as they welled up in the corners of his eyes and ran down his pallid cheeks. All pain pales when compared to the pain of a child. His blood left my hands slippery, and I was having trouble keeping my hold on him. I stumbled and almost fell. We never stopped looking at one another. I saw misery and turmoil in those brown depths of his. And blame. I was his big brother. I was supposed to protect him. I don't know what he saw in my own eyes.

"I was calling for you, Donny," he mumbled, his voice finally low and subdued, as if he might be falling asleep.

I was afraid of that. All of a sudden I wanted him yelling again. "I know, baby," I admitted. I was sobbing now, tears of rage and guilt. A scream I've never let go grew within me, a wrath that has boiled in me all the years I've lived. "Hey, stay awake. Okay?"

He whispered, "I want Mommy."

And then he collapsed in my arms. I held onto him, staggering toward home. Every step left me changed, left me hard and cold. Whatever might have been left of my childhood was shed during that journey.

As I neared my house, I could hear voices raised, all calling out for my brother. Like a distance runner closing in on the finish line, I dug down and increased my speed. I was carrying Terry across both arms, trying to keep his body from flopping around like a dead fish. I was worrying about the comfort of his head when I ran out in front of the car. A blaring horn and squealing brakes jolted me back to the more common concerns of a kid living in the city, like watching for motorists when darting across the street.

I dove one way and the car swerved the other, or I might have been joining my brother in his trip to the hospital. We fell hard, but I managed to keep Terry cradled against me. The dude in the car stepped out, cussing vehemently. I caught an impression of a jacket with patches on the elbows and one of those fancy hats men often wore to church. I gathered myself and hefted my brother as carefully as I could manage.

"Sweet mother of God," the stunned man whispered as I continued on, Benji still close on my heels. We must have looked a mess, all cold sweat and blood. I felt like a dead kid carrying the corpse of his little brother, two ghosts in the light of day. *You're still dreaming,* I prayed.

By the time I delivered my brother to Betty and the waiting authorities, I would trust nothing and no one. It would be decades before anything ever truly touched me again.

Everyone reacted differently as I rounded the house. Betty took one look at Terry and started wailing and waving her hands in the air like a Jehovah's Witness. Mrs. Simmons fell to her knees and began sending prayers everywhere, her ample bosom heaving as she sobbed. Lynn and Mrs. Lorret stood stark still, like statues erected in the middle of our street. One cop cursed bitterly and took my brother from me, holding him up and pressing an ear to his chest to check his breathing while his partner dove onto the radio and sent out instructions for an ambulance.

For a while that day I lost time, but in weird intervals. It was like I was a record playing in a slow-moving car. Every time the car hit a bump, time skipped, only my needle took a long time to come back down. I remember my mother climbing into the ambulance with my brother. The flashing of the lights atop the emergency vehicle kept drawing my attention, the flickering pattern mesmerizing me. I watched the attendants close the doors to the ambulance through the strobe. My brother never woke up while they rushed him to the hospital.

There was a crowd.

"Where'd you find him, kid?"

I was sitting on my front steps.

"Don't worry about your brother. He'll be okay."

Chip was clinging to my leg.

"Hey, what's your name?"

Benji was standing against my back, grumbling at the cop questioning me.

"His name is Donny." That was Mrs. Lorret, answering him.

"Donny? You need to talk to me, pal."

Someone in the crowd asked if the little boy had been hit by a car.

"Donny?" That was Mrs. Lorret again.

"Hey, Donny?" said the cop again, shaking me gently by the shoulders.

Someone in the crowd told someone else my brother hadn't been hit by a car. They said he'd been molested.

Molested, now there's a word for you. Rape, there's another. Webster's says these words mean the act of an unwanted or improper sexual advance. Let me assure you Webster's definitions fall significantly short. It should read more like: Ugliest and most sadistic of all acts performed by man, usually involving torture and extreme pain, loss of blood, scarring of body and soul, draining of confidence and hope, often culminating in the ruin of human life.

"I found him at the park," I mumbled. The cop standing behind the one kneeling in front of me was scribbling in a notebook. "I mean... he was in an old house across the field." My head was clearing. "They took him there to..."

"Yes?"

The assembled crowd had fallen silent, listening in.

"Do we have to fucking do this in front of all these people?"

That startled the cop. "No, why don't we step inside."

His partner began dispersing the crowd, urging them on their way.

Ruby tried to follow us inside. "You can go," I told her.

"Your mom asked me to keep an eye on you two until she gets back."

299

With my back to her I said, "Go home, Ruby."

"Donny, I—"

"Go home, Ruby!"

I didn't need anyone's help. I especially didn't need the help of one of my mother's whoring friends.

"Someone should be with you and your brother," the cop told me, attempting to regain control of the situation.

"I'll keep an eye on them tonight," Mrs. Lorret told him.

Our kindly neighbor was the only other person from the throng of onlookers who'd followed us into the house. Even Mrs. Simmons had slipped away, or been shooed off by the police. Lynn was probably at home calling people from the church. *She'll tell Bess.* I wished Bess was here. I accepted Mrs. Lorret's offer with silence. The elderly lady was good people. Ruby didn't like it, but I heard the groan of our porch as she lumbered down the steps and left, leaving me with no more excuses not to answer their questions.

My needle was bouncing around again.

"There were two of them?"

I kept getting cold, but I wasn't shivering.

"What makes you think they were brother and sister?"

It was like I had a chunk of ice inside me, numbing from within.

"How tall would you say they were?"

I was answering questions through the frost, my breath spraying a mist none of them could see.

"You're sure it was a Chevy?"

I liked the cold.

"The hood was gray?"

The numbing felt safe.

"Anything else you can remember?"

The cold was indifferent and callous and mine. It was me. I would embrace it forever.

Hours passed. *What time is it?* It was pushing four in the afternoon. The TV was on. Mrs. Lorret was cleaning up our kitchen, washing dishes. Chip was nestled up against me. Benji was lying across my feet. Tiki was under the chair, trembling and watching the front door, waiting for Betty. There was a man in a suit with a badge hanging out of his pocket, sitting on the coffee table in front of me.

"It was the tan house?"

I nodded.

"The one with the rusted-out oil tank in the back and the orange spray paint?"

I nodded again.

"Did you go in?"

That hurt. After a moment I shook my head.

"Did your brother say anything after you found him?"

That *really* hurt.

"Donny, did your brother say anything after you found him?"

I searched for those words. They were there. Every screamed phrase and gurgle of pain my brother had uttered was etched into my bones. I would carry them forever. Just like I would always see his blood on my hands, feel his fingers clawing at my back. I would remember the terror in his eyes and the clamminess of his flesh, the stink of urine in my nose. What he'd told me was there, but covered by layers of lovely ice, protecting me. *Donny, I was calling you.*

"He said they hurt him."

The detective waited. His eyes kept searching my face. I didn't care. He could wait and search forever. I cuddled up with the cold and stared back at him.

"He cried a lot. He wanted his mom."

He had a radio setting next to him. It squawked, and he answered. They had them. He was needed downtown right away. "Do we need the kid as a witness?" the detective asked. A wave of panic washed over me. I didn't want to face the cross-eyed siblings. I wasn't sure I could look at them without losing it. Fortunately, they didn't need me, at least not immediately. I was so relieved when he stood up to go without me. I had to remind myself to breathe.

Mrs. Lorret and the detective talked for a minute. The drone of their conversation couldn't hold my attention, and I skipped again. Having an artist's eye was proving costly in this instance. Every time I closed my eyes they were there. She had those crossed eyes and overlong forehead, with thick, dirty blonde hair that fell wild and tangled around her ugly face. I could see her lime green YMCA T-shirt and unbuttoned jeans, remembered how one sock had stuck out of the pants leg of her jeans as she ran toward their van.

But her brother was worse, even though I'd shared less time with him than his sister. What I could recall about him was far worse than his Frankenstein forehead. It was those eyes, devoid of anything resembling humanity. No fear. No remorse. He'd simply been in a hurry to get away. He didn't want to get caught. I looked into the eyes of a demon that day, an entity loosed from the very source of evil.

"Donny? Donny, the detective asked you a question," Mrs. Lorret drew me out of my trance, forcing the needle back against the vinyl spinning in my mind.

"Just one more question. How long would you say your brother was missing?" He was standing at the door, ready to leave. I didn't understand his question. "Just give me your best guess." Mrs. Lorret was looking at him strangely.

"I was asleep. I don't know exactly." I scratched my greasy scalp and flipped hair out of my eyes. The abrupt movement hurt my head. I had a throbbing headache. I wanted to go back and stay near the cold. "My mother said over an hour."

"Actually, it was longer than an hour, perhaps closer to two," Mrs. Lorret informed him.

"That's funny," he mumbled. He flipped a page and read something. "Your mother told the officer at the scene you were the one who was supposed to be watching your brother."

Mrs. Lorret covered her mouth and gasped. I was going to need more ice.

CHAPTER 22

We were afraid to say anything to my brother. I kept looking at him like he was a visitor from outer space who'd just landed in our backyard and dropped in for cereal and toast. He noticed me staring for about the fifth time and asked, "What you looking at?" Terry had asked his question around a mouthful of puffed wheat, and milk drained off his lower lip and dripped down the front of him. Nobody yelled at him because of his sloppiness. Hell, the kid could've spit chewed-up cereal on the walls, and we wouldn't have said a word.

Terry was eating fast, but eyeing me with caution. You had to eat puffed wheat or rice almost immediately after the milk hit it. It turned to mush in about twenty-two seconds. After that you might as well have been eating shredded bread with milk poured over it—which we had way too often. My brother took the time to fling another spoon of sugar over his bloating wheat puffs and dove back into them, trying to watch his cartoons but still wondering what was wrong with me and Betty.

My mother was scared. *So are you.* This was really freaky. Terry had slept late. I wasn't sure exactly what the doctor at the hospital had done for my brother, but I knew he'd been checked for broken bones and internal injuries, been given a few stitches the doctor claimed would dissolve on their own, and handed to Betty by a nurse with a good luck see ya later attitude. (Hospitals weren't too keen on admitting folks with no money or insurance, no matter how pathetic their plight.) Betty had put Terry to bed at about one in the morning.

Yet here he was, as obnoxious as ever, choking down cereal and hogging the tube, just like any other morning. He had some bruises on his face and told Betty his behind was sore, but nothing more than that. My mother stood next to the toaster perched on the stove, watching him as he ate. She hadn't moved. She just stood there with one hand clutching her breast, her puffy eyes studying every motion Terry made, as stupefied as I was.

I knelt down next to my brother. "Hey, buddy, how you doing?"

He tipped his bowl up and slurped noisily at the leftover milk, eyeing me with suspicion over the rim as he sent more of the sugary cream down his chest than into his mouth. He'd been eating out of one of Betty's Tupperware bowls, and the stupid rim that allowed for the airtight lid made neat slurping all but impossible.

"What's wrong with you?" he asked me after draining the bowl.

I shrugged. "Nothing."

"If you change the channel, I'm telling Mom."

"No." I spread my hands. "No, watch whatever you want. I was just wondering how you were feeling."

He set the bowl down, and Benji began doing his best to lick the bowl dry. "Did you bring me any doughnuts?"

"No," I shook my head slowly. It felt like I was dreaming again, as if this nightmare was going to run on forever. I was sure my brother was going to flip out any moment. "I didn't work at Pops' last night." *And he's going to let me know about that, too.* I remembered my promise to the old guy. But I was pretty sure the events of yesterday qualified as a good excuse to miss. "I'll run over to the store and get you guys some doughnuts though. How's that sound?"

"Chocolate?"

"Is there any other kind?"

My brother didn't know what was going on, but he knew an opportunity when he smelled one. Betty had passed her instinct to take advantage of others on to her middle son. "Two packs?"

"You got it." Terry scrunched up his face, probably kicking himself for not asking for three.

"Jack jacks?" the baby asked.

Chip was lying on the couch. The little weirdo was on his back with his head draped over the edge of the sofa, watching cartoons upside down. I didn't know how he did that. I'd tried it once and gotten nauseous.

"Why didn't you work?" Terry asked.

"Because…" *Because you were assaulted and I was becoming someone else and because our lives were changed forever and because of the police and the paramedics and because I had to stay up with the baby while you and Betty were at the hospital and because of the ice and because I didn't sleep at all last night. Because. Because. Because.* I didn't say any of that, though. I wasn't sure what *was* safe to say. All I said was, "I was too tired."

He made a queer face at me and looked over his shoulder at Betty. Our mother was still standing near the stove, watching us like we were a horror picture. I realized my brother wasn't faking. I stared into his eyes and found no trace of the tormented child from just yesterday. Except for the scrapes under his chin and the yellowing along one of his cheeks, he showed no visible signs of trauma.

He leaned in closer and whispered, "What's wrong with her?"

What isn't wrong with her? I didn't feel like picking on Betty at the moment, and let the chance to zing her slide. "Terry, do you feel sick?"

"No." He looked at me like I was a clown who'd escaped from the circus. "Why? Do you feel sick?"

That actually got a chuckle out of me. "I'm fine."

My brother rubbed at his lower back and squirmed against the floor. "My butt hurts, and my chin is sore. I think I fell out of bed." A thought occurred to him, and his eyes lit up. "Maybe I fell off my bike."

I heard my mother cry out. I think a chill ran down my spine, but I was still too cold inside to fully feel the sensation. I tousled the kid's hair. "Maybe."

"You going to get those doughnuts now? I'm still hungry."

Even though I was uneasy, I laughed again. "You're always hungry."

He turned back to his cartoons. Yogi Bear was stealing someone's lunch basket, bragging to Boo Boo as they tiptoed away. "Puffed wheat sucks," he told me absently, his attention on the antics of the animated bear now being chased by the park ranger.

"Sucks," the baby agreed with perfect clarity.

I felt a tear escape my eye. The fact that I could still feel good about anything surprised me. "Yeah, they do," I admitted. "I'll go get some doughnuts for you guys."

"Chocolate," he reminded me.

"Jack jacks," Chip added.

I glanced at the baby, and he gave me a funny-looking upside down grin. Smiling released a pool of drool that ran up his face and forced the kid to wipe his eyes, but he refused to roll over and watch the tube like a normal kid. *Maybe the world looks better to him that way?* I had to wonder, heading for the door after checking to make sure I had enough money on me.

"Donny?" Terry called after me. Pausing in the doorway and knowing what was coming, I just waited. "Can I have some M&Ms too?"

Today he didn't need to plead. Today he didn't need to turn those big beseeching brown eyes on me and beg for all he was worth. At that moment, all I had was his for the asking. If he'd have known this, my brother would've had me jumping through hoops for hours, but all he wanted was some doughnuts and candy. I'd have bought or stolen anything he asked for that morning. As far as I could tell, he was somehow managing to elude any memory of the entire sickening ordeal.

"Sure."

Call it a miracle or just a little boy's mind shutting down to protect him from something too unbearable to live with, but Terry didn't remember a thing. And it wasn't anything akin to what I was undergoing, not shielding memories or blurring images, not numbing the pain. He woke up and blocked out the whole torturous day. He never spoke a word about it. Nothing. My brother continued to pester me and whine for Betty and complain about life as if he'd decided to skip that day, kind of a twenty-four-hour do-over.

Betty called the doctor in a panic. She was told to be thankful for my brother's amnesia, and that it was common in such cases.

Later that day, I answered a knock at the back door and was surprised to find Tommy standing there holding Terry's Big Wheel. He had his hair braided tight to his head and was wearing a T-shirt with a pack of cigarettes rolled up in one sleeve. He set the bike down and tossed his smoke into the dirt beside our cracked concrete walk.

"I got this back for you," he said, snuffing out the cigarette with his foot, twisting his sneaker back and forth like he was squishing a bug. "I heard about your brother, man," he added when I didn't say anything. "How's he doing?"

I sat down on the step, letting the ripped-out screen door bang shut behind me. "It's weird." I checked to make sure Terry wasn't within earshot. "He doesn't remember shit." Insuring Terry wasn't nearby to overhear when we talked about the attack would become an ingrained habit among my family members.

Tommy whistled as he sat down next to me, but then he mumbled, "Ain't that a good thing maybe?"

"Yeah, I guess so," I had to admit. Then, "You hear about Rupe?"

Tommy stuck out his feet and crossed his legs. "Fuck Rupe. He didn't belong 'round here no way."

I was wishing I didn't belong around here either, amazed that Tommy would continue to hold a grudge against someone he was probably never going to see again. "Maybe so."

"You found him, huh?" I only nodded. "What was that like?"

Terry had wiped his mind utterly clean. I'd only managed to submerge yesterday. It was there somewhere, the memories occasionally bumping against layers and layers of protective ice. But those visions didn't really want to be free, and I didn't really want to find them. Tommy wasn't a great student, but he was perceptive enough to have mercy on me and let my silence be answer enough.

"Hey, thanks for talking to Sutton. He says I'm gonna get out of this shit with that white motherfucker 'cause Irving did the cutting." Tommy lifted his chin and spit a loogey. The wad of phlegm arced high into the air and landed out in the yard. He laughed. "Did you get a load of my bitch of a lawyer?"

I laughed back and nodded. "Yeah, Sutton hates her ass, too." I spit my own loogey and outdistanced Tommy's shot. I had to protect the honor of my home field.

"Nah, her *ass* ain't bad. It's just her attitude needs adjustment." We chuckled like we were just the guys to do it. "You should hear her and Sutton go at it. That's some funny shit, man."

"Speaking of asses, how's Lucy?"

Tommy gathered ammo in the back of his throat and took another shot, cheating by leaning forward as he sent his loogey skyward. His bullet landed close to my mine, but it was hard to tell if he'd beaten my mark or not. "Fuck that bitch."

His tone warned against further interrogation, so I let the subject of Lucy drop. I cleared my throat and filled my lungs, then sent a filmy wad of mucus about ten feet past our previous battleground. *Game over.* "Damn nice shot," Tommy admitted, bowing out and letting me keep my title.

"You going to be in school?"

Classes began this Thursday. I wasn't looking forward to the early mornings and the hassles. I couldn't believe the summer was already gone.

Tommy shook his head. "I'm suspended until this shit is cleared up."

"That right? Damn, I guess I should've gone with you."

We chuckled at my joke, but I was cautious. I still wasn't exactly sure how Tommy felt about me not going along with him to pay back the dudes who'd jumped us.

"Hey, Candy wanted me to ask you to drop by. He wants to know if you going to run for him or not." Tommy let me chew on that. The sun was out but it was breezy. The wind blew my hair down over my eyes, and I flipped it out of my face. "You been thinking about it?"

"Not really."

He checked to make sure my mother wasn't listening and lowered his voice. "Come on, man. You gots to step up. We ain't little kids no more."

I was going to be thirteen on the fifth of October. I felt a lot older than that.

"You run for Candy and you home free 'round here. No worries, baby. Candy told me to tell you we gonna take down those freaks who jumped your brother, just a matter of time and nothin' but a thing." Tommy was staring at me like this should be the easiest decision in the world. "Let's just go rap with him."

But it *wasn't* an easy decision. On the surface Candy made everything sound real smooth. You carried grass, and he paid you, only he made more money than you did while you took the risk. You ran his numbers, and he paid you. You ran his errands, and he paid you. You stole shit for him, and he paid you for it. He gave you money to make him more money, and all the while he remained practically untouchable. *Unless you talked.* Candy made unforgettable examples of anyone who incriminated him in anything.

"You coming or what?"

"No."

"Why not?"

"Because there's nothing around here I want, man. What'll happen to me running for Candy? Maybe I'll get to be Irving one day, and cut some dude's face and go to jail. Or maybe I'll get to drive for him like Jo Jo."

I flipped my hair again, irritated. *You're going to have to let Betty cut it.* There was nothing like a botched-up head on the first day of school. Tommy looked pissed but I didn't care.

"I know, maybe one day I'll get to sit on the front door of the pool hall like Isaac, with a gun tucked into my pants and warrants out for me so it isn't safe for me to walk around outside."

Tommy shook his head at me. "What you gonna do? Where you gonna go?" He flicked my forearm and twisted his lip at me. "You think just 'cause you white you gots some magical ticket out of this shit hole?"

"You, too?" I flicked his arm right back. "What the fuck does my skin have to do with shit? What? You have to work for Candy because you're black? You don't have a choice?" I gave him a sneer of my own. "I want to get out of this fucking place. You should, too."

"How you gonna pull that off? Where the fuck you think you gonna go?"

"I don't know. But Dave says—"

"*Dave?* That churchgoing motherfucker from the magic bus? What the fuck does he know 'bout living down here?"

I pursed my lips. I didn't like when Tommy argued with me. In this contest he was certainly ill-equipped for battle. "He doesn't know shit about down here," I admitted. Tommy spread his arms in exasperation, as if I'd proven his point. "But he knows a lot about *not* living down here. And he says if we work hard and stay straight, we can get anything we want and *be* anyone we want."

Tommy snorted. "And you believe that shit?"

I did. I had to. It was all I had. "Yes. I guess I do."

"Good luck with that, man." Tommy stood up and brushed off his jeans. "Maybe that shit works for white folks."

"That's not fair. Why do you have to keep pointing out that color shit?" I stood too. "It's not like I'm doing any better than you, man. Shit, I'd trade my fucking mother for yours any day."

"*Why?* How often you called nigger? And I don't mean like look at that crazy nigger. I mean, move, *nigger!* What the fuck you looking at, *nigger?* What you doing in here, *nigger?*" He clapped his hands as if an idea had occurred to him. "Wait. I got a few more for you. How 'bout rug head or tar baby or Sambo? You ever been called one of those?"

Tommy was better at this type of arguing than I'd counted on. But I still didn't think he was being fair. "Okay, I get it."

"Oh, I forgot my favorite." I could hear real emotion in his ragged voice. "Coon! You ever been called a coon?"

"No."

"Ever heard your mama called a fine nigger bitch by a bunch of fat-ass rednecks at a rest stop?"

"No."

"You ever been jumped by some white boys 'cause your black ass is rappin' at one of their white girls?" I was tired of saying no when he already knew the answer. "Then you don't know, man. And you ain't ever going to." Before I could respond, Tommy stalked away. "Good luck with the church man's plan. I'm going to stick with shit I know."

It felt like there was something I should say as I watched him strut stiffly down my walk and out into the alley. But what we were going through was well beyond me. What was tearing us apart was still beyond an entire nation, and would be for years to come. Maybe it still is.

Years later, when I was long gone and my brother was struggling with poverty, puberty, and his own Betty tribulations, something on TV would trigger his memory and start an avalanche of grievous recollections. Terry's back was bowed from scoliosis. He underwent agonizing surgery to have metal rods inserted along his spine. I visited him in the hospital. All I remember of that visit was him begging to die, wanting someone to end his anguish. He's lived a life mired in physical agony and mental torture. Of Betty's three misbegotten sons, Terry has suffered the most.

As for the cross-eyed siblings who assaulted my brother? We were never allowed our day in court, never even granted an update on what, if anything, my brother's attackers were ever charged with or convicted of. We were told they were juveniles, and that was that. I remember hearing the boy was seventeen, gender-confused, had an IQ barely above retardation, and an extensive history of being sexually abused. Much the same was said about his nasty younger sister. We were never told if my brother was their first venture into child abduction and rape or not. I'm sure it wasn't their last.

Meanwhile, our bleak lives continued on. Everyone adjusted. Everyone except me. Terry forgot (for the time being). Chip was too young to understand. And Betty wasted no time twisting the circumstances of Terry's attack to her advantage, transforming pity and commiseration into guilt and obligation, and guilt and obligation into cash and assistance.

Betty could have won an Academy Award for her performances in the days following my brother's assault. She was in her glory, and had a whole church with which to ply her trade. You give my mother a sympathetic ear and she could turn minutes into gold, entrapping people by using their own human frailties against them.

It wasn't the congregation's fault. These people wanted to believe in certain things: kindness, honesty, goodness, and a mother's love. They had no way to prepare for Betty. Even I didn't know the full extent of her depravity and lack of moral fiber. This was a woman who would one day work a hospital waiting room full of visitors for handouts while her father passed away just down the hall.

My life was full of faces I couldn't put names to and places I vaguely recalled. Betty lived a transient lifestyle, always moving on, always just a step ahead of the law. We were gypsies. It was all I knew.

Rupe and Tommy were already friends I'd left behind, one because of distance and the other due to circumstance. I wasn't going to get involved with Candy. My rejection of Candy and his schemes had nothing to do with honor or moral character. I was developing neither. It had nothing to do with God or wanting something better for myself. I was simply afraid of Irving and Candy and just about every other dude roaming in and out of that pool hall. It was fear and nothing else.

Rupe, I never heard from again. But I must assume the kid grew up and did well for himself. He was smart. I've always figured he grew up and went off to college and then started a business of some kind, where he could live out his days lording his superior intellect over hired minions.

Three decades after leaving the neighborhood, I went back and sniffed around. There was a nice young couple living in Tommy's house. They'd only lived there a few years and were probably many occupants removed from the days when my friend lived there. Sid's Tavern, where Pops had run his card games, had burned to the ground many years earlier. (I had to wonder if the old man hadn't dropped a cigarette and maybe cooked himself, but no one remembered anything about the torched place.) The pool hall where Candy once reigned had been bulldozed, the man himself replaced by even more dangerous gangs of villains barely older than I'd been while living there.

I did manage to find Dorsey's sister, Loretta, chasing after one of her kids. She'd lived in that same house her entire life. She told me Dors worked for the city of Chicago and rarely visited Ohio. She didn't remember me, but she thought she remembered Tommy Washington. She was pretty sure he went to prison a couple of times. Loretta was also fairly certain Tommy had been killed while incarcerated. I've always hoped she was wrong, that maybe she had my friend and his older brother confused. I've always thought of Tommy as my friend. I hope he doesn't mind that.

Terry was face-deep in his pizza, and kept pulling the box closer to his churning mouth whenever I wasn't looking. He had sauce dripping from the end of his nose and dribbling down his forearms. My brother didn't like to eat the crusts, so he had those piled up in the other half of the box he was tugging on. It looked like he was gathering firewood. The kid was six years old and half my size, but could eat more pizza than I could manage without bothering to belch.

"Donny boy, would you fetch me another beer?" Leon asked.

He *did* belch as I rose to fulfill his request. My brothers cracked up, and Betty began complaining. My mother swore his burps smelled worse than his farts. Terry decided to let fly as well.

"That was pretty good," Leon told my brother.

"See what you're teaching them?"

The baby tried to force a belch and only managed to spit pizza on the table. Betty smacked Leon on the shoulder when he began cackling, still bitching about the smell and the poor manners he was displaying in front of her children. *Oh, God, he's going to ruin all that hard work you put into us.* But I didn't say anything. I was in way too good a mood to bother with Betty.

"You don't smell that?" she kept asking us, waving a hand delicately in front of her face to disperse Leon's rank breath.

Leon winked at me as I handed him his cold can. I'd even opened it without being asked. "Smell what?" He hiked one of the sides of beef he used as an ass and ripped a fart. "There. Smell that." Betty smacked him again while my brothers and I applauded. Even Chip put his sauce-covered hands together and clapped, standing up in his chair and joining Terry and me in our open admiration of Leon's talents.

"Honey, get me a Pepsi," Betty asked.

"Ding dong the dick is dead, the Dago dick is dead," I sang as I went to the fridge.

Leon had moved back in today. His beer was in the fridge, his grease-stained work clothes were stacked up in boxes beside my mother's closet, and his tools were back in the useless bathroom off the kitchen. I'd helped him unload the El Camino while Betty ordered the pizza. If Leon had wanted me to, I'd have carried his stuff in all by myself. *And unpacked it for him.* I'd have happily lugged in a whole truckload of crap to get Leon living with us again. It was going to mean more laundry and having to handle Leon's dingy drawers again, but even the thought of that abysmal chore didn't bother me at the moment.

Not that I thought he'd be here all that long, or that he and Betty were going to get along any better than they had before. But Betty plus Leon meant no Tony. *At least not when Leon's around the house.* My mother would sneak around with Tony if she wanted to, especially if the loser was still washing dishes at the diner, but keeping the dude away from here was good enough for me. *Anyone* was better than Tony.

"Donny, watch your mouth," Betty warned me. I didn't look at her as I picked up another slice of pizza. Some of the topping tried to slip off, but I held it over my head and let the sauce and cheese plop right into my gaping mouth. "We don't need that."

"Aww, leave the kid alone," muttered Leon. *Yeah, leave the kid alone. You tell her, Leon.* "If some asshole punched me in the eye when I was a kid, I'd call him a dick, too."

I thought about pointing out that smacking women around wasn't much of a step up, but didn't. I didn't intend to give Leon any guff during this stay.

"Ding, ding, ding, dong, Tony's a dead dick," Terry piped in around a mouthful of pizza, out of tune.

"Ding, ding, dick," the baby chattered, and I lost it, practically gagging on my food. Chip stood up and clapped, all proud of himself for nearly choking me to death.

I could tell my mother was restraining laughter, but she still said, "Really. Can't we talk about something else?"

Leon ignored her. "I can't believe you flattened his tires," he told me yet again, shaking his head. "That took some big balls to stand up to him." Betty got up from the table and tossed my brother's cast-off crusts into the pizza box we'd already emptied and then carried it away to the trash. She didn't like to be reminded of her motherly shortcomings. "You did good. If that skinny little bitch comes sniffing around here, I'll give him a foot up the ass for you," Leon promised. I was thinking I might start calling the big lug "Dad."

The phone rang, and Betty answered it. I could tell it was someone from the church inquiring about Terry by the way she lowered her voice and pretended to be all weepy. There were gifts of food all over one of our counters. The Simmons sisters had gone on a baking spree. We had enough cake and cookies to keep Terry happy for at least a week. Mrs. Lorret brought over a sugar-cured ham and a pan of baked beans, both of which were favorites of mine, but Leon already had his eye on the ham and beans.

"We're doing the best we can."

Betty wasn't about to tell anyone how well Terry was truly doing.

"That would be *so* appreciated."

Letting folks know my brother had blocked out his attack wouldn't invoke the greatest level of pity.

"Well, I'm so far behind on my utilities I might never catch up."

She was even going to make me keep him home from church for the next week or two, so people wouldn't find out just how well he was adjusting.

"Would you?"

That was fine with me. I didn't want to go anyway.

"Yes, I'll be there this Wednesday." Betty summoned up a sob for effect. "Yes, thank you."

Leon grinned at me and shook his head.

"No, he's not really ready for visitors."

I didn't have a grin in me to give Leon.

"No, he's not eating very well yet."

In fact, I felt kind of sick.

"The doctor says it may take a while."

"Donny, who's Mommy talking about?" Terry asked me.

Leon lost that smile real quick.

"She's talking about some guy from work," I lied. I dropped a paper plate on the floor and tore up a piece of pizza for Benji. Leon gave me a scowl but didn't bitch. Betty tried to move into the living room, but the cord on our phone didn't allow her to get very far away. "Eat your food and forget about it."

Terry leaned back in his chair and rubbed his distended bare belly with both hands, smearing himself with pizza sauce. "I'm full." He grinned at me and then burped again. At the moment he was one happy kid.

"Yes, thank you for that. Your prayers are appreciated more than you'll ever know."

Just not more than your money.

"I'm looking forward to it."

Our eyes met.

"He's shaken up a little, but you know how tough he tries to be."

Whoever she was talking with had inquired about me.

"Sure, I'll tell him."

She could see my shame, and that hardened her face.

"Okay, I'll see you then."

Betty kept the anger out of her voice.

"Yes, and thanks again."

She sounded like a dying woman. I couldn't take any more and looked away.

"I'll be there for sure."

You can count on that, I told whoever she'd been talking to as she hung up the phone.

Leon chuckled as Betty continued to clear the table. "They taking up a collection for you Wednesday night?" he asked my mother. Her rigid posture and silence were all the answer we needed. "Laid it on a little thick, didn't you?"

Betty was stuffing plates down into the trash can. "Mind your own fucking business."

But Leon only laughed. "Woman, you're something else. What're you going to do when someone sees him and finds out the truth?"

"Leon!" My mother glared at him. "Can we try to remember little ears?"

"My ears aren't little," Terry informed her. They weren't, either. He pulled at his ears to illustrate his point. "And who's not eating right?"

Uh oh. The kid was getting suspicious, and he was learning to watch and listen. "I told him you were talking about some guy from work."

"Was it Tony?" Terry asked hopefully.

"I wish," I muttered. Chip hopped off his chair and headed upstairs to play. He had a hunk of pizza crust hanging out of his mouth like a cigar. I let him keep it. The kid was always chewing on something. "Stay out of my room," I yelled at the baby as he took the stairs on all fours, crawling like a bug.

"See what you've done?" Betty asked Leon.

"Get me another beer," he told me, crunching the can and throwing it in the general direction of the trash. The can clattered across the floor and wound up in the corner by the back door. "I didn't *do* anything," he shot at my mother. She was already pissing him off, and he hadn't even slept here a single night. "Maybe my moving back in was a mistake."

"Maybe it was," said Betty.

I picked up the crumpled can so Betty didn't have to, then scurried to the fridge to get Leon's cold one. "I thought we were going to play rummy?" I reminded them. Leon loved to play cards. He'd taught me to play poker so well I almost always beat him, but rummy was his second favorite game. I grabbed a dishtowel and wiped off the table, praying they'd stop arguing.

Leon drained half his can in one noisy gulp. "You got cards?"

I winked at him. "I've got a brand-new deck to beat your ass with." And I did. In fact, I had two new decks. I'd stolen both of them from behind Pops' counter when the old guy wasn't looking. "Come on, don't be scared."

"Kid, you couldn't beat my ass with a stick," Leon growled at me, but he was joking. He grabbed me and put me in a headlock, rubbing his knuckle back and forth against my scalp until it began to burn. Leon called this move a noogie. I just called it pain and humiliation. But he let me go after only a few seconds of torture. "Okay, get the cards." He laughed at me as I rubbed my head, pretending it hurt more than it actually did.

"You won't be laughing when you find all your tires flat in the morning," I told him. He made a fist and I grinned.

"I want to play," Terry chimed in.

"You can sit on my lap and play my cards. We'll beat his ass together."

That pleased my brother. I wasn't letting anything drive Leon away if I could help it. "Yeah, we'll beat his ass," Terry agreed, making a face at Leon.

"I'll give *you* one of these, too," Leon warned, raising another fist and waving it at the face Terry was still making at him.

For just a second I was afraid Betty was going to throw a monkey wrench in my plans to smooth everything over, but all she said as I went upstairs to get the cards was, "I'll make some popcorn." Terry squealed like a hungry pig, delighted at the mention of another of his favored foods, having already forgotten he was supposed to be so full.

CHAPTER 23

All you heard was the roar of the engine. All you felt was the tremendous power of the engine. It was a glorious sensation, unlike anything I'd ever experienced. *It would be a lot better if you were driving instead of hanging onto this seat for dear life.* Normally, I hated roller coasters or thrill rides. I shied away from sensations I couldn't control. But even though we were weaving in and out of traffic and passing most everyone, it never felt dangerous or reckless. Nicky handled the Harley with grace and confidence.

Faces flickered at me from car windows as we passed, like one of those homemade movies you made by flipping cards real fast. The expressions were varied. Some drivers glared at us as we roared by, obviously annoyed to have their windows rattled and their radio momentarily drowned out. Kids plastered their faces against the windows or actually leaned out of their cars and gawked. The more timid drivers kept a tight grip on their steering wheels, just clinging white knuckles with eyes glued straight ahead, too meek to even glance at us.

The ride was sun and wind and speed. Crazy speed. I felt free. *I'm going to do this! I'm going to drive fast! I'm going to pass everyone one day!* I wasn't sure if it would be on a motorcycle or behind the wheel of a fast car, but this was one bad habit I was most definitely going to pick up.

It didn't take me long to learn how to lean into the turns, and by the time we were thundering down the first stretch of highway I felt safe enough to actually look around and try to enjoy the ride. When I got brave enough, I began craning my head to the side, the wind ripping through my hair and pulling at the skin of my face as I peered ahead with squinting, tearing eyes. Bugs whizzed by like bullets, and after having more than one unlucky insect embedded deeply into the pores of my flesh, I learned to keep my mug safely between Nicky's shoulder blades, wondering how the hell he rode this fast with nothing protecting his eyes. *And mouth!*

When the ride ended at an open expanse of farmland about an hour or so outside the city, I climbed off that bike thinking of nothing but the ride back home. Nicky parked in a field already littered with what looked to me like at least a hundred other Harleys. There were bikes of every conceivable shape and color. Some were basic but many were ornately painted with skulls or flames. Some bore flags on long flexible poles, while others had colors or symbols painted on the fuselage. I even noticed some bikes with sidecars and a couple of really cool modified three-wheelers.

"Don't touch anything," Nicky warned me with a grin. I nodded, stepping back a bit from the bike I'd been examining. "Some of the animals at this party will bite." He waved at some dude roaring by. "And they get worse as the day grows long. But I don't have to tell you what happens when you mix alcohol with morons, do I?"

"No."

"So, here are the rules. You do what I tell you, and stay where I can see you." We headed toward the picnic area, following footprints in the slightly muddy field standing between us and the tents. "If I look around and can't find you, you'll be sorry when I do." He smacked the back of my head playfully. "Unless I tell you different, in which case you'll just have to fend for yourself and stay out of trouble."

I readily agreed to everything. I would've agreed to anything. School had started Thursday, and after two days it felt like I'd been grueling along for months.

After trundling the bottles in Chick's garage down to the Kroger this morning, I'd knocked on the door to hand over the loot, hoping I wasn't waking anybody up. There were more bikes in the yard than normal, and I could hear a lot of movement going on in the house as I waited. In fact, I had to knock louder to get anyone to answer.

I was pleasantly surprised when Nicky opened the door. "Hey, man. How you doing?"

"Fine," I lied.

"That right?"

The way he was looking at me had me wondering if he knew about my brother. *Why wouldn't he?* The whole neighborhood knew about my brother. Bad news traveled faster than cheap drugs around here. Kids asked dumb questions, and teachers looked at me like I was dying. One of the school's guidance counselors had called me down to her office and asked me if I wanted to talk about anything. I'd asked her if she thought the Reds were going to win the Series again, and she'd let me go on to my next class.

"That the kid?" Chick called from inside. He stuck his meaty bald head out the door behind Nicky and gave me a thrust of his thick chin. "We heard about your brother, kid. That was pretty fucked up." It got all quiet behind him, and Nicky's face hardened a bit. "That my money?" he asked, reaching for the six bucks and change in my hand.

Before I could give it to him, Nicky put a hand on Chick's face and shoved him back inside. I heard someone in the kitchen smacking the big guy as the door closed. "Just keep that," Nicky ordered me, waving my outstretched hand away. I did as he instructed, tucking the money in my front pocket. "Fat ass in there has a Rock 'em Sock 'em Robots game down in the basement. The game works but the blue robot's head always pops off as soon as you hit the damn thing, so the game's no fun."

I wasn't sure how to respond. I looked at him with uncertainty. I could tell he'd been expecting exactly the reaction I was displaying. "Okay...?" I shrugged. "Are you trying to give the game to me?"

Nicky finally grinned. "No. If I did that Chick would start blubbering." He stepped down off the stoop and punched me softly in the chest. "What I'm saying is you look a lot like that blue robot."

I got it. We both laughed. I thanked him for the money and turned to go, but his hand on my shoulder stayed me. "What are you doing today?"

It was Saturday. I didn't have plans until working at Pops' tonight. I told him as much. "Ever rode on a Harley?"

Now I had.

I was also attending my very first (and last) gathering of bikers. As far as social groups go, I can best describe the experience as a prison yard without the bars or walls. There were women, food, and lots of beer and grass thrown in just to keep everyone loose and happy. I was exposed to bare midriffs, thin T-shirts and sheer halter tops (made more so with beer poured all over them), a few fistfights, and a constant barrage of coarse language. There was an old tree that most likely died after being pissed on a few thousand times. The women had to trudge about half a mile to an old farmhouse if they wanted a proper bathroom. More than one of them squatted near that poor tree as well.

Around noon, there was a wild tackle football game Nicky wouldn't let me near that ended only when some dude broke his leg and had to be carted off to the hospital. I was glad I hadn't been allowed to play when one poor bastard got his front tooth knocked out, and the guy who did the damage held up the tooth and screamed, "We've got chicklets!" Hot dogs, hamburgers, and even steaks were cooked on open fires and portable grills. There were few kids around and someone was constantly giving me a smile and handing me food.

Grass and harder drugs passed hands, and beer was consumed by the keg or from bottles floating in tubs of water and ice. Dudes who drank too much and fell out were just left where they collapsed like ignored wounded on the field of battle. Couples making out on blankets outnumbered the couples making out more seriously in tents or *under* blankets, but not by all that much. One of the best sights was a tug of war across a muddy ditch that eventually ended with both sides diving into the mud.

I passed some time with a shifty dude sporting a Fu Manchu mustache with quick hands running a game of three card monty. He was so good even I donated a buck just to see if I could beat him. Later in the day, there was a more serious fight that had to be broken up when a guy pulled a knife. I listened to a hippie-looking dude playing Jim Croce songs on a guitar, singing "Time in a Bottle" so well he had some of the drunks crying. A couple of hours later, I passed by him again and found the dude passed out and slumped over his guitar. I also stumbled across one of the passed-out guys stripped naked by his friends. All they left him wearing was the dirty bandana wrapped around his head.

As Nicky had predicted, the bikers got pretty wild late in the day and as the sun set. I was peeking in on a tattoo artist working out of a tent near the road (I watched him put a heart on the flabby bicep of a dude so high he couldn't remember how to spell his true love's name) when the three card monty guy passed by, being dragged through the mud with his feet tied together by a horde of crazy bikers. As dusk settled, a really loaded couple stripped down to their birthday suits and plunged into a little pond near the picnic area. In mere minutes just about everybody decided to join them for a dip in the pond to wash away the day's grit or show off how drunk they were.

It was a great day.

My personal highlight came during a baseball game played with one old wooden bat, a dried-out baseball as hard as a rock, and not a single glove to protect your hands. It was our gang against some other bunch of drunken bikers. We used a stack of hay bales as a backstop so nobody broke a finger trying to catch a pitch, but whoever dared play first had to have tough hands and no brains. Chick played first for us. Almost every recorded out came by way of strikes. There were no walks. You had to wait for a pitch you thought you could hit and take your swings, with the other team mocking if you took a ball they thought was in the zone and should have been swung at.

Our team had the lead late in the game when a ball was hit deep to center. While the other team exhorted their teammates around the bases, I raced back, my eyes never leaving the ball and my quick feet skimming mucky earth. Running full speed, I lay full out and caught the petrified ball, holding it aloft in my throbbing hand and rotating my body so no one doubted I'd caught it clean as I skidded to a stop on my back. I scrambled up and threw the ball in so quickly our team tagged two more guys out before they managed to get back to their bases.

"Fucking triple play!" Chick boomed, throwing me up in the air and catching me as if I weighed no more than a baby.

"Great catch, kid," the dude who'd hit the ball admitted as he took the field.

Others agreed. I accepted my due praise with the usual aplomb, bowing for the audience and enjoying the attention. It *had* been a great catch. Nicky told me it was the greatest catch he'd ever seen. He called me Willie Mays. The next inning I even got a hit, but the game ended when the bat split right down the middle. We were ahead so Chick named us the winners. Nobody on the other team argued with him.

It was a really great day.

When it was good and dark everyone gathered around huge bonfires and settled down. Someone played taps on a bugle, and the mood grew somber. But not for long. "Here's to those left behind," a raspy voice said from across the fire. Everyone drank, and a few mumbled assents. Others just remained silent and stared into the leaping flames. The fire spit orange embers into a pink sky, where the sparks died and went black before wafting away.

"That was a great catch, kid," Chick told me again.

He handed me a beer and plopped down, propping himself against one of the hay bales we'd dragged over. Nicky walked up and set down a plate with a burger and some chips, along with a bottle of Coke. He took the beer away from me and tossed it unceremoniously at Chick, who caught it without spilling too much.

"What's your problem? Did you see that catch? The kid's old enough."

"Eat up," Nicky told me. He sat down on a bale behind me and crossed his feet. I'd been eating pretty much all day, but I didn't say anything. Nicky said eat, so I did. "Sure, Chick, why don't we get him laid, too?"

Chick liked that idea. "Yeah! I'll bet that Helen would break the kid in." He rose up on his elbows and began looking around. "I just saw her somewhere too."

"Helen? I'm not even sure Helen's a woman."

"Sorry about that, Nick," Chick grumbled. "We can't all fuck them skinny bitches. Some of us like *real* women."

"When do they get real? What, at about three bills?"

Everyone laughed at that, but Chick didn't mind. He just spit beer into the fire and grinned at the hissing protestations of the flames.

"Hey, big girls need lovin' too, boys," Chick informed us. "Plus they can usually cook, and act way more appreciative when they find a man strapped well enough to drill past the bullshit and still hit bottom."

Some girl behind us piped up. "You better talk to Helen then, Chick. She never said a thing about you hitting bottom of shit. Matter of fact, she was complaining that you didn't drill long enough to really reach much at all."

Chick spit more beer. The fire cursed back, like it was laughing at the big guy with the rest of us. "Helen don't count." Chick was blasted, and feeling good. He acted like he was waving a flag of surrender. "That bitch is too real even for me." He settled back, making himself more comfortable against the hay. It looked like he was going to fall asleep soon. "All I know is I got mine, and that's what's important."

Most of the men around the fire appeared to agree with that. One of them spouted a heartfelt "Amen brother!" while a couple of the women booed.

All the talk about women reminded me of Mandy. I'd asked Nicky if she was going to be here, and he'd said only no. He'd offered no further explanation about her absence and his tone hadn't invited any more questions, so I didn't pester him. I was learning what subjects were safe to talk about with him and what weren't. His ex and his daughter were off limits. I was pretty sure Mandy was taboo now as well. I reminded myself not to bring her up again as I threw my paper plate into the fire like a Frisbee and watched it fold up and incinerate.

Eventually everybody who was still there settled down for some fireside philosophy. Across the field, you heard the occasional Harley boom to life and clamor away as people left. I listened to outlandish lies and heartbreaking memories. They talked about fallen brothers and slant-eyed whores, old ladies who'd cheated on them, and kids they missed. I heard great tales about being chased by troopers, living in prison, busting heads, and breaking every known law. One dude said he'd just lost his license. More than one chuckled and admitted they were currently driving without theirs, too. They bitched about "the man" and how they detested the government. Most of them just called what and who they hated "they." "They" did this and "they" did that. I wasn't sure who "they" was but I didn't want any part of them. Some bragged, a few wept, but every word and sentiment was welcomed and listened to.

As I looked at the faces glowing around the fire, I realized that this was why most of them were here. Sure, the food and the drugs and the booze and the casual sex were good reasons too, but those could be had elsewhere. Not this. Tonight they were among brothers, bonded by common experiences and sympathetic hearts. The men circling these fires could feel at ease and vent tonight. What was said didn't really matter. That you could say whatever you wanted to and not be chastised or judged was the allure.

I was half asleep when Chick drew me into their world. "You want any help with what happened to your brother, kid, you just let me know."

The faces in the firelight were all turned toward me. I didn't know what to say. This wasn't the kind of attention I relished. I knew what he meant by help. It wasn't that the thought of exacting some form of revenge hadn't already crossed my mind, but nothing concrete had formed as of yet. The whole prospect of facing those deranged siblings scared me shitless. And looking for payback hadn't gone very well for Tommy; I didn't want to follow his example without putting some serious thought into my plans.

"Donny won't be needing any help," said Nicky, coming to my rescue. I suddenly realized Nicky hadn't said a word tonight. "The law already has them."

The guy who'd broken his leg snorted. They'd brought him back with his leg jutting up in the air from out of a sidecar, bouncing him around roughly and laughing at his screams of pain. "They won't have them long if they're underage," he said. *They all know too!* I realized. His name was Roman, and he had his cast propped up and his head in the lap of a woman. She kept making over him and running her hands through his hair.

"He still won't be needing any help," insisted Nicky.

"What you want the kid to do, Nick?" Chick had his eyes closed, but he sounded wide awake, and irate. "Maybe he should run around the neighborhood with his hands covering his asshole, hoping nobody decides to stick it to him, too? Give me a fucking break. I know what you'd do if that shit fell on someone you cared about."

"Chick, what you know wouldn't fill a fucking thimble," Nicky grumbled.

But Chick wasn't cowed. "I know economics, Nick. I grew up in that house we roll out of. I walked the same fucking streets this kid does. You didn't." Chick was still lying on the ground with his eyes closed, but his deep voice was tense and poised for battle. "What happened to his little brother was fucked up. Worse than fucked up, but did you see any news crews? What kind of shit is that? The fucking kid wasn't even worth a blurb in the *Dispatch*. Now you tell me true, Nick… That same shit happen to a kid where you grew up, and how much shit would've hit the fan?"

Nicky's silence spoke volumes. I felt sorry for my friend. It seemed this was one subject Chick knew more about than Nicky. Way more.

"In our neck of the woods, the cops and the people who live in nicer places don't care what happens, as long as we keep the shit in house," Chick continued. "Down there, if you get hit you better hit back. If you don't you're damn sure going to get hit again, and then kicked. And then maybe kicked some more." Chick finally sat up and looked at Nicky and me as well. "You keep taking shit and eventually worse happens to you." Chick locked gazes with me. "I say fuck waiting for worse. Me? I say when they hit you kick first, and if they kick back you get a hammer and cave in some asshole's skull.

"The kid ain't got no dad to help him out. His mom's just some dumb fucking whore." *There's no arguing with that.* "And don't blame your dad for cutting out, kid. Nam killed some of us with bullets and others with shit I can't explain. The man fucked up a lot of us. The drugs aren't his fault. Your mom dropping her pants for other dudes ain't his fault. It's a fucked-up world, and there just ain't no getting around that." Murmurs from around the fire agreed with Chick. Everything he'd said sounded logical to me.

But then Nicky began clapping. Everyone fell silent and listened to him. "Well said, preacher Chick from the church of latter day wasted fat assholes that haven't got a goddamn clue how to live in the real world." I stifled a laugh. *That was good.* Some woman across the fire giggled. "I swear to God,

I'm going to sell my bike and start hanging out at a disco joint if you don't grow the fuck up."

Chick groaned and fell back, covering his face with his hands. "Oh, God, here we go," he moaned.

"Every time we get together it's the same tired shit." I twisted around so I could watch Nicky talk. "It's just not that fucking complicated. If you drive too fast you're eventually going to get a ticket." Nicky lifted his hands in exasperation. "By the way, if you get enough of them you lose your license. That's the law. The same law everyone else has to live by. None of us are special. We went away, and our wives and girlfriends cheated."

Nicky pointed at a guy across the fire. "Hey, Granger?"

"Yeah?" Granger mumbled.

"Who's that sitting next to you?" asked Nicky.

Granger looked at the woman next to him. I couldn't see her very well. "My wife, Sue Ann."

"How long you been married?"

Granger thought about that. I decided Granger wasn't too bright.

"Be ten years come November," Sue Ann answered, bailing out her husband.

"Wait. So you were married before he left to go overseas?" asked Nicky.

"Sure were," she replied proudly.

"And you didn't leave him?"

"I waited, and I wrote him every day." Nicky let us absorb that. Sue Ann was crying when she further said, "And I prayed every morning and every night for him to come home safe." Nicky let us absorb that, too.

"You didn't cheat on him or run off?" Nicky finally continued.

"Screw you, Nick," Sue Ann shot back.

"There you have it. Some of us married wrong, and some of us married right. Shit happens. Cry in your fucking beer, and move on." Nicky chuckled. "I swear to God this whining makes me sick. And you're the worst, Chick."

"Me?"

"Yeah, you. Telling this kid to crack skulls." Nicky kicked Chick's boot with his own. "Don't brag to me about your rough neighborhood and expect me to be impressed. The reason you know so much about the fucking place is because you're too goddamn stupid and lazy to do anything but live in your mom's rent-free house and work part-time jobs until you get fired for showing up hung over or high."

"That's not my fault—"

"The fuck it isn't!" Nick cut in. "I love your fat ass like a brother, but don't preach to me unless you want to hear truth in return. It's about choices. Drink too much, and you get drunk. Take drugs, and you get high. Don't show able and ready to work, and you get fired. Add all that shit up, and guess what you get?"

Nobody ventured a guess. Without really meaning to I said, "You get to live in a crappy neighborhood and have no future."

Nicky chuckled and pointed at me. "There you go." He kicked Chick's boot again. "The kid goes to the head of the class while the dunce keeps his floppy pointy cap and stays on the stool in the corner."

"Whose side you on, kid?" grumbled Chick.

"His," I responded without hesitation.

Chick groaned like he had a bellyache. "Great, the world gets another knight in shining armor."

"I don't get you, Nick." That was Roman again. "You saying we don't have no right to bitch? What? Nam was okay with you?" He tossed a bottle into the fire and kicked up a cloud of angry sparks. "You got some fucking secret for dealing with this shit, I want to hear it."

Others did too. Mutters and comments peppered Nicky from around the fire. "Go ahead, Nick. Give it to them," Chick prodded.

"No, Roman, I'm not defending our war," he admitted soberly. "Nam was wrong. Lives were wasted. Our government's corrupt. All that shit's true."

"So what are you saying?" a man's voice on the other side of the fire asked.

Nicky sighed. "My grandfather fought in the second big one. He came home with one eye. My father fought in Korea. He came home with a permanent limp. Neither one of them ever uttered a single word against this country. I've never heard them say much about what they went through. Unlike most of you, I volunteered to fight in our war." Nicky drained a bottle and swallowed, his eyes staring into the fire as he began passing the empty from one hand to the other. "I figured I was no better than the men who raised me. It was what we did. We answered the call.

"I watched my grandfather work his farm every day of his life. Through rain, drought and bugs, falling prices, he just plugged along. When my grandmother came down with cancer, he just added the burden of caring for her and kept right on going. One morning I couldn't help myself, and I asked him why he did it. Why he never complained. Why he didn't sell the farm and put Grandma in a nursing home and take it easy."

Nicky paused and dropped the bottle. He had me mesmerized. He had the men around the fire enthralled as well. His face was bathed in the fire's light, serious but reflective, and his eyes shone with unnamed emotions. I wasn't sure if he was sad or defensive. I don't believe Nicky cared if the men around him bought what he was saying or wanted to tell him to go to Hell.

"That old man looked at me like I'd spit on him. He told me a man took care of his responsibilities. He told me a man worked every day, and when times got tough he worked harder still. He told me life was simple, and not to be looking for excuses to fail or making up opinions to complain about. He said if there were changes needed God would make them. Before he went out to the fields he told me he thought he'd taught me better than that."

There was a silence.

"What happened to your grandparents?" Sue Ann asked.

Nicky chuckled softly. "Gran died in his arms of the cancer. A few months later my grandfather was plowing fields and had a heart attack." Nicky grinned in the firelight and held out his hand, flattened and with the palm down. "He just drove that tractor right out of the field, through the fence, across the highway, and into the woods on the other side, still working even after he died."

Some of the men laughed, but with respect.

"And your father?" Sue Ann queried hesitantly.

Chick sat up, watching Nicky closely. After a sigh Nicky said, "Hundreds of acres have been repossessed. My dad works for a chicken plant and struggles to keep about sixty acres to play with and the house and barns my grandfather left him."

Roman snorted. "I'll bet he doesn't share your grandfather's faith. Fucking bankers swoop in and take your goddamn soul as soon as a man can't make a payment or raise enough cash to pay his taxes."

"My father? My father's an even stronger man. He works five to six days a week in that plant and puts another thirty or forty in his fields or repairing old farm equipment. He never complains or blames anyone for what he's lost." Nicky held out that hand again. "I'm pretty sure he intends to die on that same tractor, plowing the same ground as his father. What he can hold onto of it, anyway."

"Then he's a fool," Roman spat.

"You want your other fucking leg broke?" Chick growled.

Obviously, only Chick was allowed to break Nicky's balls.

But Nicky just chuckled again. "Let it go, Chick." He pulled a bandana out of his back pocket and fit it over his hair. "You know, Roman, I've often thought that very same thing about him. But you know what?"

"What?" Roman asked in a surly tone.

I was thinking if he kept it up Chick *would* break Roman's other leg.

"Right about now my father's had his supper and is probably sitting in the living room with my mom. She's probably knitting something. He's smoking his pipe and reading the paper, or maybe watching *M.A.S.H.* or a *Hogan's Heroes* rerun. In an hour or two he'll go off to bed and sleep until five in the morning and get up to work the place, since tomorrow's Sunday and he's off at the plant. He's happy and content. He's fulfilled. And he's going to die that way." Nicky stood and stretched. "At least he's not sitting out in some muddy field killing brain cells and whining about how hard life is, or blaming somebody else for his troubles. The whole bunch of us aren't worth five minutes of that fool's time."

"That's still a crock, Nick," Roman insisted. "That's a great story. If you want to follow the 'don't ask questions and accept what you're given' trail, go ahead. But that simple shit won't work for the rest of us."

Nick gave Roman a shrug. "Who said it worked for me? I hate farming, and I don't believe in God." Nicky motioned for me to get up. "I'm just pointing out how much more whining and bitching our generation seems to do than those before us."

"They fought real wars. We were in Nam."

Nicky chuckled. "Yeah, you've got me there, Roman. Their wars must have been birthday parties. All those wounds must've been inflicted by popping balloons or wild games of pin the tail on the donkey."

"So where do you find your strength, Nick?" Sue Ann asked. For a while nobody spoke. The fire crackled and popped.

"My last detail before getting back stateside was hauling body bags. I can't tell you how many kids and pieces of kids we hauled onto those 130s." He paused, as if maybe he was trying to come up with a number. "Whenever I get down about anything I just try to remember the weight of those bodies and that slick rubber in my hands. I remember matching up dog tags and the guys joking about how it really didn't matter if the right pieces were in the right bags, because you couldn't recognize them anyway." Nicky shrugged. "I bet you any one of those boys would trade me for the chance to have a few worries and deal with a few problems if they could. And I just drink one for them and climb on that bike."

"You got that straight, Nick," somebody said.

"Amen," murmured Sue Ann. She laid her head on her husband's shoulder.

Nicky told Chick he had to be getting me home. The big guy got up, and they embraced in the rough manner of men who could get away with doing so in front of other men. Chick hugged me too, squeezing my shoulder blades together before letting me breathe again. I felt woozy when he set me down. His breath had reeked of beer and he'd smelled something awful, but I was glad the big bear of a man considered me his friend.

"Hey, Nick, you ain't leaving because I pissed you off, are you?" Roman called out.

"Roman, your dumb ass couldn't get to me with a flame-thrower," Nicky told him. "You boys roll safe," he told the rest as we headed out.

It sounded like everyone threw him a good-bye, but I could hear another discussion starting up before we were even out of earshot. Chick told some-one Nicky was a fucking guru. Someone else said Nicky was soft. I was pretty sure the soft comment had come from Roman. Sue Ann said the rest of them could learn a lot from Nick.

"Those dumb hicks will bitch at you all night, if you let them," was all Nicky said. For a little while I listened to the scrunching of Nicky's boots in the soft earth, trailing after him as we made our way to where the bike was parked. "So, what did you get out of all that bullshit?"

I knew what he wanted to hear. Even if he didn't believe in God, he was preaching the same message Dave did, just with a different spin. "Work hard, and you'll make it. No excuses, that kind of thing."

"You ever heard the saying about excuses, Donny?" he asked. I told him I didn't think so. "Excuses are like assholes: everybody's got one, and they all stink." I hadn't heard that before. *That was a good one.* I was going to use that line. (Little did I know the rest of the world was already spouting those sage words on a daily basis.) "Did you have a good time?"

This had been one of the best days of my life, and I told him so. "Thanks for bringing me along. If you're leaving early because of me you don't have to. You don't have to keep being nice to me because you feel sorry for me, either. I'm not a little kid."

Nicky took out a cigarette and sat on the seat of his bike, looking at me while he lit up. "I'm leaving because I get sick of listening to them after about ten minutes." He blew smoke into the darkness. "You smoke yet?"

"No."

"You ever going to?"

"I don't intend to."

"Why not?"

I laughed and scratched a mosquito bite on my neck. "They stink, and they kill you."

Nicky chuckled. "Donny, *that's* why I brought you along." I didn't get it. "You're a bright kid, and you have a chance if you dig in and want to rise above the shit you live in." *Chance at what? Dig in at what?* "There is no great hidden secret to life. Just live. That's it. Don't give up, and don't make excuses. Find out what you want, and go get it."

"Okay."

What he was saying sounded well and good, but I wasn't sure what he wanted me to do with the information. I'd been told for years that science and history class were just as important to my future as English and math, but as of yet I'd still come across no evidence to support that claim. A lot of what Chick had said made sense to me, just as a lot of what Nicky had said did too. I figured the truth was somewhere in the middle. Maybe you simply applied as much as you wanted to accept from either position and made it fit your wants and beliefs. *Damn, that's pretty deep for a twelve-year-old.*

"At the risk of totally embarrassing myself I'm going to tell you something my grandmother used to say all the time." I just nodded since he acted like he wanted a response. "She believed people were no different than rain, and our lives were just the journey from Heaven to the earth." Nicky took a long drag and chuckled as he exhaled. "She had some Indian blood in her from somewhere. My Gramps claimed she'd have danced around a fire chanting and singing every time it rained if he'd have let her."

"I have Indian blood in me. Supposedly, my dad's grandmother died on a Sioux reservation." I remembered that the man whose name was typed on my birth certificate wasn't sure I was actually his. "If the guy's really my dad, that is."

Nicky nodded. "That doesn't surprise me. So anyway, she believed we kind of chose our own journey. She said some rain was angry and waited for a storm, just wanting to hurt and harm, while most rain was happy just to feed the earth and life in general. She believed some rain was just plain mean and confused and wasted itself by dashing against rocks and cliffs, trying to change what couldn't be changed." His voice took on a faraway lilt, as if he was seeing his dead grandmother. "But she used to insist that some raindrops weren't afraid to fall alone, and traveled through the sky choosing their own paths. My grandmother said one of these special drops from Heaven could land in still water and cause a ripple that lasted forever, a wave of change that ran on and on until the end of time."

"That's a cool story. Did you believe her?"

Nicky flicked the cigarette away. "Nope. Not until the first time I held my little girl. It wasn't until then that I understood my grandmother's legend. My daughter's definitely one of those drops from Heaven." He looked at me gravely. "What about you? What kind of rain do you want to be?"

"I don't know. I haven't thought about it much." He patted the seat, and I climbed aboard. "What about you, Nicky? What kind of rain are you?"

"Me? I want to fall all by myself, waiting until I catch Olivia Newton-John sun bathing in the nude. I'm going to land right between her tits, roll slowly down around her navel, and then spend eternity..." He glanced back at me and grinned. "Let's just say I'm going to die happy." Before I could respond, Nicky kicked the bike's starter. The engine roared to life on the second try. I spent most of the ride home lost in my thoughts. I was tired, and I was thinking I might skip working at Pops', especially since I was already so late. The ride wasn't as cool at night. You couldn't see as much. The faces in the windows of the cars we passed were blurred and obscured. I was hoping my life was about to settle down for a while. *After what happened to Terry, it can't get any worse.*

CHAPTER 24

Central was different without Tommy or Rupe around. I had no one to play paper football with in study hall, nobody to cut up with in the hallways between classes. Cutting a boring subject or ditching school altogether was always easier when you had other guys sneaking out with you. I had to watch my mouth a little more, but Collins and his crew were pretty much leaving me alone, so even that wasn't a problem. In fact, the worst problem I had was avoiding Patrick, who figured I needed new friends and wanted to be the first in line. The poor kid kept giving me change and following me around, hoping I'd take him under my wing. But that wasn't going to happen. *Then why do you keep taking his money?* I wasn't so lonely that I needed Patrick's company, but I *was* usually broke.

I was weaving my way through the hall when Marsha Hughes stepped in front of me, forcing me to pull up. She'd blossomed over the summer, and was well aware all the guys had taken notice. Marsha was wearing a thin lavender sweater that did little to conceal what Leon called a rack and Tony had called the twins. *Doesn't anybody call them boobs anymore?* She just stood in front of me popping her gum and watching me while my brain fluttered and my tongue swelled up.

"What's up?" I finally squeaked.

Marsha fired off an especially loud pop, then stuck out her pink tongue and licked part of the escaped bubble off her lower lip, still eyeing me frankly. "My friend likes you," she finally said. She thrust her chin toward an adjacent hall, where the new girl from Mrs. Gill's history class stood. She looked away when I glanced in her direction. "At least she thinks she does." Marsha didn't sound like she was too keen on her new friend's tastes.

Obviously, my lack of boob etiquette wasn't my only shortcoming when dealing with the opposite sex. I didn't have a clue what I was supposed to do or say under these conditions. I looked at the new girl again. She turned around and began adjusting her hair. She looked a lot like Marsha. Both girls were slightly taller than I, with dark hair and brown eyes, slender and pretty. They could have been sisters. The only distinction I could see was that Marsha's twins were bigger than the new girl's.

"Well?" Marsha snapped.

I wanted to be James Bond, to have something witty and clever right on the tip of my tongue. But all I managed was, "Well what?"

Marsha laughed at me. That hadn't been the response I was hoping for. "I told her you were clueless. I think the only reason she's interested is because she had to read your stupid story."

Now that was hitting below the belt. Our first English assignment had been to write about something we'd done over the summer. Knowing my classmates would tell tired tales about Disneyland or boring trips to Niagara Falls, I'd crafted an ingenious story about striking up a friendship with a cockroach named Skitters who could talk and play chess and loved to eat pizza and watch TV late at night.

Skitters slept all day and only came out when it was dark, but we became fast friends. The best part of the story was when my mother's boyfriend Tony moved in and started pushing me around. Skitters, who was secretly a leader of millions of other cockroaches, ordered an attack on the drunken Dago after he passed out on the couch one fateful night. Within seconds, all that was left of the bum was a polished skeleton with an Italian horn hanging around its neck. The fable had a tragic ending: Skitter's skittering days came to an end when Betty stepped on him while staggering through the kitchen in the middle of the night, out of her mind on Valium.

The teacher had us read each other's stories aloud, and she chose the new girl to read mine. She did it well, using a weird voice for the cockroach and really getting into the dialogue. The class loved it. The teacher gave me an A, writing across the top of my paper, "Imaginative and creative but not actually what I was looking for." What sucked was that I couldn't remember the new girl's name. Dull as I was, I knew better than to let Marsha in on that little fact. *Great, you have one fan, and you forget her name.*

"So? Do you like her or not?" Marsha was getting impatient. How the hell was I supposed to know if I liked her? "Are you still going with Bess or what?" As far as I knew I'd never *gone* with anybody. Marsha stopped chewing and leaned toward me, cocking her pretty head. "Are you stupid, or what?"

I never used to think so, but I was feeling awful stupid at the moment. "No." *That was good. That'll show her, you idiot.* "I mean… no, I'm not stupid."

"Well then? Do you like Sarah or not?" Marsha puckered her lips and began blowing a bubble, waiting for my answer and glaring at me from above the growing ball of sweet-smelling gum. *Sarah!* Her name was Sarah. Maybe I could still crawl out of this confrontation alive. She popped the bubble and sighed. "Is that a hard question or what?"

Marsha finished most of her questions with *or what?* I thought about pointing that out and then decided against it. "Sure, I like her," I managed to get around my swollen, numb tongue. At least I liked her as much as you *could* like someone you didn't even know.

"Why?"

"Why what?"

Marsha grinned. I'd seen that same wicked leer on Bess's face. Maybe all girls were born with the instinct to sense weakness and uncertainty in boys. I was beginning to form a theory that they enjoyed inflicting pain even more than attracting attention. She stuck a finger in her mouth and pulled out a string of gum which she then began wrapping around her index finger, her narrowed eyes boring in on me as she asked, "Why do you like her?"

Sweet Jesus, this girl's merciless! I was going to have to add to my budding theory that girls grew meaner as they aged. *Think, man!* There had to be a way out of this. Without knowing exactly how, I knew I was at some devious crossroads. This was a test of sorts. If I said the wrong thing Marsha would embarrass me. That, or maybe grow fangs and paralyze me before devouring my body like black widow spiders did after they were through using their mates.

"Well?" she persisted, still playing with her gum.

Time slowed. Kids flowed past us in the hall. Sarah waited across the way, wondering if I would pass Marsha's test or wind up as an after-school snack. Marsha kept wrapping the gum around the tip of her finger and searching me for weakness, her soft brown eyes narrowed and piercing. Then I had it! Saying what I'd come up with would sting, but I could think of no other way out of this. *Man up, Mary!* I told myself, wondering where I'd heard that saying.

"Well?" Marsha snapped yet again, growing impatient. "Do you know why you like her or not?"

I swallowed, steeled myself, and then said, "Because she's pretty. She looks a lot like you."

Marsha froze. She slowly stuffed the gum back into her mouth and bit a little clump off her polished fingernail. "Oh," she said quietly. Her cheeks were flushed, and I could tell I'd said the right thing. *Thank God.* "Well. Okay. I'll talk to you tomorrow." She headed toward the waiting Sarah, but then she collected her composure and threw at me, "Maybe we can all hang out at my house this Saturday or something."

"Sure," I replied, nodding.

I thought about my triumphant encounter as I walked home. I was remembering my kissing session with Bess and wondering if I'd soon be experiencing something along those same lines with Sarah. The thought was petrifying but exciting at the same time. My theory about girls had taken a serious blow. Marsha had practically melted when I'd told her she was pretty. Betty was fond of telling men that flattery would get them everything. Maybe my mother was on to something.

The house was empty when I walked in. That meant Betty had probably dropped the boys off at Lynn's place on her way to work. I found a note on the kitchen table, confirming my suspicion. The thought of having to walk over there and drag them home didn't bother me much, though. I was in a good mood. Before heading out I tossed some bologna and cheese between a couple slices of bread to eat on the way.

Out of habit I tore a piece off for Benji. It wasn't until that moment I even realized my mutt hadn't met me at the door. "Hey!" I called out, listening for him on the stairs. I heard only silence. That silence was one of the most frightening sounds I've ever listened to, then or since. I checked my room and found nothing. I checked outside and found only a chewed-up stick my dog and Chip had been playing with before I'd left for school.

I tried to stay calm as I headed out for Lynn's. Maybe she had my dog. Betty had never taken him there before, but there was always a first time. *She'd have put that in the note she left.* "Maybe Lynn took the boys for a walk, and he tagged along. They're probably playing on the slide outside her apartment," I said aloud just to ease my anxiety. *Maybe.* But I was trotting before making it halfway there, and I was breaking speed records as I turned into their parking lot.

Lynn answered the door, concerned because I'd knocked so urgently. "What's wrong?"

"Is Benji with you?" I asked, out of breath.

"What's all that noise?" one of the trolls growled from behind Lynn.

I ignored that. "Have you seen Benji today?" Lynn shook her head. "Could you walk the boys home? I'm going out looking for him." And I was off as she was nodding.

When he was younger, my dog would run off now and then, but never very far. It had been years since he hadn't been where he was supposed to be. He knew my routine. My going to and from school was something he had not fretted over for a long time. *Don't panic.* Everything from being hit by a car to Tony sneaking around and hurting my dog to get back at me was racing through my mind.

After checking the house again, I circled my block, working my way farther and farther from where we lived. I inquired about him with everyone I came across. I searched every alley and pile of trash. As the daylight began to fade, I checked with Lynn at the house to make sure he hadn't wandered home. My last recourse was searching places where he might have gone looking for me. He wasn't at any of them. No one had seen him. Poof, he was gone.

I found other strays—including a mutt who looked a lot like my own but was smaller and missing patches of hair. *Probably mange.* The wary little pooch didn't let me get too close but acted interested in my constant whistling and calling. Cats burst from bushes and out of abandoned houses I searched. A younger kid named Chester helped me look for a while, but slipped off after an hour or so. I even questioned a wino by the car wash who kept swearing he'd help me find my dog if I'd give him a dollar or some change.

Something's wrong. I ran home and checked the house again. When he still hadn't shown I knew he was hurt, detained, or worse. *Don't even think it.* Without bothering to ask Lynn if she'd mind sticking around, I left her to look after my brothers and ran off to the only place I thought I might find assistance. Even though it was fairly dark by now and my vision was limited, I kept calling for him as I made my way there.

Some dude I didn't recognize answered the door at Chick's place. He was an older guy. There were gray streaks in his ponytail and deep creases in his face, especially around his eyes. Faded blue tattoos covered his bare arms, and a poor replica of the Harley Davidson emblem sagged along with the loose skin on his thin, hairy chest. It might have been at that very moment I made the lifelong and steadfast decision to stay clear of tattoos.

"Is Nicky here?" I asked, out of breath from running. The dude looked high, but he understood my question and shook his head. "How about Chick?"

"Haven't seen Nick, and Chick's off seeing to his mom."

"I can't find my dog," I told this complete stranger, as if he cared one bit or could actually help me in any way.

"Dogs run off sometimes," he told me as if he were imparting great wisdom.

"Not mine," I muttered. I decided to go back home. There was no help for me here. I wasn't sure what I'd expected from Nicky or Chick anyway.

"Maybe the dogcatcher got him. Check the pound." And he closed the door.

"Shit!" I slapped my forehead. I hadn't thought of that. The notion that some lowlife dogcatcher would snatch my mutt really pissed me off, but at the same time it was something of a relief. *That has to be it!* By the time I got home, I'd convinced myself that Benji had gotten himself snagged and was scared and homesick but safely locked away in a cage down at the pound.

Betty was home when I arrived. Benji wasn't. *Talk about things going from bad to worse.* She was eating something she'd brought home from the diner with Leon and my brothers as I burst into the kitchen.

"Lynn tell you Benji was missing?" I asked. Betty nodded, but Leon didn't say anything. "He hasn't shown up?" Terry told me he hadn't. "Okay, I'll be back later."

My mother said something as I left, but I ignored her. I didn't bother to tell her where I was going or ask Leon for a ride. It was best I make this trip alone, and let no one know where I was headed or what I intended to do.

I broke speed limits on my recently repaired bike that night. Fear lent me strength. Hopping curbs and cutting through the glare of headlights, I rushed to the rescue of the only friend I had left, sure I'd find him huddling in some cold metal cage. Wind ripped through the long hair I'd yet to cut, and the nip in the cool September air stung my surging lungs. Horns blared as I ignored red lights and crossed medians. People cursed as I brushed past, just a blur and a whisper in the gloom that briefly startled them before vanishing.

When I was in the general vicinity of the pound, I stopped at a Shell station and asked a mechanic taking a smoke if he knew where the place was. He gave me pretty good directions. "Won't do you no good tonight, kid. They're closed," he called after me as I sped away. I responded with only a lift of my hand and stood on the pedals. *That's what they think.* A few more blocks of headlights and curbs and I was wheeling into the empty parking lot. The sign called the place a shelter, but I knew I'd found the pound.

The closest residence was a good half-block away, and it looked dark and quiet, as did the rest of the houses I could see beyond it. This was a dead-end road, so through traffic wasn't a concern. Behind the pound was a tall chain-link fence with some city trucks parked in a lot. Sporadic lights mounted on telephone poles illuminated the rows of vehicles, but there didn't appear to be anyone moving around. As far as I was concerned, my mission was a resounding *go!*

I hid my bike behind some bushes and approached a rickety and rusting wire fence surrounding the sides and rear of the building. The lights were all off except for a streetlight in the parking lot. Dozens of dogs began raising hell as I jumped off that fence and rattled the gate. I didn't care. One of those yapping mutts was mine, and I meant to bring him home. I paused just long enough to make sure nobody responded to their racket, but when I heard nothing and saw no lights come on, I continued on up to the building.

I found two doors, both locked, but further investigation turned up a small window just above a dormant air conditioner, also locked. After climbing up and peeking inside (just a small bathroom with no lights on), I pulled out the screwdriver I'd brought with me and punched it through the window, shattering the glass enough to safely pick away the broken remains and stick my skinny arm inside to unlock the latch. The yammering of the dogs had hopefully drowned out the sound of breaking glass, but I waited a moment or two just to make sure no alarm was going to blare and no one was near enough to have heard anything. With my heart pounding, I lifted the window and dropped into the bathroom, taking care not to slice myself.

My sneaker slipped on the closed toilet seat, and I had to catch myself on the sink. All I heard once I was inside was the thud of my heartbeat and the scrunching of the shards of glass under my feet. The hallway outside the bathroom led in only two directions. To my left was a lobby with a pair of glass doors, secured with one of those bolts you had to unlock with a key from either side. That meant I would probably have to go out the window unless I found an easier exit elsewhere. To my right there was a gated enclosure. In the distance I could hear the uproar of a bunch of excited mutts.

I kept telling myself I was just a minor. *Cops can't do shit to a minor,* we always told each other, repeating what Candy and the older guys who were always trying to talk us into running for them promised. Besides, they'd stolen my dog. What was mine was mine. They had no right to steal from me. *Like they couldn't tell he was well-fed and had a home.* But I was still scared half to death once I was inside that unfamiliar building, no matter how hard I tried to justify being there.

The gate leading to where the dogs were penned had a padlock on it, and for a moment I thought my mission was thwarted. But there was a gap beneath the fence I could just shimmy under if I pushed up on the gate and used my feet to force my head and body through. I stood up on the other side of that gate, scraped and dirty, and feeling more trapped than ever. As far as I could see there wasn't another way out except back under the gate. *Too far to turn back now.*

There were four rows of cages in front of me, but it was too dim in the room to clearly see how many of the pens were occupied. The only light came from a weak bulb in the hallway on the other side of the gate. The first row I searched was empty. The second had only a few dogs, but all of them were too big to be mine. The next two rows were full of pitiful dogs that whined or growled, some scrabbling at their prisons while others slunk as far away from me as they could get. None of them was Benji.

By now my eyes were completely adjusted to the darkness inside the building, but I had to search the pens again. I could hear my mutt calling me. He had to be here! I'd been so sure I was going to find him here. I found a light switch and flicked it on. Hanging lights in the ceiling began buzzing like disturbed beehives, groaning as if they were protesting being summoned to life in the middle of the night. One bulb after another flickered and brightened as I ran up and down the aisles again. The imprisoned mutts went crazy as I searched. They were raising such a racket; I knew it was only going to be a matter of time before I was busted.

Desperate, I found another pair of doors along the wall. Beyond them was another room with some caged cats, but no dogs. I searched every pen twice anyway, just to be sure. Another locked door led to some kind of room where they tended to injured animals. I could see a table and some cabinets of medical supplies through the wire meshed window of the locked door, but there were no animals in the room, so I hurried on.

Another door led to a room where I was fairly sure no animal went to be cared for. I didn't stay there long. I found a large oven-like incinerator and an enclosure hooked up to tanks of some kind of gas. *They wouldn't gas a dog so quickly.* There was a box of collars next to the oven, and I searched it despite the chill running the length of my spine. Benji's collar wasn't there, and I quickly left that sinister chamber.

Somebody was waiting for me as I came out, and I flinched as they came toward me. *It's only your shadow, stupid ass,* I chided myself. I checked the dog pens one last time. Every instinct I possessed was screaming *enough!* I knew I should be getting out of here, but I had to be sure. *He isn't here,* I told myself. And suddenly I was struck by the image of Benji waiting for me at home. The vision of him was so strong and clear, I was squirming back under the gate and carefully negotiating the broken window, knowing I was going to find my mutt waiting for me back at my place.

Outside, the lot where the trucks were parked was brighter. I could see that a smallish square building beyond the vehicles was lit up, and I heard at least two men talking, so I didn't waste any time hopping the fence and climbing on my bike. Intuition told me to cut across a few yards and take a different side road back to the streets leading home. It was a good thing I did. It wasn't very long before the first cop car roared down the lane I'd just vacated, siren silent but lights flashing as they raced toward the pound.

Back home, my hopes were dashed. My dog wasn't there.

I sat on the top of the steps in the darkness with my chest constricting and tears rolling down my cheeks, the salty taste of my grief mingling with sweat and dripping from my lips. I could hear my brothers' constant, heavy breathing from their room. At my back was silence, even though the door to my mother's room was cracked and Leon's El Camino was parked in the yard. I knew Betty and Leon were awake. Both of them snored loud.

"Did you find him, honey?" my mother called out.

"No." I couldn't risk saying any more than that. I didn't want them to know I was crying.

"Maybe he'll show up tomorrow."

It didn't feel like I was going to see my buddy tomorrow. In fact, I was oddly sure I was never going to see Benji again. *Stop it.*

"He's a smart little guy. He'll be all right."

"Hey, Leon?" I called.

After some hesitation Leon answered, "Yeah?"

"You think maybe Tony did something to him?" Leon didn't answer. Something wasn't right. He'd acted funny earlier as well. *And Betty called you honey.* "I mean, he might have hurt him or hauled him off to get back at me for fucking with him."

I heard Betty whispering. "Maybe," Leon admitted eventually.

"You think maybe we could check up on that bastard? If he's hurt my dog I swear I'll kill him."

There was more whispering. "Sure, Donny," Leon finally agreed, but hesitantly.

"Try to get some sleep, honey," my mother urged. "Things will be better in the morning. I've got some great news for you."

What is it with all these honeys? "What news?"

"In the morning."

I went on in my room and fell onto my mattress, but I knew I wouldn't be sleeping anytime soon. The room felt colder without my mutt lying nearby. My hand kept slipping down to where he normally snuggled up against me. I tossed and turned, staring up at the ceiling and wracking my brain to come up with a plan to find my buddy. I was still twisting around and worrying when the harsh snores of Betty and Leon dozing off drowned out the breathing of my brothers.

Unable to rest, I got up and went downstairs. I stepped outside and whistled softly. Nothing answered but rare solitude and darkness. After taking a seat on the steps, I picked up the stick Benji had recently been gnawing on while playing with Chip. My fingers ran along the gaps where my dog had chewed away the bark. I carried the tattered little branch inside with me when I finally decided to quit sitting and hoping in the cool of the night.

I'd fallen asleep watching the tube. (Needing the glare and drone of a television to fall off to sleep would become a habit that would stay with me for the rest of my life.) At the moment I was stuck in a place I called limbo. If I wanted to I could concentrate real hard and snap myself awake. I could hear the TV buzzing and feel the stick in the hand lying across my chest, but those sensations were dull and far away.

Waiting for me was a dream, almost there and yet not there at all. The choice was mine. If I chose to dive into my dream, it might be one of those visions I could control and enjoy, but there was also the risk of getting ensnared by a nightmare I couldn't negotiate and wasn't prepared to handle. *Just wake up.* Instead, I let myself slip into the waiting dream.

I might have slept a while before it began, but I wasn't sure. I was walking barefoot through a fresh snowfall, searching the alley near our house for my dog. This dream was starting out weird, because the snow wasn't cold or wet, and when I looked behind me I was leaving no sign of passage. Not a single track marred the snow. One of the great things about snow was how it could make even a neighborhood like mine look pretty for a little while. All the ugliness was covered by a perfect blanket of white powder until the shovels scraped the sidewalks, and the cars and trucks churned the snow into filthy gray slop.

Suddenly there were tracks in front of me. I realized quickly they were dog tracks. *Benji's tracks.* I stooped to study them and found they faded away if I tried to touch them. In fact, the trail stretching out before me was sifting down into the snow as I stood watching the signs leading to my little buddy slowly drift away. *This is only a dream,* I told myself. But I went running and stumbling through the snow anyway, chasing the fading tracks.

No matter how fast I ran, they melted away before I could catch them. I stumbled and fell. Snow filled my mouth and soaked my shirt. And now it was wet and cold. Shivering, I sat up and decided to go home. *This is stupid.* But when I looked behind me there was not only no trace of disturbed snow, but no alley or buildings, no neighborhood. There was nothing. All I could see was unbroken snow stretching out forever, a cold, barren wasteland that had dropped all trace of its earlier suggested beauty.

I spun around and found my neighborhood in front of me, still cloaked in fresh powder, but I was blocks from home, and afraid to move, even though my bare feet were stinging from the cold. *Maybe you can make turns and circle around until you can get back home?* I thought that was a pretty good idea if I didn't freeze to death first. But before I could test my new strategy Rupe said, "That won't work."

I wasn't surprised to find him standing beside me, but it pissed me off that he was wearing a coat, gloves, boots, and even a scarf, while I was walking around barefoot like an idiot. *What kind of shit is that?* Rupe was gazing at me all smug, like he always did when he knew something I didn't. Apparently, I was caught up in one of those dreams I couldn't control, because I couldn't whip up some shoes or a coat for myself no matter how hard I tried.

What are you doing here?"

Rupe shook his head at me like I was a moron. "I'm not really here. You're dreaming."

"No shit?" I was wondering if I could punch him right in his pink face. "I know I'm dreaming."

I turned to my left and found the same expanse of snow I'd seen behind me. Frustrated, I wrapped my arms around my chest in a vain attempt to warm myself and cursed bitterly. My expletive sent a cloud of vapor skyward.

"I told you that wouldn't work," said Rupe.

"How the fuck would you know what works and don't work in my dream?" I asked my friend. *He's not really there.*

"Because I'm smarter than you."

He sure sounded like the real Rupe. "So you keep telling me."

"Well, I'm not freezing and lost."

"This is just a dream."

"You're still freezing and lost."

"So?"

"How are you going to get home?"

"I'll be home when I wake up."

"What if you freeze to death first?"

"You can't freeze to death in a dream."

"Then why are you so cold?"

My teeth were chattering, and I was shivering. A thought occurred to me. "How about if I just take your coat and boots away from you?"

Rupe looked at me sadly, clicking his teeth and shaking his head. "That won't work either."

Somehow, I knew he was telling the truth. "You sure seem to know a lot about my dream." My feet felt like ice cubes. This was so weird. I couldn't remember the sensation of cold or heat in any of my previous dreams.

"I know how you can get home," Rupe told me, but at least he didn't sound as smug as before.

"Oh, really? And how would you know that?"

I began jumping up and down to get warm, peeking over my shoulder to make sure the frosted wasteland still spread out behind me. It did. Tiny fragments of ice glittered like stars in the flowing waves of snow, refracting light. Whether this light was caused by sun or moon,

I didn't know. When I looked up everything was gray and formless. There were no clouds or any other distinctive features.

I knew what Rupe was going to say before he gave voice to his reply: "Because I'm smarter than you."

I had no choice but to accept my friend's infinite wisdom. I was way too cold to argue. "Okay, genius. Tell me how I get back home."

Rupe grinned at me. "Just walk backward without looking behind you." He demonstrated a few steps for me just in case I was too dense to understand his simple instructions, shuffling backwards while keeping his eyes trained on my shivering skinny form. "Like this. See?"

"Yeah, Rupe, I get it."

I followed his example, stumbling a bit due to my numb feet. I took a good ten steps past my friend before really looking around, but I wasn't surprised to find his odd maneuver worked. The buildings were there at the periphery of my vision. It was a slow process, and awkward, but at least I would be able to get back home. *So what?* I hadn't meant to say that, and didn't want to explore why I had. This dream had remained vague and harmless so far. I was hoping to get home before anything hairy went down.

Progress was slow and arduous, but I'd managed a couple of blocks before long. Whenever I thought to look for Rupe, he was there, gliding beside me with an arrogant smile across his cherry-cheeked face. Neither of us was leaving tracks in the snow. The only sounds were my labored breaths and the plops of my shuffling steps breaking the drifts behind me. I was still freezing, but I felt hopeful when I recognized some of the houses on my block.

And then I saw Benji's tracks again. I stopped. They stretched out away from me much like they had at the beginning of my dream, only this time they weren't melting into the snow. "Remember what happened last time," Rupe said from behind me. I wasn't cold anymore either. I looked behind me and there was Rupe, standing in my backyard and gesturing toward my place. "Go home, Donny," he told me.

"I need to find my dog."

"Those aren't his tracks."

"You don't know that." I turned away from my friend and gazed upon the beckoning paw prints once more.

"I knew how to get you home."

"So what."

"Those aren't Benji's paw prints," Rupe said again.

I decided Rupe was right, but before I could step out of the alley I heard my mutt yapping off in the distance. He sounded close. And the paw prints became more vivid, clearer somehow, almost as if they had my dog's name written on every track. Instead of leaving, I knelt down and reached out. This time the track I tried to touch let me feel it. The indentation was warm and comforting. The paw print even felt like my dog.

"I can't leave him out in the snow," I told Rupe.

"That's not Benji barking," insisted Rupe.

"It is."

"It isn't." The barking was louder now. "Go home, Donny." Benji was whining, as if maybe he was hurt. "That's not your dog."

"You don't know that!" I snapped. Hot tears turned to ice on my face. They fell away from me and struck the snow at my feet like fragments of hail. "He could be hurt out there somewhere! He needs me!"

"That's not your dog. You know that's not your dog."

"Just shut up!" I would've hit Rupe then, but I couldn't turn around. If I did he'd see my tears. "I have to find him." I took a step forward, and the tracks began to melt away. I stepped back, and they materialized again. I braced myself like a sprinter in the starting blocks, preparing to dash after the fading prints as fast as I could manage.

"Donny, don't."

I was cold again. *You're dreaming.* Rupe was acting as the voice of reason in my dream. I knew I should listen to him. But before I could make that sage decision, the snow at the end of my alley began to skirl and whip around. Standing in the middle of the compact maelstrom was a shadow, no more than a blurred figure in the violently swirling snow. But it sure looked like my mutt. And when the shadow stumbled and fell and I heard Benji whine again, I bolted down the alley.

"That's not your dog," Rupe sent after me as I raced away, his tone promising woe.

I ran and ran, freezing again, my bare, benumbed feet slipping in the snow and ice. No matter how fast I ran, I couldn't reach the storm my mutt was trapped in. Before long I gave up and collapsed into the snow, burying my face in a drift and growling with rage and frustration. Somewhere ahead of me, my dog began to whine and cry again.

Stop it!

"That's not your dog," Rupe said from nearby.

Wake up!

"I told you not to go."

I just lay there, chewing snow and crying. I was through with this dream, even if it wasn't through with me.

CHAPTER 25

I was sick for the next two days. My mother's big news caught me completely by surprise. People from the church swooped in on us the next morning. While I lay on my mattress huddled beneath three blankets, suffering cold sweats and intense fevers, they boxed up our stuff and prepared us for a move to Pickerington, a town just outside of Columbus. Terry's attack and Betty's mewling had convinced some gullible and generous church member to reduce the rent on a decent duplex in their quaint little town.

My mother had managed to turn my brother's assault into a veritable gold mine. Kindhearted people were donating money and time, bringing us food, assisting Betty in finding another job, and even physically moving us to the new place. These hours passed in a haze of shivering and sickness. My mouth broke out with cold sores, and my skin actually hurt when I forced my body to move. (Many years later I would learn these attacks of fevers and sores were attributed to a disease known as Crohn's.)

Debilitated as I was, I still didn't let anybody handle my most prized possessions. I managed to box up my baseball card collection and comics on my own, as well as my artwork and supplies. The church people pitched a lot of Betty's junk, including most of our clothing. They threw out more shit than we took with us. Betty tried to protest, but there was little she could do and less she could say. Our sorry little family was now in the hands of God. In this case, God was working through a half-dozen hard-core church ladies who weren't about to let us transport the cat-pissed-on clothing they were scraping off the nasty floor.

What clothes they decided we could keep, they took down to the 'mat and washed before packing up. They also washed the dishes and sorted through my brothers' assortment of hand-me-down broken toys. Our last morning there, some men from the church hauled all our furniture and soiled mattresses out to the alley. How Betty continued to look those people in the eye I'll never know. I couldn't. The shame of what we were made me mean and sullen deep inside.

Those two days were a blur. I kept my stuff stacked in a corner of my room, just in case one of the harpies decided God felt there was no place for comics or baseball cards in our new place. I also had a pillowcase stuffed with my favorite pair of jeans, a couple of T-shirts and my only remaining pair of new Keds from our last rip-off job. Benji's stick was in there too. Church ladies were unpredictable; you never really knew from day to day what they were going to label as evil. I kept a wary eye on my belongings.

My brothers were having a grand time. They were so excited to be moving. Betty promised them some new clothes and a big yard to play in, complete with their own swing set. There was even mention of a new toy or two, which had my brothers giddy and eager to be off to magical and wonderful Pickerington. My mother tried to butter me up as well, telling me how great the new school was going to be and all, but I was having none of her bullshit. I kept my distance and didn't say much to anyone, using my illness as an excuse to keep to myself.

They were wasting their time and efforts. No new job was going to fix Betty. No change of surroundings was going to make anything better for very long. My mother had been down this road before. She'd been handed jobs and monetary assistance by her father, other relatives, other churches. She would use up what resources they donated and then amass debts she could never repay. She would lie and steal. She would sleep with landlords or bartenders or some guy she met at the gas station and drag home extra problems.

Running from place to place was a way of life for me. I'd once attended six different schools in the same year. But I was beginning to hate the constant change of people and surroundings as I got older.

I wouldn't admit that I needed friends, long-term. I told myself I just wanted a comfort zone; I wanted to know what to expect every day. *I guess you won't be kissing on Sarah.*

Benji never showed. I felt guilty for not feeling up to looking for him, but I did take a tour of the neighborhood our last afternoon there, scouring every nook and cranny for any sign of my lost pal. As the last of our stuff was being loaded up, I crossed my street and knocked on Mrs. Lorret's door. I asked if I could call her every few days and check to see if Benji might have shown up, and also asked her to keep him for me if she found him anywhere. She promised to do so and gave me her phone number, but I thought she was acting a mite strange.

"You take care, baby," she told me as I turned away. "You're a special boy. You get away from that mother of yours as soon as you're able. And you watch out for your brothers." I promised on both counts. "Where are they moving you?"

"Pickerington."

The old bird nodded. "It's nice out there." She had to close the door to the porch because her excited little dog was trying to get to me, all caught up in a humping frenzy. We waved at each other one last time through the blurry glass before I left.

Betty was waiting for me next to Leon's El Camino, holding an agitated Fluffy. The cat was wriggling around and growling, round eyes bulging, wanting no part of the car ride to our new home. The last of our stuff was strapped in the bed of the car, including my own things. It was going to be a tight fit on this ride. I'd have to sit in the middle of the single seat with Terry on my lap, while Betty would hold Chip and the freaked-out feline.

I was still coming out of the funk of my recent illness, but I finally noticed the absence of another of our family members. "Hey, where's Tiki?"

Leon looked at my mother along with me, acting as if he hadn't a clue what I was talking about. To her credit, my mother didn't blanch. "She went missing the same time Benji did," Betty informed me.

I thought that odd. Tiki rarely ventured but a few feet into the yard. "Why didn't you tell me?"

My mother shrugged. "I thought I did." She motioned for me to get in the car. "You were so upset over Benji I guess I just figured you'd noticed Tiki being gone too."

"No, I didn't."

What she said didn't made sense. Nothing about my dog's disappearance was making sense. *She knows something. So does Leon.* I promised myself I'd get to the bottom of this mystery as soon as we were settled in and I was feeling better. At the moment I was dreading the long ride and close quarters. The thought of being stuck between Leon and Betty for an extended period of time was a frightening notion. I was already sick. In my weakened condition I was hoping to survive the trip.

The car swayed a bit as both she and Leon settled in. I was hoping the old rust bucket wouldn't break down. I didn't even glance back at our house as we drove away, but I kept searching for my dog as we cruised out of the neighborhood. The loss sat heavily upon me as we made our way onto the highway and headed away from the city.

Fortunately for me, I dozed off and slept through most of the trip. The drive wasn't all that far. We arrived in less than an hour. Our new home was a two-bedroom second story of a nicely kept older Colonial house, with a wraparound porch. *Whoever lives under us is in for it.* My brothers were going to make a lot of noise, especially running up and down the stairs and around that porch. As soon as Betty opened the door, they both went thumping up the steps, and Chip began wailing when Terry shoved him down so he'd be the first to make it to the top and see inside. *Might as well get used to that,* I sent to our unfortunate neighbors.

I had to admit, it was one of the nicest places I'd ever seen. The carpet was new, and the walls were freshly painted. The baseboards and switch plates were stained wood, not painted the same color as the walls. All the lights had fixtures instead of bare bulbs, and they all worked. The kitchen appliances were new and shiny, and the linoleum floor didn't have a single tear or cut in it. The bathroom tub and sink had no rust around the drains. The toilet flushed when you pushed the handle, and hot water came out of the faucets when you twisted the knobs marked with an H.

The bedrooms had beds with dressers. Someone had donated a toy box and a small bookshelf for the boys. The kitchen had a nice wooden table with four chairs. There was a couch, two end tables, and an older color TV in the living room, hooked up to a large outdoor antenna. *What? No aluminum foil bunny ears?* I looked upon our new furnishings with misgivings. Betty would take all of this with her when we had to run. That, or sell it before bolting. Christian mercy was one thing, but this was ridiculous. *These people must be crazy,* I told myself sadly.

Even though this place was quite a bit smaller than the dump we'd just left behind, it felt like a mansion. The boys tramped back down the steps and went out to explore the yard and swing set while I helped to sort and unpack boxes. Betty was getting one bedroom and the boys the other. That left me with the couch, but my mother granted me the hall closet to store my personal stuff and clothing. It was a bit stuffy as we labored, so Leon opened a couple of windows in the living room to let in the cooler air. I wasn't surprised to find all the windows had serviceable screens and freshly painted panes.

Betty locked Fluffy and her cat box in the bathroom after tearing up some fresh newspaper our glassware had been wrapped in. The curious cat kept yowling and scratching at the door, wanting out. I figured the damage the cat was doing to the door frame was just the beginning. Betty was stacking box after box of ceramics along the rear wall of her bedroom, and I was wondering how many cockroaches had made the move out of the city along with us. *Fluffy probably won't be the only one exploring her new residence tonight.*

Leon lit up in the kitchen, and it wasn't long before the rancid smell of cigarette smoke consumed the lingering aroma of fresh paint. By the time I'd brought in two boxes from the living room to the kitchen, he'd left his first clump of ash on the bright unblemished linoleum. Leon was one of those guys who kept his cigarette hanging out of his mouth and let his ashes fall where they may, like the whole world was an oily garage floor or the inside of a filthy over-the-road tractor cab.

"You're going to burn the new floor," I told him, waving at the air and pointing at his dropped ashes.

"Don't get stupid, Donny."

"Right, you actually pay money for those foul smelling things, which are killing you, by the way, and *I'm* the one who's stupid?"

"Keep running your mouth and maybe *I'll kill you,*" Leon warned, blowing smoke directly at me.

He was joking. I stuck my tongue out at him and pointed to where a second pile of his cancer stick's ash had drifted down while he'd threatened me, but he only grinned and kept handing Betty dishes so she could stock them in the cabinets. There was another door in the kitchen with some steep steps descending to the back yard. *One or both of the boys are going to go tumbling down those stairs.* I made a mental note to keep this door locked and forbid the boys to use these steps whenever they were my responsibility.

There was a window in the door, and I could see my brothers taking turns climbing the ladder and swooping down the rickety metal slide. The baby draped across one of the swings and pushed off with his stubby legs, clinging to the chains and rocking back and forth on his belly. A deep sadness overwhelmed me as I watched them play. This was all nothing but false hope, and our stay here would end up especially cruel for my brothers.

"Why are you doing this?" I asked, still watching the boys with my back to Leon and my mother.

"What did you say, honey?"

"Quit calling me honey." I turned around. Betty's face was already flushed with anger. She knew what was coming. "I asked why you're doing this. How long do you think this will last? Who's paying all the rent and utilities you owe? Who's paying off all those credit people who keep coming after us?"

"You just let me worry about that." Leon wandered on into the living room and didn't come back with a box. "We have a lot to do."

I wasn't going to let her off that easy. I felt mean. "Tell me who's paying our way."

"Some people from the church donated money to pay off the old utilities and turn them on here. They also paid our first and last month's rent so we could have this nice place."

"What about the creditors?"

"Never mind that."

"Tell me."

"The pastor called them and promised to handle my money and pay them off a little at a time," she said in a rush. "There. Are you happy now?"

"Does he know about all the bad checks?"

"Yes."

"Even the ones you've been writing with the fake names?"

That had her sucking on her dentures. Her false aura of motherly concern and the brief bliss of starting over in a new place fell away, replaced by eyes filled with hatred, and a face hard and cold. This was the Betty I knew and was comfortable with. It made me uneasy when she tried to pretend things were good or normal between us. I liked the friction. It kept our relationship as open and honest as it could possibly be.

"How do you know about that?" she asked carefully, clipping her words.

"I do is all."

She took a step closer to me and leveled a talon. "You just keep your fucking mouth shut. If you fuck this up for me I'll claw your eyes out." She meant it. "Why don't you go check on your brothers?"

"Why don't you?"

She slapped me. The sting of her hand had this place feeling more like home already.

"That pastor doesn't know about all of it, does he?"

She gave me another smack.

"You're going to take him and his church for as much as you can before running out, aren't you?"

This time she hit me across the ear, setting my head to ringing.

"How can you keep conning these people after they do so much for you?"

She made a fist before swinging, so I had to duck. The momentum of her missed blow made her stagger.

"Get away from me!" she screamed. She was still clenching her right hand, so I decided to take her advice. "Why don't you keep going? Go live with your goddamn father! I don't care where you go! Just stay the fuck away from me!"

I sat out on the steps, enjoying the crisp air and watching the boys play for a while, listening to her rant, wondering what the people downstairs thought of their new neighbors.

Despite this rocky start, for the first time in my life, home became a refuge for me. As bad as Betty was, she wasn't nearly as cruel as a group of teenage rich kids. The new school was a living hell, every day worse than the one before. At Central, there were those who had and those who didn't have as much. Belonging to the group who didn't have as much wasn't all that bad, since we outnumbered the other crowd. Being poor at Central didn't make you anything special. Holes in your jeans and dingy socks didn't make you stand out.

The new school was different. There were those who had, and there were those who had *a lot*. Everything about me stood out. Their hair was all styled or freshly cut while my mop fell haphazardly wherever it would. Their clothes were new and trendy while I wore the same bargain basement shit I'd walked around in at Central.

The school was massive and had long hallways leading to different wings, which were newly constructed. It was more like a college campus than the blunt rectangle of old brick I was used to attending. I attracted eyes in those hallways, and giggles. I was getting taller and my jeans weren't. Hardly anything I wore matched or was in style, and nothing I wore was expensive or new. Looking back on those days, I often get angry. I was ridiculed for being dirty and wearing shabby clothing. I like to think I was just grunge before grunge was cool.

Questions sucked. "When's the last time you had a haircut?" "How'd you get that broken tooth?" "Who gave you those jeans?" "Do you take baths?"

Kids wanted to know where I lived. They were curious how a poor dude like me could manage to infiltrate their uppity society. I wasn't about to tell them my family was being supported by a local congregation. But it didn't take long until someone or another who attended my mother's church spilled the beans and everybody knew my story.

Bad as the students were, the teachers were worse. I detested sympathy. If I detected a hint of pity in the way someone treated me, I was done with them. I suppose most of the teachers were simply struggling to find ways to get the others to accept me, but I'd have preferred they just let me alone. I stood out in art and gym class (I blew away the entire school the first time we had to run a timed mile), but kept quiet in the rest of my classes. The kids in this school were a lot further along in their studies than we'd been at Central, especially when it came to math and English. I'd never even taken a geometry or algebra class. Some of my classmates were already into calculus and trigonometry.

Some of the grief coming my way I made worse by being so stubborn. Everyone was supposed to wear red shorts and a white T-shirt in gym class, and shower afterwards. I didn't have any red shorts, and I didn't have the five bucks to buy them. Betty sure wasn't forking over any cash for gym clothes. I tried to cut off some old red sweat pants to wear, but the gym teacher, who was also the school's baseball coach, wasn't having any of that.

I also wouldn't shower with the other guys. Many of them were a lot more physically developed than I was, and a lot of them played grab ass in the showers, flicking each other with towels and pretending to be homos. There was no way I was giving them a chance to poke fun at me by walking around naked in front of them. At this school, practically every guy was a Collins. I usually just pulled my jeans right up over my shorts and tried to slip out of the locker room without the coach noticing.

"Nice shorts," one of those physically developed brutes named Connor quipped one day as we filed out of the gymnasium and into the locker room.

I hadn't yet completed my first week in this school, and I already hated Connor. He was tall and muscular, with curly sandy-colored hair, blue eyes, and a wide, perfect smile. Leon said women fell right onto their backs for guys who looked like Connor. So far, I hadn't noticed any of the girls around here proving that proclamation wrong. I'd managed to knock Connor out of both games of dodgeball today, so he wasn't particularly fond of me at the moment. He and his pack of cronies strode the halls like they owned the school. They weren't supposed to lose at anything.

"They grow 'em kind of scrawny in the city, don't they?" one of his pals said, purposely bumping me as he passed. He was a chubby red-headed kid with orange freckles dotting every inch of his otherwise pale flesh. His name was Fletcher.

"They grow them dirty too," Connor added. His buddies all laughed on cue, just as if Connor had held up a sign that said "applause." "You going to put your dirty clothes on over your dirty shorts and run out without taking a shower again?"

I had one of my socks in my hand, just sitting with my back to them and silently taking their shit. I wasn't sure if this was the time or place to make a stand. To make matters worse, I'd ripped one of my socks when I'd pulled it on before class. I needed new socks and underwear worse than I needed a pair of red shorts. The damn sock had practically ripped near in half right along the top of the ankle, from dry rot.

"Look at that holey sock," one of the boys said with a chuckle.

"It's almost as yellow as that tooth of his," another added.

Connor stood in front of me, smiling and shaking his head while everyone laughed. Some of the guys at the lockers near us began pulling their shirts over their heads and slipping off their shorts. Fletcher reached out and pulled on some kid's athletic supporter and snapped him above the ass with the elastic strap. The crowd erupted with hoots of hilarity again. Except they weren't laughing at the guy who was holding his ass cheek and wincing. They were still laughing at me.

Athletic supporters were also mandatory apparel in gym class at this backward-ass hick school, but I hadn't even begun to think about acquiring one of those ridiculous-looking articles of clothing. *And I'm not going to, either.* I was hoping Connor and his boys were about through. They'd picked at me like this yesterday but dropped it after I'd ignored them. Fletcher gave me an almost rough shove and asked me if I was going to cry. It looked like they were going to push the issue today.

"Are you afraid of water?" Connor asked. I decided I was going to hit Fletcher right on his freckled nose if he pushed on me again. "I asked you a question, shithead."

"Nah, fuck face, it's not the water I'm afraid of," I informed him. I was pleased at the way they all fell silent and stared at me in disbelief as I stood up and turned around. I was pretty sure nobody messed with Connor and his bunch. "I just don't want no part of the way you faggots dance around, lathering each other up and giggling while you wash each other's backs. Just because Fletcher don't mind if you soap up his fat freckled ass and lick his butt hole don't mean I want to join your fucked-up little Mickey Mouse club."

All of that had flown out of my mouth without thought. My indifference stunned the group of country boys standing around me. They'd probably expected me to cower and be afraid of Connor because he was bigger than me and popular. But I didn't respect bigger and hated popular. All these guys could do was beat my ass, and that possibility didn't faze me at all. I'd been beat down by way worse than these good old boys. At least now *I* was smiling at *their* consternation, instead of the other way around, even if only for the moment.

"What'd he say?" Fletcher asked.

"*You're* a faggot," Connor managed, but stammering.

"Good comeback," I snorted.

"Yeah, *you're* a faggot," Fletcher quickly repeated.

"Great, an overweight freckled gay parrot," I declared, grimacing at Fletcher. A few of the guys laughed at his distress. Fletcher looked like he wanted to hit me. I didn't care if he did. I held up my hand and said, "Hold on a minute, Fletch. I'll pull down my pants and turn around so you can play with my ass and make all the guys think you're cool." *That* really broke up the crowd of suddenly very interested onlookers.

The big freckled idiot lunged at me, but I'd been expecting his clumsy advance and stepped clear. His momentum carried him into the bench in front of the lockers. The bench was made of steel and wood and mounted securely to the floor, so it didn't give an inch when Fletcher stumbled into it and fell over like a dead tree. We all felt him crash against the locker room floor in the soles of our bare feet. *They might have felt that impact in China.* Everyone was roaring except Connor, who was all red in the face and glaring at me.

Fletcher was struggling to get to his feet, enraged and talking in tongues. Connor was moving closer and spouting something at me I couldn't make out over the uproar of laughter. I figured I was about to get jumped, so when Connor put a hand on me I decided to get my licks in and hit the asshole as hard as I could, aiming for his smug lips. My blow missed the mark and glanced off his chin, and before I could get off another shot Fletcher swallowed me up and drove me into the floor.

Our encounter had an anticlimactic ending. Fletcher was struggling to get me in a headlock while I strained to breathe, pinned as I was beneath his blubbery bulk. Connor had a hold on one of my arms, pulling at me while the crowd egged us on. Then Mr. Howard roared, "Cut it out!" Everyone shut up, Connor let me go, and Fletcher was hoisted off his feet by our brawny gym teacher as if he was a wee piglet instead of being well on his way to a full-grown hog.

"What's going on here?" Mr. Howard asked me as I stood up.

I shrugged and examined my torn T-shirt. "Why don't you ask Connor or his fucking trained spotted pig?"

"Watch your mouth." Mr. Howard glanced around, stifling the chuckles and smirks my pig joke had garnered. "What about it, Mr. Kennedy?" he then asked Connor.

"He started it," Connor muttered, pointing at me. I thought it strange how shook up everyone was acting. As fights went, this one hadn't even really gotten going. As far as I could see, none of us was even scratched. Not a drop of blood had been spilled. "You hear how he talks."

"Yeah, he started it, coach," Fletcher added, as if his word would be enough to convince the gym teacher of their innocence.

I grinned and shook my head at them. "Yeah, that's me. I always go around trying to get my head busted by starting fights with multiple guys who are bigger than me." I paused and looked directly at Connor before saying, "Multiple means more than one, for you fucking retards."

Mr. Howard stepped close and looked me sternly in the eye. "Not another word." He had to look around again to put an end to the laughing. "All of you, get cleaned up and get to your next class," he instructed, dispersing the crowd. "And you three are done with this." He glared at each of us in turn. "And I mean *done* with this." He waited for each of us to nod our compliance. "Connor, you and Fletcher get moving." He tapped me lightly on my bony chest with his forefinger. "And *you* step into my office before leaving."

"I've got an extra pair of socks you can have," a kid sitting near me offered quietly as I dressed. His name was Greg. He was about my size, only he was shy and could hardly run three or four steps without his knees banging together. Connor and his boys picked on Greg constantly. "That is, if you want them."

I'd already tossed my ripped-up socks and put my sneakers on. It wouldn't be the first time I'd worn shoes without socks. "That's okay. I'm fine."

"My name's Greg." He glanced at me and flashed a toothy smile. Greg had the biggest forehead and the biggest teeth I'd ever seen. Both his head and his smile looked like they belonged on a guy twice the poor kid's size. "That was great the way you gave it back to Connor."

"Yeah? Fuck Connor."

Greg beamed, but then his face became concerned. "But you can't cuss like that around here. The coach might let you slide a little, but most of the teachers will give you detentions if they hear you use foul language."

I pulled on my shirt and faked a shudder. "I'm scared to death. What will I ever do if they give me a detention?" Greg laughed. He had a corny laugh, more like a cough, and little bits of spit flew off his teeth as he chuckled. *Okay, no more jokes for you.* "Anyway, thanks for the warning."

"Say, where do you live?" Greg asked.

Warning, Will Robinson. Warning, Will Robinson. "In town." The last thing I needed was the school bumpkin as my henchman. "I'll see you around. I got to go see the coach."

Greg looked bummed. "Yeah, maybe I'll see you tomorrow." Tomorrow was Saturday, but I didn't feel like reminding Greg of that. *Unless he means to find you over the weekend.* I said nothing more, inviting no further conversation and leaving to go give Mr. Howard his pound of flesh.

I knocked on the door. The coach's office was no more than a glass cage connected to the metal meshing where they locked up all the sports equipment. Mr. Howard was sitting at his desk writing in some kind of ledger. "Enter!" he barked, not bothering to look up as I came in and stood in front of his desk. He kept on writing for a while, letting me stand there, thinking he was making me sweat. *As if.* If he thought these tactics would scare me, the dude had a lot to learn about kids from the inner city.

Trophies lined two bookshelves behind the coach, probably awards from his baseball teams. He had more pictures than awards. There were pictures of teams and pictures of him standing with players and parents.

There were even pictures of him holding babies and smaller children. I was disinterested until I spotted a signed picture of him posing with Pete Rose. Across the bottom of the picture was written *Thanks to Coach Howard. Never let up.* And it was signed *Charlie Hustle.*

"Don't let that picture fool you," the coach said suddenly. "It's the only picture in here I really don't care for all that much. I had to pay him to sign the damn thing after attending a manager's clinic at Riverfront. But you got to admire the way the sonuvabitch plays." He waited for me to say something, but I wasn't about to be baited. "You prefer to be called Donny?"

"That's fine."

It was then I noticed the board with our mile times written on it. My name was at the top with a time of five minutes and thirty-four seconds. The next best time had been Connor's, but he'd barely broken six minutes. What intrigued me was the five minutes and seventeen seconds the coach had written beneath my time and circled. Something told me I hadn't been asked to see the coach simply because I wasn't doing so swell at making new friends.

He caught me looking at the times and grinned. "Well? Think you can beat the record next Monday?"

I assumed the five seventeen was the record. "I don't know."

And I didn't. I wasn't sure how much faster I'd have to run to take another seventeen seconds off my time. Hell, I wasn't sure I wanted to waste the effort to break the stupid record. *Sure you do.* Okay, so I was going to try and break the record, but not to please Mr. Howard. *Then why?* I didn't know the answer to my own question.

The coach studied me for a while. I tried not to break eye contact but couldn't help glancing away. Mr. Howard was a heavyset guy with thick jowls and a meaty head. His face kind of hung down around his mouth, so that when he talked only his lower teeth showed, giving him the impression of a bulldog. His eyes were intense, and his bushy eyebrows sprung in every direction like ruffled fur.

"I've noticed you not only run fast, but have good strength and agility as well," he told me, leaning back in his chair. "You're killing my guys in dodgeball. Have you played any other sports?"

"Baseball and football mostly. And a little basketball."

"Are you any good?"

"Better than anybody you have at this stupid school," I told him before taking the time to measure my response. "I was an All Star in the city league last year." Of course that was a lie. I'd never played in any league. But Collins *had* been an All Star, and I was way better than him at both sports. I figured that made my lie as close to a truth as it needed to be.

"Which sport?" Mr. Howard asked, forming a steeple with his fingers and leaning forward on the desk.

"Huh?"

He smiled. "Which sport were you an All Star in? Baseball or football?"

"Both." What the hell? I was on a roll.

The coach raised his eyebrows and nodded. "I see." He leaned toward me. "Well, if you're going to play baseball around here, you'll be playing for me. I coach the high school team *and* the middle school team when I have the time. If I think you're good enough, you can practice with the older guys during the season and summer workouts." The coach jabbed a thumb toward the locker room. "But you'll have to start getting along with guys like Connor Kennedy. He's one of my best players, and a good kid if you take the time to get to know him."

"Fuck Connor Kennedy. He's an asshole and so are his dumb country buddies."

"That's enough with the language," he said, pointing at me for emphasis. I kept silent, but shut my mouth and twisted my lips before looking away. I heard Mr. Howard sigh. "Look, I know it's not easy to break in a new school." His advice almost made me laugh. "But just settle down a bit and give it time. Once the guys get to know you, they'll warm up."

"They don't need to warm up. I'm not going to be around here that long."

"Oh? Why's that?"

"My father will be sending for me soon. He's rich. I probably won't be around here much longer, maybe only another week or two." Just in case he didn't believe me, I added, "He owns a horse ranch out in Indiana." What? There'd been some horses in the pictures my father's wife had sent me. How many horses do you have to own before the place can be called a ranch? "Really, I'll be leaving in a week or two. I'm out of here as soon as he and my mom get all the details worked out."

"I see."

As I sat there I began to entertain the questions that were undoubtedly racing through Mr. Howard's brain. *If you have such a rich and caring dad, why can't you pay for some shorts and buy yourself some new white T-shirts and socks?* That would be hard to explain. I opened my mouth to spill another lie and help cover up my previous whopper, but then closed it. Fortunately, Mr. Howard was either really dense or extremely perceptive. "Well, if you're still around this spring, I hope to see you try out for the team," was all he said, letting me off the hook.

"Sure," I hesitantly agreed.

"In any case, I've got something for you." The coach pulled open a drawer and lifted a stack of clothing out of it. There were socks, a couple of white

T-shirts, a pair of the red gym shorts, and an athletic supporter in the pile. Everything was new. He shoved them toward me and said, "These are for you."

I felt my face heating up. "That—that's okay," I stammered.

"Donny, I'm not asking you to take these. I'm *telling* you." I looked at Mr. Howard. He wasn't fooling. "This isn't charity. I want peace around here. I want you to get along with the other guys. All you have to do to make that happen is become one of them." The coach shrugged. "It's not that hard. Dress like them. Go to class with them. Compete with them. Just do what they do and pretty soon you're one of them."

"I don't want to be one of them. I want—"

"That's enough. I don't want to hear another word." I closed my mouth and stared at Mr. Howard in stupefaction. "Listen, kid, my grandmother raised me and my two sisters on copper pennies and prayers. You aren't the first guy to have things a little rough." I glanced away. "Look at me when I talk to you, son!" I wanted to tell him I wasn't his son, but I didn't dare. "That's better," he told me after I gave him my full attention once more.

The coach sighed and fell back in his chair. "Listen, Donny. I like you. You've got some real piss and vinegar in your veins." I didn't have a clue what that meant, but I liked the sound of it. "I'm not going to coddle you, and I'm *never* going to lie to you. I'm just poor boy who became a Marine who became an old teacher and coach." He waved a hand at all the pictures on his walls. "That's what I'm most proud of. All the guys who I helped become men. And I can help you too."

My first impulse was to tell him I didn't need any help, but he'd said not to say anything more. I kept silent and stood there. Something inside me was reaching out for his direction, actually responding to his stern manner. *You're just scared.* But that wasn't it at all. Mr. Howard was believable. It wasn't just me he was talking to. I was just an extension of every other kid he'd taught or coached over the years. The coach was just being who he was. I could sense that he was genuine and someone a guy could trust.

Whatever he saw in me, Mr. Howard seemed satisfied. "Okay. Here's the deal. You need something…" He leaned nearer and drew my gaze in. "Anything. You come to me if you need someone to talk to or money for lunch. Hell, I'll even get you help with homework or a roll of toilet paper." He smiled at me, and I grinned a little. "But there is one rule." He held up one thick finger. "I'm the boss. Numero uno. The big cheese. The coach. What I say goes."

He stared at me, waiting. "Is that clear?" I nodded my head. He grinned. "Speak."

"Yes, it's clear."

"You have no problem with that?"

"No."

"No, sir."

"No, sir."

The coach chuckled. "You will. But don't worry. All my guys have a problem with discipline and guidance at one time or another, but if shit was easy we wouldn't have to clean up after it." He pointed at the pile of clothes, and I picked them up. "I expect that to be worn. And I expect to see you showering and getting along come Monday." I wasn't sure about the showering, and I definitely wasn't wearing the supporter. But I couldn't tell the coach that.

He stood up and waved me toward the door. "Go on. Get out of here. Tell the teacher in your next class I held you up." I turned to go, but he stopped me at the door. "Donny, we'll do all right around here. You just give this old country school a chance." I nodded, but he wasn't done. "And I wouldn't mind seeing you break that record." I just returned his grin before leaving.

I never broke that record. In fact, I never had the chance to try. And I never gave Mr. Howard a chance to turn a snotty punk kid into one of those pictures on his walls. But tiny pieces of those few minutes in the coach's office always stuck with me. His no-nonsense manner had cut right through the false bravado I'd used to bluff so many other adults. I like to think that gruff old Marine had looked inside me and seen something worth a shit, something more than welfare and food stamps, more than dirt and shabby clothing, something more than a skinny boy cursing like a grizzled sailor.

I hope he saw something more than Betty.

I guess you could say Mr. Howard was a man's man. I've always liked blunt, honest people. The coach was that if he was nothing else. I put the shorts, shirts, and socks in my gym locker for Monday. I still wasn't sure I would shower, but that dilemma was a whole weekend away. I tucked the athletic supporter under some trash in one of the receptacles in the hallway outside the locker room. It would take more than the Marines to force me to wear one of those stupid things.

CHAPTER 26

My thirteenth birthday came and went with little fanfare. Betty put candles on some store-bought chocolate cupcakes, and Leon ordered pizza and handed me a crumpled ten dollar bill. The best part of the whole sorry ordeal was listening to the baby try to sing and watching him lick all the extra frosting off his face and fingers. Betty and I were barely speaking. *Voila! You're a teenager!* I realized. But I didn't feel any different, and I sure didn't feel like celebrating.

As soon as the cupcakes were devoured, my mother and Leon collapsed back onto the bed in her room, where they would lay watching television and calling out for me or Terry to fetch beer or Pepsi or bags of potato chips or whatever other dumb shit they wanted from the kitchen. Betty wasn't working much, and Leon wasn't working at all. My mother was doing a lot of whispering with Leon, keeping secrets from me.

Our new place was already in shambles. Unwashed clothes were mounting like Betty's unpaid bills. Clutter was everywhere. We were using some of the unpacked boxes as coffee tables. Leon's cigarette smoke permeated the entire house. Fluffy was pissing on everything Betty left on the floor, spraying the place like she was trying to put out a raging fire. It was a wonder the people downstairs weren't already complaining about the stench. *Or the noise.*

Some information got passed along to me by Bess, who never missed a whispered rumor in the church. I still sat with her during the Wednesday night services. The church people were practically forcing me to attend every function, now that they were the ones supporting us. On Sundays, Bess sang in the choir and chased Gordo around. She told me the pastor had called Betty into his office and counseled her because the church felt her living with Leon was immoral in the eyes of God, and a terrible example for her children. *They should have seen some of the other guys.* Leon had taken to parking his car a block away and sneaking up the back steps, and hiding in the bedroom if one of the church people stopped by unannounced.

The pastor was also trying to keep tabs on my mother's income so he could attempt to appease her creditors. He wanted her to make at least a small payment every month, as he'd so foolishly promised. *What a dope*, I thought sadly. I knew Betty had held out at least one of her more recent paychecks from the Big Boy, even though I hadn't a clue what lies she might have spun to convince the pastor she hadn't been paid. My mother was an even better liar than I, and that was saying something.

It didn't matter. She could lie all she wanted to. The pastor could counsel and pray or preach and stomp his feet. Nothing he or his entire congregation could do would hold off the inevitable. That preacher could call down the wrath of God Himself and Betty would still use his flock and run. That was just how it was. Every dime that church had spent on us, every hour they'd given up moving us, every prayer they'd uttered on our behalf was wasted.

I skipped school the next few days after my talk with Coach Howard. Showering with a bunch of randy hicks wasn't something I was ready to do, but I didn't want to disappoint Mr. Howard either. I was only running from my problems. *You have to go back to school sooner or later.*

I found a pool hall run by a retired Navy man a couple of blocks from our house, and I convinced the old guy I'd just moved into the area and wasn't enrolled in school yet so he'd let me hang around. The place was nothing like Candy's. It was clean and not as crowded. A bunch of older men drank beer and held pool tournaments two or three nights a week. The glow of the hanging lights bouncing off the green felt was familiar and comfortable, the reek of cigarette smoke and the backroom poker games common among men of every color or social station.

His name was Joe, and he let me shoot for free after I offered to sweep up and take out the trash, as long as one of the four tables was open. The old guy bent my ear with constant stories about his days at sea and all the women he'd had in faraway ports. I didn't mind. Some of his tales were on the lewd side, which was always cool when you were thirteen, and I was shooting pool for nothing and not in school. As far as I was concerned, I was the one making out on this deal.

Joe talked about beautiful exotic women and war. He told me about places I couldn't pronounce and narrated countless heroic and outlandish deeds. He talked about fallen comrades and complained about two deadbeat sons. I just listened and practiced bank shots, accepting everything he said. Joe didn't ask very many questions about my own situation. I was grateful for that.

He showed me a picture of his wife. She'd died a couple of years earlier. After that, he showed me more pictures of himself and his wife. After that, he showed me more pictures of his deadbeat sons before they were deadbeats. And then there were scrapbooks of his service days. I must've looked at two or three thousand black-and-white photos in the span of one afternoon. *Okay, this might be worse than school.* Joe lived alone in the rooms above his pool hall, and I had the feeling his evening gatherings with his buddies were about all the old guy had left.

I was heading up my front stairs that Wednesday afternoon after cutting school at Joe's when a couple of men in sport coats and dress slacks surprised me. They were sitting on the landing at the top of the stairs. I hadn't noticed any strange cars out front, and that in itself was a real warning. They stood up as I paused to gauge what danger I might be in. They remained relaxed and didn't act threatening, neither of them even taking a step down in my direction.

One of them was short and balding, with sunglasses pulled up on his head. His jaws were silently working a wad of gum. He gave me a grin and said, "Don't run, kid. If we'd wanted to hurt you, we'd have waited until you came inside and followed you in."

That was true. I went on up the steps, but cautiously. "Who you guys looking for?" I asked as I neared the landing.

"You Betty's kid?" the other man asked. He was taller, with a big nose and a perm. Unlike his pal, the dude asking me about my mother wasn't smiling. "That a tough question?"

I shook my head and leaned against the wall. "What about it, kid? You know the ropes?" the more pleasant of the pair broke in. *Don't be suckered.* A friendly smile didn't mean shit. The guy doing the grinning could be the more dangerous of the two.

"My mom owes you guys money?"

"Something like that," the taller guy muttered.

"Your mom around?" asked the other dude.

I shrugged. "She's supposed to be working a day shift at the Big Boy."

The guy with the curly perm snorted. "That what she's been telling you, kid?"

"What my partner is telling you is that your mom doesn't work there anymore."

"What I'm telling the kid is that his dumb bitch of a mom got canned and owes the wrong people some money her ass better come up with."

"There's no need to get personal. He's just a kid."

"He's old enough."

I held up my hand, and they stopped bickering—like I was the collector and they were the kids, instead of the other way around. "I know what my mom does." I looked at the taller man. "I *am* old enough. I've been old enough for a long time. But she ain't here, and we ain't got any money that I know of. Some church put us up in this house, moved us and everything. Some preacher's taking every cent my mom gets her hands on to pay off creditors. We don't have a dime."

"That preacher better send some of that money our way," he muttered.

"You'll have to take that up with him."

That was a mistake. The sullen dude stooped down a little and said right in my face, "I'm talking to *you* about it, kid. Why don't we have a look inside and see if there's anything of value setting around?" He sounded serious, and that scared me a little.

"Cut it out," the shorter guy told him, slowly urging him away from me with one outstretched hand. *I guess he actually is the nice one.* "Look, kid. Just tell your mom we stopped by."

"I don't know your names."

"Just tell her it was Bert and Ernie." I didn't know if the hard ass wanted me to smile or laugh at his joke, so I just kept my face blank. "She'll know who we were."

They began descending the stairs, and I realized I'd been more frightened than I'd first thought. My heart skipped a beat as the mean dude brushed past, but I was relieved when he didn't bother to glance at me. The bald guy smiled as he passed. I heard his partner bitching about driving out to the boondocks for nothing from down near the door.

"Hemorrhoids," the guy nearer to me said, jutting his chin toward his partner. "Hey, kid, who's your mom running with right now?" He stayed close to me. I could smell spearmint on his breath, and strong aftershave. "What I mean is… Is Tony living here with you?"

"No."

"You wouldn't lie to me, would you, kid?" he asked softly. His partner popped his head outside to have a look around and then closed the door again, silently watching my interrogation. I suddenly realized how smoothly they'd taken control of the situation, and how close the bald guy was to me. "I don't like being lied to."

"Tony gave me this." I pointed to the still pink scar above my eye. "I punctured the tires on his rusted-out Caddy and threatened to lay out in the street until the cops went after him for beating up a kid." I let what I'd said soak in. I heard the guy down by the door chortle, and I was pretty sure I'd just beheld the first genuine grin on the face of the dude asking me questions. "He split weeks ago."

"That so?" He reached up and poked at my scar with a fingertip. "Gave you a good one, didn't he?"

"I guess so." I tried not to flinch at his touch, but I could tell he knew I was getting scared.

"How about Ruby? She been around at all?" I shook my head. "You sure?"

"I'm sure. I hate that bitch. If she'd been around I'd tell you." My voice sounded small in the narrow corridor. "I wouldn't care what you did to her or Tony either."

"How about your mom?" asked the dude down by the door. "You going to care what happens to her?"

I wanted to say I didn't. I wanted to say they could have her, too. But I couldn't. As much as I liked to pretend I hated my mother, the thought of her being hunted by these dudes frightened me half to death. I heard someone downstairs moving around and thought about screaming for help, but decided against it. *They haven't done anything. Yet.*

"Sure I care," I admitted, although the words nearly burnt my throat.

"Aren't you supposed to be in school?" I nodded. "You cutting?" I just nodded again. "You need to go to school, kid."

Great, fatherly advice from a thug. "I've cut every day this week. I'm having trouble adjusting."

"What do you do all day?"

He pulled a handkerchief out of his pocket and dabbed away the glistening beads of perspiration dotting the receded hairline along his forehead. There was a window above the door that let in the sun. As he dipped his head I saw my reflection in his sunglasses. My face looked frightened. *Get a grip*. It was Betty they were after. *No, it's money they're after.* If they thought they could get their money through me, I was as good as got. I took a breath and tried to stay cool.

"I sleep in. Watch *Big Valley*. Play pool and eat lunch down the road."

He grinned for real again. "I love that damn show. Nick's my favorite. I crack up at the way the old bitch has to fall down every other episode."

I wanted to make a smart comment on how ironic it was that he liked the meanest of the Barkley brothers, but thought better of it. "I kind of like Heath," was all I said.

Pretending I had a normal family somewhere was one of my favorite fantasies. I loved to imagine running off and finding a rich father who'd never realized Betty had given birth to me. *That is so lame.* At least Heath's mother had cared about him, even if she had screwed around with married men.

"You two watch a show with that gorgeous blonde in it and you like the men?" the tall guy grumbled. "Hurry this up. I'm getting a little nervous being stuck in here with you two."

We all shared a quick laugh. "Look, kid." He handed me a matchbook with a pair of dice on the cover. Across the top was a simple name in black lettering: Snake Eyes. Both dice showed single dots. "Your mom and her dumb friend passed some bad paper at our place." I wasn't sure if the dumb friend was Ruby or Tony. *Does it matter? Keep your mouth shut.* "There's a phone number on the inside flap of those matches. Tell your mom to call it." He finally continued down the stairs, releasing me just as effectively as if he'd had me pinned against the wall by physical force. "Tell her we better hear from her real soon."

"*Real* soon," the other dude repeated before he shut the door behind them.

On the way to church that night I was sitting in the back seat feeling low, just staring out the window at the boring fields of the Ohio countryside. My mother had the radio on. Gordon Lightfoot was singing about someone reading his mind. I was humming along and mumbling the chorus. Betty borrowed Leon's car sometimes (the El Camino was broke down and he was currently driving his mom's loud, smelly Buick), especially when he was into his third six-pack and way too gone to drive. *Or care.* By now Leon would probably be asleep in front of the television, lying in my mother's bed with a cigarette hanging out of his mouth and an empty beer can in his fist.

I was thinking about my dog. It was hard to sleep at night without him near me, and I was getting more irritable every day. There were so many memories, so many times he'd lifted a lip and growled to keep one of Betty's buddies off my back or out of my room. *How about the time Terry ran over that kid on his Big Wheel and the little boy's mom and aunt came after you?* Benji had scattered them like crows, busting out of our screen door and chasing them across the street and up onto some parked cars.

He saved you from Tony. But I knew that. *Stop torturing yourself.* I'd never realized how much the little mutt meant to me. The loss of my furry companion was hitting me hard, and weighing on me more every day. He was gone, and all I had left of him was an old stick. I didn't even have a single picture of him. I found myself waking up in the middle of the night and reaching for him, searching for the comfort of his warm body.

Everything was pissing me off. I couldn't stand school. I couldn't stand my mother. Terry was driving me nuts. My brother sat up front with Betty, pestering the baby by sticking his head up over the seat and making faces. Chip was trying to ignore him, but Terry stuck his tongue out and blew a raspberry whenever he failed to get a sufficient rise out of the baby.

Spittle landed on my arm. I waited for my brother to stick his head up again and flicked his ear so hard it sounded like I'd smacked him. "Mommy, Donny hurt me!" he wailed instantly, his cries bouncing off the interior of the car like a police siren had fallen through the roof.

"Cut it out!" Betty barked.

"Tell him to keep his head down and his spit in his mouth, or I *will* hit him."

"You will not!"

Chip and I were sharing a laugh at Terry's expense. I was opening my mouth and making faces like Terry's cries were coming from me. My brother heard the baby giggling and looked back at us, his red face glowing brighter as he realized we were making fun of him. Betty was warning me about something or other. Terry was crying so loud I thought the kid was going to pass out.

"A couple of guys came looking for you today," I said as my brother continued to throw his fit.

"What?" Betty murmured. "Shut up, Terry," she said, turning down the radio. My brother continued to lift his head and bawl. Her hand shot out and smacked him across the crown of his skull. I heard her rings clack against bone. "I said shut up!" Terry sucked air and went silent, holding his head and mewling softly. Even her favorite child didn't matter when it came to preserving her own ass, but the baby and I shared a few more grins while our poor brother suffered. "What did you say?"

"I said a couple of guys came looking for you today."

"Who were they?"

I laughed. "They said to tell you they were Bert and Ernie."

"Ernie?" the baby asked.

"What'd they say?"

"They said you and Tony and Ruby were passing bad paper at their place. They gave me a number for you to call. They said call real soon." I was watching my mother closely. Her mind was racing and her thoughts weren't on the road. A car honked at us as it passed because she'd slowed down so much. "You better watch where you're going."

"Shit! How the fuck did they find me so fast?" She checked the rearview and put her foot on the gas, speeding up. "I was so careful."

Why my mother always thought moving would solve her problems was a thing I never figured out. She never realized every problem we had came right along with us no matter where we went. And it always surprised her when the law or people she owed or conned caught up with us. As if she was supposed to be smarter than they were. As if she knew some angle they hadn't seen before. Like no other criminal ever used flight as their first resort to getting away with their crimes.

"Maybe Ruby narced on you," I proposed.

"Ruby doesn't even fucking know where we moved," she said, but she was talking to herself more than me.

"Maybe they followed you from the Big Boy."

"No. I'm not—" She stopped talking and glanced back at me.

I waited until she looked forward again, and grinned before saying, "Not working there anymore?" She didn't say anything. "That pastor isn't going to like you getting fired after sticking his neck out."

"You just let me worry about the preacher," she snapped. *Can't smack me while you're driving, huh?* I thought with some pride. I was wondering how proud of himself my brother was for whining until he got to sit up front, now that he'd gotten himself whacked while I was safely out of Betty's reach. "You just keep your fucking mouth shut. Do you hear me?"

"I hear you," I muttered.

"No." Her voice went all husky and deep with anger. "Do you *hear* me?"

It was hard for me not to laugh at her. I made my voice sound as much like hers as possible and replied, "Yes. I *hear* you." The baby giggled at me. Terry was doing his best to stifle tears, whimpering. Betty was lost in her thoughts, probably pondering her next move. "So, when are we taking off?" My mother didn't bother to respond, and just kept on driving without deigning to spare me a glance or a word.

The service was reserved that night. Bess was all in an uproar because of the rumors about good old Brother Kim. She kept crying to me about how people were saying the pastor had been sleeping with a young girl who'd been living with them. The rumor was his poor wife had caught Brother Kim and the girl going at it and ratted her husband out to old Pastor Grady, who was now putting off that retirement for a while. Other whispers claimed it was the girl's parents who'd brought down the wrath of the church on Kim by threatening to involve the police. I didn't care either way. The word was that Kim wouldn't be back, and the church was searching for another assistant pastor and youth director. I couldn't figure out why everyone was acting so surprised that he'd done such a thing. Kim had been a pompous jerk from day one.

"Can you believe it?" Bess hissed during the dismissal prayer.

"The dude was a snake."

"He was seduced by the Devil."

I chuckled, and some lady behind us shushed me. "I doubt if the Devil was there when his wife caught them."

Bess gave me a dark look and said, "Amen," as the prayer ended. "You're terrible." She left to gossip with someone more responsive.

I wandered on down to the basement. There was a narrow stairwell with painted concrete steps under the balcony, and I slipped away without any trouble. Two quick left turns and I was at the office behind the steps. The door was locked, but if you pulled up on the knob and shoved just so, it opened right up. Inside there was a desk and some file cabinets, but I wasn't there to steal anything. I just needed a phone.

I closed the door and hunkered down next to the desk, pulling the phone down beside me. There was enough light to see the numbers on the rotary dial. I pulled out Mrs. Lorret's number and dialed, remembering to use the area code because there was some sort of bogus long-distance charge for calling from this far outside of Columbus. The whirring of the circular dial returning home sounded awful loud in the stillness, and I had to pause on the last number while somebody tramped by outside.

For a second I thought I'd messed up the call by pausing, but then the line clicked over. "Hello?"

"Mrs. Lorret?"

"Yes. Who's calling, please?"

Duh, tell her who you are. "It's me, Donny, the kid who lived across the street from you?"

"Hello, honey. How are things going out in Pickerington?"

Things suck. "Okay, I guess."

"That's good."

There was a long silence. "Uh, I was wondering if maybe you might have seen my dog."

"No. No I haven't."

More silence. "Well, okay then," I said, unable to conceal my despondence. This was only the second time I'd called. I was hoping she didn't mind me checking in with her. "Well, I'm sorry to bother you. Is it okay if I call again next week?"

There was a longer pause. "Donny, honey, I have to tell you… Your dog's not lost."

"What?" *Here it comes.* But I'd known. Deep down inside I'd never believed Benji had simply wandered off. I'd known all along. "What do you mean?"

"Baby, that young preacher came and took both your dogs off while you were in school that day. He dragged your dog out on a leash and put him in his car. That little dog of yours was just snarling and snapping to beat all, but he got the poor thing in his car and drove off big as you please." It sounded like Mrs. Lorret was crying. "I'm so sorry, honey, but I just didn't have the heart to tell you."

"What do you mean, the preacher? Do you mean one of the bus workers?" I couldn't believe Dave would do something like that to me.

"No. It was that pretty young preacher. Ken or…"

"Kim."

"Yes, that's it."

There was a tornado in both my ears, a whirlwind churning around violently in my head. "That's okay, Mrs. Lorret." My voice sounded funny. I couldn't breathe. "Thank you." She was talking as I hung up, asking me to forgive her for not telling me sooner.

I don't remember going upstairs, or who else I might have bumped into until I eventually found my mother. Somehow I wound up outside. Betty was standing next to the car chatting with Lynn. She saw me coming and knew in an instant something was wrong. So did Lynn. I was seeing everything through a haze of pain and fury. *They've all been laughing at you. They've all known the whole time, the whole church.*

"*Where's my dog?*" I screamed at my mother. She backed away from me. Lynn scurried off, gravel crunching under her shoes in the silence that had fallen over the parking lot. "You knew they took him! You knew all the time!"

"Donny, wait—"

"You fucking knew!" I heard church people gasping at my coarse language. Someone told me to settle down. But I had eyes only for my mother. I glared at her, my fists clenched and rigid at my sides. "You let me run around looking for him! The whole time you knew he wasn't lost!"

"Donny, there was nothing I could do," she said weakly.

I felt hot tears and ignored them. "The fuck you couldn't! You could've told—"

Suddenly I was swallowed up, picked right up off my feet and carried away. I tried to move my arms and felt them pinned against my sides. "Let me fucking go!" I screamed, writhing and twisting my head around to try and see who had me.

"Just calm down!" Dave ordered, carrying me down the steps and back into the basement of the church. He ducked into the first classroom he found and set me down, kicking the door closed behind him. "Settle down," he urged.

"They took my dog!" I yelled, as if maybe he hadn't heard what I'd been bellowing about.

Dave looked pained. He lowered his face and said, "I know."

This was getting worse by the second. "What do you mean you *knew?*"

"Donny." Dave swallowed and steeled himself. "We needed to get you out of that neighborhood and into the best place we could find… The house we put you up in… Well, the truth is, there were no dogs allowed. Your mother was fortunate the owner agreed to let her keep her cat. Pastor asked me to do it, but I couldn't. I wanted to tell you myself, but your mother warned us against telling you. She said you'd run off with the dog if we forewarned you."

"I thought you liked me. I thought I could trust you."

"You *can* trust me."

"Like hell I can."

"You need to calm down and quit cursing. This is still a church." Dave leaned back against the wall and rubbed his eyes. "I knew this was going to happen. I didn't want them to do it this way."

"I'll bet Kim didn't have any problem with it." I was seething. "Mrs. Lorret said he dragged Benji out of the house on a leash."

"This isn't about Kim."

"Fine. Where is he?"

"Where's who?"

"My dog!" I yelled.

Dave pointed at me, warning me to settle down. "Donny, I don't know. I truly don't."

"Did he take him to a pound or a shelter?"

"I don't know."

"Jesus, Dave! What *do* you know?"

"I'll find out. I promise you. I'll find out and let you know in the next day or two." Dave came over and sat on a chair near me. "But you have to understand… no matter where your dog is, you can't get him back. Your landlord won't allow dogs."

"Don't you understand how stupid that is? Don't you get it? Betty's ripping you off! All of you. She's writing bad checks and lying to your preacher. And when we run she's going to take all the furniture in that place and leave this whole church feeling like idiots for trying to help her!"

"Donny, your mom's trying."

"Oh my God! You don't know her!" I stared at Dave in earnest, doing my best to convince him. "She always does this. We've conned more churches than I can count. You don't know her. She doesn't care about you people. She doesn't care about me or my brothers. Dave, she ripped off her own father when he tried to help her! She's sick! And she's going to run again real soon, and when she does Benji will have died for nothing. For nothing, Dave."

"God can change every life," Dave said solemnly.

"Not Betty's." My voice cracked. I was almost bawling as loud as Terry had on the way here. I tried to compose myself and said, "Benji's all I have, Dave. Please help me get him back. Don't let Betty kill him."

He put a hand on my shoulder and said only, "Donny, you have to understand—"

Whatever he said next I didn't hear. I was on my feet and out the door before he could try to stop me, probably up the stairs and out of the church before he was on his feet. I could run. And I was running now. I could barely see through my tears. But I lifted my knees and churned by arms and raced away from that place, leaving behind those well-meaning Christians and all their biblical nonsense. I found a street and then another, never looking back, never slowing, trying to outrun what couldn't be escaped, attempting to flee from something I was carrying right on my back.

But I ran until my lungs burned and my legs ached. As much as I hated to cry, I let those tears roll. Dusk was giving way to nightfall when I spied a playground and collapsed against a slide. I laid there whimpering like a child, cold steel against my sweating back and the blurry night sky in my eyes. I grieved for the dog I'd never see again. I grieved for my friend. When I was done crying, I vowed to kill Kim. I promised myself I would do so even if I had to wait ten years to do it.

CHAPTER 27

After that night, I was done with everything, listening to no one and ignoring all advice or instruction. Betty threatened to call the school, the pastor, and even the police when I skipped school the rest of that week, but I wouldn't be cowed or intimidated. They'd hurt me real good by snatching my dog. *Killing your dog,* I corrected. I was through being kicked around. Anything I could do to be a pain in the ass happened with great regularity.

The school couldn't call because we didn't have a phone. They had Betty's work number but she didn't work at the Big Boy anymore, so they didn't have any easy way to contact us. We received a notice of unexcused and extended absence in the mail that Saturday, but my mother didn't let me get a look at what else the letter said before she took it from me and stuffed it in her purse. *Do you care?* I asked myself. I didn't care. I didn't intend to go back. I didn't intend to do anything at all.

I was sitting on the floor, rolling a rubber ball back and forth with the baby. Every now and then I'd bounce it off his head and catch it, making the kid crack up. He pointed toward the back door and asked, "Play outside?" The kid was talking more clearly all the time, even though he was still extremely shy and quiet.

I faked a shot at his head and he flinched. "Sure."

Fluffy was perched on the arm of the couch, watching both doors for any opportunity to escape. Betty wasn't letting the cat outside because she was so afraid of losing her. Of course, keeping the crazed feline trapped inside only made her act more nuts. Fluffy was popping her claws in the furniture and tearing at the bottom of the doors. The evidence of her wrath was everywhere. And she was still pissing all over the place. I heaved the ball at her and sent the cat scrambling for Betty's bedroom, so I could open and close the back door without her trying to dart around my feet.

"Where are you going?" Betty asked as I crossed the kitchen.

She was sitting with Leon at the table. They'd had their heads together hissing and whispering again. My mother was wearing her early morning bed head hairdo even though the day was well into the afternoon. She didn't have her teeth in and had yet to apply any unpaid-for war paint. She looked like a ghoul with a hangover. Leon was wearing only his saggy yellow underwear, dangling lit cigarette, and ever-expanding hairy beer gut.

"To Hell if he don't change his ways," muttered Leon.

He always repeated the same dumb clichés. My previous joy over my mother getting rid of Tony and letting Leon move back in was gone. He'd known about them killing my dog too, and I'd told him as much. Leon tried to lay the same line on me as Dave, whining that he'd only done as Betty requested. Everybody seemed to think I was so much better off, trading a few weeks in Pickerington for the life of my only true friend.

I thought my mother's question fairly ridiculous. I was carrying the baby under one arm and heading for the back stairs leading to the swing set, where Terry was already playing. "Chip dropped the ball and pissed me off. I'm going to throw him off the balcony to teach the little shit a lesson."

"Airplane?" the baby asked.

"We want to talk to you," Betty offered.

I continued on toward the door. "No thanks." If we talked, we'd fight, and I wasn't in the mood.

"You're going back to school on Monday," Leon broke in, trying to sound all parental. His attempt at fatherly concern fell way short. Leon was spending less and less time around here. I had a feeling he had some trouble nipping at his heels as well. *What a shock.* "You're too young to quit school."

I paused at the door. Chip wanted down, and I set him on his feet. "Is that right?" I returned, grinning boldly at Leon.

"Donny, you have to go to school," Betty whined. Something in that letter from the school had her worried. *Good.* "If you don't go to school the police could be involved."

"So?" I opened the door and let Chip out. "Use the handrail and go slow," I warned my brother as he started down the metal steps. "Why should I have to go to school? Neither of you have a diploma and look how great you're both doing." I stepped outside and shut the door behind me before they could respond, leaving them to stew in my belligerence.

I half expected Betty or Leon to come after me or call me back inside, but nobody bothered. Terry chucked a buckeye at me that rolled to a feeble stop in the brittle grass at my feet. I picked it up and whipped it back at him, sending it clanging off the metal frame of the swing. That first melee grew into an hour-long war between my brothers and me. We ran around the yard collecting buckeyes and winging them at one another, although I took care not to hit them too hard or in the head.

One of their favorite games was hiding from me. I would pretend I couldn't find them until I got bored, or sneak up on them and do my best to scare them right out of their skin, which they enjoyed even more than hiding. I let them run me ragged for a while, pretending I couldn't find them, even though half the time they hid in such lame places a deaf and blind kid could have stumbled on them without breaking a sweat. Chip hid beneath the slide three times, tucking his head between his knees and closing his eyes. I guess he thought if he couldn't see me I couldn't see him. I worried about that boy sometimes.

Terry eventually gave me some trouble. He climbed inside an old tin storage shed along the back fence and hid beneath an upside down wheelbarrow. I'd checked the damn thing twice, really listening for him more than digging through all the junk. I was getting ready to check the house, thinking maybe he'd snuck back inside, when I heard him fart before I closed the shed doors after my second search. *Scared the shit out of him,* I thought, suppressing laughter. Instead of leaving, I closed the doors but remained inside.

The interior of the shed was gloomy, but a wide crack between the closed doors let in more than enough light to see by. My brother giggled, thinking I'd left and just tickled pink that he'd pulled one over on me. I let him have a moment of glory and then reached out and rustled an old bag of grass seed. "What was that?" he asked, suddenly frightened. I shook the bag again and let loose a low but throaty growl. "Donny!" he yelped, scrambling out from under the wheelbarrow and racing past me, bursting through the thin metal doors and outside as fast as he could manage.

I sat there cackling until he came creeping back, all sheepish but grinning. We spent some time rummaging through the stuff in the shed. There were old tools, bags of seed and fertilizer, gardening implements, cans of screws and nails, a stack of lumber along the rear wall, and a lot of other dust-coated junk. The only thing I found of interest was a faded calendar hanging on the wall from '72 with a woman in a bikini posing on the hood of a Ford Mustang.

"Donny, can we build a fort?" Terry asked, hefting a hammer and pointing at the stack of wood.

That wasn't a bad idea. *It's just another thing they'll have to leave behind,* I reminded myself. That was true. "Maybe later," I told him.

"Let me have a turn!" Terry whined. Chip had climbed up on a rusty lawn tractor and was pretending to drive it. Terry began pawing at him, trying to pull him down, but our youngest brother was having none of that and kicked his antagonist right in the jaw. "Donny, Chip kicked me!"

I shook my head at my brother, flipping hair out of my eyes. "So?"

Last summer, the baby had clocked Terry above the eye with a wooden building block. The resulting gush of blood had made Terry stop pestering Chip for at least a month. I didn't think it was going to take many more years until my youngest brother's fiery temper would teach Terry to leave him alone once and for all. But I still took the hammer away from Terry and put it back in the toolbox he'd found it in.

When our exploring grew tiresome I found an old rake hanging inside the shed and made a huge pile of dead leaves. For a while we ran and jumped into the crunchy heap, sending leaves exploding into the chilly October air. The baby crawled beneath the mound and hid. Terry and I had to pretend we were going inside to get him to come out on his own. I picked Chip up and tickled the kid after he finally emerged, and then tossed his wriggling little body back into the pile. He burrowed back within the drift like some demented giggling rat.

Terry began whining to be thrown too, so I obliged him. That lasted until my arms throbbed with the strain of spinning each of my brothers in turn, hoisting them as high in the air as I could. Terry kept yelling *Superman!* and pretended he was flying. Chip just spread his arms wide and closed his eyes, cartwheeling through the air as stiff as a board. My brothers would have worked me to death, but Terry got tar from a pine cone in his eye and ran inside screaming for Betty. *Great, I'll catch shit over that, too.*

For some odd reason my youngest brother loved to gather up pinecones and pile them on the flat end of the slide. I sat on the swing and watched him at his labor. The kid worked his way farther and farther away from the swing set, collecting the cones with dogged determination. Before long he attained a heap the slide could scarcely contain, but still he continued, carefully piling each of his treasures on the growing mound.

I knew this was going to end up in a disaster. Terry would cry and get Betty to wipe his tears and clean out his eye, but when he came back outside he was going to make a beeline for that slide and Chip's pile of pine cones. If Terry swooped down the slide and destroyed Chip's mound of cones, the ensuing fight would end our peaceful outing, and Betty would blame the whole mess on me.

"Hey, you want a cookie and a drink?" I proposed when the kid wandered near, hoping to tempt him into going inside and forgetting his eccentric work of art.

"Hmmh?" he murmured, gazing up at me with his hands full of cones. The baby gave me a look that said *Can't you see I'm working here?* but paused long enough to let me repeat my question. Pine tar covered his hands and fingers, and debris from the pile of leaves was tangled in the long strands of his thin blond hair. His sweat pants were muddy, and his diaper was probably soiled. Yet something in the big blue eyes staring up at me always lightened my burden, the innocent beauty of his grimy face always made me feel a little better about our sorry lives.

"You want a cookie and a drink?" I asked again.

He didn't answer, but he did drop the pine cones, clutched in his tiny fists, and headed for the stairs. I followed him up and ushered him inside. No one was in the kitchen, but I could hear Betty and Terry in the bathroom, probably working on the tar in his eye. "Chip's inside... He needs cleaned up and changed and a drink... I'll be back later!" I yelled before quickly locking the door from the inside and slamming it. I descended the steps in three bounds and was out of the yard and down the street before my mother could stop me from leaving.

Joe was brushing down the pool tables when I came in. "Hey there," he said by way of greeting, flashing me a big smile.

"Mind if I shoot a while?" I asked, coming straight to the point.

He pretended to think it over. "Dump the ashtrays and empty the trash and a table's yours," he told me.

Joe made a couple of phone calls while I shot. I could overhear him setting up a card game and placing an order for some cases of beer to be delivered. Eventually he wandered over and watched me play for a while. "You're getting a lot better," he told me when I successfully drew the cue ball backwards after sinking the six in the corner. Joe had taught me how to use english by striking down on the cue ball, and how to use the dots along the edge of the table to better line up my bank shots.

"Thanks." I was hoping he wanted to play a game. "Want to give me another shot at beating you?"

"Young fella, you couldn't beat me with a stick," he returned, but grinned and reached for a cue.

He had a special two-piece cue in a case behind his counter, but I wasn't worth the effort to get it out. Joe was *really* good at pool. *You would be too, if you owned a pool hall.* I'd once heard a kid in school say they had a pool table in their basement. I was thinking it would be cool to have your own private table.

Before we could begin our game, the phone rang, and Joe left to take the call. I racked the balls and waited a minute or two, but when his conversation dragged on I broke and continued practicing on my own. Whatever Joe's call was about forced him to make a couple more calls, and then he told me he had to run upstairs for a few minutes and asked me to watch the place as I was sinking my last ball. I told him I would and began retrieving balls from the hanging leather pockets.

I just tossed the balls and let them roll to a stop where they would, then tried to sink as many in a row as I could, practicing my bank shots and trying to leave the balls nearer the pockets until I needed them. Even though pool was a fairly straightforward game, there was a lot more strategy involved than I'd previously thought. Joe taught me that. I was trying my best to practice the few lessons he'd imparted, tricks like leaving your ball blocking pockets, recognizing bank shots, running rails, and purposely leaving the cue ball where you had a good chance of making another shot.

"Nice shot," a man said as I banked the yellow one ball into the side. I looked up and found Dave standing on the other side of the table. "You alone in here?"

A toilet flushed upstairs. I pointed toward the ceiling with my cue and said, "This is Joe's place." I grinned. "He's upstairs taking care of business."

Dave didn't look pleased. "Your mother told me you were probably here." He watched me chalk my cue and line up another shot. There was a lot of green but I sank the ball cleanly. "You think this is the kind of place you should be hanging out in?"

"What kind of place would that be, Dave?" I gestured around. "You think this is bad? It's just some old guy's downstairs with a wall knocked down to make room for the pool tables. They throw some darts and play a little poker in the back room. What's so wrong with that? You should have seen Candy's place." I flicked the hair out of my eyes and sighted another shot, extending my cue to assist me in lining up the angle.

"They serve alcohol here, Donny. And you're a minor." I stopped shooting and faced Dave's piercing stare. "You could get yourself in trouble. You could get the man who runs this place in trouble too."

"Hey, look." I felt rising anger. "Joe's a good guy. He's about the only friend I have right now. Why don't you leave him alone?"

"Do you want me to feel sorry for you? Is that it?"

I chuckled and resumed lining up my shot. "Yeah, you've got me all figured out. Why don't you leave me alone?" I missed my shot and cursed under my breath. Dave was making me nervous. "I don't need this right now, Dave."

"What you *need* is to be knocked down a peg or two."

I chuckled. "That's what I like about you, Dave. I just love the way you sugarcoat what you have to say so it doesn't sting so bad."

"Is that what you want me to do?"

"I don't care what you do." And I didn't. In the past I'd played coy with Dave and the other church people, acting like I couldn't care less if they chased after me or not, but secretly enjoying the attention. Not now. "Just leave me alone."

"I thought you and I had something going? I thought you were going to give God a chance to work in your life?" That made me feel a little bad. Dave sounded genuinely hurt. "The gift of salvation doesn't always manifest itself in ways we can easily understand."

"Salvation? You mean when we prayed that night?" I put my cue on the table and gave Dave my full attention. "Let's see?" I pretended to think, striving to recall my recent circumstances. "Just how did that go down? Wait! I remember. I think it went kind of like… pray, find my brother raped, have my dog snatched by your rapist preacher, and then get moved out to the boondocks and shoved into a hick school where I stand out like…? Well, like *me* walking around pretending I fit in with *them*."

"There's nothing wrong with you, Donny."

I snorted. "You better look again."

"I'm not going to do this with you."

"Do what?"

"I'm not going to pretend I have all the answers, or that I can promise everything's going to be easy for you in the future. Sometimes things just are what they are. We do what we can with what we have." Dave looked away as Joe came back in. The old man could tell we were involved in a serious discussion and stayed behind his counter. "But I do know that giving up or quitting isn't the answer to your problems."

I didn't like being called a quitter. "You don't know what you're talking about."

"I think I do."

"Okay, fine. You do. Just leave me alone."

"You're heading for a bad time, Donny. What you're doing is going to hurt not only you, but your brothers as well." Dave nodded toward Joe. "Him, too."

Bad time? As far as I was concerned, I'd been living in a *bad time* for as long as I could remember. "What are you talking about? I'm not going to hurt Joe."

Dave shook his head at me. "What do you think is going to happen if the authorities find out you've been skipping school and hiding out here? I suppose you told him some lie about why you aren't enrolled yet?" I didn't bother to reply. We both knew I'd deceived Joe. "He could lose his license. At the least he'll be answering some difficult questions, and be none too pleased with you for bringing trouble down on him."

I hadn't thought about it that way. And as much as I hated to admit it, Dave was probably right. I suddenly wanted to be away from Joe's. The last thing I wanted was for the kind old guy to have problems because of me. *Or find out you've been lying to him.* Joe was still watching us. I lifted a hand to say good-bye and left without even a mumbled word, Dave trailing behind me like a hangman with a noose dangling from his hand reserved just for me.

"What about your brothers?" Dave asked once we were outside and heading toward my place.

"What about them?" I muttered without looking back. Dave was walking behind me, the hard soles of his dress shoes striking the sidewalk a loud contrast to my silent sneakers. "Don't tell me the cops will arrest *them* if I keep skipping school, Dave."

"No, but they'll ticket and fine your mother." He let me absorb that. "How are you going to feel when she has to pay out money she doesn't have because you won't go to school?" I didn't respond. "Worse than that, they just might cart you off to juvenile court and have some judge make you a ward of the state for your own good." *That* I wasn't buying at all. Getting money out of Betty would be a miracle in itself, but I wasn't about to be a ward of anything no matter who said what. "You have to go back to school. You're being too hard on your mother."

I had to laugh at that. "Did you go inside when you talked to Betty?"

"Yes, I stepped in. Why?"

"See anybody else?"

"Just your brothers."

I laughed again. "Well, you should have looked in the bedroom or bathroom. You would've found a hairy fat guy in his underwear. He parks his car down the block and hides whenever someone from the church comes around." I stopped and turned to face Dave. "Did you know she quit her job at the diner? Or that she's got a lot more bad checks floating around than she's admitted to? Some of them aren't even in her real name."

"I'm not really interested in any of that right now," he said. That surprised me. "At the moment I would be happy with you going back to school and coming back to church."

I turned and kept walking. "Please, Dave. No sermons. Not now." There were only a hundred yards or so left to our front steps, and the silence behind me was all the evidence I needed to know Dave was no longer following me.

I paused at my front door and turned to see him resume his approach. Dave had something more on his mind. There was a moment when I thought he might turn back and leave without saying anything further. But he didn't. He walked slowly to the base of the steps and gazed up at me, his forehead crinkled by some unnamed emotion. I thought he was preparing to give me another lecture, but I guessed wrong.

"Will you come to church tomorrow?" he asked. I shook my head and flipped my hair back. Dave grinned, but sadly. "I didn't think so." He made a gesture toward my shaggy head. "Don't you get tired of all that hair hanging down in your face?"

I shrugged. "I don't think about it much."

"How about I pick you up after church?"

"What for?" I asked, suspicious of his motives. Dave usually helped get the bus kids home after services. "What about your bus route?"

"Jewel can handle them. I promised the pastor I'd bring you in for a little sit-down."

I wasn't sure what he meant. "Sit-down?"

Dave chuckled, trying to reassure me. "A talk. He just wants to talk to you."

"What about?" The thought of facing that preacher was intriguing, but frightening. *What have you got to be afraid of?*

"Oh, life. You. How things are going. Whatever." There was more. Dave was nervous, and noticeably unsettled. I could see he wasn't his normal confident self. "What would you like to talk about?"

"Nothing."

"Are you afraid?"

"No." *Liar.* Dave knew I was lying too. I scrunched my face up, letting him see that I was a little squeamish. "Maybe a little."

"The pastor's a good man. You have no reason to fear him."

"It's not him, Dave. It's Betty. I don't want to cause any more trouble for him than she already has. She's told that man so many lies I might not be able to keep up with them."

"It's not her he wants to talk about, it's you," Dave informed me.

Then I got it. Betty was trying to use me in her con. She'd probably told that man I was causing her problems, maybe stealing even. *Okay, Mommy, let's play this game your way.* If the preacher wanted to talk to me, I'd talk. I was sick of my mother's shit. I was sick of Leon and his dingy underwear and his beer and rancid smoke. I was sick of feeling ashamed of myself at the church. Maybe it was time to let people know what was really going on.

"Okay, Dave. I'll talk to him."

"Make sure you're here when I come to pick you up."

"No, that's okay. I'll come to church so you don't have to make the extra trip." I was actually excited about the upcoming meeting, already preparing answers and statements in my mind. "The kids from the neighborhood need you more than I do."

"Thanks, Donny. I appreciate that." Dave stuck a hand in his front pants pocket and sighed. "This is hard for me, but I promised you an answer."

He brought out his hand and extended my dog's collar.

It was one of those moments… frozen forever but gone in a flash, nothing but a scintilla in time that's meaningless to the rest of the world but alters your own path forever. The day was crisp and clear. A semi roared by on the road out front, and I felt the rush of wind in its wake. Birds scattered out of a tree near the road. Dave was swaying slightly. I realized it was me who was wobbly.

But then a cold rage rose up and steadied me. His hand was still waiting, so I took the collar and held it down at my side where I couldn't see it, trying to be brave, clinging to rage and fighting back tears of frustration. My dog was dead. *You knew that.* But knowing something and *knowing* something were entirely different. *He could've lied to you and said Benji was fine.* I was thinking I'd rather he had. But Dave wasn't like that. Dave was honest and blunt to a fault. *You always liked those traits in him.* I hated them more than ever before at the moment.

"I'm sorry, Donny. A man at the shelter said he was limping so badly no one would adopt him. I guess the older a dog is, the less likely anybody is inclined to adopt it. He also said they couldn't clean him up or handle him because he kept snarling and snapping when anyone tried to touch him."

I didn't like my buddy being referred to as *it.* "He does that when he's scared. They took him away and put him in a damn cage, Dave. Wouldn't you be scared if someone did that to you?"

"I guess I would," Dave admitted. He didn't even bother to scold me for cursing.

"I need to go on in, Dave."

"I'll see you tomorrow?"

"You bet." I was looking forward to the talk with the pastor more than ever. I had a lot to talk about. I intended to blow the lid off Betty's whole scam. "See you then." I left Dave there and went on inside, feeling numb and tired.

Betty followed me around for a while, doing her best to sniff out what Dave had wanted with me. My dead dog's collar was stuffed in my pocket so she wouldn't see it and try to act motherly or concerned. I decided to keep her in the dark and let her worry. Leon was back at the kitchen table reading the paper, but at least he had on a greasy stained T-shirt and some jeans. I managed to get Betty off my back and slipped into my brothers' room with my record player and a small stack of 45s that had miraculously survived the witching hour.

Chip and Terry followed me in before I could get the door closed, so I let them stay. We spent a couple of hours singing along with Marvin Gaye or James Brown, only I flipped the switch over to 33 so the Motown sounds were slow and slurred. Leon especially hated when I did this. I made sure to keep the volume as high as I could without busting the lame speaker behind the cardboard facing.

I didn't feel like crying, so I pushed thoughts of Benji out of my mind and concentrated on my goofy brothers. They were singing along and dancing around, jumping off the bed and shaking their hips. But I still dreaded trying to sleep that evening. One of my worst habits was brooding over things I had little control of, or had already happened and couldn't be changed. My dog's death qualified on both counts.

Later that night, I was lying on the couch, suffering through the first of many bouts of melancholy when my mother came into the living room and plopped down beside me, forcing me to scoot over to make room for her. For a while we stared at the fuzzy television, watching an old black-and-white western starring Gary Cooper. Betty reached out and tried to stroke my brow, brushing the hair out of my face. I stiffened and pulled my head away.

"I wish you wouldn't do that," she told me.

"That makes two of us." My harsh retort made her flinch and withdraw her hand. "What do you want?"

"Can't you tell me what Dave wanted today?"

"He wants me to go back to school and come to church. The same old shit." I rolled onto my back and covered my face with a pillow. I was tired. I wanted my mother to let me be. "I'm going to sleep."

"Are you?" she persisted.

I groaned beneath the pillow. "Am I what?" She tried to pull the pillow away but I held it firm.

"Are you going back to school?"

"Maybe." My answer was muffled, and my face was getting hot. I adjusted the pillow so I could breathe more easily. "I'm going to church in the morning."

"Why's that?"

Oh no you don't. "Because I promised Dave," was all I said. I wasn't about to let her know I'd be talking with the pastor.

"That's good," she hesitantly agreed. "Dave likes you."

"Yeah, I'm a swell guy."

Betty sat quietly for a time, the stillness broken only by gunshots and horses' hooves. "I wish we could get along better," she eventually said. "I don't know what to do." She began to cry. "Nothing pleases you." I knew

Betty. These were real tears. "I swear to God I do the best I can with what I have. Do you think it's easy for me?" But she wasn't crying for me. "Do you think I like living like this?" She was crying for herself. Something big was coming.

I removed the pillow and looked at her. The glow of the television revealed the tracks of her tears. "How soon until we run?"

"A week, maybe two."

"Where?"

"Probably Indiana." She sobbed. "Maybe Texas. Leon's trying to get a job driving for a guy he knows down there."

"So Leon's going with us?" She sobbed and nodded. "Great."

"I thought you liked Leon?"

I didn't answer. I'd already decided I was still going to let the pastor in on a few things, just to get back at all of them for killing my dog. He was a gullible fool, and I was going to inform him of that fact. I didn't care if he got pissed and tossed us out on the street, either. I was beginning to hate that church almost as much as I hated my mother. Everyone had the answer to your problems. Everyone had a worthless opinion.

Believe this. Say this. Don't listen to this. Pray. Walk down to the altar. Move here. Kill your dog. All their nonsense kept running through my mind. They were all so full of shit. I was sick of preachers reaping souls by day and raping the congregation by night. *Trust me. Kill your dog.* Looking down on everyone who didn't believe the way they did.

What about Dave? I had to give them that. Dave was for real. *What about Holly and Jewel?* Okay. They were on the up and up, too. *What about how you felt the night you prayed?* I didn't want to think about that. *Why not?* I wanted to believe something about that night had been real and meaningful… that there had been something almost sacred laced in those whispered words. Dave's promises had given me hope, and made me believe I could be something more. *Like what?* I didn't know.

"Donny?" Betty called softly.

"Yeah?" I mumbled, sullen and tired.

"Why can't you understand?"

"Understand what?"

"How hard this all is for me. Do you think I want to live this way?"

"It sure seems that way sometimes."

"What do you mean?"

"The losing jobs and running around spending money you don't have. The checks you write knowing there's no money to cover them. Writing checks not even in your name." Her face hardened in the gloom. "And the men…" I whistled. "I'm telling you, Betty, the men you drag home are real winners."

"Don't call me Betty."

"I'm sorry. *Mother,* the men you let crawl on you leave *so* much to be desired."

"Stop it!" she snapped. "I hate when you get like this. You act like you're so much better than everyone else. I suppose you're going to live high and mighty. You're going to find out how hard life is one day. You'll see."

I laughed at her. "Yeah, you *will* see. I *am* going to live high and mighty. I'm going to have money and cars and whatever else I want, and I'm not going to rip people off to have what I want."

Betty was strangely silent. "I hope you do." She was still crying a little. Part of me felt bad for her, but a bigger part still hated her for the dog collar I was clutching beneath the sheet that covered me. "I believe you will. Make money, that is. But I don't believe anyone will ever love you. You're cold. You won't let anybody close. You can barely stand to be touched."

Now she was just babbling about bullshit that had no bearing on our current circumstances. "So?" I sat up on my elbows and stared at her, my face impassive. "Are we done?"

Betty wiped at her tears. "Why do you hate me so much? Why can't you understand what this is like for me? You think you have it so rough."

I held out Benji's collar for her to see. My mother stopped talking. "I had one friend in the world." *Don't you fucking cry in front of her.* "I counted on him, and he counted on me. Now all I have is this." She wanted to leave now, but I wasn't done. "For what? So you and Leon can swindle a few more dollars out of the church people while you decide where we go freeload next? I'm not going to have Benji around the next time one of your out-of-work alcoholics decides to choke the shit out of me."

"I'm going to bed," she murmured, rising to leave.

"Was it worth it?" I asked as she left. I heard her open and close the door to the bedroom she shared with Leon. "Was it worth it?" I hollered again.

My mother never answered me.

CHAPTER 28

The pastor's wife told me to take a seat and wait while her husband finished up with someone else in his office. *I guess I'm not the only problem child,* I told myself while I did as she'd requested. For a while I sat and eavesdropped on the conversation, picking up just enough to know that some blubbering lady's husband had a drinking problem. The preacher kept his voice down, so I couldn't hear what advice he was doling out.

And then Bess arrived and made any further reconnaissance impossible. She kept rattling. Every word struck my brain pan like she was firing nails out of a pneumatic gun. She talked about her brother David and his crazy new wife. I had to listen to all the details concerning her and Lynn's latest fight. In between babblings—and breaths—she periodically inquired as to what the pastor wanted to see me about. I wasn't stupid; Bess was dying to know why I was being hauled into Pastor Grady's sanctum. But I wasn't in the mood to explain myself. I wasn't sure I knew exactly why I was there myself.

"Did you know the church is going to expand their school?" Bess asked me.

I couldn't be my normal sarcastic self due to the fact that the preacher's wife was sitting within earshot, even though she was acting as if she wasn't interested in a thing we were saying, busying herself with a stack of files at her desk. Mrs. Grady wore those half-circle reading glasses on the tip of her nose, complete with the thin chain draped around her neck. She peeked over those glasses and smiled at anyone who passed through the breezeway, but appeared to be paying us no mind whatsoever.

"That's great," was all I responded, just in case.

"As soon as the higher grades are established, I'm going to attend. Maybe you can too?"

"Don't count on it," I said before I could stop myself. Mrs. Grady's eyes glanced briefly in my direction. *I knew she was listening.* "I'm sure the school will be nice," I quickly added. I liked Mrs. Grady. It was hard to act disrespectful around a lady as nice as she was.

"Charles got arrested for shoplifting, but he didn't do it," Bess continued, bouncing from one subject to another with no rhyme or reason. *Of course not.* One or another of the trolls was always getting picked up by the fuzz. And they were always innocent of the charges if you asked Bess or Mama. David, the oldest troll, had a serious hankering for little boys, even if he *had* married some whacked-out lady. "He didn't get locked up or anything, but he has to go to court in a couple of weeks," she added, as if I might be worried.

"That's good," I mumbled.

"I heard you haven't been going to school. Is that why pastor wants to see you?"

I sighed. "I'd say that's one of the things he's probably going to bring up."

"What else?"

The girl was persistent if nothing else. "Betty thinks I'm possessed. She wants the preacher to excommunicate me."

Bess smacked my shoulder. "You're awful. And if you were possessed he'd have to perform an *exorcism.* Excommunication is what Catholics do if they want to kick you out of their church."

For all I knew that was exactly what the man was going to do. I probably deserved to be kicked out. "Thanks for clearing that up."

She was quiet for a bit, looking at me with those soft brown eyes. Bess was prettier when she wasn't yakking so much. "I'm sorry about Benji." That stung. I looked down at my feet and tried not to show it. "I know he meant a lot to you." *Not now,* I wanted to say. I was trying to prepare myself for my imminent meeting. This wasn't helping. "I guess there isn't much to say about it, but I'm here for you if you ever want to talk."

I didn't and I wouldn't, but all I said was, "Thanks."

A gaggle of younger people swarmed through the breezeway, the twins leading the throng. Two of the Fuller boys trailed along behind them. The youngest, a guy named Carey, barely younger than I was, saw me and lifted a hand, so I waved back. Gordo was in the pack as well. Our eyes met, and I stuck my tongue out at him, hoping he'd flip me off and get busted by the preacher's wife. He didn't, and Mrs. Grady cleared her throat, shushing them all as efficiently as if she'd screamed and cussed. The twins led their adoring fans on outside in silence.

The door to the pastor's office opened up and set my heart to pounding. *What are you scared of?* "I'll see you later," Bess whispered as the preacher and a still-sobbing elderly lady said their good-byes. I kept my seat while he nodded and she blubbered, trying to find something of interest on the ground in front of me. It took forever for the lady to finally leave, but I found myself wishing she'd stick around a little longer as she descended the steps.

"Go on in and take a seat while I have a word with the missus," the pastor instructed me. I ducked under his shoulder and did as he asked. "I won't be but a moment," he told me as he pulled the door almost shut behind him.

Nervous as I was, his office enthralled me. The walls were lined with polished, well-stocked bookcases. I've always loved the smell of books. I'm one of those people who stick their nose in the pages and inhale like a hippie using a bong. The desk was huge, the chairs leather and sturdy. One standing lamp over in the corner and a soft reading light were the only illumination, both casting a warm glow on a room I believed was one of the most beautiful and wondrous I'd ever beheld.

The pastor had a picture of his wife on his desk, and another of his kids. I stole a quick peek at them. The one of Mrs. Grady showed just her smiling face, but the one of the kids was when they were younger and standing together outside, all smiles and sun and green grass. Pastor Grady had more pictures on his walls and others perched on shelves amid the books. I would've liked to look at more of the pictures but I didn't dare.

I climbed up in the chair facing the desk and was annoyed when I couldn't keep my feet on the ground, unless I scooted closer to the front edge. If I rested against the back of the chair, I felt like a little kid. *How revolting.* I was wondering if the pastor had chosen chairs like this on purpose when he came back into the office. He didn't say anything right away. I watched him while he tucked some papers into a manila folder and dropped them into a small filing cabinet behind his chair before taking a seat.

"Well, I'd say this meeting was long overdue," he began. The pastor clasped his fingers together in front of him and finally let his gaze rest full upon me.

I was already intimidated, but for none of the reasons I'd fretted over. There was nothing menacing about Pastor Grady. His hair had long ago lost its color, the patches at his temples so white they practically glowed even in the dimness of the office. There were deep creases at the corners of his eyes, but other than those lines he wore his years well. The man looked tired, but not daunted, and not at all worried about anything I might say to him. It was that aura of certainty and confidence that troubled me. It wasn't going to be easy to tell this man how big a sap he was.

"Before we get started, let's pray," he told me, bowing his head and beginning without waiting to see if I'd comply, which I hastily did.

He prayed for guidance and wisdom. He asked God to help him find a way to help me. He prayed for my mother and my brothers. Most of all, he prayed for me. Over the years I've run into a lot of people who wear their religion on their sleeve, and many others who use regular church attendance as an excuse to let priorities slide. I've known preachers who seduced women in the congregation and stole money from tithes. I guess I've encountered about every type of fake you can imagine.

The Reverend Lawrence Grady wasn't one of those as far as I could tell. When he prayed the words weren't merely spoken; they were delivered. The pastor seemed for real, even if he'd chosen poorly by allowing Kim into his church. Every word he uttered to God floated across the short distance between us and fell squarely upon my thin shoulders. I felt that weight, and the burden of truth and faith and sincerity was heavy upon me as he finished his prayer and lifted his head.

"I was pleased to hear you accepted Christ into your heart, Donny," he said softly as I lifted my own head, now totally sure I was going to have a lot of difficulty being mean to this man. I only nodded. "How has that decision affected you so far?"

A lot of smart answers surged through my brain and danced around on my tongue, but I held them there, unable to give voice to any wisecracks. "Okay, I guess."

"Have you felt a change?" I shook my head. "Are you praying for guidance? Are you reading your Bible?" I just lowered my eyes and searched for loose change on the carpet. "I've noticed you haven't been coming to church lately. You must understand that to better your life you must better your habits. Fellowship with those who can show you the way to accomplish this is very important, especially early in your decision to accept salvation."

I had a lot of problems with salvation and the Bible. So much of the stuff I was being told made absolutely no sense. I had so many questions. Who did Cain marry after he clobbered Abel? Who did Noah's family marry after the flood? How did people get across the ocean before there were boats big enough to make the voyage? Why weren't dinosaurs mentioned in the Bible? And just how could Jonah survive for days inside a damn whale?

I also felt the admission qualifications to afterlife were a bit too easy. According to those supposedly in the know, a guy could rape and murder hundreds of people, but if he asked for forgiveness right before he died, God had to grant him eternal life in Heaven right along with Bing Crosby and John-Boy Walton. I was sure hoping God was too smart to get conned into agreeing to a stupid deal like that. If God wasn't careful, Heaven would get turned into some kind of housing project in the clouds.

But I couldn't say any of this to the pastor. I knew before spouting the words how feeble and petty my comments would fall. *You better say something*, I told myself. The preacher was watching me, making me nervous. I felt like he could look into my mind and read my thoughts if he wanted to. *Maybe God lets him do just that.* It wouldn't have surprised me. I felt powerless and childlike in this office, perched awkwardly on this oversized leather chair and peering across the expansive polished surface of his desk.

"I'm not so sure church is for me," I finally said, hoping he'd let at least that much go.

The pastor thought a moment. "From what I hear, you've decided school isn't for you either."

And we're off! I held his gaze somehow. "I guess not."

"Why's that?"

"I don't like that school."

"What don't you like about it?"

Again, a lot of responses were given birth and then slain by better judgment. There were many honest answers I could have given the pastor. I could have told him how poorly I fit in with the other kids, or how awkward it was to be dressed like…? Well, to be clothed like one of Betty's kids when the rest of the students were walking around like they'd just stepped out of some advertisement in a catalogue. But I didn't say any of that. I was too embarrassed.

Some of what I was being teased about would be nearly impossible for me to openly discuss. There was nothing I could do about my broken tooth or ratty clothing, but I was old enough to start taking better care of my appearance. Leaving my long hair dirty and unkempt only made it all the more noticeable, and not bathing very often just because Betty rarely did so and allowed her children to follow her filthy example was no longer a viable excuse, not even to myself. There was no way I was giving a guy as wise as the pastor a chance to chastise me for not taking a bath now and then.

"I just don't like it," was all I answered.

"Unfortunately, at… How old are you now?" I told him. "At thirteen you really aren't qualified to make those sorts of decisions. Attending school is required by law. And attending church may very well make an even more influential difference in the direction your life takes. What I'm trying to say is you don't have a choice in these things. You're going to have to do as you're told."

"Told by who?"

"By *whom*," he corrected me as if I was one of his children.

"Told by whom?" I repeated, playing his game.

"By your mother."

Now he was going too far, man of God or not. "If I follow my mother's example, I'll wind up dead or in prison before graduating from high school."

"Your mother loves you very much."

"You may know your Bible, but you *don't* know Betty. My mother only loves herself and will squash anyone if it gets her through the day and keeps her big butt out of jail."

"If you're speaking of the problem with the checks she wrote, you're being too hard on her. She wrote those checks to keep a place for all of you to live and to provide food." I smirked at the pastor, and he didn't like it. "You might think it easy for a single mother to provide for three children on her own, but I can assure you it's not." I was getting ready to drop the first bombshell on the poor man, informing him about how many other check schemes she was running and letting him in on the fact that she was planning on skipping out on him, when he said, "Especially when the oldest of those three kids is stealing from her and, worse yet, hitting her."

I lost my grin. "What did you say?"

The pastor's face hardened in the soft light. "You heard me. Your mother has told me about her problems with you."

"She told you I steal from her?"

He nodded. "She said you do so all the time."

"She told you *I* hit *her*?"

"I've seen the marks on her, young man," he said, his accusation cold and dripping with derision. "I must tell you I absolutely loathe physical abuse.

I have no respect for men who mistreat women, especially when the lady is his own wife, or, as in this case, his own mother."

"She told you I'm the one who laid those bruises on her?"

He nodded stiffly. "She did."

I hadn't been prepared for this. "Leon hit her a couple times, but most of those marks came from Tony," I mumbled, still reeling from his accusations.

"She warned me you'd try to say something like that." The pastor leaned back in his chair, watching me with his stern mien. "Besides stealing and hitting your mother and brothers, I've also been informed that you have a problem with constantly straying from the truth."

Yikes. "What are you talking about?" I asked so softly I barely heard my own question.

"How many people have you told that your father was going to have you come and live with him? I can understand how difficult it might be to not have a man around, but it's not healthy to continually spin lies about a father you've never met while a mother who cares for you very much is struggling to raise you."

I ignored that. I just had to ignore that. "She told you I hit my brothers?"

"She did."

"I don't steal from her."

"Is that so? Then explain the new tennis shoes you wear that she never bought. Explain the box after box of baseball cards we moved for you that she never bought. Explain the stacks of comics she didn't pay for." I wilted beneath his onslaught of questions. Somehow, telling the man I stole all that stuff from the stores and not Betty didn't make me sound any better than the vision he'd already formed of me. "She tells me you sometimes take her welfare check and cash it if you get the mail before she does. And you hit her and threaten her if she presses you for the money. I understand this has happened more than once."

This was too much. Betty had laid a trap for me, and I'd stumbled right into it like any other of her dumb marks. She'd been using me as an excuse for coming up short on money, and the pastor had bought it. She'd used me as the reason she had bruises on her face, and the pastor had believed her. She told him I lied and stole and abused her and my brothers, lacing her own lies with just enough truth to ensnare me with my own actions. I *did* lie and steal, and I *was* abusive toward my mother, even if she was the one who did all the hitting. I found myself wondering how many people she'd worked this angle on. *More important is how many believe it.*

Stunned as I was, I had to admit this was a work of art, a true masterpiece by a craftsman with no peer. *The bitch is good.* I'd underestimated her. This was *her* game, and she knew how to manipulate the rules and work people far better than I ever would or could hope to. She'd worked me good. I was an overconfident boy floundering for a lifeline, flailing about in churning waters I'd no business trying to swim in.

"Just for giggles, where was I supposed to be cashing these checks?"

"When you lived in the city, I'm told you did work for a man who ran a bar. I guess he cashed them for you."

"When was the last time I stole a check from her?"

The pastor's eyes narrowed. "Must we play this game?"

"Please, just tell me."

He sighed. "Just last week. Your mother informed me you've been skipping school and spending the money you stole from her after stealing her check."

I chuckled. "Of course, and I suppose I cashed this one at the pool hall I've been hanging out in?"

He narrowed his eyes and said, "You tell me."

She'd thought of everything. "Would you believe me if I told you I've never stolen any check from her? Or that I've never hit her?"

He didn't bother to mull my question over. "No, I'm afraid I wouldn't."

"Then what do we have to talk about?"

"A serious change in your behavior," he said with a resolute firmness and supreme authority.

"Is that so?" I was trapped, and I didn't like it. Being outsmarted by Betty was hard to swallow. Knowing the man sitting across from me thought I was hurting my brothers fell harder yet. But wondering if Dave and Holly and some of the other people I liked at this church thought me capable of my mother's false accusations was more than I could bear. "So what's next?"

A quick knock at the door resounded, as if answering my question.

"Yes?" the pastor answered in a soft voice, still eyeing me.

Mrs. Grady poked her head inside, and her husband nodded at her. She then opened the door wider and ushered in my mother. The pastor rose and assisted Betty into a chair he scooted much too close to my own.

Betty and the preacher shared a brief and hesitant smile as he sat back down.

"Donny and I have laid the groundwork for our discussion," he told my mother, who nodded.

I was impressed by her demeanor: unsure but ready, diffident but calm, the perfect expressions of a woeful mother seeking assistance with her unruly son. She didn't look at me, even though I continued to stare at her. I didn't look away until the pastor cleared his throat and called my attention back to him.

"You look angry, Donny. Are you mad because your mother has come to me for help?" She finally cast me a quick peek. I was hoping to see some shred of doubt in that brief glance, but all I detected was vengeful gloating. "Answer me, son."

"I'm not your son," I said, sounding spiteful and insolent. *Get a grip.*

"Answer the question."

"I guess so."

"Who else was she supposed to go to?"

I shrugged.

"We need to talk about this. We need to put some new rules in place, to do what's best for your family."

"We sure do," I agreed.

"To start with, I want to know if you still have any of your mother's check left. That money has been promised to people I convinced to drop charges against her." He waited while I tried not to laugh, or scream. "Well?"

I took a deep breath. "I didn't steal her check, and I don't have her money. She and Leon are planning on skipping out of here pretty soon. She's got a lot of sh—" *Oops!* "She's got a lot of crap getting ready to fall on her head. She's not going to give you money to pay people she's already ripped off when she needs that money to get away."

Betty looked at the pastor, all sad and forlorn as she shook her head. "I told you to stop with the lies. Do you have any of that money left or not?" the preacher asked. There was going to be no convincing this man that Betty was conning him. I was a liar and a thief, and that was that.

I was suddenly done with the pastor. "No, I don't have any of her money."

He looked disappointed. "I see."

I just sat there for what stretched out like an eternity while my mother and the preacher gabbed about our new place and how they needed to get me back in school. The preacher brought up the new school the church was forming, and lectured us on how badly we children needed this guidance and that teaching. I felt like a kid caught in a bad soap opera. Betty kept going on about how bad we had it and how we needed clothes and food, and how hard it was to get to work now that she lived so far away from the diner. I thought about informing Pastor Grady that she no longer even worked at the Big Boy but let it go. *Why bother?* Betty had the man hooked so deeply she could have yanked him right across his fancy desk with a cane pole and one hand.

The preacher kept assuring her that things would get better and promising to help her find work closer to home. He kept saying to have faith and take it to the Lord in prayer. But he was also a practical man. He gave her ideas on where to look for work and who to call for help with financing a car of her own. The piece of information concerning the car excited my mother. She couldn't conceal her avid interest on how she might pull that one off. I put my head in my hands and sighed.

Betty loved any transaction that involved her supposedly paying at a later date for something she could possess now. She had Tupperware, jewelry, furniture, and clothes she'd acquired in such a manner. *And soon, maybe a car.* If she made one payment it was a minor miracle. If she made a second it was only because we were related to the person she was about to rip off and felt a little bad about it. Eventually, she always took off and kept the financed items without paying for them, or sold them to someone and claimed they'd been stolen from her, as if that meant she was no longer obligated to pay for them.

"Are we boring you?" the pastor suddenly asked me.

I lifted my head and shook the hair out of my eyes. "Yeah, kind of," I said back without pausing to think. *Add that to my list of bad habits you think you know so much about,* not flinching as the preacher's face hardened.

"Watch your tone," my mother warned.

I ignored her and kept my attention on the preacher. "I have a question."

"Go ahead," he said, but with caution.

"You know the checks you're helping her with?" He nodded. I could feel my mother tensing beside me. "She probably told you a lot of lies about how she *meant* to deposit money before this one cleared and *thought* she'd deposited money to cover that one and so on and so on, right?" He didn't answer. I went on. "But I probably know something you don't. If you check, you'll find out she made only the one deposit to open the account, probably the least amount possible, and then went right out and wrote as many checks as she could, including as many as she could pass for cash."

"Shut up!" my mother snapped.

"Now why would someone open up a checking account and write so many checks without ever making another deposit?" I continued, watching the first doubts cloud the preacher's eyes, pleased to finally crack his veneer of confidence. "Especially when that someone has warrants out for her in several states for doing the exact same thing there?"

"Stop lying!" she shot at me. It may have been like spitting in a hailstorm, but at least I'd managed to get off a decent jab before falling flat on my back and being counted out of the fight. "I told you how horrible he was," she told the pastor, trying to lower her voice and compose herself.

I could see he still believed her, but at least he was now listening to me. That was enough to rattle Betty. I couldn't expect anything more. I was beginning to realize that I was always going to be Betty's child. I was never going to escape the stigma of living life the way my mother did. Accepting something for nothing once or twice can become a bad habit; expecting something for nothing as if you're entitled to it is a downward spiral into utter ruination. But outright stealing and lying to people in order to con them into handing over money because they felt sorry for you had to leave you rubbing elbows with the worst of society's bottom feeders. The man sitting across from us really wanted to help, but I didn't need to be all that perceptive to see what he truly thought of us.

"What are you so angry about, Donny?" he asked. It hurt a little because I could see he meant well. "Why won't you give God a chance in your life? You need to let someone in. You need to talk."

"Where was God when they drug my brother off to rape him?" I asked without intending to. "Where was God when my mother's boyfriend split open my eye? Is God going to stop her sick buddies from creeping around in our bedrooms after she falls asleep? No. But the one friend I had who *did* keep us safe is dead now because of your stupid church, and you expect me to thank you for it?"

"What friend?" he asked. He looked to my mother for the answer but she wouldn't speak up. "How did the church hurt any friend of yours?"

"My dog. Kim hauled my dog off to some shelter, and they put him to sleep."

The pastor shook his head sorrowfully. "I'm sorry, but I don't know anything about a dog."

I must have looked ridiculous: I sat there with my face going blank and my jaw hanging askew, while my mother explained to him about how our new landlord didn't allow pets and they'd had to take the dogs off while I'd been at school to avoid a confrontation. He nodded his understanding at her. I tried to collect myself. Why would such a busy and important man give two shakes about some poor kid's dumb mutt? I suddenly felt even more foolish than when I'd first entered this office, and I wanted out.

And not just out of this office.

A wave of unreality washed over me. One of those weird moments when you look around and wonder how you came to be standing where you are, or how the person with you came to be walking beside you. I've had moments like this periodically throughout my life. Sometimes I shake my head and can't believe my good fortune. Often I've succumbed to stupidity or mindless anger to get myself caught up in events I was extremely fortunate to have survived.

A new emotion welled up inside me. I looked at the preacher and suddenly didn't care what he thought of me, or what he had to say. Betty was sitting in her chair beside me. I could feel her studying me. I think she might have felt some change in me, or in *us,* just as I did. I think she asked me if I was okay and called me honey, but I really wasn't listening to her anymore. Pastor Grady said something as well, but I wasn't listening to him anymore either.

I sat there for a moment, trying to figure out why I'd come here in the first place. What had I been trying to accomplish? Had I been hoping this man would be able to chant some magic word and make my life better? Maybe ask God for a favor? Nicky had claimed God had nothing to do with men. He said no God would allow the horrible things he'd witnessed to happen. *He told you to change your life yourself, and that you didn't need any help.* I was beginning to see that Nicky knew exactly what he was talking about.

Betty put her hand on my arm. I flinched, jerking my offended extremity away. I heard her gasp and granted her a dark glance. For the briefest of moments, for one flickering scintilla in time, we were alone in the world, her looking at me and me glaring at her. In that instant I saw her as she was: hurting and scared, a woman more demented with each passing year, more desperate as the end she was summoning drew near. Regret flashed behind her eyes. Maybe for just a second or two, she felt bad about what she was doing to me. But the regret and shame soon passed, replaced by the same chaos and madness I always saw in her face.

One day my mother would be alone. She would age and eventually have nothing but the same cruel indifference she'd lived by during her days on this earth. She would die mean and desolate. Of course, she had a lot of scamming left in her, and maybe another husband or two, but in that moment we'd both seen her undeniable future. She quickly grew uncomfortable with me and turned her attention back to the pastor and the con job at hand.

But I savored it as long as I could. And I smiled at her as I said, "I hate you." My statement was devoid of emotion. My mother stopped lying and gave me her full attention. "I'm going to get away from you."

"Here we go again," she said, struggling to stay in character. The pastor said something but I wasn't going to acknowledge him anymore. "I suppose this is where you start babbling about going to live with your father." She shook her head at me, gnawing on those dentures. "Go ahead. Call him. See if he'll put up with the way you run loose and do whatever you want, like some stray dog wandering the streets."

I shrugged. "I had a good teacher." She looked like she wanted to hit me. I hoped the preacher noticed. "I know my father doesn't want me, and I don't care about that. But I *am* going to get away from you." I stood up to leave. "If I have to stay around you much longer I *will* hit you, or wind up just as loony as you are."

"Donny, sit down. You haven't been excused, and we aren't done here," Pastor Grady urged, still calm but realizing he was losing control of our conference. He stood up behind his desk, unsure how to proceed.

I opened the door but paused before exiting. Mrs. Grady was staring at me from where she sat, the dark hair above her glasses streaked with gray, her eyes peering at me over those half-moon lenses, concerned and earnest. Outside, I heard tires scrunching in the gravel parking lot and people talking. Off in the distance, one of the twins shrilled something, and her fans laughed like they were supposed to. I felt sad. I suddenly realized how much I'd needed this place, how much I owed Dave and Holly for taking the time to risk my neighborhood just to bring a little light to the lives of kids like me.

Betty had taken this away from me. These people believed her lies. They thought I was a liar and a thief. *You are a liar and a thief.* That realization hit hard. *But I'm not like her!* I told myself. Except I wasn't all that convincing. The truth was, I didn't *want* to be like her. But I was, and I was scared that maybe I was trapped, that I couldn't change or get what she'd passed on to me out of my system. I had to run. I had to get away, and soon.

"Donny," the pastor said again. I turned to him. "Come back here and sit down." He gestured toward the chair. "Please."

"No thanks," I told him. And then, "Preacher, you'll find out for your-self how many of her lies you've swallowed." Betty was glaring at me. "And about the other checking accounts she has that you don't know about, one of which isn't even in her real name. *And* about how she's hidden paychecks from you and told you I stole them. *And* about the men she drags home who get drunk or drugged up and then hit on her."

"Shut up!" she growled.

"*And* about how she'll probably be taking that car you told her how to get without paying for it. *And* that she's been planning on taking off for a week or two now. But by then it'll be too late. I wish we weren't like we are." My mother began to weep, but not because I'd hurt her. She was getting scared that the preacher might believe what I was saying, that I might ruin her plans. I looked at her. "Right on cue."

The pastor said something more as I left but I ignored him. Betty could do nothing but follow me to Leon's car. She flipped out on me all the way home, screaming about how I was always trying to ruin her life. She kept swearing she was going to get rid of me, to get me put in a home for boys. I didn't say anything back. I didn't care to. If I pointed out how she'd caused all this, her raving would escalate. I didn't want her hitting me. I was afraid I might actually start hitting back.

When we got home she told Leon what I'd done, again leaving out the details about me supposedly giving her the bruises Tony had laid on her. Fortunately for me, Leon was plopped on the couch with one hand tucked down inside his sweat pants and the other clutching a cold beer, his glazed eyes glued to a ball game on the tube. I didn't have anything to worry about where he was concerned.

We had Hamburger Helper for dinner, my brothers and I sitting at the kitchen table while Betty ate with Leon in the living room. She'd carried his food to him since the drunken lug was still permanently affixed to the couch. Betty was still going on and on about me. She wanted Leon to make sure I went to school tomorrow. She kept telling him how important it was that I go to school so nobody came sniffing around or called her pastor.

"You tell him. He's your kid," Leon mumbled, more interested in his ball game and his beer than my yapping mother.

And that really got her ranting and raving. Poor Leon was in deep shit before he was even paying attention to Betty. My brothers and I got a lit-tle entertainment out of their arguing, but it didn't last long. Leon had to threaten to leave and actually struggle to his feet to get my mother to calm down. Before the fight had managed to really get going, Leon was back on the couch, and Betty was flinging plastic dishes onto the heap in the sink, again cursing me and warning me about the juvenile jail she was going to have me locked up in.

I was making faces and mimicking her behind her back, and the baby began following my example. We were having a good time until Terry piped up and told on us. "That's right. Just pass on your bad attitude to your brothers." Betty spun away from the sink and came over to the table. I thought maybe she was going to start swinging, but she didn't. Something about the way I was acting had unnerved her. She was no longer sure how I was going to react. "Maybe you can teach them how to make things harder for me, too."

No, you'll do that all by yourself, I thought but wasn't brave enough to say aloud with her standing so near and on edge. She gave me a look that promised this ordeal wasn't going to be over any time soon and went back into the living room. I flicked Terry on the ear so hard he fell out of his chair like he'd been shot and started screaming for his mommy. Chip was cracking up and spitting Hamburger Helper as I slipped out the back door before Betty came back.

That night I had strange dreams. In one of them, ants and roaches had crawled into a bag of our puffed wheat, but Betty was still trying to feed the cereal to my brothers. I was trying to warn them but couldn't talk. Then the dream took a turn for the worse, and she tried to give *me* a bowl. I took one look at the cockroaches swimming in the curdled milk and switched the nightmare off as easily as I'd turn the knob on a television.

But even though I could alter my dreams to some extent, I couldn't stop them from coming so I could rest. The worst one had Betty's mom in it. Her name was Beula, and she was a big crazy woman with hands like talons. I remembered how her shriek had been louder and viler than Betty's. Her husband was a little bald man named Danny who trembled like a human Chihuahua and shook more violently when the big hag screamed at him, which was pretty much all the time. Danny wasn't her first husband. I was pretty sure the poor man was so scared all the time because he was waiting for whatever had happened to the previous fools to happen to him.

Beula kept her bedridden father, my great-grandfather, tucked away in a tiny stuffy room off the kitchen. When I was younger and we'd visit Betty's mom, I usually spent most of my time in there with him, playing go fish and listening to the old veteran tell war stories or dumb jokes. Beula treated him like an old dog she kept chained to a stump in the back yard and threw scraps to now and again, having someone carry him out to spend time with the family at Christmas or maybe letting him sit at the table with us on Thanksgiving. I still cherish a black-and-white photo of us together, and I keep that picture propped next to his bronze star medal that I managed to get a hold of.

But in my dream I was the one who was bedridden, and Betty was the one who was supposed to take care of me. I kept trying to drag myself out of bed but couldn't move. Nor could I turn this dream off or make myself wake up. I was sure if I didn't get up and get out of the darkened room I was stuck in, I would die, slowly and in great pain. The thought of wasting away in agony and solitude threw me into a panic. I kept trying to get up, struggling to rise or even roll over, calling out for help in a weak, strained voice that sounded nothing like my own.

Falling off the couch and hitting my head on the floor woke me. I sat there until I gathered my wits. The TV was whispering at me, nothing but crackling noise and a gray, formless picture. My toe caught the leg of the coffee table when I moved, and I cursed quietly. *Wake up.* The pain helped with that. I switched off the tube and listened to Leon and Betty snore for a minute, then stole a can of my mother's Pepsi and went out to sit on the back steps.

The night was cool and quiet. I sat there mulling over ideas on how to get away from my mother. I couldn't call my father. *Why not?* I didn't know why not, exactly. *Run away.* That was a grand notion. But to where? And how would I survive? *You're just scared.* That was true. I was afraid to strike out on my own, and I was afraid to stay with Betty. There were so many emotions churning inside me that I had no way of coping with. I felt like running until my body exploded.

Instead I just sat in the late evening breeze and drank my stolen Pepsi. Little did I know that my existence with my mother was about to take an unforeseen turn, and one not of my doing, even though mine would be the finger that triggered it. I am a firm believer in old adages; most of them are grounded in old truths and harshly learned lessons. My wife is fond of saying, "What goes around comes around," or "For every Jack there's a Jenny."

Ever hear the one about being careful what you ask for? I was about to learn the meaning of that passed-down saying the hard way.

CHAPTER 29

For a day that would forever change my life, it started out pretty much like any other in the bizarre voyage of Betty and her brood. Another week or so had passed since our meeting with the preacher, and I'd yet to relent and return to school. My mother was pretty much incensed all the time. She was so sure the school was going to send some authority to the house to find out why I wasn't attending that she had me expecting a knock at the door at any moment.

Leon was close to losing his mind. My mother was riding him harder than Roy Rogers rode Trigger when he was chasing down a runaway stage coach, only Leon wasn't half as smart as the horse, and even less tolerant. He was drinking one beer after the other, but Betty wasn't letting up. There was a real mean fight brewing. I was hoping he'd get fed up and just take off for a while, but his mom's place was a ways off and the beer was here.

"Get me another one," Leon mumbled. His tone was sullen and his rheumy eyes never left the tube. The fact that he hadn't used my name or acted as if I had any choice but to do what he'd asked didn't escape me; I moved quickly, hoping he wouldn't decide to turn his irritation on me because my mother was berating him so much. "Turn the channel," he ordered as I handed over his cold one.

"Which channel do you want?" I asked pleasantly as I moved to the television.

"How the fuck should I know until I see what's on?" he returned, ending his surly question with a belch.

I ignored his belittling tone and began casually flipping the knob. Finding what he wanted shouldn't have been much of a problem. We only had four clear stations and a couple of others that were so fuzzy they were hard to watch for long. "How's that?" I asked, leaving the tube on an old John Wayne Western. You couldn't go wrong with the Duke.

Leon didn't answer so I tried to leave. "Where the hell are you going?"

"I was—"

"I don't give a shit what you *was*," he snapped. I heard my mother stop moving around in her bedroom, probably trying to listen in on our episode. "You know, if you'd act like a normal fucking kid and go to school, maybe your mom would calm the fuck down and get off my back."

"Maybe," I admitted. *Don't get wise with him.*

Leon took a swig. Beer dripped down his chin and splattered his already dirty wife beater. "I'm getting a little tired of listening to her go on about you." His eyes were still on the tube. The Duke was doing his best to draw the dumb bastard's attention away from me.

"That makes two of us, little fella," I drawled, doing my John Wayne imitation. *Careful.* Now Leon's dull wet eyes were trained on me.

"I can't take much more of her shit," he told me with drunken sincerity.

I shrugged. "So do what the other four thousand, seven hundred, and sixty-two dudes before you did. Throw some change on her bed and split."

What the hell was that? I hadn't meant to say something so antagonizing, but at least Leon grinned. *That was pretty good.* Betty was standing in the hallway glaring at me.

"Keep running your mouth," she warned.

"What? Did I miss somebody?"

Leon tried not to laugh and gagged on a swallow of brew. My mother craned her head around the corner and included him in her dark gaze. "You're not helping," she told him.

"I'm not fucking trying to," he shot back, wiping at his face and chest and then sucking the sticky wetness off his fingers like an overgrown drunken toddler.

I attempted to slip away again and made it as far as the corner of the living room, where the two egg cartons of baseball cards I was sorting were waiting. The move had gotten them all mixed up and out of order. Before I could begin unpacking them, Leon and Betty started going at it. He threw half a can of beer against the wall near her and actually got up off the couch. The fact that he'd wasted brew and moved his hairy bulk told me that he was really angry, and that this was going to be a nasty and drawn-out encounter. I slipped into the kitchen and out the back door.

From the stairs, I could see my brothers digging around in the old shed. The yard and walkway at the bottom of the steps were soaked. Terry had left the hose running after turning on the spigot so he and Chip could get a drink. I saw the lady downstairs staring at me from her kitchen window as I turned off the water. She'd been complaining about my brothers leaving crap from the shed strewn around the yard. *Now she can add them leaving the water running to her list,* I thought, ignoring her and heading toward the boys.

"Look at the mess you're making," I told Terry.

He looked around the yard with innocent wide brown eyes, as if he was shocked by the clutter I'd pointed out. "Chip's doing it too." As if to emphasize Terry's accusation, Chip came tottering out of the shed, carrying a broken hammer handle in one hand and a rusty old water nozzle in the other. I tried to let him know I wasn't happy with the mess he was making by turning my best big-brother glare on the kid, but he just lifted the nozzle toward me and made a sound like he was shooting me with a gun. That made me smile, and the boys continued their foraging.

I didn't feel like dealing with the crap they were dragging out into the yard, or hearing my mother or the nag downstairs bitch about it, so I went into the alley behind the house and decided to wander around. It still felt weird being out and about without Benji trotting along with me. It was an empty feeling. I tried to ignore the hollow place inside my gut as I turned toward the park. The day was clear and warm, and even though it made me feel guilty I tried to push thoughts of my little buddy out of my head.

Pickerington reminded me of a little town in Indiana we'd once lived in called Royal Center. The yards were mowed and neat, complete with trimmed hedges and well-kept flower beds. There were very few broken-down cars, and almost all the garbage cans were capped tightly or tucked away out of sight. Even the dogs yapping as you passed seemed more polite and urbane, as if they just wanted to let you know they'd noticed you but didn't really want out so they could tear off a chunk of your hide.

My memories of Indiana were hazy. Almost all my recollections were hazy. I could hardly remember where we'd lived when, or place teachers and friends with schools and towns. But I did remember beating up some kid who'd stolen my mom's purse out of her car, and ripping open my lip while racing bikes down a steep hill and across a narrow footbridge. *Yeah, and you were winning until you decided to make out with that old sign post.*

What about the baby-sitter's crazy boyfriend? The dude had gotten drunk and tried to break in our back door, and the sitter had locked herself in a car out front with Terry, who'd only been a few months old at the time. I'd woken up and stumbled into the kitchen to find the crazed boyfriend's face leering at me, just a creaking door chain barring him from entry into the house. He'd threatened me and told me to open the door, but I'd been spared having to make that fateful decision by the sound of a breaking chain and the snarls and snaps of our dog, a collie mix named Blaze. The enraged mutt bit the dude so many times, the cops were able to follow the moron's blood trail even in the dark.

I didn't remember the baby-sitter's name. I didn't even remember what had happened to Blaze. What I could recall was how scared my mother had been. She'd run quite a few blocks to reach the house. I'd called her before I'd called the cops. She'd jumped all over the sitter for leaving me asleep in the house, and hugged me so many times I'd gotten all embarrassed in front of the police. My mother and I had gotten along better when I was younger. I also remembered the time when two older guys across the street had stolen all my best baseball cards. Betty tried to make their parents give them back, but the thieves' folks backed them up and told her I was lying.

And I had some great memories of Terrance Senior coming home from the war. He drove me down to the hardware store and bought me a new bike the first Saturday he was home. Even though he had a sore back and still-healing wounds, he played baseball with me in the backyard and took me fishing. When he found out about how I'd been ripped off, he limped across the street and had a very different discussion with the thieves and their parents. When he came back, he was carrying all my missing cards and then some.

Those good days in Royal Center didn't last long. Terrance and Betty didn't get along for more than a few months at a time. Eventually they began fighting, and when Terrance fought he tended to get physical. Arguments led to bruises and cuts on my mother's face, which led to cops and arrests, which led to Terrance deciding to go visit his brother in Kentucky and not coming back. Not long after Terrance's departure, we were packing up and running out on the rent and some other bills my mother owed.

I resisted the urge to go to the pool hall. Dave had me scared that I'd get the nice old guy in trouble for letting me hang out there when I was skipping school. *Now it's just you and the family from Big Valley.* I had a few other good old black-and-white reruns to pass the time with as well. I'd been playing solitaire and making up other card games when there was nothing interesting on the tube. I had to admit I was getting bored with the long hours due to my school hold-out. *Go on back, then.* But I wasn't *that* bored yet.

I passed some guys playing basketball at the park but kept on moving so that none of them would have a chance to invite me in. I wasn't up to the task of trying to fit in with a new group of friends just yet, and I wasn't that good at basketball to begin with. They were arguing about somebody fouling as I left the park and slipped into the wooded area behind the expanses of grass. There was a winding ditch with a stream meandering through the trees, and I followed it.

The afternoon was getting on, and the shadows were long. I hopped a few exposed rocks to gain the other side of the creek. *Terrance would have called it a crick.* Terrance said a lot of words funny, due to being brought up in Kentucky. My mother always threw that fact up to him, telling him how he was a hick and stupid and lazy. And then Terrance would smack her around for running her mouth, causing a real dilemma over exactly who was dumber. For me it was a matter of simple mathematics; Terrance plus alcohol plus Betty equaled disaster. I knew that he and my mother couldn't live together without somebody getting killed, and that Terrance would never be coming back.

I gathered up some rocks and spent some time imagining that the trees I was aiming for were enemies, bouncing stones off trunks and branches until my arm grew sore. After the war I took off my sneaks and waded around in the water, looking for arrowheads or anything else that caught my eye. I found a piece of fishing line tangled in a jutting branch and removed a red and white bobber that was still serviceable, jamming it into my pocket for safekeeping before continuing on around the bend. The water rose up to my knees, soaking the legs of my jeans.

There were small fish darting around in the water here, hardly more than streaks of color in the murky greenish water, and I came up with the bright idea of forming a makeshift spear out of a stick and trying to impale a fish with it. I stood still and waited until a fish swam near enough for a shot, then jabbed at it as quick as I could, growing more and more disappointed with each empty attempt. It didn't take me long to realize I wasn't going to catch a fish this way, although I was pretty sure my spear had actually touched at least one of them before I flung the useless weapon away.

Soon after deciding I wasn't the great white hunter, I found a rope somebody had rigged up where if you jumped and caught it just right, your momentum would carry you safely across the creek. I had a great time playing Tarzan. The branch the rope was tied to creaked real loud when you jumped out and brought your full weight to bear on the fraying line, but not even the risk of getting my head broken by a falling tree kept me from leaping higher and farther. I eventually realized if you ran fast enough, you could hit the rope with enough force to swing out and then all the way back to the bank you'd originally leapt from.

"Who said you could mess with our rope?" I was asked as I thudded back to earth after yet another successful and daring run.

I looked at the far bank and saw a couple of the guys who'd been playing ball at the park. Both of them looked a year or two older than me, but neither of them appeared much of a threat. I wanted to say *I didn't see your fucking names on it,* but I decided on, "Sorry, I didn't mean to hurt anything."

The bigger of the two guys, a kid with sandy hair and a broad nose, gave the speaker a shove and said, "Leave the kid alone, he ain't hurting anything." He smiled at me, revealing a noticeable gap between his front teeth. "Don't mind him. He's just pissed 'cause he falls off every other time he tries to swing all the way back."

"I do not!" the smaller guy returned. He had dark hair and thin features. Something about him reminded me of Tony. I decided I didn't like him on the spot. "I fell in one time!"

Gap Tooth laughed. "You should have seen it," he told me, chuckling while his companion fretted. "He fell right on his face and came up spitting mud."

I made the mistake of smiling at his joke. Tony Junior decided it was my fault his buddy had cracked on him. "I can jump a lot higher than *you,*" he declared, turning his agitation upon me instead of where it belonged.

I doubted he could back up his bravado. "Congratulations." *Different guys, same bullshit.* "Well, I got to go."

"Hey, you just visiting or did you move around here?" the taller guy asked before I could get away.

I paused, but Tony Junior answered for me. "He lives in the upstairs of the old Landry place." His demeaning tone made it sound like we'd invaded his bedroom. "My mom knows Mrs. Bailey downstairs, and she said they're trash." *Word travels fast, even out here in the boonies.* "My mom says some church moved them out here."

The kid was getting close to finding out what I thought about Mrs. Bailey *and* his mom. We shared a stare for a moment, his face hard and challenging while I tried to remain aloof and disinterested. The last thing I needed in my life was a country bumpkin enemy.

"Yeah, I live above Mrs. Bailey."

I could've readily confessed to the rest of what he'd accused without flinching, but I wasn't going to give Tony Junior the satisfaction. I gathered up my shoes and continued on my way, hoping he'd keep quiet.

"Hey, we play baseball here on Sundays if you want to come out!" Gap Tooth shouted after me as I continued to head home. "And basketball most every afternoon!"

I just tossed my hand up in acknowledgment and kept going. I was relieved when neither of them said anything more or followed after me. It occurred to me as I slipped out from beneath the canopy of tree foliage and into the early evening dusk that we hadn't passed out our names. It didn't really matter. I would forever think of them as Gap Tooth and Tony Junior.

The walk home was taxing, the air humid and heavy now that I was out of the woods and away from the water. The thought of Betty and Leon waiting for me was heavier yet. I felt like a condemned prisoner walking death row, only my mother was worse than an electric chair. *At least the chair would just kill you.* What Betty had in mind was the torment of running again, of finding a new place to live and new people to rip off. *Another school.* I winced.

But then a heartening notion occurred to me. No matter where my mother ran to, it would be better than here. I found myself longing to be among kids who shared my fate, who didn't notice me for all the wrong reasons as soon as I walked in the door. I wanted to be safely cloaked in the midst of my peers. Poverty was easier to bear when it was shared by your neighbors.

I wasted some time kicking a can along one of the alleys, stirring up every dog within range of the racket I was raising. A man mowing his lawn smiled and waved at me, and I waved back. The guy had a beer in one hand and was guiding the mower with the other. He wasn't wearing a shirt, and the gut hanging over the waistband of his shorts rivaled Leon's. All of my relatives told me my real father was an alcoholic. *I wonder if he looks like some combination of this guy and Leon?* I was fairly certain he would. *Or worse.*

My footfalls slowed to a crawl as I entered our back walk and negotiated the clutter my brothers had left all over the yard. I took the steps slowly, listening for the sounds of fighting, prepared to flee like a coward if they gave me the slightest reason. The flickering of the TV reflected in the glass of the back door, and I peeked in to find my brothers sitting in front of the tube, mesmerized. There was no sign of my mother or Leon, so I quietly slipped into the kitchen.

As I tossed my shoes in a corner and walked into the living room, I could hear my mother's bedroom window fan thrumming away at the highest speed and the radio Leon kept next to the bed. It was currently blasting some stupid commercial. They only generated background noise like that for two reasons, the most common being when they wanted to hiss and whisper without me overhearing what they were planning or hiding, and the other… *Don't even think about that!*

Terry asked me where I'd been, but I ignored him. He asked me again, and I told him to shut up. After rummaging around in the fridge, I slapped a couple pieces of cheese between two slices of old bread and stole a can of Betty's Pepsi. My hunger overrode any fear of her reprisals, and there wasn't any Kool-Aid left in the plastic pitcher, although the empty container was still sitting in the fridge. I sat the pitcher on the kitchen table to remind myself to make some more—*if there's any sugar left*—and went on back into the other room.

Terry pointed at my stolen Pepsi while I dragged out my first box of baseball cards. "I'm going to tell Mommy," he happily declared.

"Go ahead, and the next time she leaves you with me, I'll hang your little ass off the back stairs," I promised him, more out of habit than anything else. I didn't care if he told her, and didn't intend to hide the can from her when she came out of her bedroom.

"I'll tell her about *that,* too," he whined, his plans crushed.

I shook my head at him while Chip got up and toddled over to me, reaching for my can, which I handed over with a warning not to spill. The kid slurped down a long swig like a pro and then handed it back. "Now you can tell on him too," I said to Terry.

"Can I have some?" he asked hesitantly.

"No."

"You gave Chip some."

"He wasn't acting like a dick," I explained around a mouthful of cheese and bread, but I handed him what was left of the can after taking a long last drink, just to keep him from crying and rousing my mother or Leon.

The next hour or so passed in relative peace. I stacked and sorted cards, the only interruption having to make my brothers some cheese sandwiches and weak, warm Kool-Aid with the last of our sugar. Before long I had piles all along one wall and surrounding and covering the coffee table. I sorted by sport and team and took extreme care with my favorites.

My initial sorting finished, I began the task of wrapping each stack with a rubber band and carefully placing them back in shoe boxes, then storing those back in the larger cardboard boxes. I marked each shoe box with necessary information, so I'd know at a glance what each contained. One of the boxes I marked as "doubles," hoping to find some other collectors in the area to do some dealing.

"Get away from there, it's almost time for *M.A.S.H.*," Leon told my brothers as he switched the channel. I'd been working so intently, I hadn't heard him come out of the bedroom. He went to the fridge for a beer and then plopped down on the couch. "Get this shit out of here," he growled, sweeping his foot across the table and knocking a row of the piles I had stacked there onto the floor.

And then I made a mistake. I gave Leon a look. One of those looks that say *Who the hell do you think you are?* I caught myself, but too late. Leon had seen it. And he was just looking for an excuse to vent on me. *And you just gave it to him.* I tried to play it off and act casual. He stiffened, then slowly came to his feet and stepped closer to me.

"What? You didn't like that?" I didn't say anything. I just kept trying to get the remaining cards off the coffee table before he knocked them around again. "I can't throw your shit on the floor?"

"I don't care what you do," I mumbled. *Jesus Christ, Donny, why don't you just spit on him?* But I was getting angry. Leon reached down and sent another stack spinning into the air, the cards tumbling to the floor, scattered here and yon. "Lay off, Leon!" I warned him, my voice squeaking as I reached for the tone of a man and found only that of a boy.

"Why?" He reached out again, and I grabbed his hand. He shoved me down and wiped the table clean of my cards, bending a lot of them as the cardboard caught in the coarse, sweaty hair on his thick arm and crumpled. "What are you going to do? Cry?"

A knock on the door interrupted us. Leon froze, and I heard Betty scrambling around in the other room. Her harried face peered out of the bedroom from above a sheet she'd hastily wrapped around her. She waved at me, silently motioning for me to come closer.

Because Leon had pissed me off, I ignored her.

Another knock broke Leon's paralysis. He tried to grab my arm and whisper something but I shook him off. He lifted a brawny fist and shook it at me. "Who is it?" I yelled, and then broke out laughing as Leon stubbed a toe on the coffee table in his haste to run first left and then right before coming to rest exactly where he'd been standing.

"What are you doing?" my mother hissed.

I shrugged, enjoying having the upper hand. "Answering the door."

I wasn't worried. *It's probably the hag from downstairs coming up to bitch about all the shit Terry and Chip left in the backyard.* But I didn't let my mother or Leon in on that. *Let 'em sweat.* Besides, even if it was the cops, they couldn't come inside without permission. I was an old hand at turning away the police or bill collectors while my mother hid in the next room.

Another rap on the door resounded, this one harder yet. I was beginning to think maybe it wasn't the old blabbermouth from downstairs when Leon snatched me by the arm and yanked me close. His grip was savage as he lifted me up and brought his face close to mine, his normally dull eyes now bright with rage.

His breath reeked as he whispered, "You get rid of whoever that is, and then you and me are going to get something straight." He dropped me and kicked another pile of my cards away from him, then tiptoed over to a position where he could hide in the hallway with my mother.

Half of me was scared shitless, remembering what Tony had done to me and now all too aware of how much more dangerous a guy Leon's size could be. Even though Leon had never knocked me around, it didn't mean there wasn't going to be a first time. But the other half of me was still pissed off and egging me on, urging me to keep sticking it to Leon as long and as best I could.

"Who is it, Donny?" Terry asked as I stepped over my brothers.

"Probably the lady downstairs complaining about the mess you two made," I snapped at him, jerking open the door.

I found two men in business suits standing on the landing, one holding up a fist he was just about to bring down on the door yet again, the other standing on the top step, holding some folded-up documents. *Cops.* The guy closest to me lowered his hand and gave me a reassuring fake smile. The other guy stepped closer and peered into our living room, obviously looking for someone. He asked me if I might know the whereabouts of Leon, only he used his full and proper name.

My brain told me to say we were alone and I didn't know any Leon, but my heart was still racing from Leon's threat, and my arm hurt where he'd hoisted me up. "Yeah, he's right around that corner," I mumbled, pointing toward the hallway and my mother's bedroom.

"…and a Mrs. Betty Williams," he finished as they both brushed past me and headed in the direction I'd sent them.

As scared as I'd been earlier, the fear coursing through me at that moment knew no bounds. *Did he say, "And a Mrs. Betty Williams"?* I thought about sneaking down the front stairs and running, but couldn't leave my brothers. *What did you do?* In the next room I could hear the cops asking for IDs and Leon mumbling like a scared kid caught smoking in the bathroom. *What did you do?* Then my mother began sobbing. *Oh shit!* And she wasn't faking. *What did you do?* As soon as Terry heard our mom's sobs, he let loose a wail of his own and ran into her bedroom, while Chip climbed up into my own numb arms.

To this day I couldn't tell you what those two cops looked like, even though I *can* recall them gently forcing me and my brothers to sit on the couch while they dealt with Leon and our mother. I can't remember anything they said, but I'll never forget the sound of those handcuffs closing on Betty's wrists or the droning tone of the deep voice reciting her rights. I sat there watching the whole scene play out, feeling like it was my fault she'd gotten snagged again.

They led Leon away in cuffs as well. He went out with his head down and near to tears himself. He no longer appeared menacing or capable of violence. In fact, I felt sorry for him, and guilty. He asked the cops escorting him down the stairs if he could call his mom, and one of them told him he could call his *mommy* down at the station after he'd been printed and booked. I remember feeling bad that they were making fun of him, but I was too worried about my own skin to waste much empathy on Leon.

My mother was doing her best to convince the cops she was worried about her children, going on and on about what they were going to do with us and asking where they intended to take us. But her tone changed drastically after they found a few checkbooks with false names and Leon's fake ID stash. I also overheard them asking her about stealing mail, which I knew was a pretty serious offense.

Betty soon forgot about us in her haste to throw Leon under the bus. According to her, everything was his fault and his doing. When they asked her about the checks in her name or some alias using a part of her name, she simply claimed he made her do it. They let her go on for a while, moaning and lamenting, playing the part of the helpless female sidekick with more passion and flair than any actress.

But then, "Did he make you do it in Florida and Indiana, too?"

My mother didn't have a response prepared for that question. She tried to play dumb, acting like she didn't have a clue what they could possibly be talking about. By now I was pretty sure she was going to jail. *And probably for a longer stretch than the last time.* Terry jumped down and tried to get into the bedroom again, only to be forced away by a uniformed officer who'd arrived to cart Betty off. He sat him back on the couch and reached out to tousle the baby's hair, but Chip flinched away from him and did his best tick impression, trying to crawl up under my skin and hide somewhere inside me.

I was worried about what would happen to us. The baby was snuggled up against me, trembling. Terry was perched on the edge of the couch, waiting for an opportunity to get to our mother, fat tears rolling down his face and dripping off his chin. I was close to crying myself but fighting it. I felt so damn guilty. *Betty's never going to forgive you for this.* At the moment I couldn't blame her if she decided to kill me the first chance she got.

Another cop car rolled up out front and left its lights flashing. They walked my mother out in those glaring strobes of blue. Terry tried to get to her but one of the cops restrained him. Even the baby began to cry harder, and I had to wipe at a few tears of my own. She was wearing baggy sweats and one of Leon's work shirts, her hair a mess and her hands cuffed behind her back. I saw her mumble something to the lady cop she was handed over to, the side of her face bathed in the eerie light.

She never even looked back at us as they led her out of the room and down the stairs.

CHAPTER 30

Terry was gone, and his sudden disappearance had Chip clinging to me like we were adrift in the ocean. They'd put us in a room together and let the boys sleep with me last night, and Terry had been holding my hand when they'd taken us downstairs to the cafeteria to eat breakfast. But they'd managed to lure him away and separate us on the return trip without my noticing. *We never even got to say good-bye.* I'd asked Rudy, the guy in charge of us for the time being, about Terry. But all Rudy would tell me was that Terry was with a caseworker, and he didn't know when or if we'd be seeing Terry again.

We were back in our room at the moment, sitting on the hard bed in a state of shock. There were a few toys in the room Chip could've played with if he'd wanted to, a Tonka truck with a missing wheel and a cracked Etch a Sketch among them, but the kid was only interested in staying near me. *Real* near. He'd found the bobber I had stuffed in my pocket and was rolling it around on the bed, content to amuse himself with the plastic bauble as long as I didn't try to get up and move away from him.

When the door opened, he scrambled nearer to me and let the bobber roll off the bed and crack against the cool linoleum floor, huddling up against me as if I could save him. Rudy and a sharply dressed lady came in. They were both wearing ID tags and bored smiles, and both looking at us without seeing anything they were overly concerned about. Rudy stayed near the door while the lady walked toward us, glancing at her clipboard.

"Is this Roland?" she asked, her gaze flicking upon my baby brother and back to her board.

"We call him Chip. He doesn't answer to Roland." Young Roland was presently digging his nails into my back and stomach, pressing himself against me so tightly I was having trouble drawing breath. "Why?"

She leaned in and said, "Well, hello, baby." But Chip wouldn't look at her. He wouldn't lift his face from my chest. "Would you like to go for a walk with me? We could get some candy, and I can find some other kids for you to play with." I winced as the baby dug in deeper, his tiny claws surely drawing blood. He wouldn't even acknowledge the lady trying to coax him away from me. "Rola—I mean, Chip, can you come with me?"

"Hey, don't—"

My warning was cut off as she reached out and touched my brother's shoulder. He lifted his head and screamed. Our visitor jumped back and almost dropped her clipboard. She covered her mouth as she waited for Chip to finally quiet down and shove his face back against me. The baby's growling and grunting quieted with each breath, but his lank blond hair broke out in a sweat. I could actually feel the heat rising off his scalp on the skin of my chin.

Rudy, our tough-looking black orderly, hadn't been so impressed by my brother's outburst. "You want me to pry the kid loose for you?" he asked her.

"No, no," she replied, lifting a slender hand to keep Rudy by the door and away from my panting brother. I was pleased by her reaction. I could see by the expression on her oval face that she was at least seeing Chip for what he was: a frightened little kid whose world was falling apart. She paused for a long moment, looking at both of us thoughtfully. "We'll do this later when I have a more secure place for him," she murmured as if we weren't even there.

And then she left as abruptly as she'd entered, Rudy eyeing me frankly and pausing in the doorway before following her. "You can go down the hall as far as the vending machines if you have any money," he told me.

I did. I'd managed to stuff around eleven dollars in ones and loose change in my front pocket before the cops had walked us out of the house. Just about everything I owned of any value was stuffed in a pillowcase stuck over in the corner, with the exception of the comics and baseball cards I'd been forced to leave behind.

"You can't go downstairs without an escort, and if you cause any problems you'll answer to me," he warned. Right now, there wasn't a whole lot Rudy could say that was going to worry me. "You mess with me, and I'll toss you down in population." He grinned like the term "population" should have scared the hell out of me. "You get me?" I nodded, even though I didn't have a clue what he was talking about. "Good," he said before closing the door behind him.

I was pretty sure they'd probably used that candy line on Terry to get him off by himself. He was probably bawling his eyes out by now. *And scared to death*. The more I thought about him being scared and alone, the more I wanted to go looking for him. *What good will it do if you find him?* But I couldn't answer that. I just wanted to find him and try to make a break for it.

Chip had loosened his hold on me, but not all that much. I didn't want to let go of him either, bloody gouges and all. *They're going to take him from you.* I needed to run, and now. Before they made their move I had to make mine. I wasn't sure if I could find Terry or where I would run to with Chip, but I had to try. If I could just get outside they wouldn't have a chance of catching me. *And how far are you going to get lugging a three-year-old, with eleven bucks?* At the moment I didn't care about the details. I decided to work on freedom first and worry about the rest later.

I thought about trying to carry my bulging pillowcase and thought better of it. The air was warmer out in the hall, but still air-conditioned. Rudy had an office with sliding windows at the end of the hallway next to the vending machines. I carried Chip toward him while he watched our progress. When I was close enough I pointed at the vending machines and asked if we could sit in the TV room. He assented but said, "Just don't be asking me to change the channel every five minutes."

I bought Chip a bag of Fritos, which was no easy task since he refused to let me put him down even for a moment. The door leading downstairs was just beyond the sliding window of Rudy's office, and there was a buzzer he had to hit so someone could get in or out. I pretended to watch the TV for a while, monitoring the light traffic of people coming and going, which happened about every ten or fifteen minutes. *Let's get on with it.* I couldn't risk sitting around. I had no idea how long the lady who wanted the baby would wait before coming back.

Getting out didn't look all that risky or difficult. They had a pair of thick mats near the door so people could wipe their feet before hitting that slick linoleum. I waited until the moment felt right and ducked under Rudy's office window and crawled over to the door. Yeah, I did all this with a toddler draped around my neck. *James Bond has nothing on you, kid.* I pulled one of the mats over just far enough to lift a corner of it against the closed door and quickly made my way back to the TV room.

Of course my plan would be a complete failure if the next person to come along wanted out instead of in and noticed the carefully arranged mat, but I was lucky. The next guy to happen along was a smooth-walking dude in a bright red jumpsuit much like Rudy's. He hit the buzzer three quick times in succession, and Rudy opened the door without even a glance in the door's general direction. The new guy didn't notice the upturned mat as he strutted in and slipped into my warden's office for a chat while the door slowly closed, only to be held ajar by the heavy rubber-backed obstacle.

I didn't waste any time. While the two hip brothers joked about a fine new girl working in the laundry, I crawled back over to the door and pushed the mat over to where it had originally been, at the same time carefully propping the door open with my foot. I was still holding the baby. And then we were in the stairwell and heading downstairs. I knew the cafeteria was two floors below and that we were four floors up, since I'd counted the levels outside the window of our room. I peeked in the next door down and saw nothing but more doors with a few people milling about in the hallway. I tried the latch, and it opened right up.

The first five or six doors led to offices with one or two people at desks within. I took quick peeks in each and tried to quietly close the doors, hoping no one paid me much mind or asked me any questions, wishing they'd built windows into the doors so I could just glance in and move right along more quickly. Near the end of the hallway, there was a door leading to another stairwell and a pair of double doors leading to another hallway. I thought about leaving without looking any longer for my lost brother, but couldn't bring myself to abandon him so easily and went on into the next hallway.

These rooms were more like the one I'd spent the night in upstairs, but the first few were empty. The only one I found with anybody in it was more populated than I would have liked. Two girls with stringy, dirty hair, and tattered dresses sat on a bed, talking with a lady who looked a lot like my own dreaded visitor but fortunately wasn't. All three of them looked my way as I poked my head inside, the girls' faces hopeful and then disappointed, the lady's face suspicious and then more suspicious.

"Excuse me," I said, closing the door and hoping to move on without her questioning me.

Fat chance. "Wait up there," she called after us, hurrying out into the hallway. "Where do you two belong?"

Be cool. "We're here with our mother," I explained casually. "She's picking up another kid like this one to take care of."

"Oh." She seemed to be buying my act, even though she was nervously fingering her clip-on ID. "Well, you shouldn't be on this floor. How did you get up here?"

I shrugged. "I just followed some guy up the stairs. You know, just looking around while my mom talked and filled out the forms."

"What's your mom's name, honey?"

"Betty, Betty Smith," I said after swallowing. *Betty Smith?* I couldn't believe I'd given her such a lame name. "Well, I better be getting back downstairs. My mom will get worried."

She wasn't buying anything I was selling any longer. "No, you just stay right there." She moved toward a phone on the far wall. "I'll call down and have somebody come up and take you back to your mother."

The jig up, I did what I did best and ran. "Hey! Come back here!"

But there wasn't much chance of that. I only had one option left, and I was going for it. I ran back the way we'd come and hit the door to the stairs so hard it banged against the wall. The heavy thud echoed down the stairwell ahead of me. I ran past two men walking up the steps, and they both paused to watch me thrum on by, my sneaks slapping the concrete steps so fast you could hardly distinguish my footfalls.

I decided to skip the second floor and go all the way down to street level, praying the door there might lead to some way of getting out of the building. But the door there was locked. I peeked in the window and found a large white man with closely cropped hair and a broad face sitting in a booth like Rudy's, monitoring the door. He looked at me while I checked him out, but as he rose from his chair I turned and ran back up the stairs, hoping the second floor door might lead somewhere more promising.

It didn't. All I found was another hallway and a lot more people than in the sparsely populated offices on the floor above. Everywhere I looked there was a dubious face and a hanging ID. But I couldn't dally. I could hear the dude from downstairs running up the steps after me. If I stayed here I was done for sure. I bolted into the hallway before me and hoped to make it to the exit at the other end. *The next door probably leads to the police station.* It didn't matter. Anywhere was better than here. Any chance was better than none.

"Whoa there…"

"Hey, kid…"

"Watch it…"

Everyone had something to say as I ran by. I felt like I was playing football in a crowded bus station, only the ball was alive and clutching me more fiercely than I was holding it. I was halfway to the other door before I heard the guard from downstairs holler out, ordering me to stop. When he realized I had no intention of following his barked instructions he began yelling for someone ahead of me to help him stop me. Only one putz tried, but he was a bald, portly man who had a better chance of making out with Farrah Fawcett than laying his pudgy hands on my fleet form.

Fortunately, the door to the stairs was unlocked and gave way as I shoved against it. Unfortunately, the door at the bottom of the steps had another dude in a jumpsuit and name tag watching over it. The guy on my tail was bellowing in the stairwell as he descended, and the guy on the other side of the door, a Latin-looking dude wearing a hair net, hopped off a stool and walked over to see what was going on. When he cracked the door I tried to force my way past him, but he grabbed me by the arm and prevented me from going anywhere.

"Hold up there, partner," he said, chuckling as he moved his hand off my arm but grabbed a handful of my shirt to keep me immobile.

The guy on the stairwell came panting to a stop at the bottom of the last flight of steps. "Goddamn, that kid can run," he gasped, then shared a laugh with the dude who'd nabbed me.

"What's a matter, Quincy? You getting old?"

Quincy whistled and bent over, supporting himself by placing his hands on his thighs and bending slightly at the waist. He was a pretty big guy, but still young enough that such a short dash shouldn't have him ready to keel over. "Something like that." He pointed at me and grinned. "You got some moves."

"Where'd he escape from?" the guy holding me asked.

Quincy stood up and tried to slow his breathing. "Rudy let him get away from upstairs in transition. He's mad as hell and running all over the place, trying to keep Martin from finding out he let one get away."

"Too late for that," my captor muttered, chuckling again.

Quincy nodded his agreement and reached out, getting a firm grasp on my shirt collar before the other guy released me. I had the feeling they'd done things like this before, as if passing misbehaving kids back and forth wasn't something they were strangers to. "I better get these two back to Rudy before he goes ballistic."

"See ya." And the door closed behind us.

"You aren't a biter, are you, kid?" I shook my head and allowed Quincy to guide me up the stairs. "I have got to quit smoking."

Rudy's angry lecture was meant to scare me, but I was beyond concerning myself with any of his threats or promises of revenge. Chip hadn't made a sound during our failed attempt at freedom, not letting out a peep or shedding a single tear. He lay against me like a kid in a coma, his sweaty face pale beneath the thin wet strands of hair hanging in his wide eyes. *Maybe he's getting sick?* He felt hot, but I was pretty sure he was in some state of shock. I didn't know if shock could cause a fever.

"You better answer me, kid," I heard Rudy say.

I didn't even know the question. "What?"

The baby wasn't the only one who was heated up. "I asked if you understood me."

"Sure, sure, I understand," I muttered.

Rudy looked exasperated. He ran a hand across his 'fro, pulling his wiry hair back and holding it there for a second, all the while eyeing me like he wanted to give me a good smack. I fell back on the bed and adjusted my head on the pillow while Chip snuggled up against me. "I'll come for you when it's time for dinner. 'Til then this door stays locked." That was fine with me as long as Rudy stopped yapping and left, which he did, slamming the door behind him. The clicking of his key turning in the lock was actually a pleasant sound.

I made the mistake of listening too closely to my brother's raspy breathing in the stillness that followed. We were tired from the events of the last twenty-four hours, neither of us having slept very well the night before. I pushed the lank hair out of the kid's eyes and laid the back of my hand against one rosy cheek, relieved to find his skin cooling. He threw an arm across my stomach and relaxed somewhat, looking up at me with a mixture of fear and trust. I shared his fear, but wasn't worthy of his trust.

Many years later, I would rarely hold one of my own children without at least a glimmer of this memory trying to intrude upon the present moment. I suppose I don't see things as they truly were. I don't see how dirty or lost we must have looked, how greatly in need of proper nourishment and parental care we were. All I remember is the blue of his slowly closing eyes as his breathing finally calmed and his tense little body relaxed.

During my younger years I was always a heavy sleeper. I was prone to sleepwalking and peeing in places where there had been a bathroom in the last house we lived in, but where there was now a sofa or a wall in the hallway. I'd even been roused and spanked as a child, but never remembered any of it come morning. So it was no shock to me when I found I'd slept right through the sound of our visitors unlocking the door to our room and sneaking in. In fact, if my baby brother hadn't begun screaming my name, I might have slept right through to the next morning and not realized a thing was amiss.

But he did scream.

There have been many times when I wished he hadn't. I jerked awake only to be expertly restrained by Rudy. Chip was screaming my name and reaching for me as the same lady carried him away. I tried to move and Rudy jerked my head still, preventing me from even crying out. The baby began kicking his feet as she opened the door, reaching and screaming, screeching for me again and again. I gagged and strained to no avail while my brother's sobs echoed in the hall, fading as he was carried further and further away. Even when they'd left the floor and entered the stairwell I could hear him begging me, calling my name again and again.

After a time Rudy let me go and locked me in the room again. I raged and threw the Etch a Sketch against the far wall, and kicked the rest of the tires off the truck. I pounded on the door and yelled until I was hoarse. But mostly I just cried. When Rudy came and tried to console me I cussed him and told him to go away. When he tried to escort me down to supper I told him I didn't want to eat and kept my face buried in the soaked pillow of my temporary bed.

That night was a long one. I was lonely and confused. Rudy wasn't angry with me anymore, and he tried to talk me into watching TV or playing some cards with him, but I wouldn't leave my room. That night Rudy came by before ending his shift and tried to introduce his replacement to me, but I wouldn't respond to anything he said or look up at them. "I'll see you in the morning, kid," he promised as he closed the door. I heard him narrating the story of my mad dash for freedom as they walked away, and I was pretty sure I detected a little admiration for me in his normally cocky voice.

Chip's cries haunted me all that night. The sounds of his sobs and his screaming my name would never fade away. The memory of the baby being hauled off still visits me. I laid there wondering what was going to happen to me, wondering what had already happened to my brothers. Chip's pain had me remembering Terry's recent attack. If I'd had much faith in God, I would have prayed to Him to protect my brothers from anything else like that happening to them, or me.

From my early years until the current day, nothing tortures me like my own thoughts during a long and sleepless night. I have a creative mind, and can imagine the worst of outcomes given the most ordinary and common of circumstances. I can worry myself into a state of melancholy if I'm not careful, and I can fret myself into a lather over nothing if I let my emotions get the best of me. My first night alone, bereft of the only family I'd ever known, was but the inception of what would be an onslaught of endless and restless midnight hours throughout my life.

Early the next day, it would be Rudy who eased my torment. "If you promise to eat this cereal, I'll tell you a secret." Still in bed, I kept my back to him and my face averted. "It's about your brother." That had me rolling over to gaze up at him. Rudy flashed a wide, white smile that I was sure he'd used to warm the hearts of many a girl. "You have to promise," he said again, holding out two little boxes of Frosted Flakes and a bowl containing a small carton of milk and a plastic spoon.

"I promise." I was famished. I took the cereal from him and proved I was as good as my word, tearing into the boxes and quickly preparing my breakfast. "What about my brother?" I asked around a mouthful of flakes.

Rudy looked around to make sure no one was out in the hall. "Ain't supposed to be telling you any of this, so you got to keep it low, hear?" I nodded my agreement. Rudy was talking street and sincere, slipping into his true persona now that we were alone, and he could see we shared similar backgrounds. I could tell he knew what was up. "A honey I rap at downstairs says your baby bro was hooked up special. She said the lady who came to get him just loved him to death since she can't have no baby of her own."

That did make me feel better. "What about my other brother?"

"Don't know nothin' 'bout him, little man. They pretty tight-lipped downstairs." Rudy was gathering up the truck and sticking the wheels back on it. The Etch a Sketch he tossed after a quick look at the completely shattered screen. "I'm sure they found a good home for him, though. They careful 'bout who they let take you kids in."

"I'm sorry about that," I murmured, pointing at the trash can Rudy had tossed the Etch a Sketch in.

He just chuckled. "They put that shit in here knowing it's gonna get busted up sooner or later."

The sound of footfalls in the hall had him standing up straighter and scrambling for my practically empty bowl. I was guessing he wasn't supposed to be bringing food upstairs and had bent a rule or two. He threw everything in the trash can, bowl and all, and gave me a wink just before an elderly lady with gray hair and thick glasses entered the room.

"Donald Davis?"

My name sounded strange when she said it, all proper and important. "Yeah?"

"Come with me, please."

"Good luck, little man," Rudy said softly as I snatched up my stuffed pillowcase and left, but I was too nervous to pause long enough to thank him for being so cool.

Some stairs and a few buzzing doors later, she led me into a busy office on the ground floor. "Please take a seat," she instructed, pointing at a plastic chair along the wall.

"Is this Donald?" another lady wearing too much lipstick and with her hair pinned up in a bun atop her head asked as she walked in.

"Donny," I corrected her.

"Excuse me?" Honeycomb Head asked.

"I said my name was Donny."

"Oh, that's nice." She picked up a file and began flipping through it. I saw my name scrawled across the top of the manila folder. "I see Judge Reed wasn't playing around with this one," Honeycomb said to Gray Hair.

"No, he wasn't." Her wrinkled face split into a grin behind her thick glasses. "His office called Donald's father directly last night. I heard the judge explained a few things to him personally."

"I would've liked to have been a fly on the wall during *that* conversation." *Me too.*

They laughed as if someone had told a really good joke. "Me too," Honeycomb said, echoing my thought.

"Can I see my brothers?" I asked.

Both women looked at me as if I'd asked them to strip and dance on the desk. The older lady peered at me over her glasses and pursed her lips. "I'm sorry. We don't do that. Information concerning each particular child is privileged. Not even your mother will be informed as to your whereabouts unless and until she is cleared by a judge to take possession of you, when and if she is released."

"Besides, your brothers have probably been placed in homes by now," Honeycomb interjected. "I wouldn't worry about them."

"You said released."

"Excuse me?" returned Gray Hair.

"You said released. Does that mean my mother is going back to jail for certain?"

The two women shared a look. "It would appear so," Gray Hair admitted.

"For how long?" I knew they couldn't and wouldn't answer my question even as I asked it. "I mean, is she going to jail here in Ohio or are they sending her back to Florida?" *Or Indiana.* But I kept that to myself. I'd already gotten her into enough trouble.

"I'm sorry. We aren't allowed to discuss things of that nature with you." Gray Hair was dialing a phone on her desk.

"Who's this judge you're talking about?" I asked Honeycomb, hoping she could at least answer that question.

"Yes, I have Donald here." I was suddenly more interested in Gray Hair's conversation than having my question answered. "Certainly." And she handed me the phone.

"Hello," I said, hesitant.

"Donny?"

"Yes?"

"This is Grace, your dad's wife."

"Yes?"

"How are you?"

Was she kidding me? *She's just nervous.* "Fine, I guess."

"We've wired money for a plane ticket, and they're going to send you to us. We'll pick you up at the airport tonight, so just do as they say, and we'll see you in a little while, okay?"

What was there to say? "Okay."

"You be careful, hon. We'll see you tonight."

"Okay."

I listened to the dial tone for a while, the whole judge thing becoming clear. *They're making your dad take you in.* I was thinking maybe I'd be safer in the room upstairs with Rudy sneaking me food now and then. *The dad you've never met.* From what I'd been told, my father was worse than my mother. *The dad who says you're probably not even his kid.* I'd been told he was an alcoholic and beat his wife. *The lady you just talked to.* All this felt surreal, like I should be waking up about now on the couch in Pickerington with Leon scratching and farting and Betty bitching and lying.

But Leon and my mother were gone, and so were my brothers. I was about to be put on a plane and sent to live with my father on a farm in Indiana. *What are you going to do on a farm?* I was wondering if I would have to feed chickens and pigs. *Maybe they have horses.* The thought of learning to ride a horse was appealing. Gray Hair realized I wasn't talking to anyone and took the receiver from me, eyeing me with curiosity while she replaced it in the cradle. "Is everything all right?"

I almost laughed. "Just great," I told her.

A few signatures and a file placed in a cabinet, and Honeycomb was saying good-bye to Gray Hair as she led me out of the office. We exited the building and descended a couple of concrete steps to a courtyard with some hedges along a little brick sidewalk that cut between the buildings. To my left were more office windows, but the glass to my right revealed a long room with a row of beds and maybe ten or fifteen younger boys. I could see the parking lot we were heading for and had almost looked away when I spotted Terry's familiar mop of unruly auburn hair.

I dropped my bag and jumped the hedge, running over to the glass while Honeycomb squealed and tried to hurry after me, mistakenly thinking I was making a break for it. At the window I tapped on the glass and tried to get my brother's attention, but he had his back to me and couldn't hear my rapping over the din the other kids were raising. Honeycomb put a hand on my shoulder and tried to pull me away, but I shook her off and told her to get off of me, knocking again, and harder, actually rattling the window in its aluminum frame. My brother still didn't hear me. He sat on the floor facing away from me, watching some of the other boys throw a rubber football back and forth while some others tried to steal it from them.

"Don't do that!" the lady at my back ordered. She put her hand on me again, and I jerked away so savagely she gasped aloud and stepped clear. "This won't help him, young man!" A door on the far wall opened and a young woman in a plaid skirt stepped in the room and called all the boys. "Donald, do you hear me?" Whatever she'd come for had the boys excited. Most of them ran over to her and began forming a line, chattering among themselves and hopping back and forth. "Donald?" Terry followed them almost reluctantly, climbing to his feet like a kid who'd just had the wind knocked out of him.

I caught a brief glimpse of my brother's face. His eyes were puffy and red, his whole face swollen from crying. Terry never did well with new kids. *He always has trouble fitting in.* If ever a kid needed their mother, that kid was Terry. His posture was defeated, and his eyes kept darting toward every loud noise. I was preparing to pound on the glass as hard as I could when the lady behind me said, "How will it help him if he sees you?"

"What did you say?" I asked. But I stayed my hand.

"Your brother is a special needs child. We have more trouble placing children the older they are, and your brother has been through quite a traumatic incident." The boys were filing out the door. If I didn't start banging real soon my brother would never see me. "Why would you want to upset him any more than he already is by letting him see you here? I can't even let the two of you say good-bye." It didn't matter any longer as Terry left the room, and the door began to slowly swing closed. "Come on, let's get to the airport."

She tried to talk to me on the way to the airport, but I didn't have anything to say. The sky outside my window was a burnt orange, and a steady drizzle began right after we climbed into the car. I watched the beads of water collect and run down the glass of my window, concentrating on the slapping of the windshield wipers instead of the chatty lady doing the driving, wishing she'd turn on the radio and leave me alone.

After a while she ceased trying to make small talk or give me advice and went into a round of telling me how sorry she was and describing how much better things were going to be for me when I was with my father. I let her ramble for a bit, grinding my teeth and holding back rage and tears. I knew if I let anything loose, I wouldn't be able to stem the tide churning around inside me. Instead I pressed my forehead against the cool glass and struck out the way I always did, the way I would react to any difficult situation for years to come: I was just plain mean.

"Is that what you do to make yourself feel better?" I asked. I didn't care that I was being rude. Everything felt so numb and lifeless.

"Excuse me?"

"You know, just make shit up? Tell a kid how great his life is going to be and then hand him off to some stranger? I guess if you believe his life is going to be better, it allows you to sleep at night, right? No matter what the truth is. Here you go, kid. Go live with some drunk you've never met and things will be just great." I said all this with my face still pressed against the glass, but felt her stiffen just the same. "Jesus Christ, lady, I'd love to hear the speech you gave my brother before tossing him in that room full of kids. What'd you tell him to do? Follow the yellow brick road?"

She didn't say anything for a while. "I was just trying to be kind."

She sounded genuinely hurt, but I didn't care. "Don't." And I meant it. I didn't want pity. *I don't need anyone.* I would spend a lot of years convincing myself of that. And I would come to believe it. "I don't need your lies."

To her credit, my escort gave me just what I asked for. She drove the rest of the way to the airport in complete silence, handed me over to a TWA representative along with my ticket, and walked away without saying a single word to me or looking in my direction. I actually felt a little guilty for popping off, but completely forgot her once they had me seated near the chute I would soon be traversing to board the plane to Indiana.

You would think a thirteen-year-old boy would find his first plane ride at least a little thrilling, but I hardly remember it. I recall feeling the power of the engine, and I remember the stewardess in charge of me trying to be sweet and checking on me once or twice, but I made that flight consumed by fear and grief. Too much was happening too fast. I felt guilt and confusion, loss and hatred, empty and yet so full of anger I could barely contain it.

In the end it would be anger that won me over. It would be a cold and almost all-consuming rage that I would embrace. Whenever pressed, I would inflict hurt before allowing myself to be vulnerable. I would deflect even the most constructive criticism with witty humor and quick barbs meant to disable my attacker. I would allow no one and nothing past my wall of apathy. The world felt so cold I had no choice but to *be* cold right along with it.

But I wasn't there yet. On that plane I was terrified and lonely, and my fear had nothing to do with flying. They'd given me a window seat near the stewardess's station and a pillow I kept my face thrust in to hide my tears. It was a short trip, and no one sat near me. I felt like such a fraud. For all my bravado and bluster, after all my attempts to act so tough and brave, despite the countless times I'd told Betty I didn't care about or need her, here I was bawling my eyes out and trembling like a newborn fawn in a chill wind.

In the end I was just another lost little boy crying for his mommy.

AFTERMATH

"Hello?"

"Hey, just thought I'd call. I haven't heard from you in a while."

The voice on the phone is my brother Chip. The unmistakable drawl and the soft, easy way he pronounces his words are almost more Southern than Midwest. He's lived most of his life in Indiana, save for a four-year stint in the Navy. "Are you there? You didn't fall asleep, did you?"

Here come the old age jokes. "No, I'm here. I just couldn't believe you didn't call collect," I counter.

"Well, you are getting along in years, old man."

The ten-year age difference gives my brother more ammo than I have at my disposal when it comes to teasing one another, so I let Chip win and laugh along with him. *Again.* Our conversation moves on to the normal questions and responses. My family is good. His family is doing okay. I'm keeping busy. He's rebuilding a couple of older cars and a motorcycle. I brush off any questions about my health, which isn't great. He brushes off any concerns I have about him being laid off from his job, which we both know is a good possibility. In some ways we're so much alike it's almost as if we've been raised in the same home.

"I read the chapter you sent me," he says, out of the blue. "If the rest of the book is as good as that was, I think you might have something there."

"I hope so," is all that comes to my mind.

"Lord knows your mother gave you enough material to work with."

For some reason, I don't reciprocate as I usually do when he begins our "*your* mother" routine, sensing something strange in my brother's tone. I sit and listen to him narrate one of his own haunting memories, my heart rate increasing. He tries to sound glib while telling me about a time he waited expectantly for the arrival of Betty one Christmas Eve. He tries to make it sound like he is telling me a good joke as he explains how she pushed him out onto a back porch when she arrived, so that she and the man with her could have the small apartment to themselves until they were finished.

He was five years old.

I think about Chip listening to those same sick noises, trembling under the onslaught of the same fears I'd so often endured. I try not to give in to my emotions. Guilt over the way I'd abandoned my brothers is not an uncommon occurrence. Of course, I was little more than a child myself. *There was nothing you could've done,* I tell myself. Chip has expressed that very same sentiment to me time and again.

But I recognize the empty place inside him. I feel the void we share, that nagging absence that never leaves you alone. It is a whisper you can never quite hear, something tugging at you that just won't be shaken off or ignored. Being unloved is a morbid pain. The hurt doesn't prevent you from living, and pretends it doesn't even require attention, but the invisible scar is permanent, soul-searing deep.

It isn't like Chip to discuss his demons. I listen quietly, and let him finish. In a way I am honored that the piece of my book I sent him has touched him enough to get him to open up this much. He was a special child, quiet and thoughtful. I remember he'd once been named "Mr. Best" during his first or second year of school. But growing up passed from place to place had a way of straining the "Best" out of any child. We were like those gifts you rewrapped and passed on because they were good enough for someone else, but not quite special enough to keep.

When he is finished neither of us say anything for a long moment. But he finally asks, "Are you going to go ahead and publish it?"

"Yes, I think so."

"You should."

I don't want to get into that right now. "We'll see."

"If you do, you should make sure to put *my* dishwasher in there," he says, laughing as if we are remembering a fond tale from our past.

And that hurts me more than anything else he's said. For a time we lived in the same city, right after I married and got out of the Corps. Columbus, Ohio. Chip was a scrawny teenager when he called and asked for my help. I drove straight to Betty's house and evicted her latest sick love interest, under the threat of serious bodily harm should he ever return or even look sideways at my brother.

Chip had spared me then when I questioned him about exactly what had transpired between the pervert and himself, swearing there had been no physical contact, only the attempt of such. Years later, my brother would admit that something more had happened. If I had known Betty's twisted friend had even touched my brother, I would have snapped.

We talk a bit about my oldest son, who is stationed in Iraq. We promise to call more often, or e-mail. Neither of us does very well when it comes to keeping in touch. Life just gets in the way. I sit there for a while after he hangs up, listening to the dial tone until the beeping and screeching remind me to place the receiver back in the cradle. Our bond is fragile and strained, but it is there, something permanent from my childhood. It is something I can hold onto.

Living with my father wasn't any better than living with Betty. But by then, I was practically impervious to pain. I shut down… drew into myself. It was what I had to do to survive. It's what most abused and neglected kids do to survive. If they survive.

If you're lucky, you make it to adulthood in one piece. But there's no guarantee the rest of your life is going to be any better. Kids who grow up with rotten parents are often plagued by fear and insecurity. They lack confidence and self-esteem. They battle depression, have trouble holding a job, have trouble with relationships. In the worst cases, abused children perpetuate the cycle. They neglect or abuse their own children. They become permanently lost souls.

But if you make it to adulthood and there is still a spark of life left in your soul, you have a chance. You start by letting go of as much of the guilt (yes, abused kids feel guilty) and as many of the bad memories as possible. But some of the worst memories—and some the deepest pains—never go away. So you learn to live with them.

At the same time, you hold on to the things that helped you survive… the things that still give you hope. For me, it's my relationship with Chip… a wariness of authority… my instincts about people… and the knowledge that you can choose your friends even if you can't choose your family. I also held onto the belief that I could be somebody more than a person who gets by on welfare and food stamps, and the notion that you can make your life better by working at it and earning it.

Other things I hold onto: the ability to laugh and joke about things, even if it gets me in trouble sometimes… the knowledge that I can't save the world, but that maybe I can do something with my little corner of it… and the feeling of freedom that comes with riding a motorcycle out into the country in the sun and the wind.

And, of course, I hold onto the memory of my best friend.

I pull an old chewed-up stick out of my desk drawer, fingering the places Benji once gnawed. My buddy probably saved my life more than once when I was threatened with physical harm as a kid. And I believe he saved my life as an adult, too. My memories of his friendship, his loyalty—his love—are the only things that kept a glimmer of emotion alive inside me during the tough times, so that when I was lucky enough later in life to meet someone who was willing to take a chance on a guy whose only saving graces were an offbeat sense of humor and a love of motorcycles, there was still a spark of life in my soul. That someone was my wife, and she gave me love and more things to hold onto: children to cherish and love the way children should be cherished and loved…. a family… a home.

Upstairs, I hear my two younger children banging around, quarreling with one another. From the kitchen, I hear my wife tell them to stop fighting and get washed up for dinner. The cat we rescued from a shelter jumps up on the desk and peers at me quizzically with his only remaining eye. I like survivors with scars.

"Donald, dinner!" my wife calls. I can tell by her tone she doesn't want to have to call me again. I gently put back the stick and pick up my cat, scratching him under his chin and holding him like a baby. He's purring as I deposit him on the couch in front of the big screen TV and head upstairs, before I get myself into trouble. I can hear the kids going at it again. My wife will need the referee. On the stairs I realize my eyes are wet and I wipe at them, laughing at myself for letting my brother get to me. But they are small tears caused by old hurts and easily wiped away. A pain quickly dulled by the family and home surrounding me.

CPSIA information can be obtained at www.ICGtesting.com
Printed in the USA
LVOW051200170313

324552LV00004B/7/P

9 780988 439016